JUNIOR CERTIFICATE HISTORY

FOOTSTEPS IN TIME 1

REVISED EDITION

Revised and updated by
Patricia McCarthy

CJFallon

PUBLISHED BY
CJ Fallon
Ground Floor – Block B, Liffey Valley Office Campus, Dublin 22, Ireland

©
Patricia McCarthy

ILLUSTRATIONS
Nicola Sedgwick
Roger Horgan

Revised Edition February 2010
This Reprint August 2011

Introduction

"Only the wisest and stupidest of men never change"
— Confucius

Footsteps in Time by Kevin McCarthy was first published in 1997 by CJ Fallon Ltd and reprinted in 2003. It proved to be an extremely successful and very popular book with teachers and students alike. The publisher, however, saw the need to update and thoroughly revise this text, and asked me to undertake this work. I was delighted to be given this opportunity and was mindful of the need to retain the structure and layout of *Footsteps in Time*, which has stood the test of time, while also trying to freshen it up and make it as student-friendly as possible.

Readers will find that information continues to be presented in a structured and readable manner in each chapter and section. To make it even more student-friendly, the language has been made more accessible, while the visuals and diagrams have been added to where possible. The book should now better suit the mixed ability classes in which History is mainly taught. Questions and exercises continue to appear at regular intervals in order to reinforce the learning process. The importance of information revision is also highlighted by the continued provision of 'Keynotes' at the end of each chapter, which have now been further broken down into sections to aid revision.

Importantly, this revised edition incorporates many updated Junior Certificate examination questions, at both Higher and Ordinary Levels, up to and including those from the 2009 examination.

In keeping with the emphasis in the syllabus on sources, both written and visual, I have updated the visual sources and text sources, as well as including an increased number of them. Moreover, once again, there are hundreds of the hugely popular '**Did you Know?**' features, many of them new. The design too has been enhanced, with the intention of improving the learning experience and making the text more accessible. Moreover, Internet links to additional information to supplement what is in this book can be found by going to the CJ Fallon website: www.cjfallon.ie

I hope teachers and students alike find this substantially revised *Footsteps in Time* useful and, of course, that it helps them to enjoy their study of History.

Patricia Bolger McCarthy,
Blackwater Community School,
Lismore,
Co. Waterford.

Contents   Volume 1

Contents   Volume 2

Section 3   Understanding the Modern World

Acknowledgements

The author would like to thank the following for their assistance in the preparation of this revised edition of *Footsteps in Time*: Fallon's Publishers for asking her to do this work, to the staff for allowing her to make whatever changes she thought necessary but also to leave well enough alone when required, and, above all, to her husband Kevin and children Elaine and Carole for their great support and encouragement during the revision of this text.

For permission to reproduce photographs and other illustrative material the publishers make grateful acknowledgement to the following:

Popperfoto; Dominic Ledwidge-O'Reilly Photography; National Library of Ireland; Bord Fáilte; Ancient Art & Architecture Collection Ltd.; *Connacht Tribune*; Dept. of Arts, Culture and the Gaeltacht; Margaret Gowen; University of Innsbruck; Ulster Museum; Ulster History Park; National Museum of Ireland; University of Cambridge/St. Joseph Collection; Richard T. Mills Photography; Irish National Heritage Park; J. Allan Cash Photolibrary; the Mansell Collection; Pacemaker Press International; British Museum; Hulton Getty Picture Collection Limited; Peter Newark's American Pictures; Peter Newark's Western Americana; Mary Evans Picture Library/Bruce Castle Museum/Explorer; Colman Doyle; Public Record Office of Northern Ireland; National Gallery of Ireland; David Newman Johnson; Imperial War Museum; Illustrated London News Picture Library; Telegraph Colour Library; Redferns Music Picture Library; Rex Features Limited; INPHO Photography; Associated Press Limited; Bridgeman Art Library; Lauros-Giraudon; Topham Picturepoint; Sonia Halliday Photographs; Colorific Photo Library Limited; Science and Society Picture Library; National Portrait Gallery; Image Select/Ann Ronan Picture Library; British Library; Camera Press; Novosti (London); G.A. Duncan; Don Sutton Photo Library; Zefa Pictures; Science Photo Library; Ulster Folk and Transport Museum; Derek Speirs/Report; Central Bank of Ireland; Iarnród Éireann; Radio Telefís Éireann; Sportsfile/Ray McManus; Bantry 1796 French Armada Exhibition Centre/Robin Wade & Pat Read Design Limited; Dept. of Defence/Airman John Daly; Aer Rianta/Robert Allen Photography; Electricity Supply Board; Blanchardstown Shopping Centre; *The Examiner*; *The Irish Times*; Jim Connolly Photography; Davison and Associates and the Father Browne SJ Collection.

In the case of some photographs the publishers have been unable to contact the copyright-holders but will be glad to make the usual arrangements with them should they contact the publishers.

How We Find Out About The Past

Section 1

Few will have the greatness to bend history itself;
but each of us can work to change a small portion of events,
and in the total of all those acts will be written
the history of this generation.

ROBERT F. KENNEDY

1 The Historian at Work

WHAT HISTORIANS DO

A **historian** is someone who tries to find out about the past.

The historian is a sort of detective, finding out about the past by using whatever clues can be found. A detective gets evidence from a wide range of sources, such as fingerprints and murder weapons. The historian, too, has to gather evidence from different sources. A detective is concerned with the reasons (motives) for crimes and the solving of each case. Reasons why things happened, and the results, are important in any historian's investigation.

Normally, the study of history begins with the time from which written records were kept. The time before that is known as **prehistory**. To find out about ancient peoples who lived before the use of writing requires a different type of detective work called **archaeology**. We will learn more about this in Chapter 2.

HISTORICAL SOURCES

There are two kinds of historical sources: **primary** and **secondary**. These are the same words that describe the type of school that you have just left (primary) and the one you are now in (secondary). Their meaning, when talking about sources of information in history, is different, as we shall see.

Primary Sources

Primary sources contain first-hand information. These can include objects, words, pictures, films and even songs. They *must* be the work of people who witnessed events or at least lived at the same time as the events described in the sources.

Objects

Objects from the past can tell historians about life in earlier times and about how things change with time. These can include almost anything: weapons, machinery, jewellery, clothing and buildings.

Even the simplest objects can show us how life has changed over the years. For example, nobody had ever heard of a compact disc in 1980, yet by 2000, CDs and CD-ROMs were already being replaced by mini discs, DVDs, MP3 players and iPods.

Pictorial sources

Drawings and **paintings** are also primary sources, provided they were done at the time of the events which they show. From these, historians can discover what famous people of the past looked like. From the background detail, it is often possible to learn about ordinary life years ago.

Since the invention of the camera, less than 200 years ago, we have other primary sources called **photographs**. From photos, we can also learn much about daily life in the past – living conditions, fashions and hairstyles, for example.

Maps can be important primary pictorial sources, giving us clues about the past. Accurate geographical maps have only existed for the past 500 years, but people made maps long before the development of writing, to identify hunting territory, for example. Ancient maps tell us many things. Old names for places can be discovered from such maps. We can also get a great idea of how places have changed over the years, especially if we have modern maps to compare the old ones with.

DID YOU KNOW?

Science can help us to investigate sources.

Old paints contain lead that shows up on *X-rays*. These can reveal details that were painted in at first, but painted over when the artist changed their mind. X-rays show that Jan Steen (see painting above) at first planned to paint himself smiling, but the finished painting shows how he changed his mind.

SOURCE A

In the past 100 years, **film** has become very useful to the historian. Films of historical events, taken as they happened, are known as **documentaries**. Since 1900, film records have been kept of such events as World War I and Ireland's 1916 Rising. The later developments of sound and colour mean that since World War II (1939–45), the quality of documentary films has improved and their value to historians has grown as well. As with photographs, we can also learn much about ordinary life, clothing, hobbies and so on from films.

SOURCE B

O'Connell Street, Limerick, in the late 19th century.

SOURCE C

O'Connell Street, Limerick, in the late 1960s.

CAN YOU SAY?

1. (a) The term 'prehistory' refers to the time before writing was invented. True or False?

   (Junior Certificate Ordinary Level 2005)

   (b) What is the main difference between history and archaeology?

   (Junior Certificate Ordinary Level 1998; similar question in Higher Level 2009)

2. What is a primary source as used by a historian?

   (Junior Certificate Higher Level 1993)

3. Complete: A film or a television programme that uses characters, objects and scenes from real life is a _____.

   (Junior Certificate Higher Level 1992)

4. Look at the map of Barcelona, **Source A**. Which part of the city do you think was built many centuries ago, when there were no cars and lorries? Which part is the more modern part? Give reasons for your answer in each case.

5. In the two pictures above (**Sources B** and **C**), list the differences you see between the two scenes, under these headings:

   (a) Transport

   (b) Clothing

   (c) Any other differences

Written primary sources

Letters and **diaries** (daily records of events), written by people who lived through important times in history, can be full of useful information. Some of the most reliable clues we have about life long ago come from the writings of such people as the ancient Roman, Julius Caesar, or early Irish saints such as St Patrick. In more modern times, diary writers have given us remarkable pictures of war, famine and, of course, daily life. Here is an extract from a diary written by a woman named Vera Brittain during World War I.

> **SOURCE D**
>
> *The loss of the* Lusitania *is confirmed, and the whole affair is worse than we thought. There were over 2,000 passengers on board, 1,500 of whom are lost. It is not yet certain how long the ship was afloat after being torpedoed but it cannot have been long, as she carried more than enough boats to save all on board.*

Historical **documents** come in many forms. In some parts of the world, such as Rome, detailed written records were kept by rulers well over 2,000 years ago. Details about battles lost and won, certificates of birth and death, as well as tax and land ownership documents survive in large quantities in some countries. Most material of this sort is handwritten, and because *manus* is Latin for 'hand' and *scribere* means 'to write', such documents are called **manuscripts**.

Most governments over the last 200 years have kept very detailed records of their populations. This type of record is called a **census**; a detailed census, taken every ten years, is particularly valuable as a source of information on births, marriages, deaths, employment and so on.

DID YOU KNOW?

The Diary of Anne Frank, written by a Jewish girl in the Netherlands during World War II, is the world's best selling diary, with over 25 million copies sold in 67 different languages since 1947.

Newspapers, which contain firsthand accounts and the words of eye-witnesses as well as photographs, can be great primary sources. This is true not just of national newspapers, but also of local ones. Many of these have been published for over 200 years. Moreover, many newspaper companies and libraries have stocks of old editions that historians can read through in their detective work on the past.

One primary written source that may be recorded some time after the events is a person's own account of her life. This is an **autobiography**. **Biography** means 'life story' and **auto** means 'self'. Such a source gives us information on past events and on how people involved felt about them.

Apart from letters, diaries and other documents, **songs** and **poems** may also be primary sources. In many parts of the world, particularly in areas where written records were not always kept, people preserved their history in ballads and in verses passed down from generation to generation by **oral** means (by word of mouth).

There is one other primary source we need to think about – **people**. Many of today's adults lived through and have personal memories of famous events, such as the first moon landing in 1969. Younger people remember, for example, the millennium celebrations in 2000. Nobody's memory is perfect, and certainly some details may be forgotten, but interviewing such people can give us an understanding of what it *felt like* to live through history.

Secondary Sources

When a historian has studied the primary sources available, the history book, textbook or article written by him is known as a **secondary source**. This is because when others read it, they are basically getting secondhand information from someone who did not live through the events described.

A secondary source may be able to bring together more information and examine it more carefully than any one primary source can. Most of the history that we study today comes from secondary sources, usually books. It is easier to study history in this way than through primary sources.

CAN YOU SAY?

6. Mention *two* types of primary source that a historian can use.
(Junior Certificate Higher Level 2001)

7. Complete: The official population count taken every ten years is called a _____.
(Junior Certificate Higher Level 1992)

8. Name *two* types of written source that historians use when finding out about the past.
(Junior Certificate Higher Level 2001)

9. Read **Source D** above and answer the following:
   (a) What exactly was the *Lusitania*?
   (b) How many people, according to the extract, survived?

10. Select *one* primary and *one* secondary source from the following list: a biography; an autobiography; an eye-witness account; a school textbook in history.
(Junior Certificate Higher Level 1999, similar in Ordinary Level 2005)

11. What is a secondary source? Give an example.
(Junior Certificate Higher Level 2005)

12. A birth certificate is an example of a secondary source. True or false?
(Junior Certificate Ordinary Level 2006)

DIFFICULTIES FOR HISTORIANS

Finding the Sources

Finding historical sources is not so difficult in the case of secondary sources. Most public libraries and large bookshops contain hundreds, sometimes thousands, of history books. It is often possible to order books that cannot be found on the shelves directly from the publishers, or through the Internet.

In searching for primary sources, there are many possibilities. Objects of historical interest (**artefacts**) are generally found in **museums**. Apart from the National Museum in Dublin, many Irish towns and cities now have local history museums. Many have websites too.

Old photographs may be found in museums, though **newspaper offices** generally have lots of them too. The National Photographic Archive in Temple Bar, Dublin, contains over 300,000 photographs.

Public libraries often contain copies of old documents, public records and newspapers, though the best place to locate documents is an **archive**. A special building or room is used for storing such sources. Today, material is often recorded on reels of microfilm, CD-ROMs or DVDs to save space. It can then be examined or copied when needed. Some websites also provide a lot of useful historical source material.

DID YOU KNOW?

The world's largest library, the US Library of Congress, has 120 million books and enough shelving to run from the top of Ireland to the bottom - and back again

Bias

Just because we find a primary source, this does not mean that we should believe that everything in it is true or accurate. The writer, artist or photographer may have been **biased**. This means that she had a strong personal opinion about an event and tried to show that this view was correct. Can you imagine how two people who support different soccer teams, for instance, could differ greatly in reporting a match between those two teams?

The creator of the source may not be deliberately biased, but when she is, even the basic facts can be altered to support her views or spread the ideas of groups or movements. This is known as **propaganda.**

● Subjectivity
Sometimes the writer of a primary source may be very emotional about what he is describing. This can make the source less reliable. Such a person is said to be too **subjective** (involved with the subject). Good historians should always try to be **objective**, recording and examining events calmly and accurately, without bias or too much emotion.

● Exaggeration
Stories, songs and poems can be unreliable primary sources. They are often written to celebrate events (they are **celebratory**) and their writers or tellers are often biased or too subjective. Stories also tend to become exaggerated over time as various tellers add in their own details or leave out other details altogether. In some poems or songs, facts may be changed simply to make the lines rhyme.

Mistakes
Sometimes, the writer of a primary source may simply have had the facts wrong to begin with. On one famous occasion in 1949, the *Chicago Daily Tribune* newspaper announced that President Harry Truman had been defeated by John Dewey in the US presidential election. However, the paper had gone to print before all the votes had been counted and Truman (pictured below with the paper) actually won the election.

DID YOU KNOW?

Even artists can be biased. In 1540, Hans Holbein was sent by England's King Henry VIII to paint a picture of a lady called Anne of Cleves. When Henry saw Holbein's lovely picture of her (above), he agreed to marry her without even having met her. However, when Henry saw Anne just before the wedding, he was disappointed by her looks and divorced her after just six months.

Likewise, in 2000, some American news networks incorrectly projected that Al Gore had won the US presidential election.

It is also common to find that a traditional story becomes widely accepted over time, even though sometimes the facts are wrong. This often happens when someone writes a play or story about historical events, especially long after the events. For instance, a William Shakespeare play (called *Julius Caesar*) tells us that Julius Caesar was assassinated on the steps of the Roman Senate building. In fact, historians have discovered that the Senate was closed for repairs at the time and he was actually killed in another place altogether.

Can you think of any Hollywood movies that have been criticised for historical inaccuracies?

DID YOU KNOW?

The place where Julius Caesar was killed, called the Area Sacra, is famous in modern times as a home to dozens of Roman cats!

Dates

Finally, a word on another problem – dates. It is important to know the dates when things happened; make absolutely no mistake about that. However, do not begin with the idea that they will prevent you from enjoying history or from being good at it. If you become interested in what you are studying, remembering events is far, far easier. You never have to force yourself to remember the score in your favourite team's last match, or your favourite song's position in the charts, do you? If you are interested in history, you will be surprised by how many dates you can remember.

History dates in Europe are either BC or AD, depending on

whether the events occurred before the **birth of Christ** (BC) or after that year, known in Latin as *Anno Domini* (AD: the year of the Lord). In the case of years after Christ (AD), the number in the date increases as the years pass, for example 2005 comes after 2004. In dates before Christ (BC), the number in the date gets smaller as the years pass. For instance, Julius Caesar was born in 100 BC but died in 44 BC, 56 years later.

Some people prefer to use the terms BCE (Before Common Era) and CE (Common Era) instead of BC and AD. In this book, however, we will use BC and AD.

A **century** is made up of 100 years, from *centum*, the Latin word for 100. The years from Christ's birth up to 99 AD are called the first century, from 100 to 199 AD is the second century and so on. The 20th century includes the years from 1900 to 1999, and the 21st century started in 2000 AD.

CAN YOU SAY?

13. Complete: A place where artefacts of historical or archaeological interest are housed and displayed to the public is called a _____.

    (Junior Certificate Higher Level 1992, similar in Ordinary Level 2005)

14. Complete: The spreading of the ideas of a particular group, movement or individual to bring about change is called _____.

    (Junior Certificate Higher Level 1992)

15. Complete: Photographic film for preserving a microscopic record of documents and which can be enlarged is called _____.

    (Junior Certificate Higher Level 1992)

16. Explain what the letters AD and BC mean after each of the following dates: 44 BC and 432 AD.

    (Junior Certificate Ordinary Level 2001)

17. Give *one* reason why historians prefer to obtain information from more than one source.

    (Junior Certificate 1996)

18. To which century does the date 1825 AD belong?

    (Junior Certificate Ordinary Level 2006)

CAN YOU SAY?

DOCUMENT 1.
This is a register from Kilmainham Gaol, listing people in the Gaol during the Famine in 1847.
(Source: OPW)

Name	Age	Crime	Sentence	Status	Read/ Write	Trade	Address
William Kinsellagh	75	Begging	3 days confined with hard labour.	M	RW	Labourer	Meishal, Co. Carlow
Margaret Toole	32	Same	3 days with labour	M	NN	None	Glen of Amale, Co. Wicklow
William Cooke	16	Rooting Potatoes	Bailed	S	R	Labourer	Killeague, Co. Wicklow
James Brennan	24	Stealing Potatoes	21 days confined	S	R	Labourer	Mountmellick, Queen's Co.
Andrew Farrell	16	Malicious injury by rooting potatoes	1 calendar month confined from 2 Oct. or pay £1 fine	S	R	Labourer	Longford
Alicia Hanlon	23	Stolen potatoes	14 days confined	S	NN	None	Crumlin

M: Married **S:** Single **RW:** Read & Write **R:** Read only **NN:** Neither read nor write

---

19. This document is taken from the list of prisoners in Kilmainham Gaol during the Famine in 1847, a time of great hunger and death in Ireland. Read it carefully.
The details of each person are read across the page, so take a little time to get used to the layout and then answer the following questions:
    (a) What sentence did William Kinsellagh receive for begging?
    (b) Name one female prisoner who was married.
    (c) How many of the prisoners could neither read nor write?
    (d) From the document, give one piece of evidence to show that the prisoners were poor.
    (e) Name a prisoner who committed a crime that you would associate with the Famine.

KEYNOTES

1. **Historians:** detectives seeking clues about the past.
   Primary sources: firsthand evidence
2. **Source types:** objects (artefacts)
   Pictorial: photos • drawings • paintings • maps • documentary films
   Written: letters • diaries • documents • manuscripts • census • newspapers • autobiographies
   Oral: songs • poems • stories • living people
   Secondary sources: historical articles • books
3. **Difficulties:** finding material • museums • newspapers • libraries • archives
   Other problems: bias • propaganda • subjectivity • recorder's exaggeration • errors; dates • difference between BC and AD • how centuries are numbered

The Archaeologist at Work 2

ARCHAEOLOGY

Much of what we know about early history comes from a special kind of historical detective work called **archaeology**. This is quite a long word, because it is actually made up of two words: *archaois*, the Greek for 'ancient' or 'very old', and *logos*, meaning 'study'. Thus, archaeology is 'the study of very old things'.

What Archaeologists Do

Usually, an archaeologist investigates places and objects from before the time when written records of any sort were kept. For example, when we want to learn about life in Ireland more than 2,000 years ago, it is the archaeologist who provides us with the most accurate information because there were no written records kept here then.

In places where there might be objects or ruins to examine, as well as written material, an archaeologist often works with a historian.

This is the case, for instance, with investigations of ancient Rome and in many investigations of more recent times.

Archaeologists perform many different tasks. Physical work, such as digging, might be involved. Archaeologists must also have some knowledge of science. Their work can bring them to city centres or vast deserts, to deep caves or high mountains. For some archaeologists, even skills such as deep-sea diving, flying helicopters or mountain climbing can be useful in their search for clues about the past.

Knowing Where to Look

How does an archaeologist know where to look for places or objects of interest? Often, the **ruins** of old buildings, churches, forts or graves are still visible above the ground and might be worth investigating.

DID YOU KNOW?

These archaeologists working at Pompeii were doing so in temperatures of 42°C, in the shadow of a non-extinct volcano! The cost of some of the digs at Pompeii is covered by sponsorship from some leading Italian companies.

Sometimes, ruins may even be located underwater, such as the **wrecks** of 26 ships from the Spanish Armada, which have been found around the Irish coast.

Even when ruins have virtually disappeared, an archaeologist can locate them with the help of **old maps** or **documents** that pinpoint their location. Irish Ordnance Survey maps from the 19th century mark the locations of hundreds of forts that have by now been built over or bulldozed away.

Archaeologists often locate places of interest with the help of **aerial photographs** taken from aeroplanes or helicopters. In places where the earth was pressed down by human feet or buildings long ago, soil colour and crop growth will be different and visible from above.

Old stories and **legends**, while often unreliable and exaggerated, can give important clues. For example, the Roman town of Pompeii remained buried under volcanic ash from 79 AD, but its location was known through local tradition for over 1,500 years before archaeologists finally investigated it.

Undoubtedly, **luck** helps. Farmers or building workers often discover ancient objects or ruins by accident, and then the archaeologists may move in to investigate the area more fully. In 1868, the beautiful Ardagh Chalice was found by a farmer and his son digging potatoes in a field. Most of the remains of Viking Dublin, 1,000 years old, came to light because of building work carried out in recent decades.

Finally, **science** is increasingly being used to help archaeologists in their search, through techniques such as soil X-rays, chemical analysis and the use of ultrasound scanners to detect whether anything of interest lies beneath the ground.

DID YOU KNOW?

The world's most famous cave paintings, at Lascaux in France, were found in 1940 by four boys while they were actually looking for a lost dog!

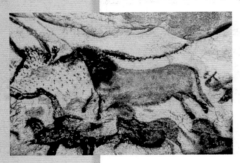

CAN YOU SAY?

1. What does the term archaeology mean?
2. Why are archaeologists particularly important in the study of Ireland's history from 2,000 years ago?
3. How can old maps help archaeologists?
4. Explain how archaeologists use aerial photographs.
5. How was the Ardagh Chalice first discovered?

THE EXCAVATION

Preparing the Site

As soon as archaeologists believe they have found a place worth investigating, it becomes an **archaeological site**. To prevent any interference with the site, it is carefully fenced off where possible. The area is then divided into square-shaped sections and identified by different numbers or letters. Pathways are marked out between the sections, so that the archaeologists can move around the site without walking on valuable objects. Then it is time to begin the excavation, often called the **dig**.

The Dig

The site may be covered in grass or topsoil. There is little chance of finding anything close to the surface, so this material is usually removed quite quickly. It is then that the really painstaking work begins.

SOURCE A

X

The archaeologists slowly dig down into each square, level by level, using small tools such as trowels or geologists' hammers to avoid breaking or missing important finds. Kitchen spoons, penknives and small brushes are also used in the excavation. Many archaeologists use toothbrushes when cleaning finds. The bristles are strong enough to clean away earth, but soft enough to avoid damaging the finds. Finds such as pieces of pottery, tools or weapons are called **artefacts**.

Anything of interest found on a dig is carefully labelled. A precise record of the section of the site in which it was discovered is also kept. This is done on a **site map**, where all the sections are marked by lines forming a grid. It is also important to record how far down the artefact was found – we shall see the reason for this later.

An archaeologist pays close attention to the colour of the earth. Any wood that has rotted back into the earth over time can cause the earth in that spot to be different in colour from the rest of the site. Careful excavation of this can reveal where the post-holes supporting an ancient house were.

The unwanted earth on a site is often passed through a sieve before being dumped, in case any objects have been missed.

SOURCE B

At the end of a successful dig, thousands of objects or fragments may have been found. Even the ancient rubbish heaps of the inhabitants of a site can provide many artefacts and bones useful to the archaeologist. Pieces of broken pottery can sometimes be put back together, a bit like a 3D jigsaw – this is one reason for marking carefully where each find occurred.

CAN YOU SAY?

6. In the picture called **Source A** above (*Junior Certificate Ordinary Level 2005*):
   (a) What work is being done by the archaeologist marked X in the picture?
   (b) What do you think the archaeologists have found?
   (c) Give *one* example from the picture of how archaeologists record information.
7. Name *two* instruments an archaeologist would use while excavating a site.
   (*Junior Certificate Ordinary Level 1998, 2001 and 2006*)
8. What is an artefact?   (*Junior Certificate Ordinary Level 1999 and Higher Level 2006*)
9. Why do archaeologists consider ancient rubbish dumps to be a valuable source of evidence?   (*Junior Certificate Ordinary Level 1997*)
10. **Source B** above shows archaeologists at work.
    (*Junior Certificate Ordinary and Higher Levels 2000*)
    (a) What is the archaeologist marked X doing in the picture?
    (b) What have the archaeologists found?   (*Ordinary Level only*)
    (c) Name *two* instruments used by archaeologists as seen in the picture.
    (d) Why do archaeologists have to be very careful when they are removing objects from the ground?
    (*Ordinary Level normally, but similar question in Higher Level 2006*)

How Archaeologists Work Out the Age of a Find

Over thousands of years, objects may become buried some metres below the surface as a result of gravity and earth movements caused by weather, floods and other factors. Usually, the further down an object lies, the longer it has been there and the older it is.

Archaeologists dig down through each layer of earth and take careful note of the depth at which each object is found. This work is called **stratigraphy.** If anything of known date is found, such as a coin, then the other items found at the same depth probably date from the same period.

Archaeologists in Ireland and elsewhere have found it useful to spend time excavating in **peat bogs** because artefacts can be very well preserved in peat. The American archaeologist in the picture (right) found a 7,000-year-old body three metres down in a peat bog in Florida.

All living creatures and plants contain a substance called **carbon-14** (or radiocarbon). When creatures and plants die, the carbon-14 in them begins to decay at a steady rate. The amount of it in the object decreases by 50 per cent over 5,568 years (its 'half-life'); then 50 per cent of the remainder decreases over a further 5,568 years and so on. By measuring how rapidly carbon-14 is decaying in a bone, for example, scientists can tell accurately how old it is. This is called **carbon dating**.

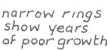
narrow rings show years of poor growth

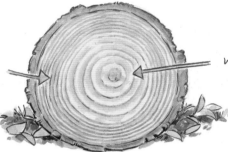

wide rings show years of good growth.

We know the age of a tree by counting the rings inside its trunk. Each ring represents the yearly growth of the tree. Thus, wide rings tell us that the weather was suitable for growth, while narrow ones might suggest a drought in any particular year. Trees from the same area have similar ring patterns, so archaeologists can even tell the age of a plank of timber if its ring or grain pattern matches those of a tree of known age. Tree-ring dating is called **dendrochronology**. So far in Ireland, the ring patterns from different trees and pieces of old timber have been matched together to cover a period as far back as 5289 BC.

Peat is composed mostly of decayed plants and so is easily dated using carbon-14. Using stratigraphy, any object found in a bog can be dated by carbon dating the peat at the same level. It is even possible to discover what plants grew thousands of years ago because pollen grains survive in the damp peat and can be identified under a microscope in a study called **pollen analysis**. Therefore, science can be of great help to archaeologists in finding and dating sites and artefacts.

DID YOU KNOW?

The Turin Shroud (below) was thought to have been the cloth that had been wrapped around the body of Jesus after the crucifixion. However, carbon dating tests done on its linen fibres in 1988 proved that the part of the shroud that was analysed was made at least 1,200 years after Jesus died.

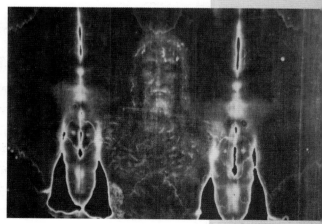

SOURCE C

CAN YOU SAY?

11. Name *one* method an archaeologist would use to date an object found on a site.
    (Junior Certificate Ordinary and Higher Levels 2000)
12. What is carbon dating? *(Junior Certificate Higher Level 1994)*
13. Explain what the rings on trees can tell archaeologists.
14. Examine the photograph, **Source C**, above and answer the questions that follow.
    (Parts (d) and (e) relate to what will be covered in the next section, but see whether you can answer them anyway.)
    (a) What work is being done by the archaeologist on the left of the picture?
    (Junior Certificate Ordinary and Higher Levels 1993)
    (b) What work is being done by the other archaeologist?
    (Junior Certificate Higher Level 1993)
    (c) What do you think the archaeologists have discovered?
    (Junior Certificate Ordinary Level 1993)
    (d) What natural element presents the biggest threat to this archaeological site? Support your answer by evidence from the picture.
    (Junior Certificate Higher Level 1993)
    (e) The work is being done in winter. If, however, these archaeologists were digging on this site in summer time, what problems could arise because of the fact that there is a beach nearby?
    (Junior Certificate Ordinary Level 1993)

PROBLEMS FOR TODAY'S ARCHAEOLOGISTS

Weather and Working Conditions

An archaeologist is at the mercy of the weather. In Ireland, digs are usually carried out only in summer time. Rain and particularly flooding are not only uncomfortable to work in, they can also seriously damage the strata on a site, making dating difficult. People who use metal detectors and dig illegally for finds, ignoring the stratigraphy, cause similar problems.

At sites in remote areas, archaeologists must often live rough in tents for months on end. Sites such as the Spanish Armada wrecks can even force archaeologists to work underwater in cold and dangerous conditions using breathing apparatus.

In city sites particularly, archaeologists may have to work very quickly. This is because the site might have been uncovered during building work and the archaeologists might have only a short time before building begins again. Such work is called **rescue archaeology**.

The blackened area on the Colosseum walls is caused mainly by air pollution from car exhausts. What look like gates on the ground level are actually rows of reinforcing metal girders. Look closely and you can see scaffolding for repair work on the inside too.

Development Problems

Pollution from car exhausts and factories can badly damage city sites and monuments, even causing stone to crumble over time. In Athens, to protect both the public and the ancient monuments, restrictions are sometimes placed on the number of cars entering the city.

In recent decades, more and more development has taken place in Ireland. Land that had been unused is now being built on. Roads, houses and factories are being built at a faster rate than ever before. One of the difficulties with this development is that it often happens in places where there may be much of historical and archaeological interest.

The route of the M3 brought it close to the Hill of Tara, Co. Meath.

At the very least, when such development uncovers archaeological sites, archaeologists are given some time to perform a dig to see what can be rescued before the development continues. However, sometimes the site can be so important that some people would prefer to see the development plans abandoned rather than have the site built on. This happened when the M50 motorway was extended through the site of a medieval castle at Carrickmines, Co. Dublin.

Even when the development work does not go directly over an archaeological site, it can cause plenty of anger when such development brings a lot of traffic near the site every day, or if the development damages the appearance of the area around the site. A recent Irish example of this is the building of a motorway through part of Co. Meath to help thousands of people trying to get to work in Dublin each day. Unfortunately, the road runs very close to Ireland's most famous archaeological site in the Boyne Valley and caused a major dispute.

Tourism and Archaeology

When the archaeologist's work is done, important objects such as pieces of pottery, weapons, jewellery and even plain household items may end up on display in a museum. Ireland's main one is the National Museum in Dublin. At several places around Ireland, folk and heritage parks have been set up, displaying artefacts and reconstructing old buildings, machines and so on. The Irish National Heritage Park is at Ferrycarrig, Co. Wexford.

Archaeology requires money – often from museums, governments, businesses and local councils. However, this can be recovered many times over through **tourism**. To attract visitors, important sites are often opened and interpretative centres built nearby. Ireland has several such places, and world-famous ruins such as the Acropolis in Athens or the Colosseum in Rome attract thousands of tourists daily. Such numbers can, of course, make it difficult to preserve these sites. The marvellous cave paintings at Lascaux, mentioned earlier, had to be closed again in the 1980s; thousands of visitors breathing on the pictures caused them to become badly discoloured. It is vital to keep a balance between attracting visitors and preserving the past.

One of Ireland's most recent archaeological discoveries – a Viking site at Woodstown, Co. Waterford – prompted a number of international experts to write the following in 2004:

SOURCE D

SOURCE E

If a sufficiently large percentage of the site were dug, it might prove possible to create a major tourist and educational resource for the south-east. The Jorvik Viking Centre at York is still drawing in 400,000 visitors a year, 20 years after its opening, when the numbers were over 800,000. If, on the other hand, the majority of the site were left without excavation, it would be difficult to realise its full potential as a resource for the people of Waterford, or to provide security against unauthorised plundering [i.e. stealing of artefacts] in the future.

CAN YOU SAY?

15. Explain *one* way in which the weather can affect an archaeologist's work.
16. Explain *one* difficulty archaeologists may have when working in a city.
17. Mention *one* way in which archaeology can help to promote tourism.
(*Junior Certificate Ordinary and Higher Levels 1992*)
18. Looking at **Source D** above, of a street in Pompeii:
Explain what you think the purpose of the iron bars in this picture is.
This site (Pompeii) is visited by millions of tourists each year. How can this help *and* harm the site? Give *one* reason in *each* case.
19. Read **Source E** above and give *one* advantage that the experts feel a large excavation could have and *one* disadvantage of not carrying out one.

KEYNOTES

1. **Archaeology:** study of very old things • prehistory • variety of skills needed by archaeologists
    Finding archaeological sites: ruins/wrecks • maps and documents • aerial photographs • stories and legends • luck • scientific methods
2. **Excavation:** protecting the site • pathways • squares • removal of topsoil – digging down through each level • spoons, trowels and toothbrushes • finding artefacts • making a site map • locating finds on a grid
3. **Problems of dating:** stratigraphy • carbon dating • dendrochronology • pollen analysis
4. **Other difficulties:** problems of weather • working in bogs and under water • flooding • destruction of layers by metal detectors • rescue archaeology • speed essential
    Afterwards: museums • heritage parks • interpretative centres • tourism • dangers and benefits

MINI-PROJECT

Write an account of the following: *An Archaeologist at Work.*
Hints:
- choosing a site
- excavating a site
- instruments used
- findings

(*Note:* This question appeared on both Ordinary and Higher Level papers in the 1999 Junior Certificate exam, with a very similar one on the 2001 Higher paper. However, the hints were not given on the Higher papers.)

Planet Earth has been existed for over 4.5 billion years. However, the earliest traces of humans found by archaeologists date only from around 2,500,000 years ago. Up to 8000 BC, these early people used tools and weapons made from stone. The objects tended to be very simple, made from roughly sharpened stone such as flint.

This first period of **Stone Age** people is more correctly known as the **Paleolithic** (Early Stone Age) period. No evidence of human life from this time has been found in Ireland, probably because it was far from the rest of what we now call Europe. In addition, great **Ice Ages** lasted from about 20,000 to 10,000 years ago and covered most of the country in a sheet of ice. However, the very south of Ireland was free of ice, so it is possible that people lived there in Paleolithic times, although no evidence of human life has yet been found.

> STONE AGES (lithos = stone)
> Paleolithic (Early Stone): The earliest period of the Stone Age dates from around 2500000 BC to 8000 BC.
> Mesolithic (Middle Stone): In Ireland, the Mesolithic period dates from around 8000 BC to 3500 BC.
> Neolithic (New Stone): In Ireland, the Neolithic period dates from around 3500 BC to 2000 BC.

THE MESOLITHIC PERIOD

As the Ice Ages came to an end, plants and trees began to grow in Ireland. At this time, we were actually joined by land to the rest of Europe, so it is likely that the first creatures to arrive in Ireland *walked* here in search of food. However, as more and more ice melted, sea levels rose and Ireland became an island.

Lefanta in Co. Waterford gave Mesolithic people places to hunt and fish, not to mention small trees that could be used for housing and a river to travel on in their dugout boats.

SOURCE A

Between 8000 BC and 3500 BC, people's use of stone tools improved a lot. This time is known as the **Mesolithic** (Middle Stone Age) period. It is during these years, according to the archaeologists, that people first arrived in Ireland.

Only a handful of Irish Mesolithic sites have been discovered and excavated, and we have absolutely no written sources to draw on for information, so our knowledge of the first people in Ireland is limited. All the sites found so far lie close to woodland and water, such as at Boora in Co. Offaly and Lefanta in Co. Waterford. Such locations provided the hunting and fishing grounds that Mesolithic people depended on so much.

Mesolithic people are often known as **hunter-gatherers**. Near the sites of their homes, archaeologists have found rubbish heaps containing bones of wild animals, such as deer, boar, fox and hare. Fish bones (salmon, eel and bass) have also been found, though no evidence of what we today call domestic or farm animals.

The absence of farm animals indicates that Mesolithic people got meat by hunting and fishing, not farming. Further finds include the remains of apples, nuts and berries, which suggests that gathering food was also important, so we can safely call these people hunter-gatherers. At **Mount Sandel** in Co. Derry, the remains of a fire-hearth, with dark post holes in the earth on either side, suggest that food was cooked over the fire on some sort of spit.

DID YOU KNOW?

It is likely that Mesolithic people travelled to Ireland and around its coasts and rivers using dugout canoes. These were made from a single tree-trunk, hollowed out by flint tools and carefully controlled fires. The longest dugout boat found in Ireland (Galway) was 16 metres, longer than three family saloon cars.

Mesolithic people differed from Paleolithic people in that they used more advanced weapons and tools. Not only have flint and other stone weapons been found in Mesolithic sites, but also ones made of timber, bone and antler. Often, objects were made from a combination of these, such as a fishing spear or saw made from tiny flints (**microliths**) attached to timber or bone handles.

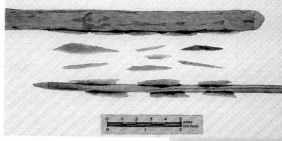

Flint artefacts from Mount Sandel.

SOURCE B

No Mesolithic sites found here so far have told us anything of pastimes, religion or burial customs. We can really only guess that the people may have clothed themselves in animal skins – weaving of cloth was not known to the earliest Irish people. Yet the work of archaeologist Peter Woodman at Mount Sandel has told us much about Mesolithic housing. During the dig, it was noticed that some spots of earth were darker than the earth elsewhere on the site. This was because they were filled with decayed timber, obviously once the posts supporting the 'house'. By fitting new posts into the holes, Woodman was able to calculate both the shape of the huts and their height. These poles were undoubtedly covered in animal skins, sods or some other covering, though we will probably never know for sure.

CAN YOU SAY?

1. Why are the earliest times called the Stone Age?

   (Junior Certificate Ordinary and Higher Levels 1995 and 1999, and Ordinary Level only in 2005)

2. Explain what the terms (a) Paleolithic and (b) Mesolithic refer to.
3. Why are the earliest Irish people called hunter-gatherers?
4. What are microliths? Give *one* example of how they were used in the Mesolithic period.
5. In the drawing above (**Source A**), list *two* activities being carried out by women and *two* by men in Mesolithic Ireland.
6. Look at the reconstruction of a Mesolithic house (**Source B** above).

   (a) What shape is the house?

   (b) What is the roof made from?

   (c) Give *one* reason why these houses were so small and light.

THE NEOLITHIC PERIOD

From around 3500 BC onwards, there are clear signs that new settlers came here and brought with them several new ideas that had a major effect on Ireland. This period is known as the **Neolithic** (New Stone Age) period. The biggest change in this period was that, instead of just hunting and gathering food, Neolithic Irish people were **farmers**.

Pollen analysis, which we learnt about in Chapter 2, has shown traces of crops, such as wheat and barley, preserved in Irish peat, carbon dated to 3500 BC. The peat contained less tree pollen than earlier peat, telling us that trees were probably cut to make way for farm land. Also, carbon dating has shown that farm animals such as sheep and cows lived in Ireland from around 3500 BC.

The remains of Neolithic **fields** have been found in places such as Céide in Co. Mayo. These walled fields were probably used not only to keep animals in, but also to mark out where each farmer's territory lay. Irish farms were generally situated on fairly high ground because soils here were not as heavy as in low-lying areas, so they were easier to plough with timber and stone tools.

The Neolithic people were generally more skilled **craftspeople** than those before them. Tools were usually made of polished stone, less likely to break and capable of chopping trees or tilling the soil. Polished stone axes and arrowheads, hide-scrapers and mattocks for farming have been found at Neolithic sites, such as Lough Gur, Co. Limerick.

DID YOU KNOW?

The knowledge of farming – of domesticating (taming) animals and of growing crops from seed that had previously grown wild – almost certainly began in what is now called the Middle East (Israel, Jordan, Iraq and so on) and gradually spread across Europe.

SOURCE C

Farming led to a need for other skills in the Neolithic home, particularly the grinding of corn. This was done between two stones. Of course, the resulting flour required another skill: bread making. Small needles made from bone have also been carbon dated to Neolithic times, and there is little doubt that sewn and woven clothing gradually began to replace animal skins.

Perhaps the greatest difference between Neolithic and Mesolithic craftworkers lies in **pottery**. Pottery, made from local clay, did not exist in Mesolithic times, but Neolithic people certainly made and used many different types. Various bowls and containers were very important for storing and preparing the food that Neolithic farms produced. Cooking was done around a fire in the middle of the floor.

Archaeologists have discovered many more Neolithic house sites in Ireland than Mesolithic ones, mainly because the population was growing at this time. Depending on what building materials were available locally, houses were made of timber, stone or a mixture of both.

Usually, the main house supports consisted of stout timber poles with walls of timber, or sometimes of wattle and daub (a mixture of

lightly woven fencing and mud). Roofing was made of straw (left after the harvest) or rushes, and probably came out over the walls of the house to protect them from wind and rain. Most Neolithic houses were rectangular, though circular ones have also been found.

How many differences between this house and a modern house can you see?

CAN YOU SAY?

7. Identify *two* pieces of archaeological evidence that prove that farming began in Ireland after 3500 BC.

8. Why did Neolithic people prefer to live in upland areas with light soils?

(Junior Certificate Higher Level 1994)

9. **Source C** above is an artist's impression of farming life in ancient Ireland during the Neolithic (New Stone) Age.
   (a) Briefly describe what type of work is going on in each of the scenes numbered 1 to 6.
   (b) In Scene 1, the man on the left-hand side has an axe. Name the *two* materials from which the axe is made.
   (c) From the evidence in **Source C**, do you agree that life in ancient Ireland was very difficult? Give a reason for your answer.

(All questions from Junior Certificate Ordinary Level 1999)

10. Mention *two* advances made by Neolithic people (New Stone Age).

(Junior Certificate Higher Level 2009)

Megalithic Tombs

The most amazing remains from Neolithic Ireland are the huge graves called **megaliths** ('great stones') or **megalithic** tombs. Around 1,000 of them survive today.

The large stones used in making these tombs were probably rolled to their sites on logs. As towns did not exist in Neolithic Ireland, hundreds of people must have gathered from far and wide to help build the tombs. At the site, the stones may have been dragged up temporary mounds of earth (later cleared away), so that they could be levered into position using timber poles.

Court cairns

In Neolithic times, three kinds of megalithic tomb were built. The earliest known tombs are called **court cairns**. There are more than 300 still in existence; the biggest is in the north-west of Ireland. These tombs are called court cairns because they had an open entrance area (**court**) and were originally covered by a mound of earth or stones (**cairn**).

Archaeologists have found the cremated (burnt) remains of the dead in the chambers inside, along with objects that may have belonged to them, such as leaf-shaped flint arrowheads, round-bottomed pottery, tools and necklaces.

Passage graves

Other Neolithic settlers were responsible for Ireland's largest megalithic tombs, known as **passage graves**. These are found mainly in Co. Meath, where there are over 30, and also in Co. Sligo, where, between the districts of Carrowmore and Carrowkeel, remains of some 70 passage graves exist.

On the outside, passage graves are circular mounds of earth or stones, varying in diameter from 8 to 85 metres. Inside, a stone-lined passage leads to a wider burial chamber or chambers – where the remains of the dead were laid. Passage graves were usually built on hill-tops, and this, plus their size and the work involved in building them, suggests that they were built for important people, probably the kings or tribal leaders of Neolithic Ireland.

Our largest and most famous passage grave is at Newgrange, Co. Meath. Those close by at Knowth and Dowth are also very large. At Newgrange, the passage of 20 metres leads to a three-sectioned chamber, and the roof over the chamber rises to 6 metres, over twice the height of a normal house ceiling. The chamber roof is **corbelled**; this means that layers of stone were placed on top of each other, each layer lying slightly inside the other until the sides eventually met each other at the top.

Newgrange was discovered by workmen in 1699 and was 'visited' after that by many people, so not much of the original contents of the chamber remained when excavations began in 1962.

> ### DID YOU KNOW?
>
> In many parts of Ireland, the skill of making grass ropes, called súgáin, still survives. These ropes are remarkably strong and could very well have been used in Neolithic times to drag the heavy boulders used in megalithic tombs.

burial chamber

court cairn

SOURCE D

However, stone basins and the remains of four bodies were found. In other passage graves in Co. Meath and Co. Sligo, mushroom-headed pins, decorated pots, pendants and a flint macehead have been found. Dating has placed Newgrange at around 2500 BC, about the same age as the Great Pyramid of Egypt.

Important evidence of Neolithic **religion** comes from Newgrange. Archaeologist M. J. O'Kelly and his team noted how the long passageway into the burial chamber was fully lit up by the rising sun only once a year, around 21 December, the winter solstice. This suggests that sun worship was important to Neolithic people. This could explain the spiral sun-like patterns carved into some of the stones at Newgrange, and the tomb facing eastwards towards the rising sun.

Newgrange shows what really advanced people its builders were, not just in their construction skills. To build it to coincide with the winter solstice required a knowledge of astronomy – and remember that, as far as we know, these people did not read or write! In addition, in a time when farming was so important, Newgrange acted as a kind of giant calendar, helping people to know when midwinter had passed and the crop-planting season was approaching.

SOURCE E

The entrance to Newgrange.

Dolmens

The third type of Neolithic tomb is called a **dolmen** or **portal tomb**. The name **portal** comes from the fact that large upright stones form an entrance or portal to the chamber (*porta* is the Latin word for 'door'). In reality, these are simpler, and usually later, versions of passage graves. A huge **capstone** rested on top of a number of smaller upright stones, while the remains of the dead were placed underneath. The capstone at Browne's Hill, Co. Carlow, is thought to weigh about 100 tonnes, while the dolmen excavated at Poulnabrone, Co. Clare, contained the remains of 22 bodies.

Dolmen artefacts (called **grave-goods**) include polished stone axes, bone necklaces and flint scrapers. As with the other types of tomb, dolmens were originally covered by a mound of earth or stone – most probably removed over the centuries for building purposes. Although very few grave-goods were found at Newgrange, those found under dolmens and in other

The Browne's Hill dolmen.

megalithic tombs seem to indicate again that Neolithic people held religious beliefs – the grave-goods, perhaps, were needed by the dead in the afterlife.

CAN YOU SAY?

11. During the Neolithic age, megaliths were built throughout Europe. What is a megalith?   (*Junior Certificate Ordinary Level 1994*)

12. Name *two* types of tomb from Neolithic Ireland.
                    (*Junior Certificate Higher Level 2005, similar in 1993*)

13. **Source D** is a picture of Newgrange, Co. Meath. **Source E** is a close-up picture of the front of Newgrange.
  (a) For what purpose do you think Newgrange was built?
  (b) The people who constructed Newgrange were great builders. Write down *one* piece of evidence from **Source D** to support this view.
  (c) In **Source E**, what evidence is there to suggest that the builders of Newgrange had some form of art and decoration skills?
                    (*Junior Certificate Ordinary Level 2000*)

14. Why were grave-goods placed inside megalithic tombs?

15. Mention *two* important advances made by Neolithic (New Stone Age) people.
                    (*Junior Certificate Ordinary and Higher Levels 1996*)

MINI-PROJECT

Write an account on: *A farmer living in Ireland in ancient times.*
Hints:
- dwelling places
- dress
- farming methods
- crops and animals

                    (*Junior Certificate Ordinary and Higher Levels 1997*)

(*Note:* A similar question was asked on the Higher Level paper in 2005 but simply as 'A person living in ancient Ireland', with no hints given.)

Mesolithic	Neolithic
1. Rough stone tools.	Replaced by stronger polished stone ones, including axes capable of chopping trees.
2. People moved around, hunting and gathering food.	With trees cleared away, people settled and used land for farming and rearing animals.
3. Food consisted of wild animals, fish and berries.	Mostly replaced by crops such as wheat and barley, and meat from cattle and sheep.
4. No evidence of pottery.	With more food to prepare and store, pottery making became very important.
5. Housing was temporary and mostly just huts.	More solid and permanent houses were made from the chopped trees and straw.
6. Clothing was made from animal skins.	Farm animals provided wool for woven clothing and leather for shoes.
7. The population was low.	As farming improved food supply, the population grew and cleared more land.
8. No evidence of warfare.	With more people competing for land, people fought each other and built forts.
9. No evidence of burial sites.	With settled communities of people, burial grounds were developed.
10. No evidence of people believing in gods or an afterlife.	Massive tombs and stone circles show that people worshipped the sun.

KEYNOTES

1. **Stone Age:** Paleolithic (Early Stone Age) period ● Mesolithic (Middle Stone Age) period ● people in Ireland ● hunter-gatherers ● tools made from flint microliths ● Mount Sandel excavations
2. **Neolithic (New Stone Age) period:** (c.3500 BC) ● beginnings of farming ● new skills needed ● bread making ● polished stone tools ● pottery ● wattle and daub housing ● Lough Gur ● Céide Fields
3. **Megalithic tombs:** huge construction tasks ● court cairns ● passage graves (Meath and Sligo) ● Newgrange ● chamber with corbelled roof ● c.2500 BC ● evidence of sun-worship ● very advanced builders ● knowledge of astronomy and seasons
   Portal dolmens: huge capstones ● grave-goods for the afterlife

The Bronze Age Comes to Ireland

4

The centuries after 2000 BC saw the beginnings in Ireland of what is known as the **Bronze Age**. The change from the use of polished stone implements to ones made from bronze took place gradually.
In Central Europe, tools were made from soft metals, such as copper, long before 2000 BC. Then someone found that a mixture of copper and tin made a much harder metal – **bronze**.

Slowly, settlers or traders from Britain or mainland Europe introduced bronze to Ireland, though stone weapons and tools continued to be made here as well. Bronze had many advantages, but it was probably hard to get in Ireland. Although we had prehistoric copper mines, like at Mount Gabriel, Co. Cork, tin had to be imported from southern England.

> **DID YOU KNOW?**
>
> A frozen body discovered in the Alps in 1991 was carbon dated to 3300 BC, 1,000 years before the Stone Age had supposedly ended, yet this 'iceman' had carried a copper axe!

SMELTING

Copper and tin are minerals that are found in rock called **ore**. Early metal workers hammered lumps of ore into shapes such as axe heads. Then the process called **smelting** was discovered; this was much more effective. Ore was heated to a very high temperature over a charcoal fire, a bit like a barbecue. As the metal in the ore melted, it dripped down through the charcoal to form a pool at the bottom. This cooled into a solid lump of metal. It could then be reheated, mixed with other metals needed and poured into a stone or clay **mould**. When this mixture cooled, the bronze implement was ready for use.

FARMING

Farming continued to develop during the Bronze Age. Hunting and gathering became less important and farming made food fairly easy to get. A better food supply also meant that people became healthier and the Bronze Age saw a big increase in population; there may have been 200,000 people living in Ireland by 2000 BC. This meant that there

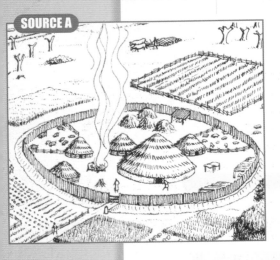
SOURCE A

was less land to go around. Pollen analysis shows that, during the Bronze Age, more forests were cut down to create new farmland. It is likely that competition for land led to fighting between Bronze Age people – archaeologists have discovered lots of bronze shields and swords. Fortified homes, rare in Stone Age Ireland, usually date from the Bronze Age onwards.

HOMES

In Bronze Age Ireland, there were two main types of fortified home.

SOURCE B

A rath in north Munster.

Raths

A rath was usually an earthen fort built by digging out a trench around a house or houses. The earth was then piled inside the trench to form a sort of ditch (rampart) against attack. Some raths had wooden fences on top of the rampart for extra protection. Entrance was by a narrow gateway.

Houses inside varied; some were made from wattle and daub (woven sticks plastered in mud), some from timber, and some even had stone walls, depending on available materials. Roofs were usually thatched. As well as protecting the occupants from attack, the rath was a farmyard to keep cattle in at night or in time of danger. Ireland once had thousands of raths. Many have now been destroyed and few of those left have been excavated.

SOURCE C

Crannógs

A rarer and more unusual type of fort was the crannóg. This was built on a man-made island, usually near a lake shore. Wooden posts were driven into the lake-bed and the inside area was filled with stones, branches and earth until a solid base was created, usually for just one or two houses. The crannóg was reached either by boat, or sunken stepping stones, known only to the owners, or by a drawbridge that was pulled onto the island when not in use.

CAN YOU SAY?

1. Name the *two* metals that were used to make bronze.
   (Junior Certificate Ordinary Level 2001 and 2005)

2. **Source A** is an artist's impression of a farming settlement in ancient Ireland during the Bronze Age.
   (a) Why do you think the fence was built around the settlement?
   (b) Name *two* materials from which the buildings were made.
   (Junior Certificate Ordinary Level 2001)

3. Mention *one* defensive feature of the fort in **Source B**.
   (Junior Certificate Ordinary Level 1998)

4. What was a crannóg? *(Junior Certificate Higher Level 1993 and 2000)*

5. Using the artist's impression of a crannóg (**Source C** above):
   (a) Give *one* reason why crannógs were built in lakes.
   (b) How did the inhabitants get from the crannóg to the mainland?
   (c) Name *two* materials used to build the dwelling and the surrounding fence.
   (d) Give *one* reason why those who build models of crannógs would consult an archaeologist. *(Junior Certificate Ordinary and Higher Levels 1995)*

DAILY LIFE

Evidence of Bronze Age clothing tells us that cloth was woven from sheep's wool and probably dyed with berries. Bronze needles and tweezers made sewing easier. Flint scrapers found in Bronze Age sites show that animal hides were still used for clothing and footwear. The Alpine iceman found in 1991 wore size 5 shoes!

Many Bronze Age house sites found had hearths (fireplaces) inside, where meat was cooked. The discovery of quern stones, for grinding grain into flour, and bronze pots suggests that foods such as pancakes, bread and porridge were also eaten. Most bones found have been of domestic animals such as cattle, sheep and pigs. Hunting was more of a pastime than a necessity.

An interesting method of early Irish cooking is the **fulacht fiadh**. This was

The reconstruction of a fulacht fiadh, which is located in the Irish National Heritage Park at Ferrycarrig in Wexford.

really a large pit, which was dug in wet ground, so that it would quickly fill with water. It was usually lined with timber planks. Stones were heated in a nearby fire and then placed in the water, so that it eventually came to the boil. A joint of meat, tied to a stick and wrapped in straw to prevent it from scalding, was lowered into the

35

water. Hot stones were added to keep the water boiling, and, as shown by the experiments of M. J. O'Kelly and at the National Heritage Park, the meat cooked perfectly at the rate of 20 minutes for each half-kilo in weight.

Crafts

Most people in Bronze Age Ireland were farmers. Pollen records show that crops such as wheat, barley and oats were widely grown.

Although several bronze sickles have been found, no Bronze Age plough has been unearthed (yet). With the amount of forest-clearing that took place, it is not surprising that bronze axes and adzes (for shaping timber logs) have also come to light.

Carpenters certainly worked in Bronze Age Ireland, making the planks and joints needed for house-building in particular. However, nothing that we might call 'furniture' has been found. Perhaps the most important craftsperson in Ireland at this time was the **smith**, who made all the bronze tools and weapons. A Co. Kildare find called the Bishopsland Hoard contained anvils, hammers and chisels used by these smiths. As the Bronze Age went on, smiths learnt how to hammer out sheets of bronze and join them together with bronze rivets. This explains why later Bronze Age discoveries include bronze shields, cauldrons and smaller pots. We also know that Bronze Age Irish people liked music, because dozens of bronze horns have been found.

Smiths also worked in gold. Much of this came from Europe, though some of the gold has been traced to Co. Wicklow. Gold objects include earrings, necklaces and bracelets. More impressive still are the **lunulae**, shaped like half-moons (*luna* is the Latin for 'moon'); these are made from hammered gold and are decorated with line and circle patterns. Lunulae were worn around the neck, as were short gold ropes called **torcs**. Hundreds of gold dress fasteners have also been found.

New types of pottery called **beakers** were made here during the Bronze Age. It is likely that crafts such as beaker making and sheet-metal working came to Ireland through trade. Although no written records exist for this period, it is certain that Irish metal products were sold as far away as Egypt, and we imported objects such as tin and semi-precious stones from all over Europe.

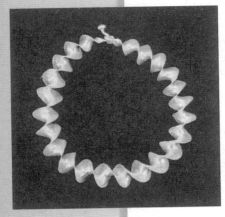

A Bronze Age gold torc.

A gold dress fastener.

CAN YOU SAY?

6. For what were querns used in Bronze Age Ireland?
7. For what purpose did early Irish people use a fulacht fiadh?
(Junior Certificate Ordinary and Higher Levels 1993)
8. Why was a fulacht fiadh usually dug in damp ground?
9. What archaeological evidence suggests that most people in Bronze Age Ireland were farmers?
10. Why were (a) carpenters and (b) smiths important in Bronze Age Ireland?
11. Identify *two* pieces of evidence that show that Ireland had considerable contact with mainland Europe during the Bronze Age.
12. Explain the meaning of the term 'torc'. *(Junior Certificate Ordinary Level 1998)*
13. Name *two* metal ores that were mined in Ireland during the Bronze Age.
(Junior Certificate Ordinary Level 1998)

BURIAL CUSTOMS

Only one new type of megalithic tomb developed during the Irish Bronze Age. The wedge-shaped **gallery grave** sloped downwards from front to back and looked like a wedge from the side; it is also known as a **wedge tomb**. In total, there are between 300 and 400 of these known in Ireland. Basically, they consist of a stone passageway roofed with stone slabs and originally covered by a cairn. Most contain just a single burial chamber, though the ones at Labbacalle, Co. Cork, and Deerpark, Co. Clare, have two.

From excavations, it seems that Bronze Age burials were much simpler than Neolithic ones. With a growing population, simple **cist burials** became the norm. The remains of the dead person were placed in a stone-rimmed grave (**cist**) in a crouched position or were cremated and put in an upside-down pot. Grave-goods placed with the remains were usually items of food or weapons. This shows (as in Neolithic Ireland) that people believed in an afterlife where such objects would be needed.

Sometimes a cist grave is found under a small mound called a **tumulus**; many **tumuli** lay undetected for centuries until they were disturbed by ploughing or building work. In the southern half of Ireland, particularly, some cist graves have been found under large standing stones called **monoliths** or inside **stone circles**.

Stone alignments (straight lines of three or more standing stones) also date from the Bronze Age. Stone alignments, and particularly

The wedge tomb at Haroldstown, Co. Carlow.

Bronze Age burial – partially cremated remains with a so-called pygmy urn.

SOURCE D

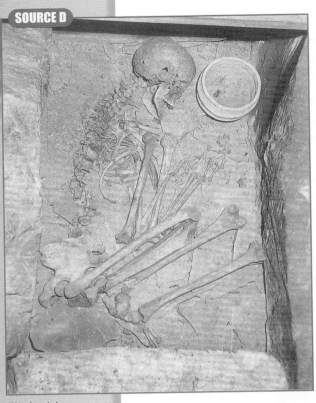

Cist burial

Can you spot the horizontal stone in this stone circle which is located at Drombeg, Co. Cork?

stone circles, offer evidence of ancient sun-worship where the rays of the rising sun shine right between the entrance stones. In some circles, a horizontal stone lies among the upright ones; this was probably used as a form of altar for making sacrifices on.

FROM BRONZE TO IRON

As we saw, the knowledge of metal came to Ireland from continental Europe. Throughout the continent, and beyond it, civilisations in different areas made tools, weapons and ornaments from metals such as copper, gold and of course bronze. One region where metal working reached a high standard was where Austria is today. Around 1000 BC, the **Urnfield** people there were among the best metalsmiths in Europe and brought their skills to a wide area of Central Europe. In about 700 BC, some of these people learnt how to make a new metal – iron – probably from contacts with Greek traders from southern Europe.

Iron was not much harder or tougher than bronze, but the ore it was made from was much more widely found in Central Europe. So iron working became very important to these people, whom the Greeks called 'Koltoi' but whom we know today as **Celts**.

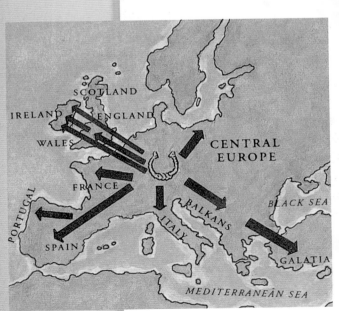

The most important archaeological site associated with these iron-working Celts is at **Hallstatt** in Austria. There, excavations in a huge salt mine and cemetery have produced a wide range of finds – pottery, iron tools and weapons. The remains of food and clothing preserved by the salt were also found on the site. These people buried their dead beneath beautifully made timber chariots. The ideas and traditions (culture) of **Hallstatt** spread to places as far afield as Portugal and Britain.

Around 500 BC, a new kind of Celtic culture developed west of Hallstatt around **La Tène** in Switzerland. These Celts were apparently more interested in art than previous Celts, probably as a result of contacts with Greek and Italian tribes. La Tène art is full of complicated spiral designs and geometric patterns, including fierce animal and serpent figures. It has been found on pots and jars, swords and shields all over northern Europe.

These Celts were also powerful warriors and their armies proved more than a match for even the mighty Romans and Greeks. La Tène Celts travelled around Europe, taking over new lands. It was La Tène Celts who first brought iron, and hence the 'Iron Age', to Ireland after 500 BC.

CAN YOU SAY?

14. Name the only type of megalithic tomb that developed in Ireland during the Bronze Age.
15. Look at the picture entitled **Source D** above.
    (a) Identify *one* way in which this type of burial is different from known Stone Age burials.
    (b) What is likely to have been placed in the pot beside the head? Explain why.
    (c) Why were Bronze Age burials simpler than Neolithic ones?
16. Explain what (a) a tumulus and (b) a monolith were.
17. In what modern country do the archaeological sites of Urnfield and Hallstatt lie?
18. What were the main features of La Tène art?
19. Roughly when did the first Celts arrive in Ireland?
20. What metal did the Celts bring to Ireland?   *(Junior Certificate Ordinary Level 2001)*

KEYNOTES

1. **Bronze Age:** c.2000 BC • combination of copper and tin • smelting of ore • pouring molten metal into moulds
   Growth of farming: more food • increased population • fighting for land
   Fortified homes: circular raths • crannógs
2. **Daily Life: Clothing:** woollen • leather
   Food: meat • cereal foods • use of fulacht fiadh
   Crafts: carpenters • smiths • weapons • tools • jewellery (torcs, lunulae, dress fasteners)
3. **Burials:** wedge-shaped gallery graves • cist • burials • tumuli • monoliths • stone alignments/circles
   Europe: Urnfield • Hallstatt • La Tène • origin of the Celts • beginning of Ireland's Iron Age, c.500 BC

MINI-PROJECT

Write an account of the following: *A farmer in pre-Christian Ireland.*
Hints:
- farming methods
- crops
- animals
- dwelling houses

(Junior Certificate Higher Level 1993)

The Celts – the Iron People

5

Celtic people began to arrive in Ireland around 500 BC. As we have already seen, the Greeks and Romans were familiar with the Celts through trade and war. The Roman historian Diodorus wrote that the Celts used to:

SOURCE A

cut off the heads of enemies and attach them to the necks of horses... embalm the heads in cedar oil... preserve them in a chest and display them with pride to strangers.

CELTIC LOOKS AND APPEARANCE

Roman writers also tell us that the Celts were generally tall and fair-haired. Both men and women seem to have kept their hair long, the men being particularly fond of bleaching and stiffening their hair with a kind of whitewash before going into battle. Most men had moustaches; another Roman writer claimed they:

SOURCE B

let their moustaches grow so long that their mouths get covered up; and so, when they eat, these get entangled in their food, while their drink is taken in, as it were, through a strainer.

Men and women wore clothing made from woven cloth. Women wore long, loose-fitting dresses and men wore long tunics and trousers (**bracae**). Clothing was usually dyed in bright colours, using juices from plants such as woad or elderberry. Both men and women also had great cloaks for travelling or for cold weather; these were fastened at the neck by brooches. The cloak doubled as a sort of sleeping bag, when men were out hunting. Archaeological finds in Ireland and around Europe also show that Celts liked jewellery made from gold, precious stones and coloured glass.

FOOD AND DRINK

The Celts were farmers and generally ate the meat of their domestic animals, as well as butter, milk and cheese. Vegetables, bread and porridge were also common. Hunting was still a popular pastime. Irish archaeologists have found the bones of deer, wild pigs and hares in Celtic sites. A Greek, Poseidonios, wrote of Celtic table manners:

> **SOURCE C**
>
> *They eat like lions, raising up whole limbs in both hands and biting off the meat, while any part which is hard to tear off, they cut through with a small dagger.*

Alcoholic drinks, such as beer and mead (made from honey), were popular with the Celts; one Roman wrote of Celtic feasts:

> **SOURCE D**
>
> *They use a common cup, drinking a little at a time, not more than a mouthful, but they do it rather often.*

SOURCE E

WHERE THE CELTS LIVED

Irish Celts generally built fortified homes for themselves, many of which can still be seen. The largest and probably the earliest Celtic forts were the **hillforts**, built mostly between 300 BC and 500 AD. These were on high ground and were often surrounded by a number of banks, for protection from attack.

Few house sites or artefacts have been found inside hillforts, suggesting that they were used only when under attack. However, Ireland's most famous hillforts, at Tara, Co. Meath, and Navan Fort, Co. Armagh, were also associated with royalty and great festivals.

Other forts from the early Celtic period also suggest that at this time defence was the main concern when building a home. We have already learnt about **crannógs** from the Bronze Age; these were also built by the Celts.

On headlands (promontories) around the coast, **promontory forts** have been found perched on the edge of cliffs. The cliff made attack from the sea impossible and the side of the fort facing the land had the usual defensive ramparts. Dún Aengus in the Aran Islands is a promontory fort (which may have existed prior to the Iron Age) with three surrounding walls and a wide area outside covered in jagged rocks called *chevaux de frise* ('horses from Friesland') to slow attackers.

SOURCE F

Later Celtic people tended to live in **ringforts**; these were smaller than hillforts, often containing just one or two houses. The remains of these houses are quite similar to earlier Bronze Age ones; walls were either of dry stone, wooden planks or wattle and daub; roofs were thatched.

Like hillforts, ringforts were protected by circular ditches (**fosses**) and banks, with timber fencing on top of the banks for extra protection. Usually there was only a single bank and ditch, probably as much to keep animals in as to keep enemies out. After 500 AD, when most ringforts were built, Ireland was a more peaceful country than in the hillfort days.

In areas such as the west of Ireland, where stone was in plentiful supply, forts were often constructed of stone and were generally called a **caiseal** or **caher**. In Celtic Ireland, most ordinary forts were known either as a **dún**, **rath** or **lios**. Thousands of modern place names have their origins in these words, such as Cashel (Caiseal), Dungarvan (Dún Garbháin) and Rathmore (Rath Mór).

A fairly common feature inside Celtic forts was the **souterrain**, an underground passageway lined with stone. Souterrains were used for storing food (being very cold) or as hiding places. Some had exits outside the forts, possibly for escape when attacked.

DID YOU KNOW?

Barley stored in a souterrain tended to rot, or ferment, on the surface. It has been suggested that this development was the inspiration for the first brewing of Celtic beer!

CAN YOU SAY?

1. Reread the four primary sources that you have come across so far in this chapter (marked **Sources A, B, C** and **D**).
   (a) What impression do they give us of the Celts? List *three* points.
   (b) Are these reliable sources? Glance back at the end of Chapter 4 before deciding on your answer.
2. Look at the picture (**Source E**) above.
   (a) What is this kind of site called?
   (b) Why were earthen fences built around the site?
   (c) On sites such as this, archaeologists have found the remains of wooden posts, pottery and implements. What can be learnt from this?
   (Junior Certificate Ordinary Level 1994)
3. Mention *two* types of dwelling place from Celtic Ireland.
   (Junior Certificate Higher Level 2001 and 2009)
4. In Ireland, after 500 AD, why did ringforts replace hillforts?
5. Describe a souterrain.
   (Junior Certificate Higher Level 1993)
6. Look at Dun Aengus in **Source F** above.
   (a) Why do you think that the people who built this fort chose this location?
   (b) Give *one* piece of evidence from the picture to show that these people were skilled builders.
   (c) Why is this period of history known as the Iron Age?
   (Junior Certificate Ordinary Level 2006)

CELTIC SOCIETY

Celtic Ireland was ruled by kings. The most powerful king was known as the **Árd Rí** (High King). However, he was not the ruler of all Ireland. At any one time, there were between 80 and 150 kings, each the **rí** of his own district (or **tuath**). In each tuath, the royal family was called the **derbhfine**. Any male member of this family could succeed a king when he died, either by election or by fighting and defeating his rivals.

Celtic **Law Tracts** tell us that each tuath had its own class system made up of nobles, commoners and slaves.

Nobles were warriors and landowners; they protected the commoners around them in return for goods and service. This bond was known as **célsine** or clientship. It was common in Celtic Ireland for nobles and kings to send their sons to the households of other nobles or kings to be reared. This custom, **fosterage**, helped to maintain good relations between tuaths.

A group of educated or skilled people called the **Aos Dána** advised a king on a wide range of matters. Aos Dána members were usually the poets, smiths, musicians, carpenters, judges and priests. We shall read about Celtic priests, or **druids**, later. The judges were known as **brehons** and were responsible for upholding the **Brehon Laws**. These laws survived in some parts of Ireland until the 17th century.

Commoners had little say in the ruling of the tuath, though they owned and farmed their own land and made up the majority of the population. One Law Tract from around 700 AD tells us of a commoner who had:

twenty cows, two bulls, six oxen, twenty pigs, twenty sheep...
a riding horse...and sixteen sacks of seed-corn in the ground.

Slaves were the lowest grouping in the Celtic class system. They were either captured in battle or on raiding trips to Britain; sometimes, poor people sold their children as slaves to avoid starvation in years of famine. Slaves worked as servants and did most of the heavy farm work. St Patrick apparently first came here as a slave, captured by Niall of the Nine Hostages.

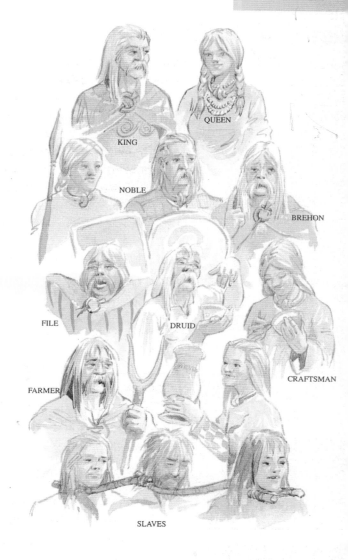

The Role of Women

Celtic society differed from most other societies of the time in one important way – women were highly respected. According to Brehon Law, Celtic women had far more independence than women in either Greece or Rome. Men were the warriors and hunters because they were generally stronger. Nonetheless, women were respected for doing what were considered to be the equally important jobs of cooking, making clothing and rearing children.

The Celts were willing to obey women leaders, even though only males could be members of the derbhfine. The Romans wrote of two British Celtic women leaders, Cartimandua and Boudicca. Boudicca was queen of a Celtic tribe in England called the Iceni; she led a huge rebellion of Celts against the Romans in 61 AD.

DID YOU KNOW?

In Brehon Law, a man's importance was based on the number of cows he owned. If someone killed him, the killer had to give that number of cows to his family in compensation.

The Irish *Táin Bó Cuailnge* legend tells of the activities of the great Queen Medb of Connacht. Although legends are unreliable as 'history', the Queen Medb story is proof that the Celts accepted the idea of women leaders. The legend also claims that Cuchulainn's weapons were given to him by a woman warrior.

CAN YOU SAY?

7. What do the terms (a) Ard Rí and (b) tuath mean?
8. Explain the meaning of *two* of the following terms:
   souterrain; fulacht fiadh; Tanaiste; derbhfine.   (*Junior Certificate Higher Level 2006*)
9. Explain *two* of the following terms relating to ancient Ireland: torc; fulacht fiadh; Aos Dána.   (*Junior Certificate Higher Level 2009*)
10. List *two* reasons why people became slaves in Celtic Ireland.
11. What does *Táin Bó Cuailnge* tell us about women in Celtic Ireland?

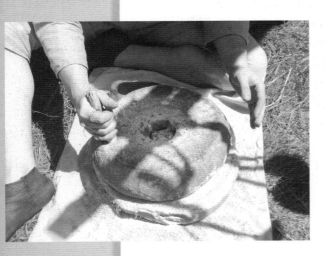

FARMING

The Celts were definitely farmers. The bones of sheep, pigs and dogs have been found at Celtic sites, but most common were cattle, the main source of wealth and importance in society. Legends such as *Táin Bó Cuailnge* suggest that wars were fought over cattle. The Annals of Ulster record great cattle losses in the winter snows of 747 AD. The Celts introduced horses to Ireland, though much smaller than modern ones.

Wheat, barley and oats were widely grown. A new type of rotary grinding quern, with a wooden handle, was used after 200 AD for making flour. Turnips, onions, beans and flax (for making cloth) were also grown.

Farm products, such as wool and flax, were spun into yarn and then woven into cloth on simple **looms**, where the threads were weighted with stones. Evidence of homemade jewellery and beads has also been found.

CRAFTS

Undoubtedly, the most important Iron Age craftspeople were **smiths**. Celtic smiths worked mostly in iron, which was quite widely found in Ireland. For the farmer, a smith made spades, sickles and some plough parts, though ploughs were largely made of wood. Clear proof that the Celts were a warlike people can be seen in other products of the smith, such as iron swords, daggers and spear tips.

Smiths also made tools for other craftspeople, such as carpenters and boat-builders. Such tools included iron hammers, axes, adzes (for shaping wood), chisels, saws and nails. Carpenters made many things: support beams for housing, gates, ploughs, chariots and even household items such as wooden bowls (very little clay pottery was used in Celtic times) and plates.

Roadways were very rare in Celtic Ireland and, as a consequence, travel by boat was very important. Boat-builders made timber-framed boats, covered in animal hide and greased in animal fat to keep water out. In 1976, Tim Severin sailed as far as Newfoundland in a boat built according to ancient Celtic design, showing just how seaworthy these boats were. They were the ancestors of today's **currachs**.

As in the Bronze Age, smiths in Celtic Ireland worked in gold and silver. Designs were of the **La Tène** variety, mentioned in the last chapter. The La Tène style was very imaginative and complicated. Spiral patterns in 's' and 'c' shapes dominate, generally coiled around beautiful objects such as necklaces or brooches, sometimes even on sword hilts. Often, these spiral patterns end by turning into the heads of animals, serpents or people and have coloured glass, enamel or jewels worked into them.

While the Tara Brooch is probably our most famous single Celtic artefact, the most important bulk find so far has been the Broighter Hoard in Co. Derry. This includes a beautiful golden boat complete with miniature oars.

A gold boat found with the Broighter Hoard in Co. Derry.

Tim Severin's boat is now on display at Craggaunowen in Co. Clare.

SOURCE F

The Tara Brooch.

Modern stage shows such as Riverdance *have been based very loosely on Celtic traditions and dance. The Celts did not look like this when they danced. However, note the similarities between the designs on some of the costumes and the La Tène style designs on the Tara Brooch above.*

PASTIMES

Celtic pastimes were quite varied. Legends such as those of Fionn Mac Cumhaill are unreliable as history, but do show the importance of hunting. More surprisingly, perhaps, we find mention of board games called **brandubh** and **ficheall** in *Táin Bó Cuailnge*. We know nothing more about these, but ficheall is the modern Irish word for chess. The origins of today's game of hurling lie in a Celtic game called **báire**.

Celts were especially fond of storytelling. Poems and stories were composed by the **poet or file**. Some families, such as the Ó Dálaigh family, were famous filí. The file was so respected that many Celts believed that he could cause people suffering and death by simply criticising them in his poetry. Training in all the rules and skills of the file took seven years. Poems were usually recited aloud at feasts or on special occasions by a **reachaire**, accompanied by music played on stringed instruments. This music, and indeed some poetry too, was composed by a **bard**.

Stories and poems were passed on orally from generation to generation because the Celts did not use writing as we know it until about 500 AD. Laws, family ancestry, land ownership rights and so on were all memorised and passed on by word of mouth alone.

DID YOU KNOW?

The *Táin* tells us that Cúchulainn played hurling on his own against an entire team, that he could hit a ball into a hound's mouth, and when travelling, used to hit the ball ahead of him and catch it before it landed! Do you believe that?

CAN YOU SAY?

12. Explain why cattle were so important to the Celts.

(Junior Certificate Higher Level 2001)

13. What was a rotary grinding quern?
14. Mention *one* achievement in arts or crafts associated with the Celts in ancient Ireland.

(Junior Certificate Higher Level 1999)

15. Why was boat-building important in Celtic Ireland?
16. In the picture of the Tara Brooch (**Source F** above), name *two* features on it which were typical of La Tène style Celtic art. (Check Chapter 4 if necessary.)
17. What were (a) ficheall and (b) báire?
18. Explain *one* of the following: bard; file; brehon.

(Junior Certificate Ordinary and Higher Levels 2000)

RELIGION AND BURIALS

Druids were the priests of Celtic Ireland before the coming of Christianity. Next to the king, druids were the most important men in a tuath. Not only were they the religious leaders but, especially before *c.*400 AD, they often fulfilled the duties of judges and, indeed, poets too. Julius Caesar tells us that the druids had:

> to memorise a great number of verses; so many, that some of them spend twenty years at their studies.

Caesar also tells us that druids took charge of the worship of the Celtic gods, performing animal and indeed human sacrifice, and that they gave rulings on religious questions and disputes. Druids were also teachers and were so respected that they were never expected to fight for their king or pay taxes to him. Indeed, the druid was the person who took charge of the ceremony when a Celtic king was being crowned. People also went to the druids for predictions of the future, which were given by a druid after watching birds in flight or examining animal entrails.

The Celts had hundreds of gods. Often, even a small local stream or well was considered sacred. It is also believed that the Celts thought that the megalithic tombs they found here were homes of gods.

The main Celtic god was **Dagda**, god of the afterlife. He was believed to be the husband of the goddess **Boann** (the river Boyne). **Lugh** was the great warrior god, particularly associated with kingship, and the sea god was **Manannán Mac Lir**. The goddess of death was called **Bodb**.

Religious festivals were popular, especially:

- **Imbolg** (February) to pray to the goddess **Brigid** for a successful lambing season.
- **Bealtaine** (May) to pray to the goddess **Bel** for healthy cattle and good crops.
- **Lughnasa** (August) to honour Lugh and pray for a good harvest.
- **Samhain** (November) to celebrate the start of the Celtic year and honour Dagda.

Samhain was the main festival, but each one involved sacrifices, prayers, games and a meeting (**aonach**) presided over by the king.

Burial Customs

Even though we have little archaeological evidence about druids, we can piece together some other facts about Celtic religion from their burial customs. Celtic archaeological excavations at Hallstatt and La Tène show that a wide range of items were buried with the dead, in the apparent belief that they would be needed in the afterlife. Finds include tools, weapons, jewellery, meat, pottery and drinking vessels. Celtic grave-goods in Ireland, such as those excavated at Carrowjames, Co. Mayo, include small offerings such as beads, jewellery and arrowheads.

At both Hallstatt and La Tène, the remains of the dead were placed beneath a chariot, along with the grave-goods, and covered with a small earthen mound. In Ireland, no chariot burial has ever been found and practically all graves were cist graves located in flat ground; some bodies had been cremated. The Hallstatt and La Tène practice of burying pottery with the dead did not happen in Ireland.

The Celts never erected monuments of the megalithic kind or size. Instead, their preference was for single stones (**monoliths**), such as the Turoe Stone in Co. Galway, which has La Tène-style curves and spirals. The earliest known writing in Ireland is found on **ogham** stones. Sometimes, these served as gravestones. Ogham stones use an unusual alphabet based on carved lines along one edge of the stone and are read from bottom to top. The lines correspond to the letters of the Latin alphabet, showing the growing contact with Romans in the early centuries after Christ. The 'Stone Corridor' at University College, Cork (left), has a most impressive collection of ogham stones.

The Turoe Stone.

CAN YOU SAY?

19. What was the role of the druid in Celtic Ireland?
(*Junior Certificate Ordinary and Higher Levels 1994*)
20. Name *three* Celtic gods and what they represented.
21. How did Irish Celtic burials differ from European ones?
22. What is ogham? (*Junior Certificate Higher Level 1995, 2005 and 2009*)
23. Explain *one* of the following terms: crannóg, lunula, druid, fosterage.
(*Junior Certificate Ordinary and Higher Levels 1992, partially in 2005*)
24. Name *two* important Celtic festivals. (*Junior Certificate Higher Level 2006*)

MINI-PROJECT

Write an account of life in Celtic Ireland under *each* of the following headings:
- Dress
- Housing
- Farming
- Pastimes

(*Junior Certificate Ordinary Level 1993*)

Or

Write about a person in Ancient Ireland. (*Junior Certificate Higher Level 2005*)
(No hints given. Try to write about ten or twelve good points.)

KEYNOTES

1. **The Celts:** Roman and Greek sources • long hair • bleached • woven clothing • great cloaks • jewellery
Diet: meat • cereals • vegetables • alcohol
Homes: hillforts • ringforts • crannóg • promontory forts • fosses • *chevaux de frise* • souterrains
2. **Society:** Ard Rí • rí • tuath • derbhfine • Taoiseach • Tanaiste • Brehon Laws • nobles • célsine • fosterage • Aos Dána (druids, brehons) • commoners • slaves • importance of women
3. **Work and Play: Farming:** cattle • sheep • pigs • horses • rotary querns • cereals • vegetables • flax
Crafts: smiths • carpenters • weaving • La Tène art
Pastimes: hunting • brandubh • ficheall • báire • storytelling • file • reachaire • bard • oral tradition
4. **Religion:** druids • worship • sacrifices • prophecies
Many gods: Dagda • Boann • Lugh
Festivals: Imbolg • Bealtaine • Lughnasa • Samhain • aonach
Burials: cists
Monuments: monoliths • ogham stones

6 Christianity Comes to Ireland

By the first century AD, most Celts in Britain and Europe had been conquered by the powerful **Roman Empire**. There is no evidence that the Romans invaded Ireland, but Roman coins and jewellery found here suggest that trade between Ireland and the Roman Empire flourished.

● THE EARLY YEARS

By the 3rd century AD, the Roman Empire was mainly Christian. It is highly likely that there were Christians in Ireland before 400 AD, either as slaves or settlers. The first Christian missionaries arrived here soon after that date. According to the Latin writer Prosper Tiro, a bishop named Palladius was sent to 'the Irish believing in Christ' in 431. Palladius, however, is never mentioned after 432 and it is generally assumed that he died shortly after arriving here. The most famous Christian missionary from the Roman Empire was called **Patrick**.

Our historical sources on St Patrick are very limited. The most important source is his own life story, called the *Confession*. In this, he tells of being brought to Ireland from Britain as a slave when he was 16, and of tending cattle and sheep here for six years until his escape back to Britain. Despite a lack of encouragement (or indeed approval from the Pope), Patrick later returned to Ireland as a bishop and began his work of converting the pagan Celts to Christianity. Tradition places Patrick's mission here between 432 and 461, though it was possibly later.

Irish written sources on St Patrick date from at least two centuries after this and so are less reliable. Patrick worked mainly in the northern half of the country, especially around Armagh. He worked on converting kings and nobles to Christianity, knowing others would follow their lead. Patrick founded

Patrick's confession.

several churches and, along with several other Christian missionaries such as Ailbe of Emly, Declan of Ardmore, Secundinus of Meath and Auxilius of Kildare, spread Christianity throughout Ireland.

The arrival of Christianity was a crushing blow to the druids, though their roles as judges and poets were continued by the brehons and filí.

There is little evidence of violence against the early Christians in Ireland and it seems that Celtic society, with its hundreds of gods, just made room for one more. Certainly, the Irish did not abandon their pagan beliefs immediately. For example, the King of Tara, who died in 560, was a pagan. Many Celts were happy to worship the Christian god and their own pagan ones at the same time. Pagan festivals continued, but gradually changed to Christian ones; Imbolg, for example, came to be celebrated as St Brigid's Day, and Samhain later became Halloween.

As Christianity slowly became the main religion in Ireland, the Church was governed by **bishops.** The area looked after by each bishop was roughly equal to that of a tuath and it was known as a **diocese.** An 8th century document tells us:

> **SOURCE A**
>
> *There shall be a chief bishop of each tuath to ordain their clergy, to bless their churches, to be confessor to rulers and nobles, and to sanctify and bless their children after baptism.*

SOURCE B

Example of a small, early monastic site.

DID YOU KNOW?

Life on the monastic island of Sceilg Mhichil in Co. Kerry was so tough that even the earth for small vegetable plots had to be carried from the mainland by currach.

Sceilg Mhichíl.

Some devout Christians chose to live apart from the rest of the population and devote themselves to God. These people formed communities in different parts of Ireland or on islands, and so we had the beginning of the first Irish **monasteries**. Around 500, the first monastery was founded by St Enda on the Aran Islands, and others such as Ciarán (Clonmacnoise), Colmcille (Derry) and Brendan (Clonfert) soon followed his example.

Early monasteries were small and resembled forts in many respects. The monks generally lived in small **beehive huts** and prayed in little churches called **oratories**. In the west, these buildings were built and roofed entirely in stone, using a similar style of corbelled roof to that used in passage graves thousands of years before. Some of these stone buildings have survived to this day. Elsewhere, monastic buildings tended to be made of wattle and daub, not much different from ordinary Celtic buildings.

CAN YOU SAY?

1. Identify *two* pieces of evidence that show that Ireland had contacts with the Roman Empire from the 1st century AD.
2. What is St Patrick's *Confession*? Give *two* pieces of information contained in it.
3. Why did St Patrick concentrate on converting kings and nobles?
4. Identify *one* piece of evidence that shows that Christianity made slow progress in Celtic Ireland.
5. List *three* duties of a bishop in early Christian Ireland (**Source A**).
6. Study the photo, **Source B**, above.
   (a) What is the building with the round stone roof?
   (b) What could either of the buildings without a roof be?
   (c) Why is there a wall around the monastery?
7. Name *one* monastic site from early Christian Ireland.

(Junior Certificate Ordinary and Higher Levels 1999)

 THE GROWTH OF MONASTERIES

By the 8th century AD, Christianity had become the accepted religion of the country and there was little fear of attack. More monasteries were built in the heart of Ireland and became less like forts in appearance. The number of monasteries also grew because huge numbers of people joined them as monks or simply lived in them as pilgrims, disciples or workers. A 9th century writer commented:

The little places where hermits settled two together, three together, are now resorts of pilgrims where hundreds, where thousands assemble.

Some monasteries were founded near the traditional homes of kings, such as Armagh. Others became so important that they became the homes of kings, for example Kildare. Thus, even soldiers, tax collectors and merchants lived within the walls of some monasteries, which effectively became Ireland's first towns.

Many monasteries had sacred and non-sacred sections. The sacred section contained the main church, graveyard, crosses and the cell of the head of the monastery, the **abbot**. The non-sacred part of the monastery was generally larger. Here lay the cells of the other monks or priests, as well as the houses where non-clergy lived. A guesthouse for visitors was usually found close to the entrance. Most large monasteries had workshops of many kinds, stables, kitchens, dining-halls (**refectories**), orchards and gardens.

The most important monasteries in Ireland around 800 AD.

● WORK AND PRAYER

Monasteries were also farming communities by the 8th century. They had **corn-drying kilns** and large **water-mills** for grinding great quantities of wheat and oats into flour, needed for the monastery's bread. **Blacksmiths** made and mended parts of ploughs, wheel-rims, axes and many digging tools. **Carpenters** made ploughs, carts and wheels, and carried out the timber work needed for walls and roofs of buildings. **Masons** shaped the stones needed by the monastery, though the more skilled ones worked on stone carving.

The coming of Christianity to Ireland also brought **writing**. The clergy of the monastery were often the only people in a district who could read or write (in Latin and Greek). Thus, many monasteries set up schools for the children of local noblemen; some, such as Lismore, became mini-universities and attracted students from outside Ireland in significant numbers.

In large monasteries, lay workers were employed to help with the daily jobs of the monastery, though the monks also did these jobs. In addition, the monks had their religious lives to lead. They rose in the small hours of the morning for prayers called **matins**, followed by others at dawn called **lauds**. Prayers in memory of Christ's crucifixion and death were said in the afternoon, while evening prayers were called **vespers**. The early monks especially believed in devotion to God through hardship. This was known as **asceticism**. They ate only small amounts of bread and vegetables, wore uncomfortable rough **habits** and shaved the tops of their heads (**tonsures**).

SOURCE C

CAN YOU SAY?

8. Give *two* reasons for the growth of monasteries after 600 AD.

9. What was the head of a monastery called?

10. 'Monasteries resembled large towns.' Give *two* examples of this.

11. Mention *two* ways in which monasteries in Early Christian Ireland promoted education and craft.   *(Junior Certificate Higher Level 1997)*

12. What was asceticism?

13. Explain *each* of the following: tonsure, refectory, matins.

14. Examine **Source C** above and give *two* reasons why this monastic site appears to be an older one than the one you saw earlier in **Source B**.

THE ART OF THE MONASTERIES

Some skilled monks made extraordinary works of art for their monasteries. Ireland had ogham stones before Christianity, but the monks adapted the ogham stone to Christianity. Some 7th century stones have been found, such as the one at Inishkea North, Co. Mayo, which have Christian crucifixes carved on them instead of ogham. Later, perhaps with improved skills and tools, these stones began to resemble rough crosses, like those at Carndonagh, Co. Donegal. Eventually, stone **high crosses** became widespread, decorated with carved scenes from the Bible, which were used to teach the scriptures to illiterate students.

Carndonagh High Cross.

St Muireadach's Cross at Monasterboice.

Irish monasteries also produced some beautiful metalwork. Most notable are the superbly crafted Ardagh and Derrynaflan Chalices. Both are excellent examples of the skill of the monastic craftspeople. The plain silver chalices are decorated with coloured glass and **enamel,** a glass-like substance that was melted and then cooled. The monasteries made some beautiful **filigree** work, in which gold and bronze wire is used to form complex patterns and designs. These were mostly of the La Tène style introduced by the Celts. This again shows Irish Christianity blending in with pre-Christian traditions.

Other metalwork produced by monasteries included brooches (for fastening cloaks), patens (for communion) and small cups.

DID YOU KNOW?

A stone wheel formed part of the design of Irish high crosses, not for any clear religious reason, but to support the arms of the cross, so that weather and gravity wouldn't knock them off.

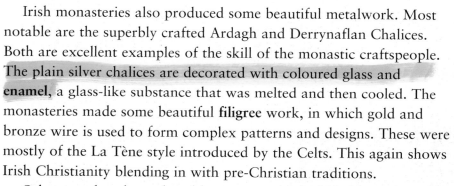

Ardagh Chalice.

Derrynaflan Chalice.

St Patrick's Bell Shrine.

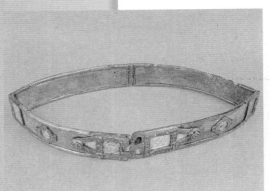

Moylough Belt Shrine.

Monasteries placed great value on ordinary objects that once belonged to their founders or other saints, and metal workers made **reliquaries** (**shrines**) to preserve these relics. These include the bell shrine made to protect what was supposedly St Patrick's own bell, and the Moylough Belt Shrine; both are examples of skilled craftsmanship using tiny glass patterns called **millefiori** as well as metal engraving. Shrines were also made to preserve the monastery's most famous works of art – **manuscripts**.

No printed books existed in Europe before the 15th century. Thus, the gospels and other religious books in a monastery had to be copied out by hand, in a special room known as a **scriptorium** (writing place). Here, monks worked for long hours, carefully writing and decorating the manuscripts with such skill that they can rightly be considered priceless works of art. Capital letters, page borders and sometimes entire pages portray scenes from the Bible, and are decorated in elaborate Celtic patterns, with a rich use of colour.

SOURCE F

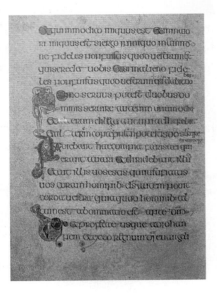

Coloured inks were made from berries, crushed acorns, metals and even beetles from Africa! The manuscript writer or **scribe** wrote with goosefeather quills on treated sheepskin (**parchment**) or calfskin (**vellum**), because the lighter 'paper' made from papyrus reeds was unknown in Ireland then. Manuscripts were mostly copies of gospels, epistles and prayers. The *Cathach* is the oldest, but the *Book of Kells*, kept in Trinity College, Dublin, is our most famous and most beautiful.

The language used was mainly Latin, then the language of learning all over Europe. However, sometimes a scribe felt that others might not understand some words, so he added in brief explanations in his own language, Irish. By studying these explanations (**glosses**), modern scholars have been able to recreate the early Irish language and so enable historians to learn much more about Celtic Ireland. Sometimes, the glosses resembled graffiti, complaining of bad ink and poor light, while one scribe even wrote a poem about his cat, called Pangur Bán, in the margin!

CAN YOU SAY?

15. **Source D** is a picture of a high cross.
    (a) What was the usual subject matter of the carvings on such high crosses?
    (b) Name *one* early Christian site where you would find an example of one.
    (Junior Certificate Higher Level 2001)

16. What is a reliquary? Give *one* example.

17. **Source E** is a picture of the Ardagh Chalice.
    (a) For what purpose do you think this object was used?
    (b) Identify *one* piece of evidence from the picture that shows that skilled craftsmen made the Ardagh Chalice. *(Junior Certificate Ordinary Level 2001)*

18. What work was done in the scriptorium of a monastery?
    (Junior Certificate Ordinary Level 1994 and Higher 2000)

19. The book shrine (**Source F**) held the *Cathach* or *Battle Book*, which the O'Donnell clan used to carry into battle.
    (a) Describe briefly what you see in *one* of the three panels – left, centre or right – of the shrine.
    (b) Give *two* reasons why such book shrines were made for manuscripts in early Christian Ireland.
    (c) Why do you think that the O'Donnell clan, who owned the *Cathach* for many years, carried it into battle? *(Junior Certificate Ordinary and Higher Levels 1992)*

20. How did the study of Latin contribute to early Irish literature and language?
    (Junior Certificate Higher Level 1993)

ROUND TOWERS

We have already seen that the first Christians came to Ireland from the Roman Empire. This great empire, which you will read about in the next few chapters, began to be overrun by tribes from northern and eastern Europe in the 5th century. Ireland escaped much of the

The round tower at Glendalough.

St Gallen, Switzerland, today. The large church in the centre of the picture is built on the site of the monastery founded by St Gall of Ireland.

destruction because it was a remote island. However, from the 8th century, the rich Irish monasteries came under attack from Scandinavian raiders called **Vikings.**

These attacks, chiefly to capture precious objects and slaves at first, led monasteries to adopt desperate measures. Protective walls were strengthened, monks were trained more thoroughly in fighting methods and **round towers** were built. Early monasteries had wooden lookout towers, but stone-built round towers were used as bell towers, lookout posts and as places of refuge for people and valuables when Vikings or other raiders came. The entrance was high above the ground and the tower was entered by a ladder, which was pulled up afterwards. Many round towers can still be seen in monastic sites today, though in some cases lightning has destroyed parts of them. The towers at Glendalough and Ardmore have been fully restored.

IRISH MONKS ABROAD

The conquest of Europe by pagans, such as the Huns and Vikings, had another effect on Irish monasteries. Some monks decided to go abroad to try to preserve Christianity by founding monasteries in Europe. St Columbanus, for example, founded monasteries at Luxeuil in France and Bobbio in northern Italy around the year 600. St Aidan set up a great monastery on Lindisfarne, an island off the British coast, and Cathaldus, from Lismore, became Bishop of Taranto in southern Italy in 680. St Gall founded a monastery in Switzerland and today the city and district is named St Gallen in his honour.

Of course, not all travellers went with the purpose of saving or spreading Christianity in Europe. St Brendan sailed a considerable way across the North Atlantic and it was his 'journey' that Tim Severin, whom we mentioned in Chapter 5, recreated in 1976. The 10th century account of St Brendan's travels includes an account of the boat landing on a small 'island', only for the crew to discover that it was in fact a resting whale!

Our most famous monastic exile was **St Colmcille**, sometimes called Columba. He founded monasteries at Derry and Durrow, before travelling to Iona off the west coast of Scotland. Tradition has it that, following his involvement in a battle over the ownership of the *Cathach* manuscript, he vowed to leave Ireland forever. Monks who chose to abandon Ireland for more uncertain shores elsewhere were later known as 'white martyrs'. Colmcille's monastery at Iona became one of the most famous centres of faith and learning in Europe; in turn, monks from it founded many other monasteries including Kells. Work on the *Book of Kells* was probably begun on Iona and finished in Kells around 800.

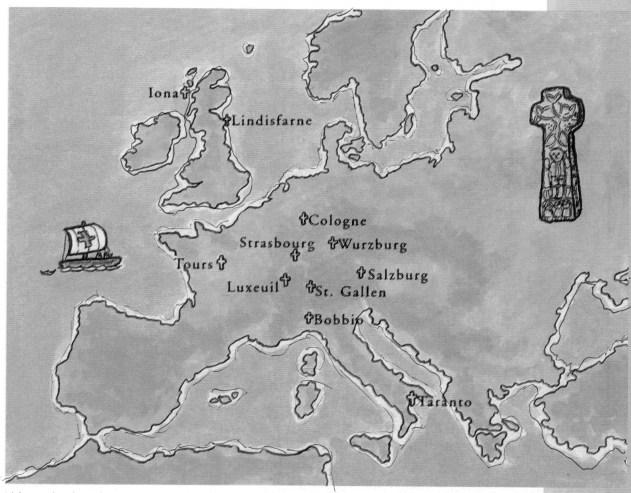

Irish monks abroad.

CAN YOU SAY?

21. In **Source G**, why do you think the entrance (marked X) was built so high off the ground? *(Junior Certificate Higher Level 2001, similar question in 2006)*

22. Right is a building from early Christian Ireland.
    (a) What is this kind of building called?
    (b) Give *two* reasons why it was built.
       (Junior Certificate Higher Level 2005 and 2006)
    (c) Name *one* place in Ireland where an example of this type of building still survives.
       (Junior Certificate Higher Level 1994)

23. Why do you think St Brendan is known as 'the Navigator'?

24. Why did Colmcille go to Iona?

25. Describe the main features of a monastery in early Christian Ireland.
   (Junior Certificate Higher Level 1996)

26. Mention *two* effects of the coming of Christianity to Ireland.
   (Junior Certificate Higher Level 2005)

KEYNOTES

1. **Irish contacts with the Roman Empire:** arrival of Christianity • Palladius
   St Patrick: slave • escaped • returned • *Confession* • later sources • Armagh
   Christianity: slow progress • added to rather than replaced pagan beliefs
   Bishops: dioceses

2. **Early monasteries:** remote and well protected • beehive huts
   • oratories (Sceilg Mhichil, Clonmacnoise, Aran Islands)
   Growth of monasteries: 8th century • Christianity widely accepted
   • huge numbers joining monasteries • resembled towns • abbot (head of monastery)
   • farming • use of corn-drying kilns and water-mills • blacksmiths • carpenters
   • stonemasons • education centres

3. **Daily lives:** matins, lauds, vespers • asceticism • tonsures • habits
   Art: high crosses • Ardagh and Derrynaflan Chalices • La Tène style • enamel
   • filigree work • millefiori
   Manuscripts: scriptorium • parchment • vellum • *Cathach* • *Book of Kells*
   • use of glosses to explain words

4. **Threat of attack:** Vikings • building of round towers
   Missionaries: preserving Christianity in Europe • St Columbanus • St Aidan
   • Cathaldus • St Gall • voyage of St Brendan, the Navigator
   St Colmcille: Derry • Durrow • 'white martyrdom' • Iona

MINI-PROJECT

Write an account of the life of a monk in a monastery in early Christian Ireland c.500–800 AD.

Hints:

- reasons for becoming a monk
- situation and layout of the monastery
- the daily life of the monk
- the missionary activities of the monks

(Junior Certificate 1995 and Higher Level 1998, very similar question in Ordinary Level 2006)

(Note: This was asked as 'Write about a monk in an early Irish monastery' in Higher Level 2005; very similar question in Higher Level 2009.)

7 Ancient Rome

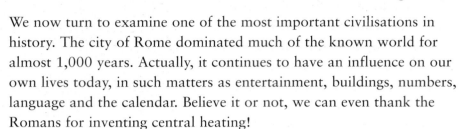

We now turn to examine one of the most important civilisations in history. The city of Rome dominated much of the known world for almost 1,000 years. Actually, it continues to have an influence on our own lives today, in such matters as entertainment, buildings, numbers, language and the calendar. Believe it or not, we can even thank the Romans for inventing central heating!

Like ancient Ireland, we can learn much about Rome from archaeologists. However, unlike the Celts of 2,000 years ago, the Romans kept very detailed *written* records of their wars, politics and trade. Thus, we know much more about how the Romans lived in 50 BC than we do about life in Ireland at that time.

SOURCE A1

SOURCE A2

The Roman Forum

The famous Roma Football Club crest is based on the legend of Romulus and Remus being reared by a wolf.

THE CITY OF ROME

Legend has it that Romulus and Remus, orphan twins who were reared by a wolf, founded Rome. In a fight over the naming of the city, Romulus killed his brother, so the city was called after Romulus. This is what is known as a 'foundation myth'.

The city of Rome was founded in central Italy on the banks of the **River Tiber**, about 24 kilometres from the sea. The site covers seven hills and it is likely that the city began as seven small villages, built on the hills for protection. These villages grew and joined together over the years.

The traditional date for Rome's foundation is 753 BC, though we cannot be certain of this. Over the centuries, trade made the city wealthy. From lands conquered by its armies, even more wealth came to the city and at its peak Rome came to control a huge **empire** of 50 million people.

SOURCE B

The centre of ancient Rome was, as in many towns, the marketplace. This was called the **Forum**. It was a busy, open space, surrounded by large buildings where politics, law and religious **temples** had their homes. The main street, the **Via Sacra**, ran straight through the Forum.

By 100 AD, Rome's population was about 1 million, so most streets were narrow in order to fit in more houses. Along some of the wider streets, **triumphal arches** and **columns** could be found. These were built to celebrate great victories by Roman armies and were decorated with scenes from their wars. Archaeologists and historians find these very useful sources of information.

Further from the Forum lay other huge buildings. **Basilicas** were law courts and offices. The **Circus Maximus** was the racecourse of Rome, and the **Colosseum** was the stadium (amphitheatre), where 'entertainment' took place. Elsewhere, open-air **theatres** and **public baths** could be found, and huge water-carrying bridges called **aqueducts**.

DID YOU KNOW?

The emperor Trajan built in ancient Rome what many believe to have been the world's first shopping centre. Shops were situated on the ground floor, with government offices above.

It is hard to imagine that the Circus Maximus, an untidy public park today, once seated over 200,000 people.

Arch of Constantine

POMPEII

Much of what we know about ancient Rome comes from excavations of the Roman town of Pompeii near Naples. Although many ancient buildings remain in Rome itself, it is still a great modern city, so some archaeological sites have been built over or destroyed over the centuries. Pompeii, on the other hand, was like a smaller version of Rome. It was buried in ash and rubble when the volcano Vesuvius erupted in 79 AD. The eruption killed many people but also covered and protected the town completely from any modern buildings or destruction.

Giuseppe Fiorelli began excavating the site in 1860, and since then Pompeii has continued to give us great information on life in Roman times. In the 1990s, for instance, life-like resin casts were made of bodies found under the volcanic ash. Fiorelli had made plaster casts of bodies in the 19th century, but these latest ones are almost see-through. They have even revealed the jewellery worn by the victims of the volcano almost 2,000 years ago.

A sad plaster cast of someone who died in a crouching position, now stored at Pompeii beside dozens of wine jars called amphorae.

Theatres and temples, streets and houses have been excavated and found to be more intact than those in any other ancient city. Loaves of bread, turned to carbon by the heat of the volcanic ash, have been found. Even the graffiti scribbled on the town walls can be read. Although Pompeii, and nearby Herculaneum, lie over 200 km south of Rome, they still give archaeologists and historians very detailed images of life in ancient Rome.

CAN YOU SAY?

1. From what you have read so far, mention *two* ways in which ancient Rome differed from a modern town or city.
2. List *two* ways in which Rome was similar to a modern town or city.
3. How do we know a great deal about ancient Rome?
4. Looking at **Sources A1** and **A2** above, list *three* features of the Roman Forum that you would not normally find in modern town centres.
5. Looking at **Source B** above:
   List *two* materials used in building the markets.
   Identify *one* item in the picture that is definitely not an ancient Roman one.
6. What was an aqueduct?
7. Why is Pompeii such a useful source of information on ancient Rome?

HOUSES

Over a million people lived among all the great buildings of Rome. It was basically a city of rich people (**patricians**) and poor people (**plebeians**). As well as having the wealth, patricians controlled most of Rome's government. They lived on the slopes of Rome's seven hills, or in the countryside. The plebeians generally lived in the low-lying areas.

Most Romans were plebeians who lived in blocks of flats called *insulae*. These were usually four or five storeys high. Inside these *insulae*, often a whole family lived in one rented room, a *cenaculum*. Streets were very narrow and strewn with rubbish thrown from the flats. Fire was a constant danger, given the hot climate, narrow streets and many thatched roofs. Rome had 7,000 firemen in 20 BC. In winter, with no heating or insulation, *insulae* were cold and damp. The poet Juvenal complained of their poor condition:

We live in a city shored up with slender props because that is how the landlords prevent the houses from falling down.

Street scene in Rome showing insulae.

DID YOU KNOW?

'Fiddling while Rome burns' is a common phrase for doing nothing in a crisis. It comes from the story that in 64 AD the cruel Emperor Nero played music while a nine-day fire destroyed most of Rome's *insulae*. (Historians now believe that Nero was probably playing a lyre, not a fiddle.)

Inside a wealthy Roman house.

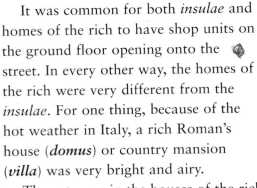

It was common for both *insulae* and homes of the rich to have shop units on the ground floor opening onto the street. In every other way, the homes of the rich were very different from the *insulae*. For one thing, because of the hot weather in Italy, a rich Roman's house (*domus*) or country mansion (*villa*) was very bright and airy.

The entrance in the houses of the rich was through a hallway called the *vestibulum*, leading to a central room, the *atrium*. Beyond was an enclosed garden called the *peristylum*. In the *atrium*, rainwater from the tiled roof dripped down into a pond called an *impluvium*; this helped to keep the house cool. Around the atrium lay the bedrooms (*cubicula*), kitchen (*culina*), a dining/living room (*triclinium*) and the master's office (*tablinum*).

The enclosed garden with wall paintings and a covered walkway of this Pompeian house.

In the houses of the wealthy, tiled pictures called *mosaics* decorated the walls and floors, keeping the house cool as well as beautiful, and wall paintings (*murals*), statues and fountains were also popular. For the winter, some houses even had central heating (*hypocaust*) – hot air from a furnace passed under floors and between the walls. Furniture consisted mostly of timber-framed beds, timber stools and couches on which people reclined.

Near the entrance to many Roman houses lay a small shrine to the gods who protected the household; this was called the *lararium*. Sometimes, however, a warning to unwelcome visitors was more common – the mosaic on the left is from a house in Pompeii and announces **Cave Canem** ('Beware of the dog')!

CAN YOU SAY?

8. What were the buildings of the poor Romans called?
9. Why was fire such a big danger in ancient Rome?
10. Where in their houses did wealthier Romans eat?
11. What did wealthy Romans do to keep their houses cool in summer?
12. How did the rich heat their houses in winter?
13. Describe the house that a rich person in ancient Rome lived in.
    (*Five* points, without using your book)   (*Junior Certificate Higher Level 2002*)

ROAMING ROMANS

Rome's Rulers

Early on, Rome was ruled by kings, but these were eventually driven out. Then came a period when Rome's parliament – the Senate – appointed two men each year to run things. These men were called consuls, the most famous being Julius Caesar.

After Caesar's death in 44 BC, Rome again turned back to having kings, though this time they were called emperors. They had huge power and some declared themselves to be living gods. Augustus was the first and possibly the greatest Roman emperor.

Expansion

As the city of Rome grew larger, it expanded into the surrounding countryside in search of valuable farmland to feed its population. To take over this land, Rome used its magnificent army. By 295 BC central Italy was under Roman control and, in the following years, all of Italy fell before the Roman **legions**.

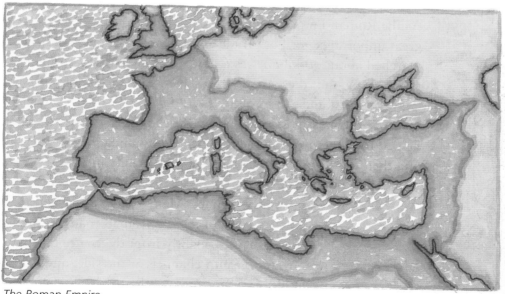

The Roman Empire.

Early in the 2nd century BC, Rome's lands began to expand beyond Italy to the east, taking land from the Greeks as far as Syria. In the west, southern France, Spain and Portugal also felt the power of the Roman military. Eventually, this Roman Empire covered much of Europe, north Africa and western Asia. It survived until the 4th century AD. From then onwards, Romans found themselves attacked by fierce tribes. Waves of Huns, Goths, Visigoths and Vandals gradually took

A Pompeii street. The stepping stones enabled people to keep their feet and clothes dry. Note also the tracks for the chariot wheels. The street slopes down to the edge in order to carry away any water.

DID YOU KNOW?

The famous Pont du Gard in southern France, over 60 metres high, carried water on top and a road below, making it an aqueduct and a viaduct.

over more and more of the Roman Empire; Rome itself was twice occupied by its enemies in the 5th century. By then, the mighty Roman Empire was a pale shadow of its former glory. From the historian's and archaeologist's viewpoint, however, there remain thousands of Roman sites to investigate all over this once huge empire.

Towns

While on campaign, the soldiers always made camp following a specific layout and design. Whenever the army set up a 'camp' at an important position, such as a river crossing or mountain pass, this camp could become a permanent base. Tents were replaced by buildings and ditches by solid walls, and in this way many Roman towns began. These were always laid out, like the camps, in a rectangular shape with very straight streets. The soldiers' central parade ground became the town's marketplace.

Roads

As the Roman Empire spread beyond Rome and Italy, roads were of great importance for both trade and the army. Roman soldiers usually marched about 30 kilometres a day and they required straight level roads. They built these roads themselves, so a shovel and pickaxe were standard items in a soldier's kit.

The straightest possible routes were chosen, and then the soldiers, helped by slaves or captured enemies, laid foundations of first large and then small stones. Where possible, especially in the case of major roads, stone slabs were laid on top to provide a smooth surface for carts, chariots and marching armies. Many roads in Europe still follow the lines of the old Roman roads.

Roads sloped slightly from the centre to drain rainwater off into channels at the side, and so prevent potholes from forming on the roads. It was not until the 19th century that the British engineer Thomas Telford built roads as good as those of the ancient Romans, using the very same ideas. The Romans also left wide open spaces on either side of their roads, to prevent enemies attacking them by surprise. If a road had to cross a river, a bridge called a **viaduct** was built. This looked like an aqueduct but carried a road (*via*) instead of water (*aqua*).

Building the Empire

An important feature of Roman Empire architecture was the **arch**. This was made by two pillars of cut stone, which curved towards each other over a timber frame to meet at the top in a semicircular style. The stones of the arch were cut to fit each other. The one at the top of the arch was wedge-shaped, so that, no matter what weight it had to support, it could not fall down. When the arch was complete, the wooden supporting frame was removed.

Amphitheatres and other big buildings relied on the use of arches. When the Romans discovered how to make concrete in the 2nd century BC, building technology developed further. The Colosseum in Rome and the El Jem amphitheatre in north Africa were built of stone arches on the outside, but the walls and seating supports inside were of brick and concrete. Amphitheatres, such as those at Arles (France) and Verona (Italy), are still used for a wide range of events, from bull-fighting to operatic concerts. How many of today's buildings will still be standing and used in 2,000 years time?

Dotted around Europe, north Africa and parts of Asia today, we can still see the remains of other constructions erected by the ancient Romans. Notable among these is **Hadrian's Wall** in what is now northern England, built by the Emperor Hadrian to protect Roman Britain from the Picts to the north. It was 4.5 metres high and 3 metres thick in places.

The Roman arch, whether made of cut stone or, more commonly, of bricks and concrete, was the main feature of many different types of building. This one at Pompeii has stood against an earthquake, a volcanic eruption, 2,000 years of time and tens of millions of tourists.

El Jem, Tunisia

Hadrian's Wall

The Romans and Ireland

Coins and other artefacts from the Roman Empire have been found in several locations in Ireland. It is generally thought that such things came here through trade between Irish Celts and people in Roman Britain. We still have no definite evidence of a Roman camp or settlement here. We know that the Roman general Agricola wrote that Ireland could be invaded with little more than a legion, but there is no evidence that he ever came here. No written sources make any mention of the Romans invading Ireland, nor do we have even one known Roman building on the island. Individual Romans, however, possibly visited Ireland as traders.

DID YOU KNOW?

Whether or not the Romans invaded Ireland, they certainly believed it to be a 'wintry' place. They called Ireland **Hibernia**, from the Latin word for 'winter' (*hiberna*). I wonder why!

CAN YOU SAY?

14. Name *one* famous Roman. *(Junior Certificate Higher Level 2002)*
15. Why did Romans take great care in building roads?
16. Why did they leave open spaces on either side of their roads?
17. Looking at **Source C** above, identify *two* things these stones tell us about the size of Roman carts. Think carefully.
18. Name *two* types of Roman construction that used arches.
19. What kind of Roman ruin would you find at the Pont du Gard?
20. What was the Roman name for Ireland?
21. In your opinion, what were the main achievements of the Roman civilisation? [Try to write four or five sentences on this] *(Junior Certificate Higher Level 1998)*

KEYNOTES

1. **Rome:** founded in 753 BC (Romulus and Remus legend) • by the River Tiber • written sources • archaeological artefacts • ruins of Pompeii
   Buildings: Forum • temples • Via Sacra • triumphal arches • columns • Circus Maximus • Colosseum • theatres • baths • aqueducts • basilicas
2. **Housing:** poor people (plebeians) • *insulae* • fire hazards • rich people (patricians) • house (*domus*) • mansion (villa)
   Main parts of a house: *vestibulum* • *atrium* • *peristylum* • *cubicula* • *culina* • *triclinium* • *tablinum* • *impluvium* • mosaics • murals • central heating • *hypocaust* • *lararium*
3. **Roaming Romans:** Roman army • expansion • Empire • camps • towns • roads: straight and level • drained water off • arches • amphitheatres • aqueducts • viaducts • Romans and Ireland • some contacts • Hibernia

Daily Life in Ancient Rome

8

CITIZENS

In ancient Rome, much depended on whether you were regarded as a **citizen** or not. Both rich patricians and poor plebeians were citizens and, for example, entitled to vote and join the army. People who came from outside the city could not be citizens. Neither could slaves nor women.

As we have seen with regard to housing, there were many differences between the lives of the patricians and plebeians.

Work and Crafts

Patricians generally made their money from land they owned outside or inside Rome. Less important rich people worked as **equites** (business people) – collecting taxes for the state, money lending, property dealing and trading in the huge range of goods needed to keep Rome and its empire going. The rich generally looked down on the idea of earning a living by getting one's hands dirty.

SOURCE A1

SOURCE A2

The poorer Romans worked at a great variety of trades. Some of these are still found in most towns and cities – butchers, bakers, carpenters, cobblers and weavers, for example. Others are less common now: **fullers** cleaned and dyed clothing, **coopers** made timber barrels, **tanners** made leather and there were many **potters** and **smiths**.

DID YOU KNOW?

Fullers generally used human urine, supplied by passers by, for the process of bleaching clothing.

Potters, of course, made most of the vessels needed for food and drink, as well as items such as lamps, candleholders and funeral urns. Huge clay containers called *amphorae* were vital products in a city that depended so much on storing and transporting goods.

SOURCE B

Tile-makers were very busy in ancient Rome. Roof-tiles were much less of a fire risk than thatch. Most Roman roofs were made of flat tiles called *tegulae*, with the gaps between them made watertight by rounded *imbrex* tiles. These tiles were made of clay and, initially, were dried in the sun; later, kiln-dried tiles proved to be more waterproof.

Many Roman craft-workers were very artistic. Some tile-makers, for instance, concentrated on mosaic-making; this involved making millions of tiny square *tesserae* of clay, marble or glass, which were used in beautiful floor and wall pictures in the houses of wealthy Romans.

Just as in Celtic Ireland, smiths produced beautiful jewellery and ornaments. Gold became plentiful as Roman armies conquered more territories. Gold rings were popular among wealthy men and women, and women also wore bracelets, necklaces and earrings. Glass making was another important craft. Glass was rarely used in windows, but was popular in the jewellery, vases, plates and drinking vessels of the rich.

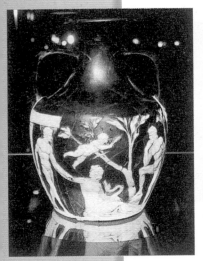

The Portland Vase, an example of the skills of Roman craftspeople.

Most Roman craftspeople had to work very long hours, from dawn to dusk, to earn a living. The idea of a weekend did not really exist and days off were limited to religious festivals. A holiday was also given whenever the Roman army returned home to march in triumph through the streets.

From the third century BC onwards, trade was conducted with the aid of coins. The most widely used coins were the *Sestertius* and the larger *Denarius*, four times as valuable. Julius Caesar actually minted a gold coin called an *Aurea*, worth 25 *Denarii*.

CAN YOU SAY?

1. Looking at **Sources A1** and **A2** above, explain *two* of the jobs being done by any of the people in the picture.
2. What were *amphorae* used for?
3. What precisely were *tegulae* and *pilae*?
4. Look at **Source B** above and identify *two* things about this picture that you would not normally find in a photograph of a modern roof?
5. Write an account [*five* points, without your book] of 'work, arts and crafts' in ancient Rome.

(*Junior Certificate Higher Level 2002*)

 ## THE NON-CITIZENS

While both patricians and plebeians could be citizens, more than three out of every four 'Romans' in the city were non-citizens. Those who lived in the rest of Italy (provincials) or around the empire were rarely citizens either, unless they were originally Roman landowners or soldiers who got land on their retirement. Yet, the role played in Roman society by all these non-citizens was a vital one.

Farmers

The people in Rome, and in Roman towns such as Pompeii, depended very heavily on farmers to produce the food and some of the raw materials they needed for their work. As the Roman Empire got larger, its people became the world's first commercial farmers. Whereas the Celts mainly produced food for themselves, large farms developed in Roman times that also produced food for the people of the cities.

Produce varied across the empire, depending on climate and conditions. In Italy itself, olives (for oil) and grapes (for wine) were widely grown, as were wheat and other cereal crops. Although France is the world's most famed wine-producing country, it was actually the Romans who introduced grapes and wine to France.

The main animal reared for meat was the pig, with its meat being salted to preserve it over the winter. Salt (*sal*) was so important that Roman soldiers were paid partly in salt, so they could preserve their meat. In fact, this is where we get the word 'salary' from. Cattle were actually used for pulling ploughs as much as for meat, and the Romans would rarely use a horse for farm work. Horses were reared as a means of transport or for the army. Farmers kept bees for honey, as the Romans had no sugar.

A Roman farm.

Slaves

The Romans, like most ancient civilisations, used **slavery**. Slaves were brought to Rome from Africa and other parts of the Roman Empire, often after being captured in wars, and bought and sold in the marketplace. They could be owned by citizens or by the Roman state. Slaves were mostly used to do heavy manual labour in building, mining or farming. However, many slaves (notably Greeks) had been educated and were used as teachers, clerks and scribes. Wealthy women and children usually had a slave as a bodyguard when they went out.

When Rome was at its height, there were some 300,000 slaves in the city. It was very rare for a slave to escape for any lengthy period – any Roman citizen who helped an escaped slave was severely punished. Some slaves eventually got their freedom (**manumission**) by buying it or in reward for loyal service. It was not uncommon for freed slaves to set themselves up afterwards in business or as state employees.

CAN YOU SAY?

6. Explain *two* ways in which farming in the Roman Empire differed from modern Irish farming.
7. How do we know that salt was important in ancient Rome?
8. List *three* jobs done by Roman slaves.
9. How might a slave achieve freedom?
10. Who was Spartacus?

WOMEN AND CHILDREN

Regardless of whether you were Roman or a provincial, rich or poor, neither women nor children were considered as Roman citizens.

Women

Roman women did not have equal rights with men. They were not regarded as citizens and so could not vote or hold public office. If a woman came from a wealthy family, her life tended to revolve around marriage, at least by the age of 14, having children and managing the household slaves. A male was always regarded as the head of the family, the *paterfamilias*. Marriages were usually arranged by parents and, for the girl particularly, the engagement (*sponsalia*) was really a sort of drawing up of a contract between her family and another, often aimed at making business or political alliances.

Although patrician women were greatly respected, it was rare for one to have any real influence in politics or business. If they did, it was behind the scenes. One woman, Agrippina, managed to marry an emperor (Claudius), while also being his niece. She allegedly had him poisoned, and then got her son installed as emperor afterwards. However, her son, the infamous Nero, eventually had her murdered.

For plebeian women, early marriage was also common. Being less well off and unable to afford good medical care, plebeian women often suffered death in childbirth. Many plebeian wives worked in their husbands' shops or market stalls. With no slaves of their own, wives also took charge of the household jobs, such as shopping and rearing the children.

Children

The children of plebeians received little or no education. They mostly learnt their crafts and skills from their parents. Some patrician children were educated at home by their parents or a **tutor**. However,

DID YOU KNOW?

It has been estimated that, among the poorer classes, only two out of every three children in ancient Rome survived beyond their first year.

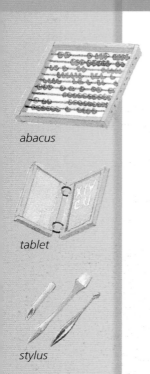

abacus

tablet

stylus

most patrician children aged between 7 and 12 attended school (*ludus*) and learnt reading, writing and mathematics.

After 12, girls were generally kept at home to learn skills such as embroidery and flower-arranging from their mothers. The boys went to a teacher called a *grammaticus* to study Greek and Roman literature, history, arithmetic and geometry. Further study after this might involve going abroad, particularly to Greece from where many of the slave-teachers in Rome originally came.

School lasted from dawn until noon and many students arrived and left with slave escorts. Writing was usually done with a pointed **stylus**, scratching words and numbers onto a wax tablet. Paper, made from **papyrus** reeds, was used only for books and documents. Mathematics were done with the help of a counting frame called an **abacus**, which is still used by children today. Unsatisfactory students were severely beaten. On market day, once every eight days, schoolchildren had a day off.

However, it was not all work and no play. Archaeologists have found evidence that Roman children enjoyed ball games and played with timber dolls and spinning tops. Carved toy swords, soldiers and animals have also been found, and at least one Latin writer complained of how the young seemed to do nothing but play and enjoy themselves.

DID YOU KNOW?

A male child officially became an adult *and* a citizen at the age of 14, when he also received his first shave!

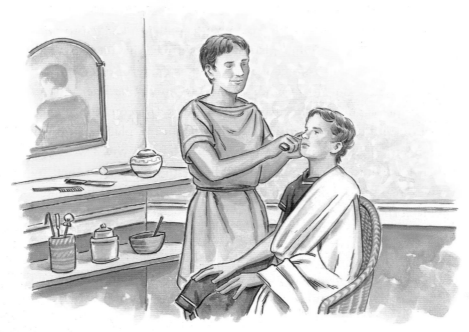

CAN YOU SAY?

11. Write down *one* fact about housing *or* women's lives from ancient Rome.

    (*Junior Certificate Ordinary Level 2006*)

12. Explain *two* ways in which patrician women's lives differed from those of plebeian women.

13. Explain *two* ways in which Roman women's lives differed from the lives of men.

14. What was (a) a *ludus* and (b) a *grammaticus*?

15. Explain *two* ways in which a Roman school differed from a modern Irish one.

OTHER EVERYDAY MATTERS

Food

The diet of the ancient Romans was quite healthy. Meat was expensive and very difficult to preserve in a hot climate, so it was rarely eaten by the poor. Corn and bread were the staple foods; many a politician rose or fell depending on his success in keeping corn prices down. Romans were very fond of corn-based foods such as porridge and pancakes.

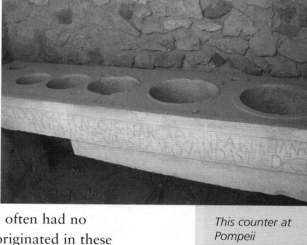

This counter at Pompeii contained hollowed out sections of different sizes. These were used to measure out different quantities of grain.

Take-aways called **thermopolia** were popular, particularly with the poor whose homes often had no cooking facilities. It is almost certain that pizza originated in these ancient Roman food bars, though with different toppings, as tomatoes were unknown in Roman times. Many poor Romans also bought a strong fish sauce called **garum** to hide the taste of their own food, which was often anything but fresh.

SOURCE C

This picture of a thermopolium from Pompeii shows the holes in the counter, which were used for containers of hot food, as well as the mural (picture) on the wall, part of the shrine to the household gods.

Among wealthier Romans, chicken and fish were popular. More unusually, perhaps, they also regarded thrushes, swans and snails fed on milk as special treats! Vegetables and citrus fruits were plentiful, as was wine.

Breakfast (*ientaculum*) was usually eaten soon after dawn. After a midday lunch (*prandium*), Romans relaxed for a few hours to escape the heat of the sun; this *siesta* is still normal in Mediterranean countries today. The main meal, the *cena*, was eaten in the evening and there the day's news, business dealings and politics were discussed.

Wealthy Romans ate their meals while reclining on couches; the meals were cooked and served by their slaves.

DID YOU KNOW?

A particular delicacy eaten by wealthy Romans was stuffed mouse! These poor creatures were reared in jars on a diet of nuts; they were then killed, stuffed with minced meat and baked in the oven. The senate eventually banned this in 169 BC.

Clothing

The most common garment among Romans was the **tunica**, which resembled a long, buttonless shirt tied at the waist. This was worn by men, women and children around the house, with light leather sandals, to keep cool in the warm weather.

In public, however, a patrician's outer garment was his **toga**. This was a long robe, made from a semi-circular cloth, draped over the shoulders and down to the feet. Togas were almost always white, though young patricians wore purple-edged ones. Although made of wool, the toga's whiteness deflected the sun's rays and kept the wearer cool.

A woman wore a long dress called a *stola* and, when going out, a wrap-around shawl or *palla*. Although wearing the *palla* over the head must have been uncomfortably warm, sun-tans were

SOURCE D

This is a detail from the Arch of Constantine.

avoided at all costs by ladies from the patrician class. Being tanned suggested that you had to work outside, which meant that you were probably a plebeian.

Men were usually clean-shaven, though beards were common after 100 AD. Women – *and* quite a few men – dyed their hair, wore wigs and used perfume and make-up. Chalk, for example, was popular for whitening the skin, while ashes were used for darkening the eyebrows.

Language and Numbers

The Romans spoke and wrote in Latin. Between 30 and 50 per cent of the words we use daily in English come from Latin. Even more of the languages of modern Italy, Portugal, Spain and France come from it, as the Roman Empire controlled these places for centuries.

For example, the first numbers in Latin are: unus (1); duo (2); tres (3); quattuor (4); quinque (5); sex (6); septem (7); octo (8); novem (9); decem (10). Here are the Portuguese equivalents: um (1); dois (2); tres (3); quatro (4); cinco (5); seis (6); sete (7); oito (8); nove (9); dez (10). See how the numbers in any language you know (even English or Irish) compare with the Latin originals.

The Roman alphabet became largely the alphabet we use today. They often wrote the letter J as an I, and U as a V, partly because these were easier to carve in stone inscriptions.

Roman numerals are sometimes used today. As far as 39, they are based on the use of fingers and hands for counting purposes. The capital I was used for 1, V for 5 and X for 10. For larger numbers, the Romans used the letter L for 50, C for 100, D for 500 and M for 1,000. Forming the numbers outside of these is simply a matter of addition and subtraction. For example:

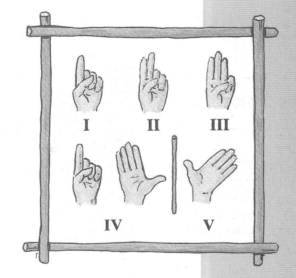

2	= II (2 x I)
4	= IV (1 less than 5)
8	= VIII (3 more than 5)
80	= LXXX (50 and three 10s)
90	= XC (10 less than 100)
1,200	= MCC (1,000 and two 100s)
1,900	= MCM (1,000 and 100 less than 1,000)

CAN YOU SAY?

16. Explain *three* ways in which the Roman diet differed from a modern Irish one.
17. In **Source C** above, explain *two* ways in which this thermopolium at Pompeii differs from most modern take-away restaurants.
18. Explain *three* ways in which the hot weather affected what Romans wore.
19. What was a *toga candida*?
20. Look at **Source D** above.
    (a) Identify and name the *two* main garments being worn by the female figure in this carving.
    (b) What background detail suggests that this carving may not be of a real person?
21. What was the language spoken by ancient Romans?
22. Write your date of birth in Roman numerals.
23. Write an account of 'food and clothing' in ancient Rome.
    [Five points, without your book]   (*Junior Certificate Higher Level 2002*)

KEYNOTES

1. **Work:** patricians – landowners; equites (bankers etc.); plebeians
   • trades (carpenters, fullers, tanners, potters, tile-makers);
   crafts: mosaics (*tesserae*), jewellery, glass making
   Commercial farming: grapes, olives, cereals, meat, honey
   Slavery: manual labour • bodyguards • teachers • gladiators • Spartacus
2. **Women:** non-citizens, early marriage, children, household management
   Children: tutors • *ludus* • *grammaticus* • stylus, papyrus, abacus, games
3. **Food:** chicken, fish, bread • corn prices • vegetables, fruit • stuffed mice • pizza
   • *thermopolia* • *garum*; meals • *ientaculum* • *prandium* • *cena*
   Clothing: *tunica* • *toga (candida)* • *stola* • *palla*
   Latin: language's influence • Roman numerals

MINI-PROJECT

Write an account on: *A young person growing up in a named ancient civilisation* (outside of Ireland).

(No hints given)   (*Junior Certificate Higher Level 2000*)

Rome's Special Occasions

9

As well as hard work, politics, domestic jobs and school, daily life in Rome had many special occasions, events and ceremonies – some were religious, some were definitely not.

BATHS

For wealthy Roman men and women, going to the public baths was a daily routine rather than a special event. Even plebeians had access to free public baths, which was just as well, as they rarely had washing facilities in their *insulae*!

The **public baths** were a popular place of recreation – for exercise, bathing or simply for meeting friends. They had three main baths – the *frigidarium* (cold), the *tepidarium* (lukewarm) and the *caldarium* (hot). Roman baths generally had very complicated heating systems beneath the floor, and these heated both rooms and water. The heat was intended to clean the skin's pores by perspiration. Most Romans actually scraped dirt off their bodies with curved rods called *strigils*, and olive oil was much more commonly rubbed on the body than soap.

Physical exercises were done in the courtyard or *palaestra*. Men and women bathed at different times of the day, though Pompeii actually had separate bathing facilities for men and women. The time spent at the baths was possibly the most important way that Romans had of maintaining business contacts and of keeping in touch with political events or even the latest gossip.

To give some idea of the scale of public baths, the Baths of Caracalla in Rome covered an area of about 11 hectares, the size of a small farm, and could hold 1,600 bathers, and the Baths of Diocletian were said to have held twice that many!

THEATRE

The Romans developed a love of the **theatre** from the Greeks, and built many beautiful theatres in the same semicircular shape as the Greeks. Some theatres could seat up to 30,000 people on stone steps. Sound quality was so good that ancient Roman theatres are still used today as venues for concerts and recitals; for example, the Roman theatre at Orange in southern France seats 9,000 people and has three doors through which actors make their entrances or exits.

Roman plays were usually either **comedies**, with happy endings, or **tragedies**, which ended sadly. Large theatres were open-air, but some smaller indoor ones called **odeons** were also popular – the Emperor Nero was fond of acting in odeon plays and no one was allowed to leave while he was performing.

SOURCE A1

SOURCE A2

CHARIOT RACING

The Romans held horse races in the **Circus Maximus**. The most popular of these were the **chariot races**, where teams of four horses pulled chariots and their **charioteers** around the course. Corners were very tight, so that accidents, serious injuries and deaths were not uncommon.

A race meeting opened with a huge procession through Rome. This was called a *pompa* and it included priests, musicians and charioteers. Over 20 races were held, each approximately the length of today's Aintree Grand National. Each team was identified according to its colour: red, blue, green or white. Rome's most successful charioteer was a 'red' called Diocles, winner of 1,462 races.

So popular were Diocles and the other charioteers that sometimes even the 250,000-seater Circus Maximus could not hold the crowd. Thousands were killed when some temporary seating fell down on one occasion. What remains of this stadium today is mainly just a public park. When Italy won the football World Cup in 2006, one million people greeted the team at the Circus Maximus.

GLADIATORS

The Romans built many **stadia** or **amphitheatres**, the most famous being the **Colosseum**. Here, **gladiators** fought each other with swords, javelins, tridents (three-pronged forks), shields and nets. *Mirmillones* were gladiators who fought with sword and shield, and their most common opponents were called *retiarii*; they carried tridents and nets. Sometimes, gladiators fought with wild animals or the stadium was flooded for mock sea-battles.

DID YOU KNOW?

At chariot races, riots between rival supporters were quite common – the Emperor Justinian had to crush a rebellion in Constantinople, which began as a riot between the 'blues' and 'greens'.

The Colosseum. You can see the underground cells where gladiators and animals waited before the games.

DID YOU KNOW?

In 106 AD, Emperor Trajan ordered 17 continuous weeks of gladiator fights. During these, 9,000 gladiators died.

DID YOU KNOW?

Spectators at the Colosseum instructed gladiators to kill or release defeated opponents by pointing their thumbs. Pointing upwards meant the gladiator survived, while downwards meant he was to be killed. The writer Pliny's description of this is simply **verso pollice** ('thumb having been turned'), and we really don't know whether thumbs down meant 'stab him' or 'put your sword down'.

SOURCE B

As with chariot racing, crowds became passionately involved at gladiatorial contests. Indeed, the Roman historian Tacitus wrote of a serious riot that took place in Pompeii in 59 AD between groups of people from Pompeii and nearby Nuceria, all over a gladiatorial contest. Several spectators were killed. Placing bets on likely winners was common practice too. Gladiator contests were held at festival times, but it was also common for an unpopular emperor to pay for such 'games' and give people free admission, in the hope that it distracted people from his misrule!

CAN YOU SAY?

1. Give *one* difference between Roman baths and modern swimming pools.
2. Look at **Sources A1** and **A2** above and identify *two* differences between Roman theatres and modern cinemas or theatres.
3. What was a *pompa*?
4. What evidence shows that chariot racing was extremely popular?
5. Where did gladiatorial contests take place?
6. What were (a) *mirmillones* and (b) *retiarii*?
7. In **Source B** above, identify *one* way in which the interior of the Colosseum resembles a modern stadium and *one* way in which it is different.

RELIGION

For over 800 years, the Romans worshipped many gods, just as the Greeks had done before them. **Jupiter** was the king of the gods and god of the sky. Soldiers prayed to Mars, god of war. The god **Neptune** ruled the sea. Romans in love prayed to the god **Cupid**, and **Saturn** was god of the harvest.

The Romans worshipped many goddesses too. **Juno**, wife of Jupiter, was the goddess of women. **Venus** was the goddess of love and beauty, and one goddess to whom all Romans prayed was **Vesta**, goddess of the hearth.

All these gods, and many more, had temples in their honour, the greatest being the **Pantheon**, which is today used as a Catholic church. Its amazing roof is made from a series of arches meeting around an opening in the centre.

Animal sacrifices were regularly offered to the various gods, and **augurs** tried to predict the future by examining the entrails of the sacrificed creatures. It was also common for the worshippers of a god to write their own special prayers on the temple wall.

Most Romans built altars to the gods in their own homes. Here, the head of the family made a **libation** – an offering of milk and wine – in honour of the household gods (*lares*).

The Pantheon today.

Rome held many religious festivals such as the *Lupercal*, which celebrated springtime, and *Vinalia*, held in honour of the grape harvest. The most popular festival of all was *Saturnalia*, in honour of Saturn. It began on 17 December and ran for seven days. During this festival, all work stopped, slaves got temporary release to enjoy themselves and gifts were exchanged.

Christianity

Around 30 AD, a new religion began in one of the most troublesome parts of the Roman Empire, Judaea. This religion was Christianity. Fearing a possible revolt, the Roman governor, Pontius Pilate, authorised the execution of Jesus Christ, but this failed to stop the spread of Christianity through the eastern part of the Empire, especially the city of Antioch.

About the middle of the 1st century AD, Christians began to arrive in Rome, hoping to spread their faith in what was the known world's most powerful city. By this time, some Romans had begun to worship their own emperors as gods and did not take kindly to the Christians.

DID YOU KNOW?

The pagan Romans believed in many spirits, as well as gods. One spirit was **Janus**, protector of the doorway. He had two faces. His name has been given to our month of January because it is a time when we both look forward to the coming year and back on the one just ended.

Emperor Nero blamed them for the great fire mentioned in Chapter 7 and had many Christians, including St Peter and St Paul, executed. Thousands of Christians in Rome and its empire suffered horrific deaths in amphitheatres such as the **Colosseum** or **Nero's Circus**, where they were thrown to lions, tigers and other wild animals.

The great breakthrough for Christianity came with the conversion of the Emperor Constantine in the 4th century AD. After this, the persecution of Christians ended and Christianity became the official religion of Rome and its empire soon afterwards. This was of great importance in helping to spread the religion to most parts of Europe – St Patrick's father, for example, was apparently a Roman soldier.

DID YOU KNOW?

A Roman high priest was known as the *Pontifex Maximus*. This title, or its shortened form of **Pontiff**, is still used today by the Pope.

DID YOU KNOW?

Dead slaves were often just thrown into pits called *puticuli*, along with the household rubbish!

CAN YOU SAY?

8. Who was the king of the Roman gods?
9. Of what were Mars and Neptune gods?
10. What did augurs do?
11. Looking at **Source C** above, give *one* way in which the Pantheon resembles any modern building you know of and *one* way in which it is very different.
12. What was Saturnalia?
13. Give *two* reasons why early Christians were persecuted in Rome.

Burial Customs

When a poor person died, the burial usually took place the following day with little ceremony. In fact, the writer Cicero wrote of poor people being buried in mass graves outside the city walls with no ceremony at all.

When a rich person died, the body could be kept in the house for up to a week, usually in the atrium. Candles surrounded the corpse, which was laid on a bed with its feet towards the door. Those in mourning often wept or beat their chests, calling out the name of the dead person continually.

For the funeral of an important or wealthy person, the family sometimes hired professional mourners (called

Most Roman funerals ended with the cremation of the body and the placing of the ashes in an urn. This is what remains of the platform where Julius Caesar's body was cremated in 44 BC. His nephew, Octavius (later called Augustus), had a temple built on the spot.

A Roman columbarium.

praeficae) to cry aloud all through the ceremony. As the body was carried on a platform through the streets, actors put on displays reminding people of the great achievements of the person concerned. A speech or *laudatio* was often given by a friend or relative of the dead person.

Even the rich had to be buried outside the city walls – many burial grounds were sited along the Via Appia; they were filled with tombstones. The most powerful patrician families buried their dead in family tombs, while those who were cremated could have their ashes placed in communal tombs called *columbaria*. Once a year, on All Souls Day, offerings of wine and milk were poured on the graves.

Tombstone.

The pagan Romans believed in an afterlife, as did most civilisations, including the Celts in Ireland. A coin was placed in the dead person's mouth because the Romans believed you had to pay the legendary ferryman, **Charon**, to carry spirits safely to the next life, across the River Styx.

Life after death was based in the underworld, known as Hades, and the spirits of people who had lived good lives were believed to go to Elysium, the Roman version of heaven. The spirits of the underworld were called the **Manes**, so many tombstones were inscribed with *Dis/Diis Manibus* ('To the gods/spirits of the underworld'), the Roman version of 'Rest in Peace'.

Over several centuries, persecuted Christians built a huge, complex network of passageways underneath Rome. These were called **catacombs**. In these, Christians found safe hiding-places during their persecution before the 4th century; they built sleeping quarters and small chapels, and buried their dead. Many of the early popes were buried in these catacombs.

The catacombs.

CAN YOU SAY?

14. Write down *one* important fact about burial customs in Roman civilisation.
(Junior Certificate Ordinary Level 1998, 2000 and 2002)

15. What were (a) a *laudatio* and (b) a *columbarium*?

16. Give *two* pieces of evidence that show that the Romans believed in life after death?

17. What were catacombs?

18. Write an account [five points, without your book] of 'burial customs' in ancient Rome.
(Junior Certificate Higher Level 2002)

KEYNOTES

1. **Entertainment and leisure:** Public baths • *frigidarium* • *tepidarium* • *caldarium*
   • exercise • meeting-places • theatre • open air • comedies and tragedies • *odeons*
   • chariot racing • Circus Maximus • *pompa* • blues • greens • whites • reds
   • gladiators • amphitheatres • Colosseum • *mirmillones* • *retiarii* • turning the thumb

2. **Roman religion:** many gods • Jupiter (head) • Mars (war) • Neptune (sea)
   • Saturn (crops) • goddesses • Juno (women) • Venus (love) • Vesta (hearth)
   • Janus (two-headed spirit) • household gods *(lares)* • augurs • temples (Pantheon)
   • libations (offerings to the gods) • festivals • *Lupercal* • *Vinalia* • *Saturnalia*
   Christianity: persecution of early Christians • thrown to the lions
   • hiding in catacombs • conversion of Emperor Constantine

3. **Burial customs:** difference between rich and poor • week-long mourning
   • funeral procession • *laudatio* • *columbaria* • afterlife • Charon • River Styx
   • Hades • Elysium • *Dis/Diis Manibus*

MINI-PROJECT

Write an account of the following: *A priest or priestess in an ancient civilisation.*
Hints:

- the functions of the priest/priestess
- forms of worship
- gods/goddesses
- places of worship   *(Junior Certificate Higher Level 1994)*

Or

A person from a named civilisation outside of Ireland.
Hints:

- food and clothing
- housing
- arts and crafts
- burial customs   *(Junior Certificate Ordinary Level 2003)*

[This was also asked in 2005 Ordinary Level, but with work given as a hint instead of arts and crafts, and on the 2006 and 2009 Higher Level papers with no hints.]

Normans, Knights and Castles

10

THE NORMANS

For reasons that we will go into more fully later, the centuries between ancient history (the Romans, for example) and more modern times are called the **Middle Ages**.

We left ancient Irish history in Chapter 6, just as the Vikings first came here to attack and plunder monasteries. Later, they began to settle and trade here, founding cities such as Waterford and Dublin. Vikings, of course, settled elsewhere too – Iceland, Greenland, even Canada! Closer to home, in 911, Vikings, under a leader called Rollo, captured land for themselves in northern France, which became known as **Normandy**, from the word **Norse**, another name for the Vikings.

William the Conqueror

A hundred years later, Normandy was one of the strongest regions in France. The Vikings (or **Normans**), led by **Duke William**, now spoke French. In 1066, King Edward of England died and William laid claim to his throne, based on a promise supposedly made by the dead king. However, before William could get to England, the English crowned Harold Godwin as their king.

William decided to invade England, an event that inspired one of the most amazing works of art of the day, the **Bayeux Tapestry**. In Latin words and embroidered pictures, it tells the story of the Norman invasion of England in 1066. William and his army landed at Hastings on the south coast of England and Harold, with his army, marched south to meet them. The Bayeux Tapestry shows us that the **Battle of Hastings** (October 1066) was a bloody one, which came to its conclusion after the death of Harold.

DID YOU KNOW?

The Bayeux Tapestry is a woven linen cloth only 50 centimetres high, but about half the length of Croke Park.

SOURCE A

The Norman victory was due to a combination of better equipment and good tactics. The Norman horse-soldier (**knight**) was the best-trained and best-equipped soldier in Europe then. The Normans also had archers who used longbows and crossbows. Twice, William's army appeared to retreat, and twice they lured the English into a trap, killing many of them.

After the battle, William marched to London where he was crowned King of England on Christmas Day 1066. From then on, he was known as 'William the Conqueror'. Over the next 100 years, William and his successors ruled England, and brought the entire country under Norman control, with the help of Norman lords loyal to them.

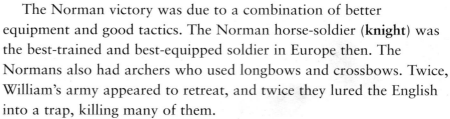

THE NORMANS IN IRELAND

We have seen in earlier chapters how Ireland had many kingdoms and many kings. One of these kings, **Dermot MacMurrough**, was driven from his kingdom of Leinster by Tiernan O'Rourke of Breifne and Rory O'Connor, the most powerful king in Ireland.

In 1169, MacMurrough sailed to Norman-controlled **England**, and eventually found the country's king, **Henry II**. Henry gave permission for the Norman lords of Wales to help MacMurrough if they so wished. These men included Maurice FitzGerald, Robert FitzStephen and Richard FitzGilbert de Clare (**Strongbow**). MacMurrough promised them land in return for help in getting back his kingdom. Dermot also promised Strongbow his daughter, Aoife, in marriage and the kingdom of Leinster after his own death.

In 1169, the first Normans arrived in small groups, but, with their horses, armour, archers and military planning, they were able to defeat much larger Irish forces. At Baginbun, Co. Wexford, 80 Normans are said to have defeated a force of 3,000 Irish. Strongbow married Aoife in Waterford and, after Dermot died in 1171, he became king of Leinster. Soon, Henry II began to worry that Strongbow and other Normans might, in fact, become too powerful and threaten his own rule, so he came to Ireland in 1172. The Norman lords, and quite a few of the worried native Irish kings, swore loyalty to Henry and declared him **Lord of Ireland**.

CAN YOU SAY?

1. What does the Bayeux Tapestry depict? *(Junior Certificate Higher Level 1994)*
2. Examine the scene from the Bayeux Tapestry (**Source A**).
   (a) Name *two* weapons being used by the soldiers.
   (b) Describe *one* way in which the soldiers are protecting themselves.
   (c) What advantage do the Normans have?
   (Junior Certificate Ordinary Level sample paper)
3. The Bayeux Tapestry was made for William's half-brother. Is it a fully reliable source? Explain. (Remember Chapter 1)
4. Give *two* reasons why the Norman invasion of Ireland was successful.
   (Junior Certificate Higher Level 1993)
5. In which order did the following arrive in Ireland? Start with the earliest:
   the Vikings; the Celts; the Normans. *(Junior Certificate Ordinary Level 2006)*

● KNIGHTS

We have seen how important horses were to the Normans. All over Europe, soldiers who fought on horseback (*à cheval* in French) were called **chevaliers**, or **knights**. These were highly trained and respected soldiers, who lived by a code of honour called **chivalry**. This involved 13 sacred vows, including vows of loyalty to the king and to God, as well as to protect women and children and never to run from a fight.

Only relatively wealthy people were ever likely to be made knights. Training to become a knight began at the age of seven when a boy went to a neighbouring castle to be a **page**. As a page, he spent seven years learning to read and write, play music and perhaps to use a bow and arrow. He also acted as a general servant.

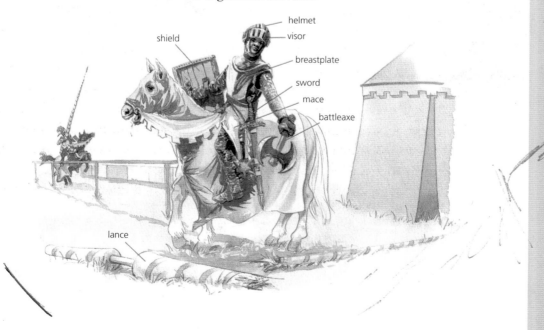

At 14 or 15, the page became a **squire**, who acted as an assistant to a knight. He now learnt to use the weapons of a knight and to fight on horseback. He also cared for the knight's horse, armour and weapons; some older squires fought and died beside their knights in battle. If a squire fought particularly bravely, he could be created a knight on the battlefield – 'a knight of the sword'.

Normally, however, a squire became a knight at 21, following an all-night **vigil** of prayer and fasting in church. In the morning, a mass was celebrated and the squire swore to uphold the code of chivalry. He then knelt on one knee, while his lord **dubbed** him by touching each of his shoulders with a sword and saying: 'Arise, Sir _____.'

Armour and Weapons

Knights were very well protected in battle. Early knights wore full-length **chain mail** made of thousands of metal rings; this helped to deflect some blows or arrows. Later knights preferred full suits of **armour**, which were heavy but gave them greater protection. A movable grill on the **helmet**, called a **visor**, protected the eyes, while a single piece of armour (**breastplate**) protected the chest. It was also usual for a knight's horse to wear a protective cloth – William the Conqueror had three horses killed under him at Hastings!

A knight's weapons consisted mainly of a sword, shield, mace and battleaxe. His shield was decorated with his **coat of arms** (a family crest). **Lances** were long, heavy poles used when charging the enemy on horseback.

DID YOU KNOW?

Armour made by riveting small metal plates to cloth or leather was called **brigandine**. This was used for a knight's gloves (**gauntlets**); the same idea is used in most modern bulletproof jackets!

SOURCE B

CAN YOU SAY?

6. During the Middle Ages, what was chivalry?
(*Junior Certificate Higher Level 2002 and 2009*)
7. Name *two* of the stages involved in the training of a knight.
(*Junior Certificate Higher Level 2001 and 2004; Ordinary Level 2002 asked for* one *stage*)
8. What was a knight's main job? (*Junior Certificate Ordinary Level 2000*)
9. **Source B** is a picture of a knight. Name *two* items of armour carried by the knight.
(*Junior Certificate Ordinary Level 1998*)
10. In this display of suits of armour through the ages (**Source C** below), the earliest ones are on the left-hand side of the picture. Identify *two* significant differences between earlier armour and the later ones on the right. Can you explain why these changes came about?

SOURCE C

EARLY CASTLES

The Normans were seen as foreign invaders and were frequently attacked by the Irish. For defence purposes, one of the first things a Norman lord did was to build a castle. These early castles were known as **motte and bailey** castles, and were made mostly of timber.

The bailey section of the castle was like a ringfort. It was circular and surrounded by a ditch with a wooden **palisade** (fence) on top of it. Inside, servants' houses, stables, barns and sometimes a small chapel were found, usually made of wattle and daub, with roofs of thatch.

Unlike earlier forts, a man-made earthen hill stood beside the bailey. This was called a **motte**; it was much higher than the ground

SOURCE D1

Source D1 is a photograph of a motte and bailey site as it is today and Source D2 is an archaeologist's drawing of what it looked like in Norman times.

SOURCE D2

where the bailey stood and was usually reached by a sloping bridge. On top of the motte, a timber tower (**bresteche**) was built to house the castle-owner and his family. Some castles were surrounded by a water-filled trench (**moat**) for extra protection, but the greatest danger to these timber castles was from fire – can you guess why?

STONE CASTLES

After a few decades, motte and bailey castles came to be replaced by **stone castles**, particularly if a nobleman felt safe and secure, and if he was wealthy enough. Although the designs of these castles differed all over Europe, they had many features in common.

A stone tower or **keep** was the strongest and most important part of the castle. It could be several storeys high. Below ground level lay prisons or **dungeons**, while above them kitchens and storerooms were found. Above them again was the **great hall**, the venue for banquets and business dealings, and the top floor was reserved for the owner's quarters, the **solar**. Rush-covered floors were usually reached by a stone staircase. Some keeps had toilets (**garderobes**), though 'plumbing' was just a hole in the wall!

As with timber castles, a **bailey** (known in Ireland as a **bawn**) lay beside the keep. Surrounded by an outer **curtain wall**, the bailey contained stables, workshops and storehouses. A large castle had a garden and a **well** within the bailey too, and some even had outer and inner baileys to provide double defences. Servants' and soldiers' quarters and a **chapel** were also found in the bailey.

SOURCE E

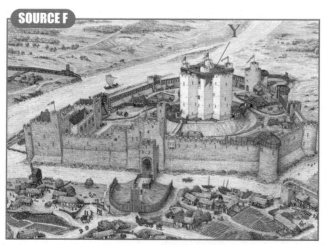

SOURCE F

CAN YOU SAY?

11. In Norman times, what was a motte and bailey?
    (Junior Certificate Ordinary and Higher Levels 1992)

12. Some medieval castles were surrounded by a moat. What was a moat?
    (Junior Certificate Ordinary Level 1993)

13. Study the pictures called **Sources D1, D2** and **E** and answer the following questions:
    (a) Describe *one* source of evidence an archaeologist would need to draw **Source D2**.
    (b) What was the purpose of a motte and bailey?
    (c) Name *one* material used to build an early Norman motte and bailey.
    (d) In **Source D2**, name the parts of the drawing marked **X** and **Y**.
    (e) Study **Source D1** carefully. State what you consider to be the most serious danger to the conservation of this historic site. Support your answer by evidence from the picture.
    (Junior Certificate Level 1996)
    (f) Why do you think the type of castle in **Source D2** was replaced by the type of castle shown in **Source E**? *(Similar question on Ordinary Level paper 2006)*
    (g) In **Source E** what was the name of the part of the castle (marked **Y**) in which the lord and his family lived?
    (Junior Certificate Higher Level 2000)

14. **Source F** is an artist's impression of Trim Castle during the Middle Ages.
    (Junior Certificate Higher Level 2002)
    (a) Name *one* form of transport shown in **Source F**.
    (b) Give *one* piece of evidence to show that many of the people who lived near the castle were farmers.
    (c) Why do you think the lord of the castle lived in the building marked **Y**?
    (d) The Normans were the first people to build stone castles in Ireland. True or False?

ATTACKING AND DEFENDING

A Castle's Defences

The main entrance in the curtain wall was the castle's weakest point in the event of an attack, so it was protected by a large iron grill called a **portcullis** and, if the castle had a **moat** around it, by a **drawbridge**. The **gatehouse** held the soldiers who guarded the entrance, as well as the pulleys for lowering the drawbridge or portcullis.

Some castles had extra towers (**barbicans**) outside the entrance for extra protection. Other defensive features included small towers or

In this picture of Roscrea Castle, you can see the drawbridge and portcullis in the gatehouse, as well as a 'murder hole' over the entrance, from which defenders could fire missiles or boiling liquid down on attackers.

turrets for soldiers at intervals along the curtain wall. Windows tended to be narrow **slit-windows**, making it difficult for enemy arrows to hit those inside, while all walls were topped by **battlements** (or **ramparts**).

This view of Cahir Castle shows the curtain wall, keep, turret and battlements.

The picture above shows a cannon ball still stuck in the wall beside a slit window.

Attacking Castles

Castles were very well defended and attacking them was difficult. Their slit-windows were wider on the inside than the outside; this made it easy for defenders to shoot arrows out – the battlements had gaps in them (**crenellations**) for the same reason. Hot liquid and missiles could be hurled from the walls down on the attackers below. A strong castle with enough supplies could hold out for months against an attack (**siege**).

Those **besieging** a castle usually surrounded it and tried to break down the gates with a **battering ram.** Alternatively, they would try to climb the castle walls with **siege ladders** or the larger **siege towers**. Sometimes, tunnels were dug beneath the castle walls to get them to fall (**undermining**). Fires lit in these tunnels could crack the stones of the castle wall.

SOURCE G

Large weapons were also used to hurl missiles at the castle's defenders, such as a giant crossbow called a **ballista** or huge boulder-throwing catapults known as **mangonels**. The introduction of gunpowder and, hence, **cannon** in the 15th century made attacking a castle much easier.

Many battles in the Middle Ages were also fought on open ground, not around castles at all. Although knights were the most important, most of an army was made up of foot soldiers. Particularly important were **archers**, who fired on the enemy using **crossbows** or **longbows**. Crossbows took time to load, but their **bolts** could pierce armour. Longbows were taller than a man, yet could be fired quickly and with great accuracy. At the **Battle of Agincourt** (1415), English archers killed some 6,000 Frenchmen before they could even reach the English army's front line.

CAN YOU SAY?

15. Explain *three* of the following terms relating to castles in the Middle Ages:
    turret; *moat*; *keep*; *portcullis*; *bailey*.
    (Junior Certificate Higher Level 2002. Two items from a similar list asked on Ordinary Level paper in 2004)

16. (a) List *two* defensive features of medieval castles.
    (Junior Certificate Ordinary Level 1995; similar question in Higher Level 2009)

    (b) Mention *one* way that an attacking army might capture a castle during the Middle Ages. *(Junior Certificate Higher Level 2000)*

17. List *five* ways in which a medieval stone castle differed from a modern house.

18. Look at the picture entitled **Source G** above.
    (a) Which numbers correspond to a battering ram, a mangonel, a ballista, a siege tower, a turret and a siege ladder?
    (b) What are the attackers marked **A** doing?
    (c) Explain *one* thing that the defenders are doing to stop the attackers.

19. Explain *one* difference between a longbow and a crossbow.

20. List *two* important effects of the coming of the Normans to Ireland.
    (Junior Certificate Higher Level 2006)

KEYNOTES

1. **Normans:** William the Conqueror • Bayeux Tapestry • Battle of Hastings • Dermot MacMurrough • Strongbow • Henry II • Lord of Ireland

2. **Knights:** chivalry • page • squire • vigil • dubbing
   Armour: chain mail • helmet • visor • breastplate • gauntlets • coat of arms
   Weapons: lances • swords • shields • battleaxes • maces

3. **Castles:** motte and bailey • palisade • moat • keep • dungeons • solar • great hall • curtain wall

4. **Defences:** portcullis • drawbridge • barbicans • slit windows • turrets • battlements • crenellations
   Attack: siege • battering ram • siege towers • mangonels • ballistas • cannons • undermining • crossbows • longbows

MINI-PROJECT

Write a detailed account of the following: *A knight in medieval times.*
Hints:
● training
● weapons
● armour
● chivalry
[Write about 10 or 12 sentences, if possible without looking at your book.]
(Junior Certificate Higher Level 1993, similar at both levels in 2005)

Feudalism and the Manor

11

The Normans were militarily powerful people who conquered northern France, England and Ireland in the 11th and 12th centuries. However, all over Europe, other people were equally powerful; they, too, ruled kingdoms, built castles and fought wars.

THE MIDDLE AGES

The period in which the Normans lived is often called the **Middle Ages,** because in history it lies between ancient times and modern times. Historians often use the word **medieval** (from the Latin *medium* 'middle' and *aevum* 'age') for this period. For most people, the Middle Ages (or medieval times) lie between the 11th and 15th centuries.

FEUDALISM

Most kingdoms in medieval Europe had a system of government called **feudalism**. The **king** granted land to his **noblemen**, including higher churchmen, such as bishops and abbots. These nobles then became the king's **vassals**, rather like tenants renting land from the owner. The actual 'granting' of the land was called **feudum**, from which we get the word **feudalism**, and the vassal's piece of land was called a **fief**.

In return for the land, the vassal swore an oath of **homage**. This meant that he became the king's 'man' (*homme* is the French for 'man'). He promised money to the king, his '**overlord**', and to provide knights to fight for the king. The number of knights depended upon the value of the land grant received. This duty was known as **knight service**. A vassal also had to give food and lodgings to the king and his followers, whenever they visited the vassal's home.

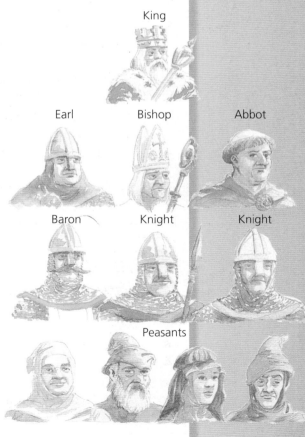

King

Earl Bishop Abbot

Baron Knight Knight

Peasants

DID YOU KNOW?

DID YOU KNOW?

DID YOU KNOW?

Strongbow died in 1176, leaving a baby daughter, Isabel. She became a ward of the king until old enough to marry William Marshal, who then became ruler of Leinster.

DID YOU KNOW?

When England's King Richard the Lionheart was taken prisoner in Austria in 1192, his vassals back in England had to pay a ransom of 150,000 marks for his return, equal to several million euro in today's money.

A feudal king had duties too. He acted as a judge in disputes between his vassals. Should a vassal be killed, the king took in his children as **wards** until they were old enough to take over their family fief or, in the case of the girls, be married. Most importantly, with the help of all the money and knight service due to him, it was the king's duty to protect the country (and, hence, his vassals) in times of war.

The most important noblemen were **earls**; their fiefs were usually so large that they kept only some of the land for themselves (the **demesne**). The rest was 'rented' out to lesser nobles, such as **barons** or knights, under similar terms to those between the earl and his king. The earl was then the **overlord** to his own vassals, and it was usually with some of *their* knights and payments that he paid his own dues to the king.

Ireland's Feudal Normans

The first Normans settled mainly on the good land of the south and east of Ireland, close to Dublin and to their original bases in England and Wales. There they built most of their motte and baileys and, later, stone castles.

The Normans brought feudalism to Ireland – the Norman and Irish lords who swore loyalty to Henry II in 1172 basically accepted him as their overlord ('Lord of Ireland') and became his vassals. Over the next century, Norman lords, such as Hugh de Lacy and William de Burgh, carved out territory for themselves, although powerful native families such as the O'Neills and MacCarthys held on to their lands.

 CAN YOU SAY?

1. Explain precisely what the term 'medieval' means.
2. Explain the following terms:
   (a) vassal (b) homage, (c) fief
   (*Junior Certificate Higher Level 2005, (a) and (c)*)
3. List *three* duties of a vassal.
4. List *three* duties of an overlord or king.
5. Give *one* reason why the majority of 'motte and bailey' castles were built in the south-east of Ireland.
   (*Junior Certificate Ordinary and Higher Levels 1999*)

On one occasion, the English vassals of King John (brother of Richard the Lionheart) were so unhappy with him that they rose in rebellion. In 1215, John was forced to sign the Magna Carta, agreeing to consult with his lords in all future decisions, so taking the first steps towards an English parliament.

Carrick-on-Suir castle.

Norman Castle in Naples.

MANORS

Stone castles were very expensive to build, so only the really wealthy noblemen in Ireland and other feudal countries could afford to build them. An earl might grant portions of his fief to many lesser noblemen, who generally lived in large stone houses with thatched roofs. The amount of land held by a lord to the value of one knight service was called a **manor**, and the house (or castle) of its lord was called the **manor house**.

As the Middle Ages progressed and times became more peaceful, even the wealthiest lords stopped building defensive castles and chose instead to live in simpler **tower houses** or in much more comfortable buildings such as the beautiful *chateaux* of France's Loire Valley. It has been estimated that nearly 10,000 castles and tower houses were built in Ireland by the 1600s. In many Irish examples, the original manor is now known as a 'townland'.

Where Were Our Manors?

The ideas of feudalism, vassals, manors, knight service and so on were introduced to Ireland by the Normans. The map on the next page will help to give some idea of the parts of Ireland that were controlled by the Normans around 1350. Feudalism (and the associated manors) took several centuries to become part of native (or Gaelic) Irish life. Therefore, what we call the 'manorial system' was found mainly where the powerful Norman lords settled.

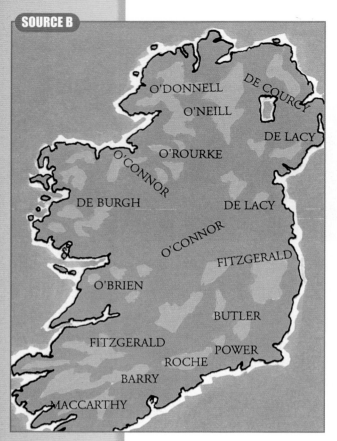

SOURCE B

Native Irish family names generally began with **O** or **Mac** (both meaning 'son of'). Norman names, however, generally began with **Fitz** or **de**. In French, *fils* means 'son' and *de* means 'of' or 'from'. Normans had names such as de Clare or FitzGerald – one very large FitzGerald was simply known as Raymond **Le Gros** ('the fat one')! Some Norman names derived from their place of origin, such as Walsh (from Wales). Many Norman names have now lost the *de* in English, for example Barry (de Barra), Roche (de Róiste) and Power (de Paor). In 1185, Prince (later King) John granted some of Munster to a loyal butler (servant) named Theobald FitzWalter, whose family afterwards were known as Butlers (de Buitléir).

Layout of the Manor

Around the manor house, or tower house in most Irish cases, the homes of **peasants** were clustered to make up a **village**. Craftspeople, such as smiths and carpenters, also lived there. Most villages had a church and, if the lord of the manor was wealthy enough, his officials might also have their own houses.

The land that the lord kept for himself (the **demesne**) lay near the manor house. Much of the remaining land was divided into three huge fields; each field was sectioned into 1 acre (0.5 hectare) strips, which were farmed by the peasants. Another field was kept for the peasants to graze their cattle (**the common**) and, for a fee, a lord who owned woodland might allow peasants' pigs to feed on nuts there (**pannage**).

The farming system on the feudal manor was an **open-field** one. The people of the manor farmed strips scattered throughout the three great fields of the manor with little or no fencing. Some could have up to 30 strips to work on, which meant a lot of time could be spent simply travelling between them.

Fertilisers, as we know them, did not exist in medieval times, so **crop rotation** was practised. Crops were grown in only two of the three fields in any one year, leaving the third idle (**fallow**), to build up the minerals in the soil. The following year, a different field was left fallow and a different field again in the third year, as the diagram

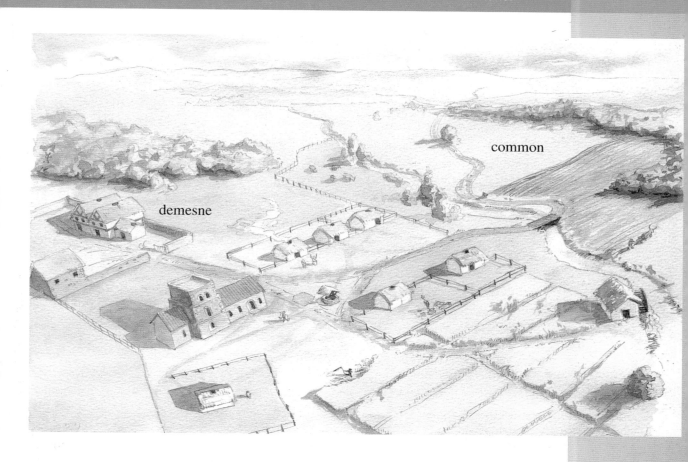

above shows. This, obviously, meant that only two-thirds of the land was actually producing crops in any one year, increasing the danger of **famine**. Wheat, barley, oats and rye were the main crops.

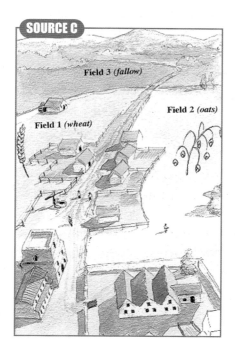

SOURCE C

Field 3 (fallow)

Field 2 (oats)

Field 1 (wheat)

CAN YOU SAY?

6. Mention *two* important effects that the arrival of the Normans had on Ireland.
   (Junior Certificate Higher Level 1997 and 2001; similar in 2003)

7. What was a medieval manor?
   (Junior Certificate Ordinary and Higher Levels 1992 and 2005)

8. In **Source A1** above (Carrick on Suir castle), identify which part of this castle was built in time of war and which in peaceful times. Then do the same with **Source A2**, a picture of a medieval castle in Naples, Italy. Give *one* reason for your choice in each case.

9. Using the map in **Source B**, and what you have read beside it, give *three* family names of Normans who introduced manors.

10. Explain the following terms: *serf; tithe; pottage.* *(Junior Certificate Higher Level 2009)*

11. Why was crop rotation practised in medieval times?

12. In **Source C**, using what you have learnt of medieval farming in this chapter, explain the following:
    (a) What the lines in these fields were in medieval times.
    (b) What the unlined area in the centre was used for in medieval times.

A ducking stool in action.

THE LIFE OF A LORD AND LADY

The lord and lady of the manor made their wealth by renting out portions of their manor to peasants. In addition, several taxes and laws gave them extra sources of income. In fact, the lord of the manor basically made and enforced the laws on the manor, which meant that he and his family had huge power in the locality. Most lords employed a number of officials to help them to run the manor effectively and profitably.

The local priest was often appointed by the lord – peasants paid 10 per cent of their crop to the priest (**a tithe**). A special tax was paid to the lord if a peasant inherited land – this tax was called a **heriot**. **Bailiffs** and their assistants (**reeves**) made sure that the peasants carried out their duties, and **clerks** worked as the lord's book-keepers and collected the rent.

Anyone breaking the law, or failing in his duties to his lord, could be brought before the **manor court**, which was presided over by the lord or his deputy, the **steward**. Punishments ranged from a severe drenching in the river, on a device called a **ducking stool,** to having your property taken from you.

Having Fun

Lords and ladies of the manor also liked a good time. In the early Middle Ages, the most important festival of entertainment was the **tournament**; this was a type of military sports meeting, enjoyed by nobles and with the peasants allowed to attend as well. **Jousting** was one of the most spectacular events at the tournament; it involved two knights on horseback charging at each other along a railing (**the lists**) to see who could knock the other from his horse with a blunted lance. A tournament always ended with a mock battle (**tourney**) between two groups of knights. Anyone who performed well might win the 'favour' of a beautiful lady – possibly the lord's daughter – and become her **champion**.

SOURCE D

Manor lords were particularly fond of **falconry**; a bird of prey, such as a falcon or hawk, was carefully trained to catch other birds in mid-flight and then return with them to its master's gauntlet. **Hunting** was also popular, particularly deer hunting.

Huge feasts or **banquets** were impressive occasions in a lord's castle or manor house. The guest list could run to over a hundred in some cases, all seated in the **great hall**. Food arrived on platters, carried from the kitchen by a procession of servants, with the lord's own taster at the front. Large cuts of bread called **trenchers** served as plates and food was generally eaten using a knife and one's fingers. Forks were not widely used until the 17th century. Meat was hugely popular – roast pig, beef, chicken, rabbit and venison (deer), or more unusual 'treats' such as pheasants, thrushes, swans and herons.

Ale, mead and wine were drunk at these banquets, while desserts consisted of fruit, tarts or marzipan cakes. (Why do you think there was no ice-cream?) At large banquets, entertainers such as acrobats and jugglers were common, as well as a professional clown called a **jester.** Musicians played pipes and stringed instruments, while, as in Celtic Ireland, poets recited their work or singers sang ballads of heroic deeds and romance.

SOURCE E

CAN YOU SAY?

13. Name *two* officials who helped the lord of a manor, and explain what each one's job was.

14. Describe *one* form of punishment used in medieval times.

15. **Source D** above shows a tournament during the Middle Ages. From the picture, give *one* piece of evidence to support this statement.

(Junior Certificate Higher Level 2004)

16. In medieval times, what was jousting? *(Junior Certificate Ordinary Level 1999)*

17. Examine the picture of a feast in 16th century Ireland (**Source E**).
    (a) State briefly what the people marked **A** and **C** are doing.
    (b) What evidence does the picture offer to support the opinion that there are clergymen in the company? (Remember Chapter 6.)
    (c) How are those seated at the table being entertained?

(Junior Certificate Higher Level 1993)

18. Look again at the picture in **Source E**.
    (a) Briefly describe the arrangements for preparing and cooking the food.
    (b) Briefly describe how the comfort and entertainment of the guests is provided for.
    (c) On the basis of the evidence in the picture, would you consider those sitting at the table to be poor people or rich people? Explain your answer.

(Junior Certificate Ordinary Level 1993)

19. Why were spices so sought after in medieval times?

(Junior Certificate Higher Level 2006)

LIFE OF THE PEASANTS

Although some peasants were **freemen**, owing no duties to their lord apart from paying their rent, about 60 per cent were **serfs**, not very different from slaves. Some serfs farmed up to 30 acres (12 hectares) of land; these were **villeins**. Most had much less than this (**bordars**), while many were no more than **cottiers** (or **cottars**), holding only a small cottage and garden.

Peasant houses were generally made of wattle and daub, with thatched roofs and no windows. A small hole in the thatch let some smoke out. Furniture consisted of a table and stools, and most peasants slept on the floor.

Peasants generally grew their own vegetables, which they made into a soup called **potage**, and kept chickens. Meat was a rare treat and could only be preserved by being heavily salted. Bread and porridge were other basic foods, but famine was a constant threat, often caused by drought or warfare. In many years, supplies of food simply ran out before the new harvest was ready, leading to a problem called **spring hunger**.

Clothing was home-made from wool or hemp, using spinning wheels and hand looms. Men wore tunics and breeches, and women wore long dresses and head dresses called **wimples** and **hennins**. Shoes were expensive and most children went barefoot.

DID YOU KNOW?

The first spinning wheels were brought to Europe from India and China around 1200.

*A wealthy couple –
the lord and lady of the manor*

*A peasant couple in
their Sunday best.*

Duties of the Peasants

Peasants had to perform many tasks for the lord of the manor. Rent was paid to him in money or in goods, such as eggs or flour. They also had to work for a few days a week on the lord's demesne and do extra work (**boon work**) for the lord at harvest time. Many lords forced peasants to cut timber and repair bridges and roads for them, while it was common for peasants to have to bring their grain to the lord's **mill** to be ground into flour, for which they were charged handsomely! The amount of time and produce that peasants had to give to their lord made survival all the more difficult. There were few doctors, so injury and illness were greatly feared.

A serf's best chance of escaping his 'slavery' was to flee to a town, where he had to remain, without being captured, for a year and a day in order to become a freeman. Temporary relief came in the form of a weekly day off, Sunday, and at festival times such as **Midsummer** in June or **Christmas**, when everyone in the village was invited to a banquet in the manor house.

SOURCE F

FARMING METHODS

The land was ploughed using teams of oxen or horses. A team of four oxen could plough roughly one strip of land (1 acre/0.5 hectare) per day. Seed was planted by the **broadcast** method, which involved scattering by hand from a sack. This was very slow and much of the seed was eaten by birds or destroyed by the sun or frost when it lay uncovered on the ground.

Harvesting was also slow, especially when valuable harvest time had to be spent in boon days on the lord's demesne. **Sickles** were used for cereal harvesting and **scythes** for cutting hay. Once harvested, the grain was beaten with a **flail** to separate the kernels containing the flour from the **chaff** or waste. Women and children followed the harvesters as they worked, collecting any precious stalks left behind. This was called **gleaning**.

Few peasants had many cattle. Those they had were grazed together on the village common. Unfortunately, this meant that diseases spread very rapidly among the cattle. Added to the fact that the average size of medieval cattle, sheep and pigs was much smaller than modern breeds and the difficulties of preserving meat, it explains why meat was a rare treat for most people.

CAN YOU SAY?

20. In medieval times, what was a serf?

(Junior Certificate Ordinary Level 2000 and 2005)

21. What were (a) tithes, (b) heriots and (c) boon work?
22. How could a serf become a freeman in medieval times?
23. Give *two* reasons why medieval peasants were under constant threat of famine.

(Junior Certificate Higher Level 1993)

24. In **Source F** above, identify *two* activities that are taking place.

(Junior Certificate Higher Level 2004)

KEYNOTES

1. **Middle Ages:** medieval
   Feudalism: vassals • fiefs • homage • knight service • Magna Carta • wards
   Nobles: earls • barons • overlords • demesne
2. **Manor:** manor house • tower house • chateau • demesne • common • pannage • open-field system • crop rotation • fallow
3. **Lord:** power • wealth • tithe • heriot • bailiffs • reeves • clerks • steward • manor court • tournaments • jousting • lists • tourney • falconry
   Banquets: great hall • trenchers • jesters • spices
4. **Peasants:** freeman • serfs • villeins • bordars • cottars/cottiers • potage • wimples • boon work • broadcast • sickles • scythes • flails • gleaning • threat of starvation

MINI-PROJECT

Write an account of one of the following:

A serf living on a medieval manor.

Hints:

- home
- work
- duties to the lord of the manor
- holidays and pastimes

(Junior Certificate Ordinary Level 1995 and both levels [different hints] in 1999)

Or

A lord living on a medieval manor.

Hints:

- dress and pastimes
- the manor house
- the lord's family
- relations with the serfs

(Junior Certificate 1997)

Medieval Towns 12

THE GROWTH OF TOWNS

In medieval times, most people lived on the land, but this period also saw a rapid growth in towns. Some European towns began in Roman times (such as London and Lyon). Ireland's earliest towns grew around the **residences of kings** or **monasteries** – Derry, Armagh and Kildare are examples.

The building of **castles** and **manor houses** in the Middle Ages attracted people to live nearby for protection or employment. The more people came to live in or around these centres, the more others were attracted by the possibilities of trade. Towns such as Newcastle and Warwick (England) and Angers (France) began like this.

Ireland's new medieval towns owed their origins mostly to trade. Towns sprang up where **trade routes** crossed, where traders could cross rivers at shallow points (**fords**), and especially where deep rivers or inlets made it possible to dock boats (**ports**).

The remains of the town walls of medieval Waterford.

After the **Vikings** attacked their first Irish monastery in 795 AD, they began to winter here and trade with the locals. By the 840s, they were settled at two shipping ports (**longphorts**), Dublin and Anagassan, Co. Louth. Permanent Viking settlements, and so towns, began soon after this, with Waterford being founded by the Norwegian King Sitricus in 853. Dublin gets its name from the **Dubh Linn**, or **Black Pool**, at the mouth of the Liffey where the Vikings settled, though the town developed a short distance away from this in the 10th century. Other towns such as Wexford, Limerick and Cork also began as Viking trading centres.

When the **Normans** arrived in the 12th century, they took over most of the old Viking towns and built castles in them. As the Normans moved inland, now building new castles, more towns, such as Trim in Co. Meath, grew up around them.

HOW TOWNS WERE RUN

When a town in medieval Ireland or Europe became large enough, the king or local lord might grant its citizens a **charter**. This made every townsman (**burgess**) a freeman, owing no services to the local lord. It allowed people the right to elect their own leaders to govern the town or city. In large towns, a number of men – never women – were elected to the **town council**, and the most senior of these (**aldermen**) chose the **mayor**.

The mayor and council were responsible for the town's defences; a lot of medieval towns had high walls, turrets and gates. **Tolls** were also collected by the council at the town gates from traders entering the town. Some of this income was used for town services and to maintain law and order.

SOURCE A

Medieval barbican gate in Drogheda, Co. Louth.

Crime and Punishment

Town councils appointed **constables** to protect the citizens from crime. With little or no street lighting, night-time was when most criminals were active. The constable patrolled the streets with a lantern and every hour called out, '_____ o'clock and all is well' to reassure the citizens.

As in the case of the manor, criminals were severely dealt with. Public executions by hanging (from a timber **gallows**) or beheading (usually with a huge axe) were held in the town centre and often attracted enthusiastic crowds. Other criminals might be condemned to a spell in the town jail (or **gaol**) or be placed in the **stocks**. These were timber planks with holes in them for the hands and feet; while the criminal sat trapped in these, passers-by hurled abuse, fruit or indeed rocks at him. A **pillory** was similar to the stocks, but it held only the head and hands of the criminal, who took his punishment standing up.

CAN YOU SAY?

1. Name *two* places around which medieval towns and cities grew.
   (Junior Certificate Ordinary Level 1999 and Higher Level 1997)
2. Name *one* defensive feature of a medieval town.
   (Junior Certificate Ordinary Level 2006)
3. Why is the Wood Quay area of Dublin of special interest to archaeologists and historians? *(Junior Certificate Ordinary and Higher Levels 1994)*
4. What were (a) aldermen and (b) tolls?
5. **Source A** above is a picture of the medieval barbican gate in Drogheda.
   (a) Where did you normally find barbicans? (Refer back to Chapter 10 if you need to.)
   (b) Why do you think Drogheda needed a gate like this?
6. For what were the pillory and stocks used in medieval times?
   (Junior Certificate Ordinary Level 1994 and 1998)

INSIDE THE TOWN'S WALLS

Each entrance gate in a town's walls was guarded by a strong gatehouse or tower. In most towns, the main street ran between the two main entrance gates and was paved with cobblestones. The other streets, however, were little more than dirt tracks and became very muddy in wet weather.

The main open space in a town was often in front of the largest church or the town hall, where the council met. Like the Forum in ancient Rome, this **square** (though rarely actually 'square' shape) was the centre of business activity and the place where everybody met.

Houses

The homes of the wealthy were usually made of stone and had slate roofs. Business premises were usually located on the ground floor, and above lay the parlour, bedrooms and **hall** for entertaining guests. Furniture for wealthy people included huge **four-poster bed**s, wooden tables, chairs and stools, and chests for storing money and clothes.

Less well-off people lived in thatched homes made from wattle and daub. Many poor families lived in just one room. While the homes of the rich generally had separate kitchens and chimneys, many homes had open fires for heating and cooking, with no chimneys. The rich also had glass in their windows and tapestries decorating the walls – not so for the poor.

Medieval houses excavated recently in Waterford and at Dublin's Wood Quay had earthen floors and no windows, whereas waste disposal and toilets consisted of little more than timber-lined pits outside.

As increasing numbers of people were attracted to medieval towns, space became more and more valuable. Buildings of several storeys in height became common and streets were often barely wide enough for one horse-drawn cart to pass through.

The narrowness of medieval streets and the height of the buildings made everything very dark down below. Medieval Amsterdam in the Netherlands was extremely crowded and the more ground space you occupied, the more tax you had to pay. Thus, many Amsterdam houses had very narrow doors and hallways; furniture often had to be winched up and brought in through the upstairs windows. One house that still stands is no wider than the doorway itself!

DID YOU KNOW?

Medieval beds were much shorter than modern ones. This is partly because medieval people were generally smaller than modern people but also because people tended to sleep in a sitting position, believing that lying down was too similar to being dead!

DID YOU KNOW?

Wood Quay, once beside the River Liffey, now lies 100 metres from it! This is because space was so scarce in Dublin that the Vikings, and later the Normans, reclaimed land beside the river, making it much narrower than it had been years earlier.

In central Europe, snow was gathered from the mountains in winter, stored in stone containers in cellars and used to keep food cool in kitchen presses. In this medieval kitchen, the 'fridge' is on the left, as far away as possible from the large fireplace where food was cooked.

PROBLEMS

Fire

Because of the narrowness of the streets, and the timber or thatch in the houses, fires could spread very easily from one side of a street to the other. Fear of fire was so great that the constable had a special duty to enforce a **curfew**. This was a law requiring all fires in the town's houses to be put out during the hours of darkness. Each evening a special bell was rung to announce both the start of curfew and the closing of the town gates to protect against unwanted intruders.

SOURCE C

A street in Amsterdam.

SOURCE D

In medieval Amalfi, southern Italy, space was so precious that this street was just about the width of a doorway. People on their balconies on one side of the street could easily shake hands with the people across from them, not to mention spread disease to each other!

Disease

Few houses had any toilets or sewerage systems and household waste was simply thrown into open pits, as at Wood Quay, or into gutters in the streets. The smell was awful, but the risks to people's health were even worse.

Rats, cockroaches and fleas were widespread in towns and spread diseases such as cholera and typhoid very rapidly in the overcrowded conditions. While peasants in the countryside worried about famine, disease epidemics were the great killers in towns and cities.

In 1348, Europe was struck by the bubonic plague, known as the **Black Death**. This deadly disease was carried from Asia by fleas living in the fur of black rats. The first signs of it came in the form of black sores on the armpits, which spread rapidly all over the body. Accompanied by a very high fever, the plague usually ended in death. Knowledge of medicine was very poor in the Middle Ages and it is estimated that some 25 million people died as a result of the Black Death.

DID YOU KNOW?

Sick people in medieval times often went to their local barber, who cut them to let some of the 'bad blood' out, believing that this made people better. Traditional barbers' signs are red and white poles, dating from the days when red blood and white bandages were common in barber shops!

CAN YOU SAY?

7. Explain *two* ways in which the medieval chest pictured as **Source B** above differs from modern furniture.
8. List *three* ways in which the homes of the wealthy differed from those of the poor in medieval towns.
9. Using **Source C** above, explain *two* unusual features about old Amsterdam houses as shown in the picture. (Look carefully!)
10. What evidence suggests that land was scarce in medieval Dublin?
11. Why was fire a major problem in medieval towns?
(Junior Certificate Ordinary Level 1995)
12. In a medieval town what was *curfew*? *(Junior Certificate Ordinary Level 2001)*
13. In the picture above of medieval Amalfi (**Source D**):
    (a) Identify *two* features common to most medieval towns.
    (b) Identify *one* feature in the picture *not* found in medieval times.
14. What was the Black Death? *(Junior Certificate Higher Level 1995 and 2001)*
15. Name *two* dangers faced by people who lived in towns during the Middle Ages.
(Junior Certificate Higher and Ordinary Levels 2001 and 2003)

● TRADE

As we saw earlier, trade was vital to medieval towns. There were no shopping centres and indeed few shops as we know them. Business was carried on at the **market**, which was held in a town's main square once a week. Here, peasants from the manors came and sold their produce; the bailiff did the same with the produce from the lord's demesne. In return, they bought goods made by the town's craftspeople or sold by the town's traders (**merchants**).

In early medieval times, goods were often swapped or bartered but soon many towns began to mint their own gold or silver coins. For example, the **florin** came from Florence in Italy, where Europe's largest medieval bankers and merchants, the Medici family, were based. Ireland's earliest known coin is of Viking origin, dating from 977 AD, though hundreds of foreign coins have been found at Wood Quay and other Irish medieval sites.

As well as the weekly markets, most towns also had annual **fairs** where an even wider range of goods, often from as far away as India and China, could be bought. From the time of Marco Polo (1254–1324), the medieval Italian city of Venice traded with these regions and sold silks, spices, jewels and many other goods all over Europe.

Craftspeople and their Guilds

At the heart of the business life of the town lay the **guilds**. These were an early form of trade union with each group of craftspeople having its own guild. If a person wanted to work in a town, he (rarely 'she') had to belong to a guild. Each group of craftspeople tended to live in the same street or the same part of the town, so we still find street-names that came from the trades associated with them – Cook Street (Dublin) or Baker Street (London).

Guilds fixed working hours and prices to maintain fair competition among their members. They also prevented non-guild members from setting up in business. Using money collected from all guild members, the guild set up a fund to look after sick or elderly members or to pay for their funerals.

Becoming a guild member was a long and difficult process. A young person wishing to qualify as a craftsman, such as a carpenter, shoemaker or tanner (leather maker), had to serve an **apprenticeship** of around seven years, doing minor tasks for a craftsperson and slowly picking up the 'tricks of the trade'. The physical nature of the work and the medieval idea that such trades were mainly for men meant that few, if any, girls trained as apprentices.

Upon passing a test set by the relevant guild, the apprentice became a **journeyman** and, for the first time, was paid in money for his work. The journeyman *might* have travelled around looking for work, but the term actually comes from the fact that he was paid by the day (*journée* is the French for 'day').

A journeyman was admitted to a guild only if his work was good enough. At the guild's meeting-house (**guildhall**), a sample of the journeyman's work was examined by the members. If it met with their standards, the journeyman was declared a **master** craftsperson, admitted to the guild, and the work which had been examined was known as a **masterpiece**. This was often placed on display in the craftsperson's shop window once he set up in business.

Source E is a modern photograph of part of a medieval town or city.
Source F is a modern reconstruction of daily life in a medieval town or city.

DID YOU KNOW?

Because of the danger that they might cause fires, blacksmiths generally had to operate outside the town walls. In many towns, the most powerful guilds were those of the merchants, who weren't craftspeople at all!

SOURCE E

SOURCE F

FASHION, FOOD AND FUN

Peasants generally made their own clothes, but townspeople bought theirs from **drapers** at town markets. Thus, although peasants' clothes were cheaper, the clothes of townsfolk had more variety. Medieval townsmen wore short tunics (sometimes two) over trousers or, for the wealthy, a stocking-trouser called a **hose**. Women wore long, flowing dresses called **kirtles** and their hair was usually covered by a veil. Whereas the clothes of the poor were made from dull-coloured wool or linen, rich people could afford silks, damasks and furs.

Food in towns was similar to that of the countryside, though it was possible to get imported figs and grapes in 13th-century Dublin. Pits in medieval Dublin have been excavated and showed that pork was certainly the most popular meat there, but huge quantities of cockle and mussel shells were also found.

Entertainment was often violent. Cock- and dog-fighting, wrestling and a form of **football** with few rules were popular in many towns – these 'soccer' players kicked an inflated pig's bladder from street to street with sometimes hundreds on each team. Different towns had different favourite 'sports' too – the people of Pamplona in Spain have enjoyed the *encierro* each July since the 1300s – loose bulls chase the people through the streets of the town (see top).

English guilds such as those in Wakefield, Coventry and York staged more peaceful pastimes in the form of **miracle plays**, based on scenes from the Bible. The actors were guild members and usually performed in a procession of horse-drawn moving stages.

DID YOU KNOW?

Football playing became so dangerous in medieval London that King Edward II of England banned it in 1314.

SOURCE G

X→ ←Y

CAN YOU SAY?

16. Name *two* trades you would find in a typical medieval city.
(Junior Certificate Higher Level 1998)

17. (a) What were guilds in a medieval city?
    (b) Describe how guilds operated.
(Junior Certificate Higher Level 1997; variations in 2001, 2003 and 2005)

18. During the Middle Ages, name *two* stages in the training of a craftsman.
(Junior Certificate Higher Level 2003, one stage asked at Ordinary Level)

19. Give *one* way *each* in which food and clothes differed between medieval towns and countryside.

20. List *three* ways in which medieval town entertainment differed from the entertainment of modern times.

21. (a) From **Source E**, name *two* features (parts) of this scene that suggest that it is part of a medieval town or city.
    (b) In **Source F**, what trade has the man working on the right-hand side?
    (c) Give *one* reason why this tradesman was important in medieval times.
(Junior Certificate Ordinary and Higher Levels 1999)

22. In **Source G** above:
    (a) Identify the crafts practised by the workers marked X and Y.
    (b) Give *one* piece of evidence to show that craftworkers were important during the Middle Ages.
    (c) During the Middle Ages, what name was given to a young person learning a craft? Choose from serf, page or apprentice.
    (d) Give *one* reason why there were so few female craftworkers during the Middle Ages.
(Junior Certificate Ordinary Level 2006)

KEYNOTES

1. **Towns:** ancient times • king's residences • monasteries • around castles • trade • longphorts • Wood Quay
Government: charter • burgess • alderman • mayor • tolls • constables • gallows • stocks • pillory

2. **Houses:** four-poster beds • curfew • narrow streets • high buildings • timber and thatch • fire threat
Disease: Black Death • bubonic plague • poor knowledge of medicine • disease threat

3. **Trade:** markets • merchants • barter • fairs • hose • kirtle • football • miracle plays • *encierro*
Guilds: apprenticeship • journeyman • masterpiece • craftsperson • guildhall
Fashion, Food, Fun: drapers • kirtles • hose • pork • football • miracle plays

MINI-PROJECT

Write an account of the life of the following: *A craftsman in a medieval town.*
Name the craft.
Hints:
- how the craftsman was trained
- where the craft was practised
- the craft guild
- the home life of the craftsman
(Junior Certificate 1994, 2000 and 2002)

13 The Medieval Church and Monasteries

PROBLEMS OF THE CHURCH

In Chapters 6 and 9, we saw briefly how Christianity suffered in its first 1,000 years through persecution by the Romans at first, and then through the invasion of Christian Europe by tribes of pagans such as the Goths and Vandals. In Ireland, monasteries were targets of attack by Vikings (and sometimes by the Irish) throughout the 9th and 10th centuries.

Christianity's problems did not disappear after this either. In 1054, a split (called a **schism**) occurred between Christians in western Europe and Christians in eastern Europe. This resulted in the Christian world (**Christendom**) dividing into the **Roman Catholic Church**, led by the Pope, and the **Eastern Orthodox Church**, led by the Patriarch of Constantinople.

Catholic churches and monasteries were often very wealthy, and many kings and other rulers wanted as much control over them as possible. For example, several Irish kings appointed their relatives as bishops or abbots. This practice changed only very slowly.

From the 12th century onwards, it became common for individuals or groups to disagree seriously with some Church teachings. These people were branded as **heretics** and expelled from the Church (**excommunicated**) or put to death.

The medieval church faced a huge temporary problem that was known as the **Great Western Schism**. A row between French and Italian cardinals resulted in there being two popes for most of the 14th century, one in Rome and one in Avignon, France.

PILGRIMAGES AND CRUSADES

Despite all these problems, the Middle Ages saw a huge growth in devotion to the Church – with many donations of money, large membership of religious orders and numerous **pilgrimages**. These were long and difficult journeys made by people doing penance for their sins. **Pilgrims** usually travelled on foot to religious centres such as

Canterbury (England) or Compostella (Spain), though the greatest pilgrimage of all was to the **Holy Land** itself.

In 1070 AD, the Muslim Turks captured the Holy Land. Pope Urban II called upon Christians to take up arms and drive them out. Over the next two centuries, several 'armies' of Christians set out for the Holy Land on what became known as the **Crusades** (from the word **crucifix**).

SOURCE A

From the Peasant Crusade of Peter the Hermit to the Crusade led by three kings (including Richard the Lionheart), all ended in failure, except for a period in the 12th century when Jerusalem was briefly recaptured. The Turks, especially under their great leader Saladin, were more than a match for the **Crusaders**, many of whom never returned from the Holy Land alive.

CAN YOU SAY?

1. What important event in Church history happened in 1054 AD?
2. What precisely was a heretic?
3. Apart from Rome, where else did popes live at one time?
4. Why were pilgrimages undertaken?
5. What was (a) the purpose and (b) the result of the Crusades?
6. Looking at **Source A** above:
   (a) Identify two pieces of military equipment being used by the Crusaders.
   (b) Explain why you think they are wearing crosses on their shields.

DID YOU KNOW?

In 1212, a **Children's Crusade** left France and Germany for the Holy Land. There were about 50,000 children taking part in it, most of them aged between 10 and 18 years old. Whether they were drowned, killed or captured by slave-traders, none of them was ever heard of again.

CHURCH ORGANISATION

Although the Pope was head of the Catholic Church, it was through his **legates** (ambassadors) and **Bulls** (letters) that his decisions and laws were handed on to the different nations of Christendom. Bulls were written in Latin and took their titles from their first words. When Pope Adrian IV, an Englishman, gave King Henry II his blessing to invade Ireland, the Bull began and was called *Laudabiliter*.

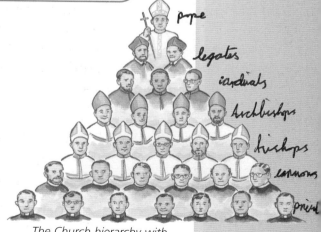

The Church hierarchy with the pope at the top.

Just as feudal kings had vassals, the popes controlled a network of important churchmen known as the **hierarchy**; it included cardinals, archbishops and bishops. Members of the hierarchy were usually very powerful men and rich landowners. The basic territory ruled by a bishop was called a **diocese**, and this was divided into a number of **parishes** run by ordinary **canons** and **priests**.

In country parishes, a priest was often appointed by the lord of the manor from among his own villeins. As well as receiving **tithes** from the peasants, the priest was given land known as a **glebe** to provide him with an income. In return, he said Mass, performed baptisms, marriages and funeral services, as well as frequently acting as clerk and letter writer for the lord. In many places, the only people able to read and write were the clergy and all official writing was done in the Church languages of Latin and Greek.

CHURCH BUILDING

In medieval times, the Church's wealth and popularity, plus improved building methods, resulted in a wave of church building across Europe. The most impressive of these buildings was the **cathedral**, which held the bishop's seat (**cathedra**). Early medieval cathedrals were generally based on ancient Roman architecture; this style was called **Romanesque**. Later, many cathedrals were built in a new style, which came to be called **Gothic**.

Romanesque

Romanesque buildings were very solidly constructed, with few high towers or spires. Walls could be up to two metres thick in order to support the roof, and inside it was common to find rows of very thick pillars, again supporting the roof. The overall effect tended to be quite dark. The most easily recognisable feature of this architecture is found in the design of the windows and doors; they are based on the ancient Roman arch, so they were all **rounded** on top. The Romanesque style was common from the 10th century on, but by the 12th and 13th centuries, better building methods led to the creation of a new type of architecture, **Gothic**.

Gothic

Gothic cathedrals were often taller than earlier ones. They usually had high bell towers and spires (called **flèches** from the French for 'arrows'), reaching to the skies as if to get closer to God. Gothic walls

SOURCE B

The interior of Durham Cathedral in England.

Romanesque gateway from Roscrea.

were thinner than Romanesque ones. They were supported by thick stone **ribs** between the windows and by unusual outer stone props called **flying buttresses**. This new style of building also meant that the inside pillars were less bulky than Romanesque ones.

As with Romanesque buildings, the easy way to recognise Gothic architecture is by looking at the doors and windows. These were always **pointed** rather than rounded at the top. Sometimes, as many as five windows were placed beside each other, with only thin stone pillars (**mullions**) between them.

These Gothic windows often had beautifully carved designs near the top, called **tracery work**. At key points in the cathedral there were huge circular **rose windows** full of stained glass. When the sun shone through these windows, the cathedral was filled with a glowing light.

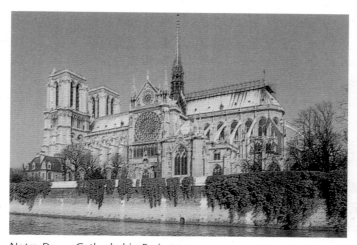

Notre Dame Cathedral in Paris.

DID YOU KNOW?

Some people disliked Gothic churches because they were often highly decorated, sometimes with hideous carvings of demons (gargoyles) to show the horrors of hell. Even the drainpipes on Notre Dame Cathedral in Paris are fitted inside the heads of gargoyles. The word 'gothic' was another word for 'barbaric'; thus this type of architecture became known as **Gothic**.

SOURCE C1

Fountains Abbey, Yorkshire.

SOURCE C2

Notre Dame.

CAN YOU SAY?

7. In relation to the Middle Ages, what were the terms Gothic and Romanesque used to describe? *(Junior Certificate Ordinary Level 2002)*

8. In looking at **Source B** above, identify *two* features of this construction that are typical of Romanesque architecture.

9. Give *one* reason why beautiful cathedrals were built during the Middle Ages. *(Junior Certificate Ordinary Level 2001)*

10. (a) In the pictures above, identify the features numbered 1, 2, and 3.
    (b) Having done so, say which of the cathedrals (**C1** or **C2**) is Romanesque and which is Gothic.
    (c) In the picture on the left (**C1**), identify *one* feature that is not usually found in this type of architecture. [Look carefully.]

11. Is the type of architecture shown on the left Gothic, Baroque or Romanesque? *(Junior Certificate Ordinary Level 1997)*

12. In **Source D** below, identify *one* feature on this window in that is typical of Romanesque churches.

SOURCE D

MONASTIC ORDERS

Churchmen living among the ordinary people were called **secular clergy**. Others preferred to join religious orders and live apart from society in monasteries, according to strict rules. These were **regular clergy** (**regula** is the Latin for 'rule').

Before 1000 AD most regular clergy or **monks** took sacred vows of **poverty, fasting** and **separation** from society. However, as the power and wealth of monasteries grew, these rules were slowly forgotten. One monk wrote:

> *I wonder how monks could grow so used to eating and drinking so much, to wearing such rich clothing and to riding all over the country … our abbots perhaps… themselves are not without blame.*

The author of these comments was **St Bernard of Clairvaux**, the leading member of a new religious order, the **Cistercians** (named after their first monastery at Citeaux, France). This 12th century order emphasised a strict rule of work, fasting and prayer, while previous 'rich clothing' was replaced by a plain white **habit**. Other new medieval orders dedicated to strict rules included the Cluniacs, founded at Cluny in France, and the Carthusians, also founded in France (at Chartreuse). Carthusians lived in almost continual silence, usually in single cells, and ate only one meal a day!

Daily Life

So, what was life like for these new **monastic orders**? Depending on the order, a monk could expect to have formal prayers (**offices**) seven or eight times a day, as well as Mass at least once a day. The main offices were 10 to 50 minutes long, including **Matins** (2am), **Prime**, the 'first hour' (5am), **Lauds** (6am), **Terce** (9am), **Sext** (noon), **None** (3pm), **Vespers** (6pm) and **Compline** before going to bed. Monks also read the Scriptures – even at meals, one monk (the **lector**) read aloud to the others as they ate.

The rest of a monk's waking hours were spent at work. Working on the land was particularly important and most monasteries were able to provide all their own food. There were many other jobs to do too, including copying and illuminating manuscripts (done by **scribes**, as in early Irish monasteries – Chapter 6). Monks also practised crafts such as carpentry and metal-working – the Cross of Cong in the illustration is a fine example of 12th century Irish metalwork.

Monks generally shaved the tops of their heads (**tonsures**) to show their devotion to God.

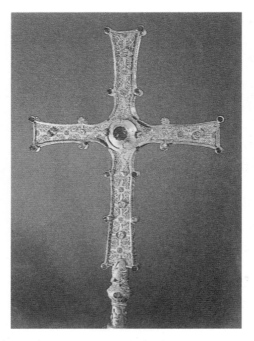

Some monks had specific duties – the **refectorian** prepared the meals, the **infirmarian** looked after the sick and the **almoner** distributed money (**alms**) and food to the poor. Large monasteries also had guesthouses for visitors, run by the **guest master**, and a monk called the **bursar** looked after the monastery's money. Of course, as with the early Irish monasteries (see Chapter 6), medieval monasteries were headed by an **abbot** (or **abbess** in the case of a convent). The abbot's deputy was called the **prior**.

SOURCE E1

SOURCE E2

If medieval monasteries had some things in common with earlier Irish ones, major differences lay in the monastery building itself. Most of the medieval monastery was made of cut stone and roofed in slate. The main church was often very large and, like cathedrals, built in either a Romanesque or Gothic style. Most monasteries had **dormitories** rather than individual cells for the monks to sleep in. Many of the other monastic buildings were built around an open courtyard called the **cloister**, where monks could walk, read or write in the fresh air. A large monastery would also have had a **chapter house** where the abbot or abbess met the monks or nuns daily.

> ## DID YOU KNOW?
> In medieval times, a person fleeing from persecution or the law could find protection, known as **sanctuary**, within a church or monastery, and his pursuers were forbidden to enter the place of refuge.

CAN YOU SAY?

13. Explain the function of (a) the abbot and (b) the almoner in a medieval monastery.
    (Part of a question in Junior Certificate Higher Level 2005)
14. **Source E1** shows the ground plan of a medieval monastery in Ireland. **Source E2** is a modern photograph of the same monastery as it looks today.
    (a) In **Source E1**, all parts of the monastery are named. Select any *two* parts and briefly mention what those two parts were used for.
    (b) Examine **Source E2** and name *two* parts of the monastery that can be seen today. (Note: parts chosen must be listed in **Source E1**.)
    (c) Briefly state *two* advantages for the local community of having a monastery in its area. *(Junior Certificate Ordinary Level 1999)*
15. What was the cloister in a medieval monastery?
    (Junior Certificate Ordinary and Higher Levels 1995, 2005 and 2006)
16. What was sanctuary in medieval times?
    (Junior Certificate Ordinary and Higher Levels 1996 and 2006)
17. Name *two* services provided by monasteries to local communities in the Middle Ages. *(Junior Certificate Higher Level 2006)*

The Friars

By the 13th century, there were many large towns and not enough clergy to minister to the people in them. As a result, new orders such as the **Franciscans** and **Dominicans** were founded. Their members were known as **friars** (from the French **frère**, a brother). These friars also took vows of poverty, obedience to their abbots and chastity (to avoid sexual relations). However, they differed from monastic orders, because they travelled out among the people, preaching and caring for the poor and sick. The friars were sometimes called **mendicant**, which means 'begging', because they depended on the good will of the people for their own survival.

Orders of Nuns

Most of what we have seen above applied to orders of nuns as well as to monks. Their monasteries, rules and main tasks were similar to monks, although the education of girls was a more prominent part of convents than farming was. There were orders of nuns associated with the Franciscans, Dominicans, Carmelites and Augustinians. It is fair to say, however, that nuns in general were more restricted to their monasteries (convents) than even the monks were. Many orders were 'enclosed', with nuns never going outside the boundaries of the convents at all. It was also common for widows of rulers to enter convents after their husbands had died.

In Ireland, unlike the rest of Europe, orders of nuns were relatively rare. Neither the Franciscans nor Dominicans established convents here, for example. Some convents (sometimes called nunneries) that existed in the 13th century had died out by the 16th. One convent was closed by the Pope when it was reduced to having just one nun in 1431.

Letter-writers and Teachers

We have already seen how medieval clergymen were often the best educated people in a country. Thus, they commonly acted as clerks and letter-writers for kings and lords, and, of course, ran schools. The medieval period saw the beginning of modern **universities** in places such as Bologna (Italy) and Oxford (England). Most of the great teachers at these universities were churchmen, notably the Dominican St Thomas Aquinas (1225–74) and Peter Abelard (1079–1144), founder of the University of Paris.

CAN YOU SAY?

18. Name *two* orders of monks or friars from the Middle Ages.
    (*Junior Certificate Higher Level 2004; one order of monks asked for in Ordinary Level 1999*)
19. Explain *one* of the following terms relating to medieval monks and monasteries:
    tonsure; abbot; dormitory.   (*Junior Certificate Ordinary Level 2006*)
20. Explain *one* way in which medieval nuns' lives differed from those of monks.
21. Apart from religion, mention *two* services that monasteries provided to people
    during the Middle Ages.   (*Junior Certificate Higher Level 2004; one service asked
    at Ordinary Level, 2002*) (*Junior Certificate Ordinary Level 1993*)
22. Write about the life of *three* of the following in medieval times:
    a craftsman, the lady of the manor, a scholar, a serf, a mendicant friar.
    (*Junior Certificate Higher Level 1995*)

KEYNOTES

1. **Christendom:** Pope • heresy • excommunication • Great Western Schism • Avignon • legates • Bulls
   Pilgrimages: Canterbury • Crusades
2. **Secular clergy:** hierarchy • dioceses • parishes • bishops • canons • priests • glebe • cathedrals
   Architecture: Romanesque • rounded arches • Gothic • pointed arches • flèches • ribs • flying buttresses • tracery work • rose windows • gargoyles • mullions
3. **Regular clergy:** monks • rule • Cistercians • Carthusians • habit • offices • dormitory • lector • scribe • refectorian • infirmarian • almoner • alms • guest master • bursar • abbot/abbess • prior • cloister • chapter house
4. **Friars:** mendicant • Franciscans • Dominicans • orders of nuns • enclosed • Ireland • universities • St Thomas Aquinas • Peter Abelard

MINI-PROJECT

Write an account of the following: *The life of a monk in a medieval monastery.*
Hints:

- daily life
- the monastic rule
- the monastery buildings
- the monks

[Write at least 10 or 12 sentences, without looking at your book.]

(*Junior Certificate Ordinary Level 1992, 1998 and both Levels in 2001* [hints vary])

14 Introduction to the Renaissance

WHAT WAS THE RENAISSANCE?

From the Middle Ages, we move on to a period known as the **Renaissance**. The word is a French term meaning 'rebirth'. It describes the period, from around 1400 onwards, when there was a great *rebirth* of interest in ancient Greek and Roman civilisations.

Over 1,000 years earlier, the Greeks and Romans had done great things in architecture, art, writing, science and engineering. After them, little further progress occurred and many of the ideas and inventions of the Greeks and Romans were forgotten.

In the 15th century, the people of Italy mainly began to rediscover what these ancient peoples had done, and to use this as inspiration to make many new strides in art, writing, architecture and so on. In fact, the beginnings of many things in the modern world can be traced to the Renaissance.

ITALY – WHERE IT ALL BEGAN

Italy became the birthplace of the Renaissance, partly because it had been the home of the **ancient Romans**. Many Italians wanted to recreate the greatness that had produced the Colosseum, the aqueducts and the works of art that they could still see around them. Even the ancient Greeks had left their mark on Italy, founding Naples in 600 BC. (**Neapolis** means 'New City' in Greek.)

Another link with ancient Rome lay in **language**. Italian is largely based on the Latin of the Romans and many Italians were able to read the works of Julius Caesar and other writers without difficulty. Elsewhere, as we saw, Latin was known only by priests and monks.

In Chapter 12 we saw how Italians led European trade with distant places since the time of the Crusades and Marco Polo. This also inspired the Renaissance, because it meant that Italians kept up to date with **new ideas** such as

Dexter
(Latin)
Destra
(Italian)

Sinister
(Latin)
Sinistra
(Italian)

Note how similar the Latin and Italian words are.

the development of geometry – vital to engineers and architects – in Arabia.

Italy was the home of the Catholic Church and, as we saw in the last chapter, the Church was hugely popular and wealthy in the Middle Ages. In Italy especially, a great period of **church building and decoration** developed, which needed thousands of architects, artists and sculptors to do the work.

In Chapter 12, we saw how towns developed in medieval Europe. Italy, in fact, was not a country, but a region of city states where **powerful cities** such as Milan, Florence and Venice had their own rulers, armies and territories. While some cities, such as Bologna, had great universities, others were the homes of wealthy rulers, merchants, churchmen and bankers who wanted to show off their wealth and learning by encouraging artists, writers and architects. These people became known **patrons** of the Renaissance.

The rediscovery of Greek culture in Italy was greatly helped by two 15th-century events. A grand council of Florence (1439) brought hundreds of Greek Orthodox churchmen to Italy and the Turkish capture of the city of Constantinople (1453) resulted in hundreds of its wealthy Greek inhabitants fleeing to Italy. These brought their language, and often works of art and ancient Greek manuscripts, with them to inspire 15th century Italians.

Although the **printing press** was first developed in Germany, the Renaissance in Italy was also helped by the availability of printed books, notably from the Aldine Press begun in Venice by Aldus Manutius in the 1490s.

Finally, for no other obvious reason, Italy just produced **more great writers**, **artists** and **architects** than any other country at the time to make it the cradle of the Renaissance.

DID YOU KNOW?

Many cookery experts believe that spaghetti first appeared in Italy as a result of Marco Polo's travels to China, where he encountered noodles.

DID YOU KNOW?

Milan was so wealthy that its rulers collected 700,000 ducats in taxes annually from its people, half of what the entire population of England paid to its king!

CAN YOU SAY?

1. What was the Renaissance? *(Junior Certificate Higher Level 1994)*
2. Which ancient civilisations inspired it?
3. Name *three* great Italian cities of the 14th and 15th centuries.
4. Renaissance artists usually had patrons. What was a patron?
   (Junior Certificate Higher Level 1992 and 2009, Ordinary Level 2005)
5. Give *two* reasons why the Renaissance began in Italy.
   (Junior Certificate Higher Level 2001 and 2003.
   One reason asked for at Ordinary Level, 2002 and 2006)

DID YOU KNOW?

This is the Ponte Veccio bridge in Florence. The wealthy Medici family used a passageway over the shops on the bridge to walk from their palace across the River Arno to the city offices without having to mix with the common people down below. The offices are now the world-famous Uffizi art gallery.

SOURCE A

PATRONAGE

As we saw, there were many wealthy patrons in Renaissance Italy who hired and encouraged artists, sculptors, architects and others. Although there were actually thousands of them, a few are worth special mention.

Lorenzo de Medici

The **Medici** family in Florence ran Europe's biggest bank in the 15th century. This was largely built up by **Cosimo de Medici**, who became a great patron of the arts and a collector of old manuscripts. His grandson **Lorenzo**, who was basically ruler of Florence (1469–92), became even more famous as a patron, earning the title **Lorenzo the Magnificent**. He allowed the family's business to decline because of his interest in literature and art. He also spent a great deal of public

Lorenzo de Medici

money to give Florence beautiful works of art and fine buildings, saying:

> **SOURCE B**
>
> *Many think that it would have been preferable to keep some of the money in the treasury; I think that our patronage was the great splendour of our regime and, in my opinion, the money was well spent.*

Lorenzo's money supported a group of writers and scholars known as the **Platonic Academy**, where Greek and Latin manuscripts were studied and translated. Artists such as Botticelli, Verrocchio and Leonardo da Vinci, whom you'll hear more about in Chapter 15, were employed by Lorenzo.

Although Leonardo da Vinci is now regarded as one of the world's most famous painters, Lorenzo used him to design parades and festival decorations to help celebrate great occasions. Towards the end of his short life (he died of gout at 43), Lorenzo set up a sculpture school in his own gardens and was very impressed by one 15-year-old student there named Michelangelo.

Ludovico Sforza

Another great Renaissance patron was Ludovico Sforza, ruler of Milan (1480–1500). Lorenzo de Medici was a politician and banker, but Ludovico was more of a soldier. Leonardo da Vinci knew this and, when he sought work from Ludovico in 1481, his letter of application mentioned:

> **SOURCE C**
>
> *I can build covered wagons, safe and unassailable, to penetrate with their artillery among the enemy ... I have plans for destroying every fortress or other stronghold ... for making cannon ... covered chariots, catapults.*

However, Ludovico also preferred to use Leonardo to plan festivals and magnificent celebrations to delight the people of Milan, and to design locks for a new canal system that he built in the city. Leonardo once went for three years without payment from Ludovico, who was occupied with affairs of state.

Ludovico was also patron to many other artists, poets and musicians, as well as to the architect Donato Bramante. Bramante was hired to

Lorenzo de Medici

DID YOU KNOW?

Ludovico was eventually overthrown by a French army in 1499, and French soldiers destroyed Leonardo's magnificent clay horse by using it for archery target practice.

design what became Ludovico's favourite church at the monastery of Santa Maria delle Grazie. Later, Ludovico hired Leonardo to paint *The Last Supper* on the dining-room wall of the monastery.

Later again, Ludovico hired Leonardo once more, this time to make a 180 tonne bronze statue of his father on horseback. Leonardo spent years making the clay model for this, which was displayed in the main square. However, before the bronze could be cast, Ludovico became involved in a war and used 150 tonnes of the bronze that Leonardo had stored – to make cannons!

Apart from these patrons, Italy had many more statesmen, businessmen and churchmen who patronised the writers, artists and others whom we will read about in Chapters 15 and 16.

CAN YOU SAY?

6. Why were patrons so important during the Renaissance?
   (Junior Certificate Higher Level 2002 and 2005)
7. Looking at the picture called **Source A** above:
   (a) What evidence does it show us of the Medici's wealth?
   (b) How does it show that Renaissance Florence was a crowded city?
8. Name a sculptor patronised by Lorenzo.
9. List *three* jobs that Leonardo da Vinci did for Ludovico Sforza.
10. What information given above suggests that Sforza was hard to work for?
11. The passages marked **B** and **C** (above) are examples of *primary* evidence. Why is this so?
12. According to **Source B**, why did some people criticise Lorenzo's patronage?
13. According to **Source C**, what did Leonardo think Ludovico's main interests were?

RENAISSANCE ART

In the coming chapters, we will read a lot about Renaissance artists. Before we do, it is worth examining how these artists changed and improved upon previous medieval art.

A new idea that influenced Renaissance art, writing and sculpture was **Humanism**. Quite simply, this was the belief that a human was important in his or her own right. Before the Renaissance, a person was seen as nothing more than a creation of God, and so most paintings, statues and indeed writings had a very strong religious theme; angels, saints and scenes from the Bible were the most common subjects. However, Renaissance artists, though still painting religious scenes, painted many more non-religious (**secular**) subjects for their wealthy patrons. Leonardo's *Mona Lisa*, for instance, shows the wife of a Florence merchant.

Renaissance Humanists were interested in ancient Rome and Greece, so many paintings dealt with the history and mythology of these civilisations. Humanism's interest in human beings for their own sake is also the reason why **nudes** are common in Renaissance paintings, something which would have been shocking to medieval people.

SOURCE D

Primavera *by Botticelli (whose name means 'little barrel').*

Medieval paintings tended to be very lifeless and not like real scenes at all. Renaissance artists often studied the bodies of humans, horses and birds in order to paint a more **realistic** picture. The artist Giotto (1267–1337) inspired many later artists towards greater **realism** by having his subjects show emotion on their faces, unlike other medieval artists. Giotto was also the first major artist to paint realistic scenery behind his subjects.

While medieval paintings seemed flat, Renaissance paintings had **depth**. Artists achieved this by using **shade**, for example, on the faces and clothing of people, and through the use of **perspective**. This meant that houses, roads, hills and so on were made narrower and smaller to give the impression that this was a real scene, going back into the distance.

Medieval paintings were often done on wood, which, over time, dried out and cracked, ruining the painting. Renaissance artists preferred **canvas**, which was light, could be easily rolled up and never cracked or dried out. The technique of painting on wet plaster, called a **fresco**, was known before even Giotto's time, but it was perfected during the Renaissance. As the plaster dried, it absorbed the paint, holding it fast, so that many Renaissance frescoes have survived in excellent condition to this day.

The Trinity *by Masaccio (1401–28) was one of the earliest masterpieces to achieve depth by using shade and perspective.*

Dull medieval paints were made from coloured powders and egg-white, which dried quickly. Renaissance artists mixed paints with **oil**, which dried slowly and allowed the artist to change his mind (called a *pentimento*) and alter things easily. Oil-paints enabled artists to paint in strong, bright colours. A method known as **impasto** involved applying layer upon layer of colour to make certain features stand out – the artists of Venice, such as Titian and Tintoretto, were noted for their bright colours.

Oil also enabled artists of the Renaissance to blend the outlines of their subjects in with the background by blurring the edges of hair and clothing. This idea was called *sfumato* ('smokiness') and is thought to have been invented by Leonardo da Vinci himself.

CAN YOU SAY?

14. Mention *four* changes that took place in painting during the Renaissance.

(Junior Certificate Higher Level 2000)

[Note: Two points were asked for at Ordinary Level in 1997.]

15. Explain the term *fresco*. *(Junior Certificate Higher Level 1999)*

16. Name *one* patron of artists during the Renaissance.

(Junior Certificate Ordinary Level 2002)

17. Why did many Renaissance artists often take their inspiration from the civilisations of Ancient Greece and Rome?

(Junior Certificate Higher Level 1999)

18. Using **Source D** above identify two reasons why you believe this to be a Renaissance rather than Medieval painting.

19. Give *one* reason why the painting by Titian, **Source E** above, is a typical Renaissance painting.

20. From the painting in **Source F** above, give *two* pieces of evidence to show that this is a Renaissance painting.

(Junior Certificate Higher Level 2003)

KEYNOTES

1. **Renaissance:** rebirth of Greek and Roman civilisations • new ideas • Italy, home of the Church • fall of Constantinople • wealthy city states.
2. **Patrons:** Medicis • Cosimo and Lorenzo • Ludovico Sforza.
3. **Renaissance art:** Humanism • nudes • realism • depth • shade • perspective • Giotto • Masaccio • Botticelli • canvas • fresco • oil-paints • *impasto* • *sfumato*.

15 The Great Italian Artists

We briefly met the artists Giotto, Masaccio and Botticelli in the previous chapter. These, and other early Renaissance artists, through their use of perspective, oil and realism, paved the way for the greatest artists of what became known as Italy's **High Renaissance**.

LEONARDO DA VINCI (1452–1519)

Leonardo da Vinci was named after his home town of Vinci, near Florence. His father had hopes for him as a lawyer. However, when he saw an incredible painting of a monster which the young Leonardo had done on a block of wood, Ser Piero da Vinci sent him to train as an artist's apprentice in Florence. Leonardo was just 15 years old.

Leonardo worked with other apprentices in the studio of the famous Andrea del Verrocchio. Here he learnt not only the skills of painting, but also of sculpture. He was very strong for his age, and legend has it that he sometimes entertained his fellow apprentices by bending horseshoes – with his bare hands!

Leonardo's first painting of note was of an angel in the corner of a larger work by Verrocchio called *The Baptism of Christ*. Apparently, Verrocchio thought Leonardo's work so much better than his own that he never painted again.

Leonardo was accepted into the Florentine artists' guild at the age of 20 and spent the next ten years working there, sometimes for Lorenzo de Medici himself. Then, in 1482, leaving two major paintings unfinished, he went to Milan to work for Ludovico Sforza.

Sforza often used Leonardo to organise engineering works and festivals. At this time, Leonardo was also compiling notebooks full of ideas for tanks, helicopters, submarines and parachutes. Unfortunately, Sforza showed little interest in these schemes, though modern research has shown that an aeroplane designed by Leonardo could have flown.

One of Leonardo's on flying machines.

Leonardo completed only six paintings in 17 years in Milan, notably *The Virgin of the Rocks* and *The Last Supper* in Santa Maria delle Grazie. He walked the streets of Milan for months on end seeking interesting faces for the characters in *The Last Supper*. Notice how Jesus is at the centre of the table. Judas, based on someone Leonardo had seen in Milan's criminal quarter, is darker and lower than the other apostles – can you guess why?

Unfortunately, in *The Last Supper*, Leonardo used a new paint mix which has flaked badly over the centuries. Dampness from a nearby swamp also harmed the painting, and, years later, the monks even cut a doorway through the bottom of it! Can you see it in the photograph? A major restoration effort, begun in the 1970s, has struggled to restore the work to its former glory.

With the fall of Ludovico Sforza in 1499, Leonardo left Milan, abandoning the huge statue of horse and rider which he had worked on for Sforza for 12 years.

Back in Florence, among other work, Leonardo did a small painting of Francesco del Giocondo's wife – *The Mona Lisa*. Now on display in Paris's Louvre Museum, this little picture with the famous smile on its subject's face has amazed art lovers for five centuries. Leonardo had music played while he painted, to keep his subject amused.

Leonardo continued to study science; he admitted to dissecting at least 30 corpses in his study of the human body (**anatomy**) and made many drawings of plants, birds in flight and horses in his efforts to further the study of biology. Many of his ideas laid the basis for great advances in science centuries later. Leonardo died in France, as a guest of King Francis I, in 1519.

DID YOU KNOW?

Leonardo's 5,000 pages of notes are written in 'mirror writing', that is backward and from right to left. This was probably an idea he used simply to avoid smudging the ink with his hand – he was left-handed.

The Virgin of the Rocks.

SOURCE A

The Last Supper.

The Mona Lisa. *If you look closely enough, you should be able to see the* sfumato *where the lady's hair and clothing blend into the background.*

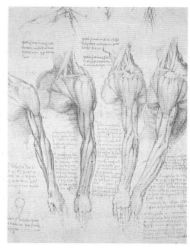

Leonardo's drawing of the muscles of the arm and shoulder.

CAN YOU SAY?

1. Who was (a) Leonardo's teacher and (b) his patron from 1482–1499?
2. Name and briefly describe *one* work of art completed by Leonardo da Vinci.
   (Junior Certificate Ordinary and Higher Levels 1996)
3. Describe *two* unusual aspects of Leonardo's notebooks.
4. In both **Source A** and **Source B** above, explain *one* way in which the artist gives the impression of perspective or depth.
5. Why did the condition of *The Last Supper* deteriorate over the years?
6. Why do you think *The Mona Lisa* is also known as *La Gioconda*?

MICHELANGELO (1475–1564)

The second giant of the Italian High Renaissance, Michelangelo Buonarroti – to give him his full name – was born in Caprese, near Florence, in 1475. Much of his early life was spent around Settignano with a family of stonemasons, and this experience set him on the road to becoming probably the Renaissance's greatest sculptor, as well as a magnificent artist.

At the age of 13, Michelangelo's father, a former mayor of Caprese, allowed him to join the artist Domenico Ghirlandaio as an apprentice. In his studios in Florence, the young boy learnt fresco-painting and, from the sculptor Bertoldo nearby, he got his first training with the chisel.

Michelangelo quickly gained a reputation for being hot-tempered; he had his nose broken and permanently flattened in a fight with another young artist named Torrigiano. Yet, even at 15, his talent was obvious and he was taken by Lorenzo de Medici himself to train at his sculpture school.

After brief periods in Venice and Rome, Michelangelo returned to Florence in 1501 and won the contract from the city council to 'do something' with a huge block of white Carrara marble which had lain abandoned there for forty years.

The result of Michelangelo's efforts was the statue of *David*, based on the character from the Bible who killed a giant with a sling. The statue stood almost five metres high and was known locally as *The Giant*. It was completely nude, in Humanist fashion (see Chapter 14), and in its detail and beauty resembled the work of ancient Roman sculptors.

In Florence, Michelangelo also earned fame as a poet and is still regarded as one of the great early Italian poets. We also know a great deal about his life from the 495 letters that he wrote to friends and relatives on a wide range of topics.

Michelangelo had a great rivalry with Leonardo da Vinci while in Florence. Leonardo had failed to get the contract that resulted in Michelangelo creating his *David*. At one time, both men even worked opposite each other in the same council chamber on rival frescoes of the *Battle of Anghiari* (in which Florence had defeated Milan back in 1440).

During Michelangelo's earlier stay in Rome, he had carved the beautiful *Pietà* of the Virgin Mary with the dead Jesus in her arms. This was done for the French Cardinal de la Groslaye, and was also carved out of white marble. In 1972, a man with a hammer damaged the statue, but it has been completely restored.

In Rome for a second time, Michelangelo was asked by Pope Julius II to paint the ceiling of the Sistine Chapel at the Vatican. Michelangelo preferred sculpture to painting. Nevertheless, he undertook the work in 1508, annoyed by the mockery of the artist Raphael and the architect Bramante, who thought he wasn't up to the task. Nor did Michelangelo get on very well with his own patron. He often barred Pope Julius from viewing the work in progress!

SOURCE C

Michaelangelo's David, which today may be seen in a museum in Florence.

DID YOU KNOW?

Leonardo painted a mixture onto the wall before painting the *Battle of Anghiari*, hoping it would make his painting brighter than Michelangelo's. Unfortunately, the paint ran off it before it dried, ruining the work. In the end, neither artist finished this particular contest, because Michelangelo left for Rome.

The ceiling of the Sistine Chapel.

On the Sistine ceiling, Michelangelo painted scenes from the Old Testament – the Creation, Adam and Eve, Noah and over 300 other figures. He hired five assistants to help him, but sacked them within days, preferring to work alone. Lying on his back, on top of 20-metre-high scaffolding, with paint dripping onto his face Michelangelo took four years to complete the work. It is now recognised as one of the greatest artistic works of the Renaissance.

Even before he had begun painting the Sistine ceiling, Michelangelo had been hired by Pope Julius II to design a tomb for him. This elaborate and expensive work occupied Michelangelo and others on and off for 40 years and was eventually completed in 1545, long after Julius' death.

In his later years, Michelangelo added to his already incredible reputation as a sculptor, painter and poet by turning to architecture. Several architects, including Bramante and Raphael, had worked on designing St Peter's Basilica in Rome, the new headquarters of the Catholic Church. Michelangelo was given the job by Pope Paul IV in 1546 and worked on it until his death. Much of the present appearance of St Peter's, especially the dome, is based on Michelangelo's design.

DID YOU KNOW?

The ceiling of the Sistine Chapel covers twice the area of a large tennis court such as the Centre Court at Wimbledon.

Over 20 years after completing the Sistine ceiling, Michelangelo was persuaded by Pope Paul III to paint scenes showing The Last Judgment *on the end wall of the same chapel.*

CAN YOU SAY?

7. Who was Michelangelo's teacher of painting?
8. Who became Michelangelo's patron when he was 15?
9. Explain *one* reason why **Source C** above, *David*, is a typical work of Renaissance art?
10. What is depicted in *The Pietà*?
11. Which Pope invited Michelangelo to paint the ceiling of the Sistine Chapel?
12. Explain *one* difficulty Michelangelo had in painting the Sistine ceiling.
13. What great architectural work did Michelangelo carry out?

TWO YOUNG MASTERS

While Leonardo and Michelangelo lived to old age, two other Italian artists won fame in much shorter lives.

RAPHAEL (1483–1520)

Raphael Sanzio was born in Urbino, over the Apennine Mountains from Florence. With both of Raphael's parents dead by the time he was 11, he was apprenticed to the great painter Perugino at the city of Perugia, learning the skills of fresco-painting and perspective.

Raphael's tomb in the Pantheon today.

At 21, Raphael moved to Florence, where he was greatly impressed by the work of Leonardo. He learnt how to create *sfumato* from Leonardo, but whereas Leonardo's figures were often deep and dark, Raphael preferred bright colours and action in his paintings. Raphael's first great work was *The Marriage of the Virgin*. Note how the paving stones narrow as they go back, giving a sense of perspective.

SOURCE D

The Marriage of the Virgin.

In 1508, Pope Julius II hired Raphael to paint frescoes in the papal apartments at the Vatican in an area known as the Stanza della Segnatura. One of these became known as *The School of Athens*; it is perhaps Raphael's greatest work. Elsewhere at the Vatican, Raphael painted several pictures of the Virgin Mary – known as the Madonna in Italian – the most famous being the *Sistine Madonna*.

Pope Julius II and his successor, Leo X, were so impressed by Raphael that he was given the job of redesigning St Peter's Basilica and the responsibility for preserving the ancient buildings and monuments of classical Rome. The young artist also earned the reputation in Rome of being quite a 'ladies' man' and became very wealthy. However, in 1520 he developed a fever and died on his 37th birthday – 6 April. At his own request, he was buried in the ancient Roman Pantheon (see Chapter 7).

CARAVAGGIO (1573–1610)

We cannot leave Italy's art Renaissance without mentioning its final genius, Caravaggio. He took the Renaissance interest in realism to a new level, often painting figures such as angels and saints as ordinary people who were bald, ugly or wore tattered clothes. His subjects were different from the perfect beauty painted by Leonardo and Raphael. Caravaggio also loved the contrast between light and shade, known to artists as *chiaroscuro*. We can even describe Caravaggio as the last Renaissance 'great' or as the first great artist of the style which became popular afterwards, known as **Baroque**.

Caravaggio's private life was very troubled. He got involved in several serious fights, was arrested twice and, in a row over a disputed score in a tennis match in 1606, he killed a man. He spent the next four years on the run until he died of fever and exhaustion, aged 37.

While Ireland has no great paintings by Leonardo, Michelangelo or Raphael, we do have an important work by Caravaggio. *The Taking of Christ* had been 'missing' for centuries, when Sergio Benedetti rediscovered it in the house of the Jesuit Fathers in Dublin's Leeson Street in 1990. Until his keen eye recognised Caravaggio's style, it was thought that the painting was the work of a little known Dutch artist.

SOURCE E

The Taking of Christ.

Since then, other experts, aided by X-rays and complicated scientific techniques, have proved beyond much doubt that Ireland, unknown to anyone, had been housing one of the greatest paintings of the late Italian Renaissance. The Jesuits had been given a present of the picture by Dr Lea-Wilson in 1930. Since the discovery of its true identity, this masterpiece has been on indefinite free loan to the National Gallery of Ireland.

CAN YOU SAY?

15. Name *one* Renaissance artist and mention one of his works.
    (*Junior Certificate Ordinary Level 1999.* Very similar questions in 2001, 2002 and 2005)
16. Name *one* of Raphael's patrons.
17. Name *one* non-painting task which Raphael carried out in Rome.
18. **Source D** is a picture of *The School of Athens* by Raphael. Give *two* pieces of evidence which support the fact that it was painted during the Renaissance.
    (*Junior Certificate Higher Level 2001*)
19. How has Dublin an important connection with Caravaggio?
20. Using **Source E** above to help you, explain *one* way in which Caravaggio's painting differed from that of Raphael and Leonardo.
21. What did Raphael learn from Leonardo?
22. **Source F1** below was painted by an artist called Cenni di Peppa in 1285 or so. **Source F2** shows *The Alba Madonna* by Raphael (1511). Give *two* reasons why the second one of them is an example of Renaissance painting.
    (*Junior Certificate Ordinary Level 2005*)

SOURCE F1

SOURCE F2

KEYNOTES

1. **Leonardo:** Vinci • Verrocchio • Milan • Sforza • inventions • mirror writing • *The Virgin of the Rocks* • *The Last Supper* • *The Mona Lisa* • anatomy
2. **Michelangelo:** Ghirlandaio • *David* • poems and letters • *Pietà* • Sistine ceiling • *The Last Judgement* • dome of St. Peter's
3. **Raphael:** Urbino • *The Marriage of the Virgin* • frescoes • *The School of Athens* • architecture
4. **Caravaggio:** Baroque • *The Taking of Christ* • Dublin

MINI-PROJECT

Write an account of the following: *A Renaissance painter*.
Name the painter (artist) and you may use the following hints in your account.
Hints:

- training
- patrons
- techniques
- works

[Write at least 10 or 12 sentences, without looking at your book.]

(Junior Certificate Higher Level 1993 and 1997, Ordinary Level 1997 and 2000
[Hints and wording vary])

Writers, Sculptors and Architects 16

We have seen how Italy gave the world some of its greatest artists in the 14th, 15th and 16th centuries. However, the Italian Renaissance involved much more than painting.

EARLY WRITERS

Latin was the language of the Church and of most educated people in the Middle Ages. However, it was not spoken by many other people and few of the great Latin writers of ancient Rome were studied.

Francesco Petrarch (1304–74)

Petrarch was born in Arezzo near Florence in 1304. Despite living before the real birth of the Renaissance, he helped greatly in the revival of interest in Latin authors such as Cicero and Virgil. Petrarch travelled, often on a mule, through France, Belgium, Holland and Germany. He recovered important manuscripts of great writers from monastery storerooms and libraries. His efforts encouraged patrons such as the Medicis to set up libraries and promote learning.

Francesco Petrarch.

However, Petrarch was much more than a manuscript collector. He wrote a number of books in Latin on different subjects. One of these, using material from the ancient manuscripts he found, was called *De Viris Illustribus* (*Concerning Famous Men*). In this, Petrarch told of the great achievements of men of the past, especially those of ancient Greece and Rome. The book inspired further interest in these ancient civilisations among Italians of his own and later days.

Petrarch's most famous writings were the poems he wrote to a woman called Laura. From the first time he saw her, in a church at Avignon, in 1327, to her death from the Black Death 21 years later, Petrarch dedicated many short poems, known as *Canzoniere*, to her. These short poems had only 14 lines each and were known in English as **sonnets** – you will hear more about them in Chapter 18.

Petrarch's *Canzoniere* were written in **Italian** and, along with the works of other writers such as **Dante** (*The Divine Comedy*) and **Boccaccio** (*The Decameron*), they began a very important trend.

DID YOU KNOW?

Although Petrarch spent 21 years writing to his beloved Laura, there is no historical evidence that the two ever even spoke to one another.

More and more writers began to abandon the idea of writing in Latin or Greek and instead produced works in their native languages. This is normally called writing in the **vernacular**; right across Europe it encouraged a huge growth of interest in books and learning – again, a major contribution to the Renaissance.

Niccolo Machiavelli (1469–1527)

Whereas Petrarch was a writer of the early Renaissance, the most famous writer of the High Renaissance was Machiavelli. Although the son of a poor and indeed bankrupt lawyer, by the age of only 29 Machiavelli was one of the most powerful men in Florence. As head of the **Second Chancery**, he worked for the government of Florence (the 'Ten') and was very involved in defence and foreign affairs.

Machiavelli was a sort of ambassador for Florence in places such as France and Rome, and also set up a local army (**militia**) to defend the city. He wrote short accounts, always in vernacular Italian, on many of his experiences, such as *The Way to Deal with Rebel Subjects* (1503) and *Arming the State of Florence* (1506). Machiavelli also once led a Florentine army to capture the nearby city of Pisa.

By all accounts, Machiavelli was a kind and honourable man. Yet his most famous work, ***The Prince***, states that a successful ruler must be ruthless whenever necessary. The message of *The Prince* is that 'the end justifies the means'; i.e. it doesn't matter what method you use (war, murder, lies and so on) as long as you achieve your goals in the end. To this day, the book is seen as a bible for dictators, despite also being one of the most famous novels of all time.

Niccolo Machiavelli.

DID YOU KNOW?

The Prince is based on the life of Cesare Borgia, a tough ruler and soldier. Cesare was actually the son of the man who became Pope Alexander VI!

CAN YOU SAY?

1. Why did Petrarch travel around Europe?
2. What was *De Viris Illustribus* about?
3. To whom did Petrarch dedicate his sonnets?
4. Who wrote *The Divine Comedy*?
5. Where was Machiavelli from?
6. What did Machiavelli work at, apart from writing?
7. Name *one* Renaissance writer and a work written by that writer.
   (Junior Certificate Higher Level 1993, Ordinary Level 2001, 2002 and 2004)
8. What exactly is vernacular writing?

SCULPTURE

We saw in the last chapter what an incredible sculptor Michelangelo was. He was not, however, the only great Italian Renaissance sculptor, and certainly not the first. Florence was also the home of the early Renaissance's greatest sculptors. As well as families such as the Medicis, Florence had many wealthy merchant and trade guilds, and it was often these guilds that acted as patrons to the city's sculptors.

Lorenzo Ghiberti (1381–1455)

In 1401, Florence's cloth merchants' guild ran a contest to choose a sculptor to make bronze panels for the north doors of a building known as the **Baptistry**. The contest was won by the 20-year-old Lorenzo Ghiberti. Over the next 22 years, Ghiberti worked on 28 individual bronze scenes from the New Testament. In the end, his patrons were so delighted with the work that he was then hired to carve scenes from the Old Testament on panels for the east doors.

Ghiberti carved the door handles in the shape of human heads, one of them being his own.

Ghiberti's ten bronze panels for the Baptistry east doors were so beautiful that Michelangelo later called them 'the Gates of Paradise'. Bronze casting was done by first making a model of the design in clay, wood or wax, then a mould (usually of plaster) was made of the model, and finally the hollow in the mould was filled with melted bronze.

As well as being some of the most beautiful sculptures of the early Renaissance, Ghiberti's 'Gates of Paradise' are also some of the very earliest examples of the use of perspective in Renaissance art; they had a great influence on painters and sculptors alike afterwards. Can you see how he achieved the feeling of perspective in the panel on the right?

Donatello (1386–1466)

Donatello actually worked for Ghiberti for a time, helping to make the first set of Baptistry door panels between 1404 and 1407. Soon, however, the young genius began to outshine even Ghiberti.

In the early 15th century, both the cathedral of Florence and the church of the Florentine guilds, known as the **Or San Michele**, were being decorated. Donatello was one of the sculptors who worked on these. He carved marble statues of saints

SOURCE A

This panel depicts the fight between David and Goliath.

The Feast of Herod.

and prophets for both the cathedral and its bell tower (**campanile**). At the Or San Michele, Donatello and others were hired to carve marble statues of the patron saints of the guilds in Florence. His most famous statue is of St Mark, patron of the linen guild.

Donatello was also skilled in bronze. The panels we saw earlier by Ghiberti are known as **relief work** – the carved figures stand out from a flat surface. Donatello's relief bronze *The Feast of Herod* (1427) shows how he too was an early master of perspective.

Yet, it was for free-standing bronze statues that Donatello was most famous. His statue of *David* – an early version of the bible hero – was the first free-standing bronze nude produced since the time of the ancient Romans, and it began a new Renaissance fashion that survived up to Michelangelo's *David* and beyond.

The ancient Romans had also been fond of statues of soldiers on horseback (equestrian figures), and Donatello revived this tradition, with his huge bronze sculpture of *Gattamelata*, standing 3·35 metres high in the town square in Padova to this day.

DID YOU KNOW?

Gattamelata, the subject of the Renaissance's first equestrian statue by Donatello, was a famous soldier in the army of Venice, though his name surprisingly means 'the honeyed cat'!

Donatello's David.

CAN YOU SAY?

9. How did Florence's guilds encourage sculptors?
10. For which building did Ghiberti carve door panels?
11. Look again at **Source A** and **Source B** above. Give *one* different reason why *each* is an example of Renaissance sculpture.
12. What was Donatello's *David* made from?
13. This is a sculpture by Michelangelo.

   (a) What is this sculpture called?
       (Junior Certificate Ordinary and Higher Levels 1994)
   (b) What material is it made from?
       (Junior Certificate Ordinary and Higher Levels 1994)
   (c) What is its theme?
       (Junior Certificate Higher Level 1994)
   (d) Name another Renaissance sculptor and *one* of his works.
       (Junior Certificate Ordinary and Higher Levels 1994 and Higher Level 2001)

ARCHITECTURE

We saw in Chapter 15 how great artists such as Leonardo, Michelangelo and Raphael also worked at times as architects. Michelangelo was easily the most successful of these artist-architects. Yet, again, to find the roots of Renaissance architecture, as with sculpture, we have to go back to Florence a century before Michelangelo worked on St Peter's.

Filippo Brunelleschi (1377–1446)

Just as the Renaissance in painting, writing and sculpture was greatly influenced by the ancient Romans, so too was architecture. *De Architectura* was a handbook for Roman architects, written by **Vitruvius**. It was the inspiration for many great Renaissance architects, notably a man named **Filippo Brunelleschi**.

Brunelleschi was a goldsmith at first and had been one of the people defeated by Ghiberti in the contest for the design of the famous Baptistry doors in 1401. Following this, Brunelleschi turned his attention to architecture, and, accompanied by his friend Donatello, he toured and learnt from all the ancient buildings in Rome.

Brunelleschi especially loved the Pantheon. Florence's cathedral had been under construction since 1296. When another contest was held to design the cathedral's roof, he based his design on that of the Pantheon and won the contest. In order to win the competition, Brunelleschi defeated his old rival Ghiberti by constructing a model dome nearly four metres high. The model alone took 5,000 bricks to complete!

In 1420, Brunelleschi began building the dome (**cupola**) to complete the building. Incredibly, he spanned a 40-metre gap using no rafters; he built it of bricks, placing each layer slightly inside the one below until the top was reached. Brunelleschi also designed most of the machinery needed during the 16 years of construction work. While the Duomo is now *only* the third largest Christian church in the world, Brunelleschi's dome is still the world's largest unsupported church dome.

In the design of other buildings, Brunelleschi used further ideas from ancient architecture. He loved to use long slender pillars with

Florence Cathedral. The bell tower on the left was designed by Giotto.

decorative tops (**Corinthian columns**), rounded arches and circular windows (*tondi*). His work produced wonderfully bright and attractive buildings such as the chapel he built for the Pazzi family, the great rivals of the Medicis; there is not a pointed arch, gargoyle or flying buttress in sight, all very different from the Gothic buildings we saw back in Chapter 13.

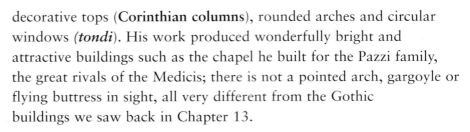
SOURCE C

Andrea Palladio (1508–80)

Later Renaissance architects such as Bramante, and indeed Michelangelo, learnt much from Brunelleschi, whereas in the design of private houses, Palladio became the later Renaissance's most influential architect. Palladio designed about 150 houses and villas for wealthy patrons, using domed roofs and porticoes (front porches) based on the columns of Greek and Roman temples.

Palladio's *Four Books on Architecture* explained his designs. Over the following centuries, these books had a huge influence on building design all over Europe. Look at Palladio's **Villa Rotonda** (near Vicenza, Italy) below, for instance, and see how many similarities you can see between it and Dublin's Four Courts, which was built some centuries later.

Villa Rotonda.

The Four Courts.

CAN YOU SAY?

14. Who wrote the book *De Architectura*?
15. What was Brunelleschi's first profession?
16. Give *two* reasons why the dome of Florence's cathedral was a great construction.
17. Using the picture in **Source C** above, explain *two* differences between Gothic architecture and that of Brunelleschi.
18. Name Palladio's famous writing on architecture.
19. What are (a) porticoes and (b) Corinthian columns?
20. Name *one* feature of Renaissance architecture.

(Junior Certificate Higher Level 1998 and 1999)

KEYNOTES

1. **LITERATURE**
   Petrarch: collected manuscripts • *De Viris Illustribus* • sonnets • *Canzoniere* • Laura • Dante • Boccaccio • vernacular literature.
   Machiavelli: *The Prince* • Cesare Borgia • the end justifies the means.
2. **SCULPTURE**
   Ghiberti: 'the Gates of Paradise' • relief bronze sculpture • perspective.
   Donatello: *The Feast of Herod* • *David* • *Gattamelata*.
3. **ARCHITECTURE**
   Vitruvius.
   Brunelleschi: Dome of Florence • Cathedral • Pazzi Chapel.
   Palladio: *Four Books on Architecture* • Villa Rotonda.

MINI-PROJECT

Describe the main changes in architecture and painting that took place during the Renaissance. *(Junior Certificate Higher Level 1994)*

Or

Concentrating on this chapter only, how many examples of the influence of ancient Greece and Rome can you discover? If you really dig deeply, you should be able to get close to ten points. Write a sentence in your own words explaining each example that you find.

17 Doctors, Scientists and Inventors

We have seen how the Renaissance involved a new interest in ancient Greece and Rome. We have also seen how, in art and architecture, the people of the Renaissance did not just copy these civilisations but improved on them. This is also true of medicine and science, where great improvements took place in many countries.

MEDICINE

In our look at medieval times, we saw how poor the knowledge of medicine was. During the Renaissance, the search for new ideas led to many great improvements in medical knowledge. Let us briefly examine some of the people responsible for making the Renaissance a great period of medical discovery.

SOURCE A

Medieval surgery, the amputation of a leg.

Andreas Vesalius (1514–64)

A vital part of improving knowledge of medicine is the study of the human body. This study is called **anatomy**. In ancient and medieval times, the idea of cutting open (**dissecting**) a dead body in order to examine it was thought wrong – indeed, it was illegal in most places. Because of this, knowledge of the human body was mostly based on the study of apes and monkeys. Unfortunately, this meant that medical diagnosis often came down to educated guesswork and was sometimes totally wrong.

SOURCE B

Vesalius demonstrates to his students at the University of Padua what a human arm looks like when dissected.

Vesalius, from Brussels, was most responsible for improving this situation and is known as 'the father of modern anatomy'. Vesalius studied in universities at Paris, Louvain and finally Padua, where he became a professor of anatomy. He studied anatomy by dissecting bodies himself and proved that many old ideas about the human body were wrong.

In 1543, at the age of only 29, Vesalius published *The Seven Books on the Structure of the Human Body*, usually known as the *Fabrica*. It was easily the most detailed and accurate study ever of the human body and contained many beautiful illustrations, done in the studios of the famous Venetian artist, Titian. Later in life, Vesalius became doctor to a number of European rulers. He died on the Greek island of Zakynthos, while returning from a pilgrimage to the Holy Land.

Ambroise Paré (1510–90)

The work of Vesalius paved the way for many others. The Frenchman Paré also preferred to learn from experience rather than accept old ideas. He worked as a surgeon on many battlefields in the service of four different French kings.

While treating French soldiers at the siege of Villane in Italy, Paré developed an ointment made of egg yolk and turpentine. He found that, when treated with this ointment, gunshot wounds healed better than before, with less suffering to the soldiers. Another time, Paré's skill enabled him to remove a lance point which was embedded in the face of the Duke of Guise (below), who was known ever afterwards as 'Scarface'.

Paré was fond of saying, 'I dressed him; God healed him.' However, there is little doubting the influence he had on improving the techniques of **surgery**. Incredibly, Paré was not even a member of a surgeons' guild; he was barred from entry on the grounds that he had little or no knowledge of Latin!

Like Vesalius, Paré was an example of the Renaissance search for new and better ways of doing things. He once declared, 'I would rather do the right thing on my own than follow the guidance of experts and do the wrong thing.'

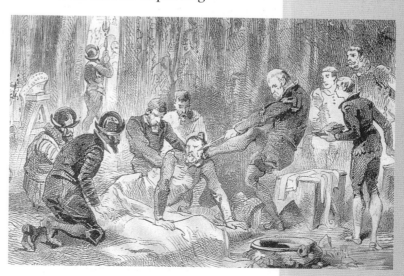

DID YOU KNOW?

Up to the time of Ambroise Paré, gunshot wounds were treated by pouring in boiling elderberry oil and then sealing the wounds with red-hot irons. It is likely that as many soldiers died in agony from the 'treatment' as from the wounds themselves.

William Harvey (1578–1657)

The final giant of Renaissance medicine was an Englishman, **William Harvey**. Just like Vesalius and others, Harvey was determined to prove the errors in existing medical theories. His greatest achievement was to prove that the blood is pumped around the human body by the heart; this is called the **circulation** of the blood. His great book on the subject was called *An Anatomical Treatise on the Motion of the Heart and Blood in Animals* (1628).

Harvey's discoveries disproved the ideas of ancient Greeks such as Aristotle and Galen. Without his work, doctors could never have fully understood the workings of the heart, lungs, liver and other organs. Like the others we have met in this chapter, Harvey's success lay in his refusal to just accept old ideas. Instead, he relied on personal investigation and experiment. Ironically, Harvey was actually banned from practising medicine in the final years of his life because he supported the losing side in the English Civil War.

CAN YOU SAY?

1. From what you have read, give *one* reason why **Source A** above is typical of medieval times and why **Source B** above is typical of Renaissance times.
2. What was the name of Vesalius's great work on anatomy?
3. What nationality was Ambroise Paré?
4. Why was Paré not a qualified surgeon?
5. Whose ideas did Harvey prove to be false?
6. Why was Harvey banned from practising medicine in his final years?

 ## SCIENCE

The most important scientific advances of the Renaissance were made in medicine. Yet, the period's greatest individual scientist was a man who gave up the study of medicine to concentrate on mathematics, physics and astronomy.

Galileo Galilei (1564–1642)

Galileo was born in Pisa, Italy. He entered Pisa University to study medicine, but soon changed his mind in favour of mathematics. This was at least partly due to a discovery he made one day in Pisa Cathedral. He noticed how a swinging lamp, no matter how high it swung, took the same time to come back down again. Years later, when he was blind, Galileo developed the pendulum clock based on this discovery.

Galileo also found that all falling objects, regardless of weight, fall at the same speed. Legend has it that he discovered this by dropping objects – some say hats, some say cannon-balls – from the top of the Leaning Tower of Pisa, but this story has not been satisfactorily proven.

Having been appointed professor of mathematics at the University of Padua at the age of 28, Galileo's discoveries continued. In 1608, a Dutchman called Jan Lippershey invented the **telescope**. When Galileo heard about the invention, he decided to make one for himself and eventually designed one capable of magnifying distant objects hundreds of times.

Galileo shows the moons of Jupiter to the senators of Venice.

Galileo used his telescope to study the stars and planets (this work is called **astronomy**). He discovered that the moon's surface is uneven, that the planet Jupiter has four smaller **moons** revolving around it and that Saturn is encircled by rings. He could even see spots on the surface of the sun – about 149 million kilometres away! Galileo published all these discoveries in a book called *The Starry Messenger* in 1610.

Before the Renaissance, people believed that all the planets orbited Earth. This was what the Old Testament suggested to them in the Book of Genesis. Yet, a Polish priest called

Nicolaus Copernicus (1473–1543) had produced a book – *On the Revolution of Heavenly Spheres* – contradicting the Church's teachings. Copernicus believed that all the planets revolved around the sun, not the Earth, but was so afraid of offending the Church that he allowed his book to be published only when he was close to death.

Galileo's telescope research convinced him that Copernicus had been right. Yet the Church refused to listen to his views. Spurred on by the work of astronomers such as the Dane **Tycho Brahe** and his German student **Johannes Kepler**, both of whom supported the Copernican theory, Galileo put his ideas in a book. When *Dialogue on the Two Chief World Systems* (1632) was published, the Church authorities were outraged.

Though many agreed with Galileo, he was called before the Church court (the **Papal** or **Roman Inquisition**) and forced to take back everything that had contradicted the Book of Genesis. If he had not, he could have been executed. As it was, Galileo was forced to spend the rest of his life under house arrest, a sad end for the Renaissance's greatest scientist.

The verdict of the Inquisition

SOURCE C

The proposition that the sun is the centre of the world and immovable from its place is absurd, philosophically false and formally heretical; because it is directly contrary to the Holy Scriptures.

SOURCE D

The proposition that the Earth is not the centre of the world, nor immovable, but that it moves… is also absurd, philosophically false and… at least incorrect in faith.

CAN YOU SAY?

7. What did Galileo first study at Pisa?
8. What did he discover about falling objects?
9. Whose invention of the telescope did Galileo improve on?
10. Name *two* discoveries described by Galileo in *The Starry Messenger*.
11. Name *two* developments in science or medicine during the Renaissance.
    (Junior Certificate Higher Level 2001 and 2009)
    [One development asked at Ordinary Level 1999, 2003 and 2006]
12. In the extracts from the Inquisition verdict (above) of June 1633:
    (a) What ideas of Galileo are attacked in **Source C**?
    (b) What evidence in **Source D** suggests that the ideas of Galileo regarding Earth were not as offensive to the Church as those in **Source C**?
13. Write an account [*six* sentences or so, without the book if you can] of science or medicine in the Renaissance. *(Junior Certificate Higher Level 2005)*

PRINTING

So far in this chapter, we have seen how the greatest general advances in Renaissance science were in medicine. We have also seen how the greatest individual scientist was Galileo. It remains for us to examine what most people regard as the greatest single invention of the Renaissance – the printing press. It is fair to say that many of the great Renaissance people who we have met would barely have been heard of in their own lifetimes had it not been for this invention. Surprisingly, its inventor was neither an engineer nor a scientist, but a simple German goldsmith.

Johann Gutenberg (1397–1468)

Johann Gutenberg came from the southern German city of Mainz, though many of his early working years were spent in Strasbourg (now a French city and home of the European Parliament). There, he and Andreas Dritzehn worked as goldsmiths and diamond cutters. When his partner died, Gutenberg returned to his native Mainz in 1448.

It was at Mainz that Gutenberg perfected the process of printing. He made small metal blocks, each with a letter standing out from it in reversed relief. Gutenberg made hundreds of these in moulds, both capital and ordinary letters. These metal blocks were known as **type** and were kept in a typecase, which had separate boxes for all the a's, b's and so on.

SOURCE E

Gutenberg made a frame and arranged the letters into words, with blank type for the spaces between the words. They were arranged from right to left along each line in the frame, so that they resembled the mirror writing of Leonardo da Vinci to some extent. When the frame was filled with words, side panels were screwed into place to keep the whole 'page' of type firmly in position. Ink was then dabbed all over the type and a sheet of parchment (sheepskin), vellum (calfskin) or paper was placed upon it. To make the ink come out evenly on the page, a sheet of wood was placed over the page and then pressed down firmly in a device that had been used for crushing grapes. The result was a clearly and evenly printed page.

The real importance of Gutenberg's invention was that it could reproduce hundreds of identical pages much more quickly than the writers of manuscripts could ever do. With the growing availability of cheap paper – made from boiled-down old rags – Gutenberg had made it possible for books to be printed more easily and more cheaply than ever before. Gutenberg's first printed book was a Bible, with 42 lines on each page. This was published in 1456; fewer than 50 copies of it still survive today. Unfortunately, Gutenberg was forced out of his own business by his financial backer, Johann Fust, and died poor.

A page from Gutenburg's Bible.

Other Printers

Although Gutenberg did not live to reap the full rewards of his invention, the printing press, with its **movable type**, spread rapidly throughout Europe. The Englishman **William Caxton** ran a printing works at Bruges (Belgium); he printed several books, among them the first printed book in English, a history of Troy, in 1478.

As with much of the Renaissance, Italy soon became the home of movable type printing. Venice alone had around 150 printers by 1500, the most famous of them being Aldus Manutius. It was he who invented the *italic* typeface. In 1500, there were over six million books in print across Europe, many in vernacular languages.

Caxton reads his first proofs.

Printing had a huge impact. Writers could spread their ideas much more easily as books became more plentiful. With fewer 'man-hours' needed to produce books, they became much cheaper, particularly when printed on paper rather than expensive animal skin as before.

The book revolution which Gutenberg had begun also led to a great education boom, bringing **literacy** to masses of people. In turn, this led to more and more vernacular writing, more schools and more universities. People became increasingly aware of what was going on in the world, of new discoveries and ideas.

DID YOU KNOW?

The present Vatican Library was begun by Pope Nicholas V in the same decade as Gutenberg's invention of movable type. Today, the library houses about one million printed books, though it still holds some 60,000 manuscripts from before Gutenberg's time.

CAN YOU SAY?

14. Where did Johann Gutenberg come from?
15. Before paper became cheap and widely available, what were books written on?
16. What precisely were (a) type and (b) the press?
17. What was Gutenberg's first printed book?
18. Explain why the invention of printing is regarded as one of the most important developments of the Renaissance.
    (Junior Certificate Higher Level 1994 and 2000, Ordinary Level 1998 and 2001)
19. Give *two* effects of the invention of the printing press.
    (Junior Certificate Higher Level 2002, 2004, and 2006; one effect asked at Ordinary Level, 2003 and 2004. [General account asked for in Higher Level 2005])
20. Look at the picture above (**Source E**).
    (a) In the case of the workers marked A, B, C, D and E, select two and state what job each of the two is doing.
    (b) Excluding information about work, mention *two* other items of information that a historian could get from this engraving about people who lived in the 16th century.
    (c) This engraving is a primary source. Give *one* reason why this is so.
    (Junior Certificate Ordinary and Higher Levels 1995)

KEYNOTES

1. **Medicine:** Vesalius • anatomy • *Seven Books on the Structure of the Human Body* • Paré • operations and treatment • Harvey • circulation of the blood • the heart as a pump
2. **Galileo:** Pisa • pendulum • telescope • astronomy • *The Starry Messenger* • Copernicus • Brahe • Kepler • *Dialogue on the Two Chief World Systems* • Papal Inquisition
3. **Gutenberg:** movable type • paper • the press • 42-line page Bible • Caxton • Manutius • literacy • huge influence

MINI-PROJECT

Describe briefly the part played by *three* of the following in the Renaissance:

- Leonardo da Vinci
- Michelangelo
- Lorenzo de Medici
- Johann Gutenberg
- Raphael
- Machiavelli

(Junior Certificate Ordinary Level 1993)

Or

Write about the following:

A printer during the Renaissance.

Hints:

- training
- everyday tasks
- materials used in printing
- the importance of printing for society

(Junior Certificate Ordinary and Higher Levels 1996)

Italy was the birthplace and main centre of the Renaissance but it was not the only centre. Let us now turn to meet some of the great artists and writers who contributed to the **Northern Renaissance** – called that because most of them came from regions far north of Italy.

ART

Jan van Eyck (c.1390–1441)

Probably the greatest early Northern artist was Jan van Eyck from Holland. Although we know very little of van Eyck's early life, it is certain that he worked for several wealthy patrons such as Duke Philip of Burgundy and the bankers and merchants of the rich cities of Bruges and Antwerp in Belgium. For a time, in fact, van Eyck even acted as an ambassador for Duke Philip.

Van Eyck was not a master of perspective as other, later artists were. He is, however, famous for the incredibly lifelike detail he put into his work. Furthermore, van Eyck was one of the early masters of oil-painting, making full use of improved varnishes and other ingredients in the early 15th century. Many of his pictures were done on wood coated in a smooth layer of plaster called *gesso*. One of Van Eyck's most famous paintings is the one showing the marriage of Giovanni Arnolfini and Giovanna Cenami, painted in 1434 and pictured here on the right.

SOURCE A

The Arnolfini Marriage

Albrecht Dürer (1471–1528)

Whereas van Eyck was the early 'great' of the Northern Renaissance, the German Albrecht Dürer was famous in the High Renaissance period. He was one of 18 children in the family of a Hungarian

Dürer painted this self-portrait in 1493.

goldsmith based in Nuremberg in southern Germany. Albrecht studied his father's trade for three years, but, as he wrote later:

SOURCE B

Though I could do that work as neatly as you could wish, my heart was more for painting. I raised the whole question with my father and he was far from happy about it, regretting all the time wasted, but still he gave in.

Dürer became an artist's apprentice in Nuremberg at the age of 15. There he learnt not only painting skills, but also those of wood and copper **engraving**. Printing works were now plentiful all over Germany, 40 years after Gutenberg's death. Dürer did engravings in wood – these were called **woodcuts** – which were then inked over and used to illustrate printed books.

Dürer visited Italy when he was 23 and was inspired by the wonderful art he saw in cities such as Rome and Venice. Around this time, with the help of a mirror, Dürer painted what most people think was the first **self-portrait** done by a Renaissance artist. He also painted **landscapes** for their own sake – other Renaissance artists used landscape painting simply to create a background to the **people** they painted.

In Germany, Dürer was patronised by the Emperor Maximilian and was made a freeman of Nuremberg in 1513. Dürer was respected not only as an artist and engraver, but also as an architect and writer. Like van Eyck, he had a great eye for detail, in his woodcuts and in beautiful nature studies, such as the one on the left entitled *A Hare*. This painting is just about the same size as a page of this book, yet we can see every hair and whisker on the animal.

Pieter Brueghel (1525–69)

After Dürer, most of the great Northern painters of the Renaissance came from the Low Countries (Holland and Belgium). Pieter Brueghel (the Elder) was famous for beautiful landscapes, and particularly for scenes depicting simple peasant life such as dances and weddings. His people tend to be quite 'well-rounded' folk who enjoy life. Some of Brueghel's pictures, such as *Netherlandish Proverb*s, are intended to be funny, whereas many contain scenes of daily life involving many different characters.

SOURCE C

The Harvesters.

Rembrandt (1609–69)

Just as Caravaggio marked the end of the Italian Renaissance and the beginning of the Baroque period, in the Northern Renaissance that role was filled by the Dutchman Rembrandt. Like Caravaggio, Rembrandt was very fond of contrasting light and dark shades and painting realistic (not necessarily handsome) figures. Rembrandt painted hundreds of works on a wide variety of subjects, though his most famous is probably *The Nightwatch*. This showed a group of civic guards (police) in Amsterdam during the 1640s. Despite Rembrandt's popularity, bad business dealings left him very poor and he died owning little more than his paints.

DID YOU KNOW?

During World War II, the Netherlands suffered bombing and invasion. In order to protect *The Nightwatch* from being damaged or stolen, it was taken from its frame, rolled up inside a giant tube and hidden in a sand dune near the coast.

The civic guards paid Rembrandt to do The Nightwatch. *One of them later stated that 'sixteen of them had each paid 100 guilders, some a little more, others a little less, according to the place they occupied in the painting'.*

Others

It is important to point out that we have looked at only a selection of the great non-Italian artists of the Renaissance. There were many others such as **Vermeer, Rubens, Bosch, Holbein** and 'Spain's' greatest artist, **El Greco**, who actually came originally from Greece.

CAN YOU SAY?

1. What nationality was Jan van Eyck?
2. **Source A** is *The Arnolfini Marriage* by Van Eyck.
   (a) Name *one* place where such pictures are normally kept.
   (b) Give *two* pieces of evidence that the couple in the picture were not poor.
   (c) This picture was painted during the Renaissance. Give *two* pieces of evidence to support this statement. (*Junior Certificate Ordinary Level 2001*)
3. What kind of man was Dürer's father? Base your answer on what you can read in **Source B** above.
4. Name *two* art forms for which Dürer was famous, *apart* from painting.
5. Dürer painted *two* special types of picture. What were these?
6. Examine **Source C** above. Give *two* activities that you can see from the painting. Do you think that the painting looks life-like? Give *one* reason for your answer. (*Junior Certificate Ordinary Level 2003*)
7. Why is Rembrandt's work like Caravaggio's?
8. Name *one* Renaissance artist from outside Italy and *one* of that painter's works. (*Junior Certificate Ordinary Level 1998, similar in 2003 and Higher Level 2005*)

LITERATURE

Whereas the quality of art in the Northern Renaissance was very high indeed, it is fair to say that its shining lights were in the field of literature. We saw in Chapter 16 how Italy produced many great writers and was the birthplace of vernacular writing. Yet, by any standards of judgement, the greatest writer of the Renaissance and possibly of all time was an Englishman.

William Shakespeare (1564–1616)

Shakespeare was the son of an alderman of the town of Stratford-on-Avon, near Birmingham. His father later became Mayor of Stratford and the young William benefited from an education – paid for by the local council – at Stratford Grammar School. We have few other records of Shakespeare's early life, but it is known that, at 18, he married Anne Hathaway, the daughter of a wealthy local landowner. They had three children and it is quite likely that Anne's money helped Shakespeare to move to London and become an actor in 1592.

The reconstructed Globe theatre in London.

He became a member of the Lord Chamberlain's Company of Players, but it wasn't long before he began to write plays rather than act in them. London had several theatres at this time, but the one most associated with Shakespeare's plays was **the Globe**. This was circular in shape. Wealthy people watched the performances from galleries, protected by a thatched roof. Poorer people – who paid one penny – stood below in the open air, watching the actors on stage above them. The Globe was destroyed a few years before Shakespeare's death when a cannon fired during a performance of one of his plays accidentally set fire to the roof. Because the rest of the theatre was made of timber, it all burned down in just an hour.

Shakespeare's plays were usually based on stories he had read or heard. For example, in typical Renaissance fashion, he was interested in ancient Greece and Rome. So, he turned to the works of the Roman historian Plutarch to get ideas for plays such as *Julius Caesar* and *Anthony and Cleopatra*. Other plays were based on English history, such as *Henry V* and *Richard III*, whereas the ideas for many plays came from stories of Renaissance Italy, such as *Romeo and Juliet* and *The Merchant of Venice*.

Although Shakespeare wrote light-hearted plays with happy endings (**comedies**), his greatest plays were his **tragedies**. He based his ideas for his four great tragedies on those written in ancient Greece. *Hamlet*, *Othello*, *King Lear* and *Macbeth* all tell the stories of great men who are destroyed by their own weaknesses, by bad luck and by the actions of others.

Shakespeare also wrote poetry, notably 154 **sonnets** – remember Petrarch, the inventor of the sonnet, whom we met in Chapter 16. Shakespeare's 14-line sonnets deal mainly with love, poetry and death.

DID YOU KNOW?

The American film director Sam Wanamaker spent years reconstructing the Globe (above). He had to go to court to do so because, ever since the Great Fire of London (1666), it has been illegal to erect a thatched roof in the city. Fortunately, the court made an exception for him.

DID YOU KNOW?

When Shakespeare died in 1616, he was a wealthy man. Curiously, however, although his will left most of his wealth to his children, he gave his wife his 'second-best bed'.

CAN YOU SAY?

9. From what English town did Shakespeare come?
10. Who was Shakespeare's wife?
11. How did the Globe differ from modern theatres or cinemas? Looking at the pictures of it on page 169 may give you some clues.
12. Name *one* play Shakespeare wrote about ancient Rome.
13. Name *one* play he wrote about English history.
14. What are Shakespearian tragedies?
15. In what ways was Shakespeare a typical Renaissance writer? (Think carefully.)

Other Writers

Some non-Italian writers continued to write in Latin and Greek. The most famous of these non-vernacular writers were the Dutchman **Erasmus** and England's **Thomas More**. Erasmus attacked stupidity and corruption in a work called *In Praise of Folly*, while More's great book was *Utopia*, about an imaginary land without laws or government.

Vernacular writing flourished too, **François Rabelais** was the greatest writer of the French Renaissance, while in Spain **Miguel de Cervantes** was responsible for the most famous novel of the entire Renaissance.

Miguel de Cervantes (1547–1616)

Don Quixote attacks a windmill.

Cervantes was the son of a poor Spanish doctor. He was mostly self-educated and was such a talented scholar that he was teaching in a Madrid school by the age of 21. Then, however, he wounded a man in a quarrel and was sentenced to have his right hand cut off.

Cervantes fled from Spain and spent the next ten years going from one adventure to another. In 1571, he fought for the Christian forces of Venice against the Turks at the great sea battle of **Lepanto**. He was once captured by pirates and spent several years as their prisoner.

When Cervantes finally felt it safe enough to return to Spain, he began writing seriously, in the dialect of his native province of Castile. He wrote his first novel, *La Galatea*, in 1585, followed by plays and poems. However, he never made money and spent time in jail for owing debts.

Perhaps all these varied experiences eventually stood to Cervantes, for in 1605 he produced his masterpiece, the novel *Don Quixote*. It is the story of an old knight from La Mancha who thinks he is a great romantic hero. In this state of mind, the hero travels around Spain on his horse, Rosinante, watched over by his squire, Sancho Panza.

This hilarious story of a knight who, among other things, charges at windmills in the belief that they are giants, made Cervantes famous throughout Europe. It also helped make **Castilian** the language of most of Spain, as it still is.

THE OVERALL RESULTS OF THE RENAISSANCE

As we leave the Renaissance, there are some important points we should consider. Firstly, we have seen that this period was responsible for the creation of many of the greatest **works of art and sculpture** in history. We have also seen that it had a huge impact on literature, particularly in the growth of **vernacular writing** and the availability of books in general, and in **science** and **medicine**.

The Renaissance also changed mankind's **view of the world**. People were encouraged to try new ideas, to investigate the world they lived in, to challenge ideas that had previously been accepted for centuries without question. We have seen this happening with the likes of da Vinci, Galileo, Harvey and others. In future chapters, we will see that this **questioning spirit** of the Renaissance also transferred itself to areas we have not considered up to now, particularly to people's desire to explore the world and to think again about their religious beliefs.

One thing the Renaissance did not manage to change very much, however, was the **place of women** in society. The traditional view of women was slightly shaken by the emergence of some female artists such as the Italian, Artemisia Gentileschi (1593–1652). It would be wrong, however, to exaggerate this. With few exceptions, just as in medieval times, women did not have access to the same levels of education as men, or to rights such as guild membership, running businesses or travelling independently. It would not be until the 19th and more so the 20th century that greater degrees of opportunity and equality for women would come about, and then very slowly. Some of Gentileschi's greatest works were wrongly attributed to her father, also an artist, showing how hard it remained for women to gain acceptance in the world of Renaissance art.

DID YOU KNOW?

Shakespeare wrote the Renaissance's greatest plays, and Cervantes its greatest novel. Isn't it strange that they died on the very same day, 23 April 1616?

DID YOU KNOW?

Georges Sand (France) and George Eliot (England) were two leading writers of the 19th century. Both were, in fact, women, who used male names to help their works become accepted.

Judith slaying Holofernes *by Gentileschi*.

CAN YOU SAY?

16. Give the title of *one* book written by the English Humanist Thomas More or the Dutch Humanist Erasmus.

   (Junior Certificate Higher Level 1996)

17. 'Cervantes was a man of action.' Explain why.
18. What is the name of Cervantes's greatest book?
19. In precisely what language did Cervantes write this book?
20. What unusual detail do both Shakespeare and Cervantes have in common?
21. Name *one* Renaissance writer and a work written by that writer.

   (Junior Certificate Higher Level 1993 and 2004, Ordinary Level 2005)

22. (a) Give *two* reasons why there were so few female scientists or artists during the Renaissance.

   (b) Mention *three* results of the Renaissance.

   (Junior Certificate Higher Level 2005)

KEYNOTES

1. **Art of the Northern Renaissance**
   Van Eyck: oil painting • *gesso* • lifelike detail
   Dürer: engraving • woodcuts for book illustrations • self-portrait • landscapes • *A Hare*
   Breughel: landscapes and peasant life • *Netherlandish Proverbs*
   Rembrandt: Baroque • *The Nightwatch*
2. **The greatest writer: Shakespeare:** Stratford-on-Avon • the Globe Theatre • history plays • tragedies • comedies • sonnets
3. **Other writers. Cervantes:** Battle of Lepanto • *Don Quixote* • Castilian Spanish
4. **Overall results:** new art • vernacular literature • new ideas in science and medicine • questioning spirit • limited progress for women

MINI-PROJECT

Write an account of *one* Renaissance writer or artist who was not from Italy.

   (Junior Certificate Higher Level 2000 and 2009 – no hints given)

[*Note:* Try to write at least ten sentences on this. You may wish to do some research in an encyclopaedia or using a computer. If so, include in your project only information that you fully understand and always write it in your own words. There are many other non-Italian Renaissance artists and writers you could look up too: Vermeer, Rubens, El Greco, Marlowe, Jonson…There's a challenge for you!]

Studies of Change

Section 2

Few will have the greatness to bend history itself;

but each of us can work to change a small portion of events,

and in the total of all those acts will be written

the history of this generation.

ROBERT F. KENNEDY

19 The Age of Exploration – Why and How?

INFLUENCE OF THE RENAISSANCE

The Renaissance was a period when a great desire for knowledge existed alongside far-reaching social and economic developments. People had confidence in their own abilities. In Renaissance Europe, anything seemed possible to people such as Leonardo da Vinci and Galileo. Over the next four chapters, we will see how this spirit of self-belief and adventure became, at the same time as the Renaissance, another tremendous force for change, leading to the **Age of Exploration**.

EARLY EXPLORATION

There were, of course, great European explorers before the 1400s. Marco Polo from Venice travelled to China and set up trade links between Italy and the Far East, which helped to make Italy a wealthy country by 1400.

Thor Heyerdahl's Ra *crossing the Atlantic. The boat was made from papyrus reeds.*

At sea, too, there had been great explorers before Renaissance times. It is unclear whether our own St Brendan reached Iceland, but it is certain that Vikings from Scandinavia sailed far and wide, and that one of them, Leif Ericsson, reached the mainland of Canada sometime around 1002.

Moreover, the great modern Norwegian explorer, Thor Heyerdahl, has shown that it is possible to sail great distances across the open sea in the types of boat built thousands of years ago by the ancient Egyptians and by the peoples of the Pacific. Despite all this, people in 1400 still knew very little about the world. Entire continents, such as America and Australia, remained completely unknown to Europeans and very little was known about the further parts of Asia or Africa.

In addition, many Europeans had badly mistaken beliefs about these unknown parts of the world. Although it was commonly understood by 1400 that the Earth is round, no one was quite sure of its size. It was believed that terrible weather, whirlpools, monsters and misshapen people lay beyond the horizon. Even after Marco Polo's explorations, Italians travelled to the Far East either by land or along very well-known sea routes – they rarely ventured off these familiar routes.

CAN YOU SAY?

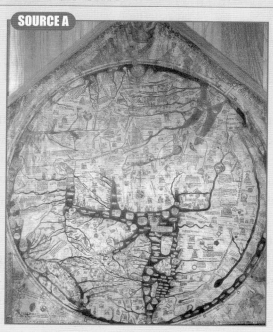

SOURCE A

1. This is a reproduction of an early 14th-century 'map of the world' (*Mappa Mundi*).
   (a) Find a modern map of the world – in your own atlas – and list at least *two* differences between the two maps.
   (b) What shape does this map suggest the Earth to be?

2. *They are courageous in battle and when they attack another tribe's territory, they persist until they have destroyed it completely. They take the women prisoners and make the men serfs. They are well built and good looking and daring, but their daring is not apparent on land; they always launch their raids and campaigns from ships. They wear full trousers and when they put them on, they roll them up to the knees and fasten them there… They wear neither coat nor mantle, but each man carries a cape which covers one half of his body, leaving one hand free.*

   In this description of the Vikings, the writer says: 'Each man carries a cape which covers one half of his body, leaving one hand free.' Why, in your opinion, was one hand free?

   (*Junior Certificate Ordinary and Higher Levels 1992*)

REASONS FOR EXPLORATION

The main reasons why Europeans chose to travel beyond their own continent had been the same for many centuries.

Trade, as we saw in Chapter 12, grew substantially in the Middle Ages. Distant places, such as Arabia, India and China, were vital to this. Gold, silver, silks, gems and ivory were all highly sought after in medieval Europe. So important was trade in these goods that the route from Europe to China was known as the **Great Silk Road**.

DID YOU KNOW?

The small dark cloves that you often find now in apple tarts were, in medieval times, highly prized for curing colds and other ailments.

We saw in Chapter 11 how medieval food was often rotten because of the lack of refrigeration. This added another reason for exploration – the search for **spices**. Merchants from great Italian cities such as Venice, Genoa and Florence brought spices, including cinnamon, nutmeg, cumin and cloves, from the Far East, notably from the **Spice Islands** (now called the **Moluccas**). Apart from being used in food, some of these spices were also used in medieval medicine. The voyage from the Red Sea to eastern Asia was easily the longest voyage undertaken by medieval sailors.

In the Middle Ages, all of Europe was basically Christian and many felt it their duty to spread **Christianity** to distant parts of the 'pagan' world. Sometimes, this involved major wars, such as the Crusades (see Chapter 13) or the struggles of Spain and Portugal against the Muslim **Moors** of North Africa. A legend, widely believed in Europe, told of a great Christian king called **Prester John** who supposedly lived beyond the regions controlled by the Turks and Moors. So, a further reason for exploration was to find Prester John and form an alliance between his kingdom and Christian Europe to crush the Muslim forces of the Turks and Moors.

Land was another attraction for explorers. The prospects of finding and taking over regions rich in farmland, minerals and other 'assets' were the main reasons for Viking exploration. In 986 AD, Eric the Red promised his Viking crew that they would find fertile farmland by sailing to the west. What they found was largely covered in snow and ice, but Eric still insisted on naming it **Greenland**.

These had been reasons for European exploration for centuries. Other developments around 1400 gave an extra 'push' towards new exploration.

Other Reasons After 1400

We have already seen in Chapter 12 how towns had expanded greatly by 1400. **Growing populations** meant a growing demand for goods and growing trade across Europe. So the prospect of great wealth lured many – no longer just the Italians – to explore new lands in search of badly wanted goods for the European market.

In the 14th and 15th centuries, changes occurred in Asia that added to the need to find **new routes**. The Mongol Empire, with which Marco Polo had traded, had collapsed by the mid-14th century, cutting off a vital trading region from Europeans. In addition, the Turkish conquest of the Holy Land (see Chapter 13) meant that, by 1453, the Turks were in control of an area running from Constantinople in the north to Egypt in the south. Although it was still possible for the traders of Venice and Genoa to pass through these areas on their way to the East, it became more and more difficult and dangerous to do so.

> **DID YOU KNOW?**
>
> 'Goods' in medieval times meant much more than the items mentioned. The term was also applied to another type of cargo – **slaves**. At this time, the **slave trade** was common throughout Europe; between 1450 and 1500, it is estimated that Portuguese slave traders alone brought back around 150,000 African slaves from their journeys.

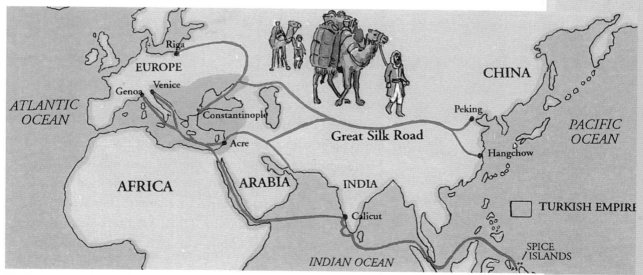

Trade routes to the Far East.

In all, with a growing population to cater for, and a greater difficulty in bringing goods from former sources along the old routes, 15th-century Europeans needed to act. They were able to do so because of improvements that took place at this time in shipbuilding, navigation and map-making.

One Portuguese sailor explained the reasons for his voyage to India:

> **SOURCE B**
>
> *And as the principal reason for this voyage to India has been the service of God our Lord and our own profit, it pleased Him in His mercy to speed them on their route. We learn now that they did reach and discover India … and great populations, among whom is carried on all the trade in spices and precious stones.*

CAN YOU SAY?

3. What *two* regions were joined by the Great Silk Road?
4. Who was Prester John?
5. What European first landed in Greenland and why was it so called?
6. What motives does the author of **Source B** give for the voyage?
   (Junior Certificate Ordinary and Higher Levels 1993)
7. Why were the Moluccas an important destination for explorers?
8. Give *two* reasons why spices were so important in 15th and 16th century Europe.
   (Junior Certificate Ordinary and Higher Levels 1992; similar in Higher Level 2002)
9. Give *two* reasons why rulers were prepared to sponsor voyages of exploration.
   (Junior Certificate Higher Level 2003 and 2004; similar in 1997; one reason asked at Ordinary Level 2000)

 NEW SHIPS

Sea travel was common as far back as the days of the ancient Romans. Medieval traders from Venice and Genoa continued this tradition, with hundreds of voyages undertaken annually between Italy and the eastern Mediterranean, en route for the Far East usually. However, the Mediterranean is a sea with virtually no tide and rarely suffers the sort of bad storms or currents that would be found in the Atlantic Ocean. Thus, Mediterranean ships were not very strongly built – at least, not for long, ocean-going voyages. They were, however, easy to handle. They had triangular sails called **lateens**, which enabled them to catch the wind and twist and turn well, vital for getting around the busy harbours and many islands of the Mediterranean.

However, the Spaniards, and especially the Portuguese, were Atlantic sailors. Their boats were strongly built, using a system of overlapping planks on a solid timber frame. This was known as **clinker-building** and was very similar to the method previously used by the Vikings. These square-sailed Atlantic ships were built for strength rather than manoeuvrability, and found it very difficult to turn quickly.

The major breakthrough in shipbuilding came in the early 15th century when the Portuguese combined the clinker-building method of Atlantic ships with the use of Mediterranean lateen sails. The new type of ship that resulted was called a **caravel**. Its strongly built hull allowed it to withstand the might of the ocean waves, yet the use of lateens at front (**fore**) and back (**aft**) made it easy to steer. Caravels often kept square **mainsails**, but the use of lateens made it possible to sail against the wind; this is called **tacking**.

SOURCE C

A Portuguese caravel from the 15th century, with two triangular lateen sails.

Later in the 15th century, larger and rounder **carracks** also became popular. The Portuguese called these *naos* and their size made it possible to carry larger quantities, both of supplies for the crew and trading goods. Thus, it was easier and more profitable to undertake long voyages.

CAN YOU SAY?

10. Explain *one* difference between medieval Mediterranean ships and Atlantic ones.
11. What does the term clinker-building mean?
12. What is tacking and why is it used?
13. **Source C** above is a picture of a ship used during the Age of Exploration.
    (a) Name the type of sailing ship in the picture.
    (b) Give *one* reason why it was more suited for longer voyages than ships during the Middle Ages.

(Junior Certificate Higher Level 2000; similar in 2003)

An astrolabe.

The only navigation device he has is a compass.

NEW AIDS TO NAVIGATION

Better ships would be of little use if sailors did not know where they were going. Even during the first half of the 15th century, many sailors were unhappy about sailing on the ocean out of sight of land. Several developments in **navigation** – the art of finding one's way at sea – made longer voyages into the 'unknown' possible.

Early explorers generally told east from west simply by noting the direction in which the sun rose and set. North was identified from the pole star at night or from the direction of the sun's shadow at noon. These methods of direction-finding were improved upon greatly by the development of the **compass**. Its needle always pointed towards the north and this made it possible to identify all the other directions.

An instrument called a **quadrant** became common in the 15th century. This measured the height of the pole star or of the sun above the horizon and told sailors how far north or south they were. At night-time, another instrument called an **astrolabe** told your position from the altitude of the stars.

The Portuguese sailor Diogo Gomes wrote of a voyage south along the African coast in 1462:

> **SOURCE D**
>
> *I had a quadrant, when I went to these parts, and I wrote on a quadrant table the altitude of the north star, and I found this better than any chart.*

The most accurate method of telling a ship's speed – and so the distance being travelled – was by using a **log**. This was attached to a rope which had knots tied on it at intervals. The log was thrown over the side and the number of knots which went over the side as the rope trailed out after it gave you the ship's speed. To this day, a sailor's term for 'miles per hour' is **knots**, though a sea mile is a little longer than a land mile.

Problems

Before you get carried away with the idea that navigation became easy in the 15th century, think again. Accurate compass readings were almost impossible to get on an unsteady ship, added to the fact that any iron on the ship could distort the direction of the magnetic needle – this was not realised until much later. Estimating distance with a log was really not much better than guesswork, as it took no account of ocean currents. Even telling the time accurately – in order to judge when noon occurred in open sea, and so find out how far east or west you were – was not possible until the 18th century.

Quadrants and astrolabes too gave a rough, rather than an accurate, guide to north and south; again it would be the 18th century before the **sextant** could do this with precision. One expert claims that navigators in the 15th century were happy if their calculations were 80 per cent correct. As this could mean they were hundreds of kilometres off course, it shows what very brave people these explorers were.

Another problem on lengthy voyages concerned **food**. Cooking on timber ships was difficult; it was generally done in a sand-lined firebox made of iron. Storing food created even greater difficulties. Meat had to be heavily salted in barrels, and even then was frequently rotten. Fresh fruit and vegetables were important to maintain the crew's health, but with no way of preserving them, supplies quickly perished. A lack of fresh fruit led to health problems, as we shall see later.

Keeping the ship in good condition was also very important. It meant that the ship's crew had to include carpenters and sailmakers, generally under the command of the **boatswain**. Sometimes, a ship had to be deliberately beached at low tide to enable repairs to the hull to be carried out; this process was called **careening**.

DID YOU KNOW?

The depth of water beneath a ship was measured using a rope with a lead weight tied to the end. Knots were tied at six-foot intervals (about two metres) along the rope; the distance between two knots was known as a **fathom**. Sailors regarded it as an easy job; hence the expression 'swinging the lead'.

New Maps

Improved ships and improved navigation methods led automatically to improved map-making. Correspondingly, as maps improved, sailors felt happier about going on longer voyages. Since the 1300s, sailors had made quite accurate maps of the Mediterranean – these were called **portolan** ('harbour-finding') **charts**. In the 1400s, these portolans were also drawn up for Atlantic regions as far apart as Iceland and North Africa, further reducing the fear of the unknown.

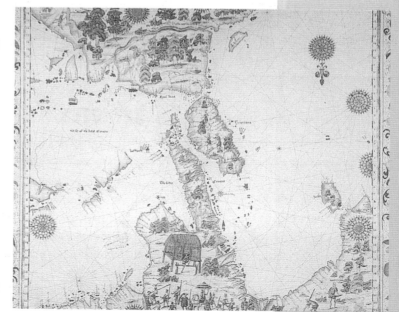

This is an early portolan chart of an area of south-east Asia.

SOURCE E

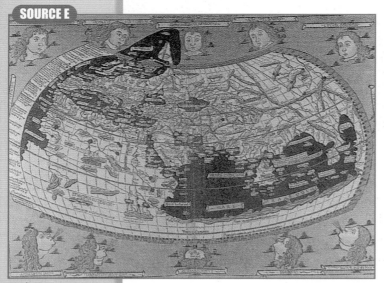

Ptolemy's map.

A great boost to map-making came in the form of an ancient manuscript brought to Europe from Constantinople. **Ptolemy's** *Geography* contained a world map far more accurate than any previously drawn. It inspired map-makers (**cartographers**) all around Europe – in Bologna alone, 500 copies of it were printed in 1477. By showing the world to be round and by dividing the map with lines of **longitude** and **latitude**, this rediscovered cartographer of the second century set the standard to follow for map-makers of the 15th and 16th centuries.

DID YOU KNOW?

A mistake in Ptolemy's map accidentally encouraged exploration. He made the Earth seem small and encouraged the notion that Asia was just a short distance west of Europe. This is not true, of course, but it inspired Christopher Columbus to sail westwards in search of Asia. Do you know what he found instead? (See Chapter 21.)

CAN YOU SAY?

14. For what purpose were *two* of the following used during the Age of Exploration? compass; astrolabe; portolan charts; log and line.

    (*Junior Certificate Higher Level 2002, 2004; one asked for at Ordinary Level in 2004; similar questions at both levels in 2006*)

15. In **Source D** above, what instrument did the sailor use and what did he measure with it?

16. Explain what explorers meant by (a) knots and (b) fathoms.

17. Look at Ptolemy's map above (**Source E**) and list *two* ways in which it is a better map than the *Mappa Mundi* (**Source A**), but also *two* ways in which it is worse than today's maps.

18. Mention *two* dangers that faced sailors on journeys during the Age of Exploration.

    (*Junior Certificate Higher Level 2000; Ordinary Level 2003*)

KEYNOTES

1. **Renaissance spirit:** the Age of Exploration • Marco Polo • the Vikings • *Mappa Mundi*

2. **Reasons for exploration:** trade • spices • search for new routes • Christianity • land • population growth

3. **Improved ships:** lateens • clinker-building • caravels • mainsails • tacking • *naos* • carracks

4. **Navigation:** compass • quadrant • astrolabe • log • knots • fathoms

   Maps: portolans • Ptolemy • longitude • latitude

We have already seen how European trade and indeed sailing were dominated by the Italians up to the 1400s. This chapter deals with sailors from a small nation on the Atlantic – no bigger than Ireland – who led the new Age of Exploration – the **Portuguese**.

HENRY THE NAVIGATOR

Much of the credit for Portugal's crucial role must go to one man, the 'Infante Henrique' (1394–1460), the third son of King John I, who is much better known to us as **Prince Henry the Navigator**.

Henry's early life was one of excitement and adventure. At only 21, he and his two older brothers were dubbed knights of the sword (see Chapter 10) for their role in capturing the city of **Ceuta** in North Africa from the Moors. Ceuta lay at the entrance to the Mediterranean and so was an important stronghold and trading centre.

Henry was appointed Governor of Ceuta in 1415 and successfully held it against a Moorish counterattack. Henry dreamed of increasing Portuguese control in North Africa. Portugal itself was a poor, mountainous country and Henry wanted to tap into the wealth of the Moorish Empire, which then traded widely in products such as gold, slaves and spices.

Henry also longed to crush the Muslim Moors and convert 'pagans' to Christianity – he later received three Papal Bulls to encourage him in these efforts. The possibility of finding the legendary **Prester John**, mentioned in the last chapter, was an added dream of the prince's.

Down the African Coast

In 1418, as Governor of Ceuta, Henry sponsored the first voyages. Two of his captains reached the islands of Porto Santo and Madeira off the African coast and claimed them for Portugal. Knowing that he would never be King of Portugal, in 1419 Henry left Lisbon and moved to southern Portugal as Governor of the Algarve.

Prince Henry the Navigator.

DID YOU KNOW?

The title **Navigator** was given to Henry, not by the Portuguese but by later English historians. Prince Henry never went on any voyages of exploration himself – in fact, he tended to suffer from seasickness when on board ships.

Over the next 40 years, he set up the greatest navigational school in the world at that time at his Algarve court of **Sagres**. Map-makers, astronomers and instrument-makers found a ready welcome there.

Many improvements were made to instruments – for example, the idea of placing the compass needle on a pivot to allow it to rotate freely. Maps became more and more accurate as Henry sent explorers further south along the African coast.

A major obstacle on the African coast was **Cape Bojador**, a peninsula jutting 40 kilometres out into the Atlantic. Several expeditions sent by Henry failed to round it because of dangerous seas. Finally, in 1434, **Gil Eanes** succeeded. In 1445, the mouth of the **Senegal River** was discovered by **Dinís Dias**. Here, at last, lay beautiful forests and fresh water.

Ptolemy had suggested in his *Geography* that nothing or nobody could live in the heat of these southerly regions, but one explorer wrote:

Sagres seaport today.

SOURCE A

Instead, precisely the contrary has been found to be true. Countless are the black people who live on the equator, and the plants there have an incredible growth, precisely because there vegetation is at its most vigorous, and the forms of the plants are quite special.

In 1441, the first gold and slaves had been brought back by a Portuguese caravel, both obtained by bartering cheap goods such as brass bells and mirrors with the Africans. The trade in slaves became so large that Henry built a special fort and 'warehouse' for the purpose at Arguin Island off the coast of North Africa in 1448. By the time of his death in 1460, the Lisbon Mint had begun issuing pure gold coins called **cruzados**, made from Guinea gold. Clearly, by this time, the sailors of Henry the Navigator had not only made many voyages of exploration but had also added considerably to their own nation's wealth.

At the time of Henry's death, Portuguese sailors had reached the area now known as Sierra Leone, just 8 degrees north of the equator. Their discoveries had already shown Ptolemy to be wrong in many of his opinions, and the hope grew that one of his most strongly held notions might yet be shown to be false. The following extract is from the writings of Azura, a friend of Prince Henry the Navigator:

Cape Verde Islands

SOURCE B

Up to that time, neither by writings nor by the memory of man, was anything definite known about the land beyond the Cape... He wanted to engage in great and noble conquests, and, above all, attempt the discovery of things which were hidden to other men... If there chanced to be in these lands some Christians, or some harbours into which it would be possible to sail without danger, many kinds of goods might be brought to Portugal. They would find a ready market, and also the products of Portugal might be taken there and the trade would bring great profit to our countrymen... His great desire was to increase the Holy Faith in our Lord Jesus Christ and to lead to this faith all souls wishing to be saved.

CAN YOU SAY?

1. What type of school did Prince Henry of Portugal establish at Sagres in 1420?
   (Junior Certificate Higher Level 1995)
2. According to **Source A** above, how did the early Portuguese explorers prove Ptolemy wrong?
3. List *two* things that Portuguese sailors brought back from their voyages.
4. What were Prince Henry's motives for exploration (**Source B** above)? Aim to find at least *three*.

   (Junior Certificate Higher Level 1994)

THE SEARCH FOR THE CAPE

If you glance back at Ptolemy's map in the previous chapter, you will see that Africa was thought to stretch as far as the South Pole. If it did not, the Portuguese thought, it should be possible to sail around its southern tip ('cape'), and then eastwards to India, China and the Spice Islands. As the Italians were finding it difficult to continue their trade links with these areas (see Chapter 19), the possibilities for Portugal seemed very good indeed.

After Henry's death, Portuguese sailors set up forts and trading posts all along the African coast. A good reminder of the goods they bought lies in the names they gave to the places where they landed. Modern Liberia was christened the **Grain Coast**, after the grainy pepper they bought there. Next to it was the **Ivory Coast** – so called to this day – whereas Ghana was then called the **Gold Coast**, and Benin was the **Slave Coast**.

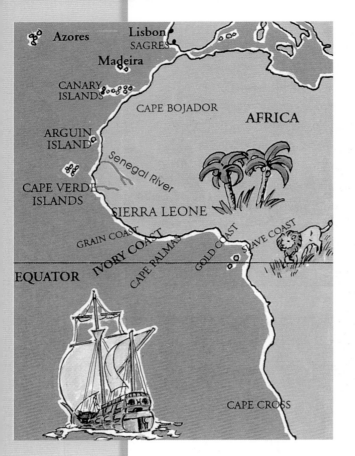

The equator was crossed for the first time in the 1470s – without the seas boiling, as some sailors had feared. Under the rule of King John II (1481–95), the Portuguese pressed further south in search of the elusive tip of Africa and the sea route to India. In 1485, **Diogo Cão** reached Cape Cross in modern Namibia, 22 degrees south of the equator.

Bartolomeu Dias

In 1487, King John ordered **Bartolomeu Dias** to go further south than Cão had gone, still in search of the tip of Africa. With his own ship, the *São Cristóvão*, and two others, Dias set sail from Lisbon in August 1487 and followed the African coast beyond Cão's last marker. Storms forced Dias to lose sight of the coast for a few days and when he turned east to find it again, he found open sea. The end of Africa had been reached.

DID YOU KNOW?

In order to warn off sailors from any other nation, Diogo Cão and others placed large stone pillars (*padrãos*) along the coast as they went, marking the area as property of the Portuguese monarchy.

SOURCE C

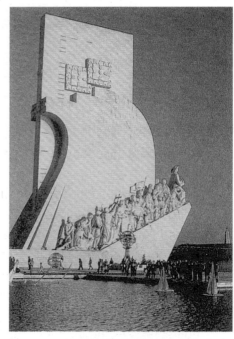

The monument to the Discoveries located on the banks of the River Tagus in Lisbon. The monument, which is 40 metres high, is built in the shape of a caravel. Along its base are statues of many of Portugal's most famous sailors.

Here, two great oceans – the Atlantic and the Indian – crash into each other, so sea conditions are often violent. Dias named the point the **Cape of Storms**. After three months of exploring the southern coast of Africa, he came home with the great news in 1488.

King John II was delighted. He and Dias decided to change the name from Cape of Storms to **Cape of Good Hope**, in order to encourage other sailors to round it and make their way to India. Dias, in fact, went on several other voyages before being lost at sea very close to the Cape of Good Hope itself in 1500.

CAN YOU SAY?

5. Why did the Portuguese want to find the southern tip of Africa?
6. What were the old names for Benin and Ghana?
7. What was Bartolomeu Dias's ship called?
8. In the above picture of Dias and Diogo Cão (**Source C**):
    (a) What was the pillar that they are putting in place called?
    (b) What was the purpose of these pillars?
9. (a) What name did Dias give to the cape at the tip of Africa?
    (b) What name was given to it later?
10. Why was King John unwilling to listen to Christopher Columbus, in your opinion?

VASCO DA GAMA AND THE ROUTE TO INDIA

Portugal's preparations for the voyage to India were interrupted by the death of King John in 1495. However, his successor, Manuel I, took up the idea and gave the job to Vasco da Gama in 1497.

Knowing that this voyage, if successful, would probably be the longest sea journey ever undertaken, da Gama chose larger ships than the traditional caravels. One of his four ships, the *Berrio*, was a caravel for exploring awkward and uncharted coastal regions. Two of the others were larger *naos*, better for holding necessary supplies and, hopefully, valuable cargoes on the return journey; these ships were called the *São Gabriel* and the *São Raphael*. A fourth, giant store ship was brought part of the way, but then abandoned along the African coast.

Because Dias and others already had mapped accurately the coast and pinpointed the location of the Cape of Good

Vasco da Gama.

Hope, da Gama and his men were able to sail directly from the tip of West Africa (Cape Palmas) to the Cape of Good Hope. They reached the Cape in November 1497 and continued beyond the point Dias had reached, erecting *padrãos* as they went. On Christmas Day, they reached the shores of a land they called **Natal**, in honour of the birth of Christ (the Nativity).

The voyage had already lasted several months and the ships had been unable to stock up on fresh food for lengthy periods, so many crew members had begun to suffer from a disease called **scurvy**. This is caused by a shortage of vitamin C. This vitamin is best found in fresh fruit and vegetables, but it was impossible to store these on a 15th-century ship for more than a few days. Scurvy caused the sailors' joints to swell up, their gums to swell and rot, and their bodies to be covered in sores. Without fresh food, death was inevitable.

Sailing up the east coast of southern Africa, da Gama's expedition reached Mozambique in March 1498, where they picked up valuable information regarding the sea route from there to India. At this time, Arab traders sold gold, gems and spices between India and east Africa.

Arrival in India

After a voyage of 23 days from what is now Kenya, da Gama reached the Indian port of Calicut in May 1498, completing one of the most important voyages in history. While the locals – experienced traders themselves – were not as fond of cheap brass bells and hats as the west Africans, da Gama managed to buy cargoes of spices for the return voyage.

Bad weather made the voyage back to the African coast last nearly three months. So many sailors died of scurvy that da Gama destroyed the *São Raphael*, taking the remainder of its crew on the other two ships. When they finally reached Portugal again in September 1498, it was to a great welcome. King Manuel gave da Gama a pension of 1,000 cruzados a year and knighted him. In a letter to the rulers of Spain, King Manuel boasted that da Gama had brought back *'great quantities of cloves, cinnamon and other spices...rubies and all kinds of precious stones ... they also found lands in which there are mines of gold.'*

Da Gama's ships in the port of Calicut.

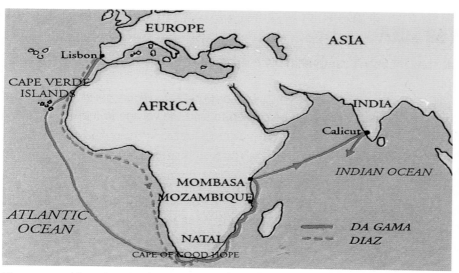

The voyages of Bartolomeu Dias and Vasco da Gama.

Results of da Gama's Voyage

The king may have exaggerated somewhat the value of da Gama's cargo. However, the voyage paved the way for hundreds of similar voyages by the Portuguese, often beyond India to the Spice Islands and China. Over the next century, Portugal became one of Europe's wealthiest and most powerful nations, remarkable when you consider that its entire population in 1500 was barely one million, roughly that of Dublin today.

A small section of the Vasco da Gama bridge in Lisbon today.

Though their army was never as powerful as those of larger European nations such as France and Spain, the Portuguese were able to take over many of the territories that they discovered and these became Portuguese **colonies**. Places such as Guinea, Angola, Mozambique and Goa (in India) remained the property of the Portuguese Empire for centuries.

It is hard to overestimate the role of Portugal in ship design, navigational techniques and voyages of discovery. As we now turn to look at the two great 'Spanish' explorers of the day, it is worth remembering something. One of them (**Columbus**) received most of his training as an ocean voyager while in Portugal, whereas the other (**Magellan**) was, in fact, from Portugal.

CAN YOU SAY?

11. Name the European country that discovered the sea route to India around the year 1500.

   (Junior Certificate Higher Level 2002 and 2004)

12. Why was da Gama fortunate to be chosen to lead the voyage to India?
13. Which *one* of his ships was a caravel?
14. Why was the land of Natal so called?
15. What causes the disease of scurvy?
16. Having read **Source C**, what do you think was King Manuel's main interest in da Gama's voyage?
17. What is a colony? Name *one* of Portugal's.
18. Name any method used by European sailors in the Age of Discovery to find their way across the oceans. *(Junior Certificate Ordinary Level 1993)*
19. Name *one* geographical explorer and *one* place he discovered.

   (Junior Certificate Ordinary Level 1998)

KEYNOTES

1. **Henry the Navigator:** Ceuta ● Prester John ● Sagres ● Cape Bojador ● Gil Eanes ● Senegal River ● cruzados ● Azores
2. **King John II:** Diogo Cão ● *padrãos*
   Bartolomeu Dias: *São Cristóvão* ● Cape of Storms/Good Hope
3. **Vasco da Gama:** *Berrio* ● *São Gabriel* ● *São Raphael* ● Natal ● scurvy ● Calicut ● Spice Islands ● colonies
   Portuguese influence on: Columbus ● Magellan

MINI-PROJECT

List five difficulties which Portugal's sailors had to overcome in their voyages, and then five ways in which Portugal benefited from those voyages.

Or

Write an account of Portugal's contribution to the Age of Exploration.

Write at least eight points.

   (Junior Certificate Higher Level 2003)

Although it was certainly the Portuguese who led the way in the Age of Exploration, probably the two most important individual voyages of discovery were sponsored by Portugal's neighbour, Spain.

CHRISTOPHER COLUMBUS (1451–1506)

The Early Years

Christopher Columbus was born in **Genoa** in 1451. Living in one of the great Italian seafaring cities, this son of a wool trader and innkeeper went to sea at the age of 14. Over the next ten years, he made many voyages on Genoese merchant ships around the **Mediterranean**, gaining in experience all the time.

In 1476, Columbus signed on as a crewman of a Flemish ship on the Atlantic route from the Mediterranean to Belgium. However, he was shipwrecked en route and swam ashore to the coast of **Portugal**. His brother, Bartolomeo, was already working there as a map-maker and Christopher spent most of the next nine years learning about Atlantic sailing and navigation from the experts.

East Is Really West!

Columbus gained more Atlantic experience on a voyage to Iceland in 1477, during which he stopped at Galway. Legend has it that Columbus saw two bodies washed ashore in Galway. They were of Asiatic appearance and apparently set him wondering about how these 'eastern' people could have drifted to Ireland on currents from the west.

> **DID YOU KNOW?**
>
> The statue of Columbus in Barcelona has the famous explorer pointing to the sea. However, as Barcelona is on the eastern coast of Spain, this means that Columbus is actually pointing east, away from the direction he intended to sail in.

By now, most people accepted that the world was round, but Columbus was convinced that Asia lay quite close to Europe, not to the east, but across the Atlantic to the west. Inspired by the writings of Marco Polo, Columbus believed Japan (**Cipangu**) lay about 2,500 kilometres east of China (**Cathay**) and so was 2,500 kilometres closer to the west of Europe.

The Italian map-maker **Paolo Toscanelli** had encouraged Columbus in 1474 with a 'map' showing Japan to be less than 4,000 kilometres west of Portugal, within reach of a caravel. Toscanelli wrote to Columbus:

> **SOURCE A**
>
> *I esteem your noble and grand desire to navigate from the east to the west...for the said voyage is not only possible, but is sure and certain.*

Sponsorship

Columbus approached King John of Portugal with the idea. However, most experts thought that Asia lay at least 16,000 kilometres to the west, much too far for a non-stop voyage. With Portugal's own sailors on the verge of finding the eastern route to Asia, the king rejected Columbus' plans. He was rejected elsewhere too, including in England.

Columbus then tried Spain, but its rulers, **King Ferdinand** and **Queen Isabella**, were busy with a war against the Moors in southern Spain. For seven years, Columbus made his case; finally, when the Moors had been defeated at Granada in January 1492, Queen Isabella agreed to sponsor a voyage.

Preparations

Royal proclamations ordered the people of the port of **Palos** to provide a crew for Columbus. Although some still believed that the Earth was flat – and that Columbus would sail over the edge – or that terrible creatures existed across the ocean, most simply feared that the journey would be too long and that those who went would be lost in the open sea or die of scurvy.

Columbus was helped by two brothers from Palos, Martin and Vicente **Pinzon**, and, through their urgings, nearly 80 crew members signed on, some as young as 12.

DID YOU KNOW?

Despite the popular legend, Columbus, in fact, never took crew members from Spanish jails. He did take four men who were on the run and these were granted royal pardons, but no more.

The Explorers of Spain

Columbus was given three ships – two caravels called the *Pinta* and the *Nina*, and a larger *nao*, the *Santa Maria*. He appointed the Pinzons as captains of the smaller vessels and chose the *Santa Maria* as his own flagship. The people of Palos also gave supplies, including one-and-a-half tonnes of hard flat bread, made with salt to preserve it, one tonne of strong local wine, salted meat, dried fish, garlic, beans and rice.

SOURCE B

A replica of the *Santa Maria* in the harbour at Barcelona, which has been destroyed by fire since this picture was taken.

CAN YOU SAY?

1. Where was Columbus born?
2. Where did he get his first sailing experience?
3. How did a visit to Galway apparently influence Columbus?
4. In **Source A** above, what words do you think were most encouraging for Columbus?
5. What rulers agreed to sponsor Columbus?
6. Who captained the *Nina* and *Pinta*?
7. Using **Source B** above, give *three* differences between the *Santa Maria* and a modern ship.
8. This (**Source C**, page 194) is a copy of Toscanelli's map, which influenced Columbus. Study it and answer the questions below.
   (a) Why was the map of the west coast of Africa so detailed?
   (b) Mention *two* errors on the western side of the map.
   (c) Describe the principal fears of the sailors on Columbus's first voyage of discovery.
   (Junior Certificate Higher Level 1994)

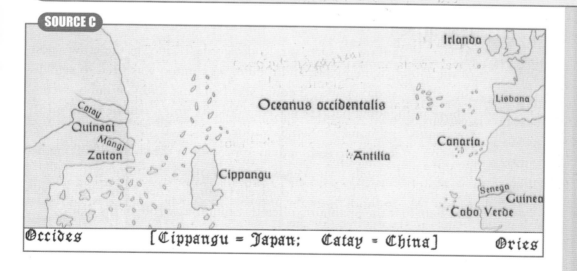

SOURCE C

Irlanda

Oceanus occidentalis

Lisbona

Catay
Quinsai
Mangi
Zaiton

Canaria

Antilia

Cippangu

Senega
Guinea
Cabo Verde

Occides   [Cippangu = Japan;   Catay = China]   Ories

The Voyage

The three ships set sail from Palos on 3 August, 1492. At the Canary Islands, repairs to a rudder and some sail changes took place; square sails replaced lateens to make best use of the winds blowing west below the Canaries. Then they sailed southwards to catch the winds for the voyage west. The weather was fine and the crew caught tuna fish. However, after 18 days at sea, many felt that they had gone far enough and should return before supplies ran out. The threat by Martin Pinzon to hang six of them from the mainmast of the *Santa Maria* prevented a mutiny.

The ships sailed further and found the sea to be a mass of floating weeds. The sailors christened it the **Sargasso** (seaweed) **Sea** – still the home of much of the world's eel population. Amid continuous grumbling, Columbus begged the crews to go on and often lied to them about how far they had actually travelled. Even the Pinzons feared that, at the very least, they were sailing at the wrong latitude and forced Columbus to turn south-west on 7 October. On two evenings, they thought they saw land, only for it to have disappeared by the next morning. Columbus wrote:

> **SOURCE D**
>
> *The people could stand it no longer and complained of the long voyage; but I cheered them as best I could, holding out fond hope of the rewards they would have. I added that it was useless to complain; I had come to go to the mainland of the west and so had to continue until I found it, with the help of our Lord. (9 October)*

Land, at Last!

At last, at 2am on 12 October, Roderigo de Triano, in the crow's nest of the *Pinta*, sighted land, and the *Pinta's* cannon was fired to signal the others. At daybreak, all could see the island and Columbus went ashore in the longboat. He placed a crucifix and a flag of Spain on the island, and named it **San Salvador**.

Soon after their arrival, natives appeared on the shore. Thinking he had reached islands near Asia, Columbus called them 'Indians'. They were happy to trade their gold jewellery for the cheap glass beads, bells and hats that the Spaniards offered. Columbus wrote in his diary:

SOURCE E

> *The whole of the island is so green that it is a pleasure to gaze upon, and these people are very docile. They ought to be good servants.*

Columbus later kidnapped six of the local people and brought them back to Spain for exhibition. The next three months were spent exploring islands near San Salvador, including **Cuba** and **Hispaniola**.

The awkward *Santa Maria* ran aground on Christmas Day 1492 and Columbus had a fort built on the shore using its timbers. Leaving 39 men in the fort, the remaining ships returned home to a great welcome in March 1493.

Columbus went on three more voyages to what the Spaniards called the **New World**. On the third of these, he reached the mainland of what he thought was Asia. He was never to learn the truth. Unfortunately, when appointed Governor of the New World, Columbus failed to control either the Spanish settlers or the 'Indians' and was brought home in chains on charges of ill-treating the natives. He lived out the rest of his life in disgrace, a forgotten man.

Columbus lands in the New World.

SOURCE F

Sunday, 14 October. *In the morning, I ordered the boats to be got ready, and coasted along the island toward the north-northeast to examine that part of it, we having landed first at the eastern part. Soon we discovered two or three villages, and the people all came down to the shore, calling out to us, and giving thanks to God.*

Some brought us water, and others food. Others seeing that I was not disposed to land, plunged into the sea and swam out to us. An old man came on board my boat; the others, both men and women cried with loud voices —'Come and see the men who have come from heaven. Bring them victuals and food'.

I set out in the morning, for I wished to give a complete report to your Highnesses, and also to find where a fort might be built. However, I do not now see the need to fortify the place, as the people here are simple in war-like matters.

Your Highnesses will see this by those seven men which I have ordered to be taken and carried to Spain in order to learn our language and return. I could conquer the whole of them with fifty men and govern them as I pleased.

DID YOU KNOW?

Columbus later refused to give Roderigo de Triano the promised reward for sighting land, claiming he had seen the island himself four hours earlier, but had said nothing.

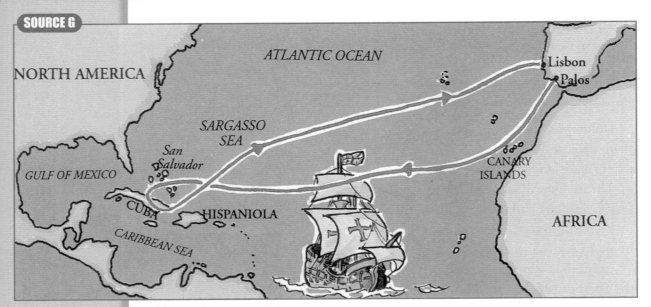

SOURCE G

The first voyage of Columbus to the New World in 1492.

Others – whom we will meet in the next chapter – would build on Columbus's achievement.

Columbus had not landed in Asia at all but, rather, on a continent, America, which no Europeans knew of in 1492. Explorers after him soon realised that this was a completely 'New World'. In 1513, a Spaniard named Vasco de Balboa found that, on the western side of the New World, lay another great ocean, stretching as far as the eye could see. Beyond it, surely, lay Asia.

CAN YOU SAY?

9. From which port did Columbus set sail?
10. How did Martin Pinzon prevent a mutiny?
11. Why was the Sargasso Sea so called?
12. (a) What does Columbus's diary entry (**Source D**) tell us about his personality?
    (b) What does Columbus's diary entry (**Source E**) tell us about his attitude to the natives?
13. Name the sailor on the *Pinta* who first sighted land.
14. What did Columbus call the first island?
15. **Source F** is from an account by Christopher Columbus of his voyage in 1492.
    (i) Which part of the island did Columbus explore on Sunday morning?
    (ii) From the account, give one piece of evidence to show that the people of the island welcomed Columbus.
    (iii) How many of the island men did Columbus order to be taken to Spain?
    (Junior Certificate Ordinary Level 2006)
16. Looking at the map, **Source G**, can you explain why Columbus went so far south before sailing west? Re-read the text for a clue if you have difficulties.
17. Explain how the natives of the American continent came to be described as Indians.
    (Junior Certificate Ordinary and Higher Levels 1996)

FERDINAND MAGELLAN (1480–1521)

The Early Years

Ferdinand Magellan was the son of Portuguese noble. When his father died, Ferdinand became a page at the court of King John II of Portugal. Here he developed his love for the sea and learnt about navigation. He was at court when Vasco da Gama left for India in 1498, and wanted adventure and wealth for himself.

After da Gama's great voyage, Portugal sent hundreds of ships and thousands of soldiers to the east, establishing trade links and, where possible, colonies. From 1504 to 1511, the young Magellan served as both a sailor and soldier in the **East Indies**, helping to defeat Arab traders who had controlled the spice trade up to then. Magellan commanded one of the ships in the first ever European expedition to the Moluccas – called the **Spice Islands** in 1511.

Back in Portugal, Magellan quarrelled with his king, Manuel, and after some years without receiving any job as, captain (a **commission**), he went to Spain. Since Balboa's discovery of the new ocean beyond America, Spanish explorers had sought a southern route around the American continent, a cape, to reach the east as Columbus had planned.

Ferdinand Magellan.

Preparations

In 1519, Magellan won a commission from King Charles V of Spain to find the elusive cape and sail to the Spice Islands, westwards. For such a lengthy voyage, Magellan chose *naos* rather than caravels, and was given five ships in very bad repair. They were called the *Santiago*, *Victoria*, *Concepcion*, *San Antonio* and his own flagship, the *Trinidad*.

The combined crews numbered 280 men and boys. Most were Spanish, though some came from as far away as Malaysia. One of the crew was from Venice. He was called Antonio Pigafetta and his diary of events has become a valuable primary source of information about the voyage. Magellan stocked the ships with enough supplies for two years. Vast quantities of provisions were taken on board, including ten tonnes of salted meat, fish, garlic, cheese and beans. Seven cows and three pigs were taken to provide some fresh meat on the first leg of the journey. Added to all this were tonnes of trading goods,

DID YOU KNOW?

Magellan was wounded in battle on a number of occasions; following a lance wound to his knee when fighting for Portugal against the Moors (1513), he was left with a limp for the rest of his life.

weapons, equipment for navigation and repairs, and even, according to Pigafetta, 'five drums and twenty tambourines given to the people of the fleet to serve for their pastime'.

The First Stage of the Voyage

The fleet set sail on 20 September 1519. Magellan soon had problems. He was Portuguese, leading a Spanish expedition, and he was not trusted by the Spanish captains of the *Victoria*, *Concepcion*

While crossing the Atlantic, Magellan's ships encountered very stormy weather.

and *San Antonio*. He could rely only on the captain of the *Santiago*, his lifelong friend from Portugal, **Juan Serrano**.

After a six-day voyage to the Canaries, the fleet sailed down the African coast. Magellan then spent almost two months crossing the Atlantic in terrible weather before reaching the coast of South America on 29 November 1519. There he found the natives friendly and anxious to trade. Pigafetta noted that it was possible to buy five chickens from them for a fish-hook or two geese for a comb.

The fleet sailed southwards along the coast in search of the cape or passageway (**strait**) which would lead beyond America. In January, they found a bay that they named **Rio de Janeiro** ('River of January').

In late March 1520, the fleet anchored at St Julian's Bay for repairs and supplies. Here, with the southern winter approaching, Magellan's Spanish captains wanted to return home – he had already replaced the captain of one ship in mid-Atlantic. Now he faced a mutiny in three of his five ships.

One biographer of the time explained:

> **SOURCE H**
>
> *The crew began to murmur about the eternal hatred between the Portuguese and the Spaniards and about Magellan being Portuguese. He, they suggested, might best win glory in his own country by working to wreck this fleet.*

In the middle of the night, Magellan and loyal crewmen attacked the mutineers and won back control of the fleet. The last of them to surrender was Sebastian del Cano of the *Concepcion*, who we will hear of again.

CAN YOU SAY?

18. In what country was Ferdinand Magellan born?
19. Which king gave Magellan his five ships?
20. Why were some of Magellan's captains unhappy with him?
21. Why is Antonio Pigafetta important to historians?
22. Why was Rio de Janeiro given that name?
23. Who was the captain of the *Concepcion*?
24. In **Source H** above:
    (a) Why did the crew members not trust Magellan?
    (b) What did they think Magellan might do to win glory?

Searching for the Straits

Sailing southwards, the *Santiago* was lost in an April storm. Pigafetta wrote of strange sights never before seen by Europeans – penguins, walruses and even tall, big-footed natives – in what is now southern Argentina. To this day, that region is known as **Patagonia**, the 'land of the big foot'.

The Straits of Magellan.

Finally, in October 1520, a wide strait was discovered and the fleet slowly made its way through. It took a month for the ships, sailing at an average speed below one knot, to reach the end of this strait, which was full of rocks and dangerous currents. Magellan called the island to the south **Tierra del Fuego** (Land of Fire) because its natives kept fires burning night and day on the hillsides.

The Pacific

At last, the ships reached a vast, calm sea. Magellan christened it the **Pacific** (peaceful) **Ocean**; to this day, the straits he sailed through are known as the **Magellan Straits**. His joy, however, was short-lived – Magellan soon found that the *San Antonio*, which carried most of the provisions, had turned around in the straits and sailed back to Spain. However, the remaining ships set sail across the new ocean, which Pigafetta tells us:

> ### SOURCE I
>
> *Well was it named the Pacific, for during this time we met with no storm.*

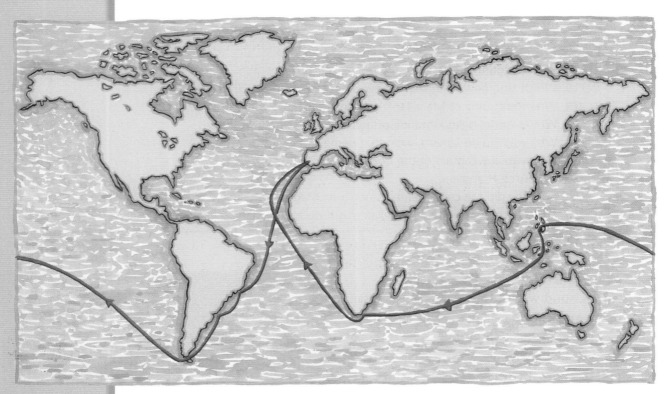

The route of Magellan/Del Cano circumnavigation of the Earth.

The crew saw shoals of flying fish; Pigafetta described how they used to:

> **SOURCE J**
>
> *spring from the water and fly about a bowshot so long as their wings are wet and then regain the sea.*

However, only two tiny, uninhabited islands were sighted in three months. Conditions on board were dreadful; 19 men died of scurvy. Pigafetta recorded:

> **SOURCE K**
>
> *We ate biscuit, but in truth it was ... a powder full of worms... We also had to make use of sawdust as food and rats became such a delicacy that we paid half a ducat a piece for them.*

Even strips of leather from the yard-arms were eaten, having been softened first by being towed over the stern of the ship for five days.

The Philippines

Finally, in March 1521, the three ships reached the islands now known as the Philippines. Magellan claimed the islands for Spain and converted the king of one of them, Cebu, to Christianity. Magellan also agreed to help him crush a rival pagan king on the island of Mactan. However, as a small force of Spaniards led by Magellan landed on Mactan, they were met by a force of, according to Pigafetta, several thousand natives. As his men retreated to the boats, Magellan was wounded in the face, leg and arm by the natives and died near the beach beneath a hail of blows.

With less than half of the original crew remaining, the fleet left the Philippines and spent three months trading in the Spice Islands. Here they bought cloves, ginger, pepper, silks and gems before heading home. By now, the *Concepcion* was beyond repair, so it was abandoned. Then, in late 1521, the *Trinidad* began to leak badly. Its crew stayed in the Spice Islands, while the *Victoria*, captained by Magellan's one-time enemy, Sebastian del Cano, headed for home.

Homeward Bound

The voyage home was undertaken along the well-known Portuguese route around Africa. Magellan's voyage had shown that the westwards route to the Spice Islands was just too long to make it worthwhile. Del Cano and 17 survivors reached Seville on September 1522, completing the first ever **circumnavigation** of Earth. Pigafetta had survived the entire journey and he finished his account by telling us how he:

> **SOURCE L**
>
> *presented to his sacred Majesty, King Charles, neither gold nor silver, but things more precious in the eyes of so great a sovereign. I presented to him ... a book written by my hand of all the things that had occurred day by day in our voyage.*

CAN YOU SAY?

25. Why was Tierra del Fuego given this name?
26. Why did Magellan call the ocean the Pacific?
27. According to Pigafetta:
    (a) In **Source I**, why was the Pacific Ocean well named?
    (b) What do you think the word 'bowshot' means in **Source J**?
    (c) What detail in **Source K** shows us how important rats were as food?
    (d) What information in **Source L** proves that Pigafetta's work is a primary source?
28. On what island was Magellan killed?
29. Who commanded the final voyage home?
30. What does the word **circumnavigation** mean?
31. Name *one* famous explorer and say why his journey of exploration was important.

    (Junior Certificate Ordinary Level 1994)

32. Select *one* named voyage that you have studied. Write the name of the voyage.
    (a) Name the ruler(s) who sponsored the voyage.
    (b) Name the sailor(s) who led the voyage.
    (c) Describe the consequences (results) of the voyage.

    (Junior Certificate Higher Level 2000)

KEYNOTES

1. **Columbus:** Genoa ● Mediterranean ● Portugal ● Polo's influence ● Toscanelli's map ● Ferdinand and Isabella ● Palos ● Pinzon brothers ● *Santa Maria* ● *Pinta* ● *Nina*
2. **The voyage:** Canaries ● Sargasso Sea ● Roderigo de Triano ● San Salvador ● 'Indians' ● Cuba ● Hispaniola ● three further voyages ● 'New World'
3. **Magellan:** Balboa's discovery ● Portugal ● Spice Islands ● Charles V ● five ships ● *Victoria* ● *Trinidad* ● Pigafetta ● Serrano
4. **The voyage:** South America ● Rio de Janeiro ● St Julian's Bay ● mutiny ● Patagonia ● Straits of Magellan ● Tierra del Fuego ● Pacific Ocean ● Philippines ● death on Mactan ● del Cano ● Spice Islands ● circumnavigation

MINI-PROJECT

Write an account of the following: *A named leader of a geographical exploration.*
Hints:

● reasons for the exploration
● problems during the exploration
● the area explored
● the results of the exploration

(Junior Certificate 1995 and 1999 – both levels – Higher Level 2009, and Ordinary Level 2001 and 2002, with different hints)

Or

Write an account of: *A sailor on a voyage of discovery during the Age of Exploration.*

(2006 Higher Level paper; no hints given)

Note: *Higher Level questions now tend to have few, if any, hints with them. You will find more results in the next chapter, but try to think of some without looking at it.*

After the Discoveries

Magellan's voyage, completed by del Cano, proved that the world was round. Despite the difficulties encountered, especially in the Pacific, the voyage helped to destroy people's fear of the unknown and their superstitions about sea monsters and whirlpools. Thus, it encouraged more exploration and further discoveries. Yet, ultimately, the voyage of Columbus probably had an even greater effect on the world.

POSSIBLE CONFLICT

Columbus, on three later voyages, landed on many more islands – Puerto Rico, Jamaica, Trinidad and others – and finally on the American continent itself. Fears grew that Spain and Portugal would end up at war with each other, especially as it was then believed that Columbus's discoveries lay very close to those places beyond Africa that the Portuguese were trying to reach. Wishing to avoid war and ensure that all newly found peoples would be converted to Christianity, Pope Alexander VI (see Chapter 16) drew up an agreement between Spain and Portugal.

In the **Treaty of Tordesillas** (1494), an imaginary line was drawn from north to south through the Atlantic Ocean, roughly 2,000 kilometres west of the Cape Verde Islands. Spain claimed all discoveries west of this line, and anything to the east, including Africa, was Portugal's. Thanks to this, major disputes between the countries over their discoveries were rare.

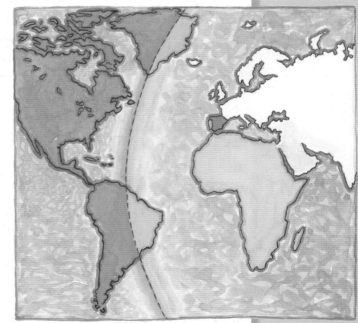

Under the Treaty of Tordesillas, lands in the New World were divided between Spain (red) and Portugal (yellow).

*Amerigo Vespucci
(1454–1512)*

AMERIGO VESPUCCI'S EVIDENCE

Apart from Columbus, Spain sent many other explorers westwards to the New World. One of these was another Italian, **Amerigo Vespucci** from Florence. He made several voyages between 1497 and 1504 – one on behalf of Portugal. Vespucci is usually credited as the first to realise that this New World was an entirely new continent (in 1502), not just the furthest end of Asia as Columbus had believed.

Unlike Columbus, Vespucci wrote accounts of his travels to the New World. When these were first published in 1507 as *Quattuor Americi Navigationes* (*Four American Voyages*), Vespucci's fame spread and it is widely believed that the name **America**, which was given to the entire continent, was based on his Christian name. Vespucci wrote in 1497:

SOURCE A

Amongst those people we did not learn that they had any law, nor can they be called Moors nor Jews, and they are worse than pagans: because we did not observe that they offered any sacrifice: nor even had they a house of prayer: their manner of living I judge to be luxurious: their dwellings are in common: and their houses made in the style of huts, but strongly made, and constructed with very large trees, and covered over with palm-leaves, secure against storms and winds: and in some places [they are] of so great breadth and length, that in one single house we found there were 600 souls: and we saw a village of thirteen houses where there were four thousand souls: every eight or ten years they change their habitations: and when asked why did so: [they said it was] because of the soil which, from its filthiness, was already unhealthy and corrupted, that it bred aches in their bodies, which seemed to us a good reason... in fine, they live and are contented with that which nature gives them. The wealth that we enjoy in this our Europe and elsewhere, such as gold, jewels, pearls, and other riches, they hold as nothing: and although they have them in their own lands, they do not labour to obtain them, nor do they value them.

DID YOU KNOW?

Like so many important Renaissance figures, Vespucci also came from Florence. Although his home city is not even built on the sea, a statue commemorates the explorer outside the Uffizi Gallery to this day.

More evidence of the results of discoveries comes to us in a letter from the year 1500 from Vespucci to his patron, the famous Lorenzo de Medici.

SOURCE B

Letter from Amerigo Vespucci to his patron Lorenzo de Medici (1500).

We were absent thirteen months on this voyage, exposing ourselves to terrible dangers, and discovering a very large part of Asia, and a great many islands, most of them inhabited. According to the calculations I have several times made with the compass, we sailed about five thousand leagues…We discovered immense regions, saw a vast number of people all naked, and speaking various languages. On the land we saw many wild animals, various kinds of birds, and an infinite number of trees, all aromatic.

We brought home pearls in their growing state, and gold in the grain. We brought two stones, one of emerald, the other of amethyst, which was very hard, at least half a span long and three fingers thick. The sovereigns esteem them most highly, and have preserved them among their jewels…We brought many other stones which appeared beautiful to us, but of all these we did not bring a large quantity, as we were continually busy in our navigation, and did not stay long in any one place.

When we arrived in Cadiz, we sold many slaves. Finding two hundred remaining to us…thirty-two having died at sea... However, we are satisfied with having saved our lives, and thank God that during the whole voyage, out of fifty-seven Christian men, which was our number, only two had died, having been killed by the Indians.

(Source: The Oxford Book of Exploration, p. 327)

CAN YOU SAY?

1. What was agreed at the Treaty of Tordesillas?
2. Why do you think America was called after Vespucci rather than Columbus?
3. Read the first extract above from Vespucci (**Source A**):
   (a) Give *one* reason why Vespucci said that the people whom he had discovered were 'worse than pagans'.
   (b) Why did they change 'their habitations' every eight to ten years?
   (c) What is the difference in attitude to wealth between the Europeans and the people described in the extract?
   (d) Give *two* reasons why the rulers and merchants of European countries were prepared to sponsor voyages of exploration such as that of Vespucci.

   (Junior Certificate Higher Level 2000)
4. Based on your reading of **Source B** above from Vespucci:
   (a) How far did Vespucci and his crew sail?
   (b) Mention *two* things they discovered.
   (c) Name *two* things they brought back.
   (d) Why did so many slaves die on the voyage?
   (e) Why did rich patrons like de Medici sponsor voyages such as this?

   (Junior Certificate Higher Level 2005)

CONQUEST

As Europeans pushed further and further inland, they came to realise the tremendous rewards that could be reaped in the New World. So, in the first half of the 16th century, in the case of Spain in particular, explorers were soon followed by armies.

Their job was to **conquer** the rich native kingdoms for Spain. These armies were known as **conquistadores**. Let's take a look at the two most famous of them.

Hernando Cortes (1485–1547)

Hernando Cortes made a name for himself as a soldier in the West Indies, helping in the Spanish conquest of Cuba in 1511. He also had further ambitions, inspired by native tales of a great empire on the American mainland, with vast amounts of gold and other valuables.

Tenochtitlan, the Aztec capital, the site of Mexico City today.

Despite opposition from the Spanish Governor of Cuba, Cortes decided to launch an expedition to invade this great empire, controlled by a tribe called the **Aztecs**, and situated where **Mexico** lies today.

Cortes raised a fleet of 11 ships with around 100 sailors, 500 soldiers and 16 horses. They sailed for the mainland in February 1519. On landing, Cortes ordered the ships to be burnt in order to prevent any of his men from deserting and returning to Cuba. The first tribes that the Spaniards met were terrified of their horses and six cannons. These tribes presented Cortes with a captured princess whom the Spaniards christened Doña Marina. She proved very useful to Cortes, especially as she was fluent in the Aztec language, Nahuatl.

The Aztec capital, **Tenochtitlan**, was a great city built on a network of islands by a lake shore. Cortes was impressed. The Spaniards saw great pyramid-style temples and found that the Aztecs could read, make fine clothing and jewellery, and had worked out a very accurate calendar. On the other hand, they still believed in human sacrifice and were unable to make iron or wheels. One Spaniard described an Aztec sacrifice to the gods:

> **SOURCE C**
>
> *They cut open the wretched Indian's chest with flint knives and … rip out the bleeding heart … They cut off the arms and head and eat the arms and … they put the heart on a rack.*

The Aztecs' beliefs proved helpful to Cortes, for their priests had told them of a great pale-skinned god called **Quetzalcoatl**. When Cortes arrived, the Aztec king **Montezuma**, and soon the whole tribe, accepted him as Quetzalcoatl. It was only when Cortes's men began stealing gold and jewellery that their doubts arose. Cortes placed Montezuma in chains to frighten the people. This did not work, however, and in mid-1520 the Spaniards were driven out of Tenochtitlan by the Aztecs, who stoned Montezuma to death for welcoming them in the first place. Many Spaniards were killed, some by having molten gold poured down their throats.

The meeting between Cortes and Montezuma.

Cortes regrouped his forces away from Tenochtitlan and found allies among tribes ruled by the Aztecs. Then, in 1521, the Spaniards returned to capture Tenochtitlan and butcher the Aztecs. One Spaniard claimed 'the lake was full of heads and corpses'. Up to this time, Cortes had acted against the wishes of his superiors and without the permission of the king of Spain, Charles V. Defeating the Aztecs led to him being forgiven and he was made Governor of **New Spain**, as Mexico was called. Tenochtitlan became **Mexico City**.

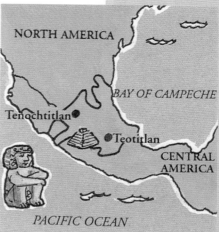

The Aztec Empire.

CAN YOU SAY?

5. Which European country did Hernando Cortes come from?
6. Why did Cortes burn his boats on landing in Mexico?
7. Name (a) the Aztec leader and (b) the Aztec capital.
8. Give *one reason each* why **Source C** above may or may not be reliable.
9. Give *three* reasons for the Spaniards' victory over the Aztecs.

Francisco Pizarro (1475–1541)

Francisco Pizarro was another Spaniard who gained vast experience of the New World in the early 16th century. He had even accompanied Balboa on the expedition that reached the Pacific in 1513. However, unlike Cortes, when Pizarro heard stories of a great, rich empire in South America, he returned to Spain and got official backing from King Charles V for an expedition to conquer it.

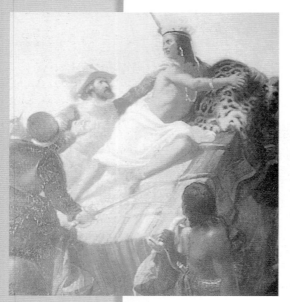

Pizarro's capture of Atahualpa.

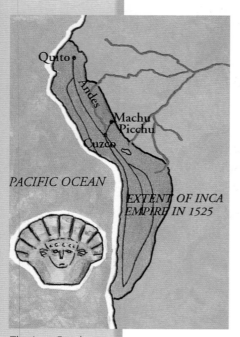

The Inca Empire on the west coast of South America.

In 1529, Pizarro was appointed governor of the land south of Panama, known as **New Castile**, and in January 1531 he and his four brothers set off southwards to conquer the great tribe of Peru, the **Incas**.

The Incas were more advanced in many respects than the Aztecs. They had a well-organised system of government, good roads and buildings, and produced magnificent artwork in gold and silver. However, like the Aztecs, they had never before seen horses, armour or cannons.

Even though Pizarro's force numbered only 180 men and 37 horses, he routed an Inca army of several thousand at Cajamarca and took their emperor, **Atahualpa**, prisoner. The Incas then surrounded Cajamarca, but did not attack because Atahualpa was being held hostage. Although a ransom of an entire room full of gold and silver was paid for his release, the emperor was strangled on Pizarro's orders. The Incas retreated in confusion and Pizarro made an alliance with one of Atahualpa's enemies named **Manco Capac**. The Spaniards continued to the Inca capital of Cuzco and proclaimed Manco Capac as leader (**Inca**) in 1533.

The Incas were basically a peace-loving people. With fresh reinforcements from Spanish-controlled Panama, and with the loyalty of Manco Capac, the Spaniards quickly took over the entire Inca Empire. Pizarro established a Spanish capital of Peru at **Lima** and, until his death in 1541, helped to spread Spain's control throughout most of South America.

CAN YOU SAY?

10. How did Pizarro's preparations for his expedition differ from those of Cortes?
11. Name (a) the Inca leader and (b) the Inca capital.
12. What did Pizarro do to the Inca leader?
13. What was the Spanish capital of Peru?
14. **Source D** below shows that it did not take long before other countries followed the lead of Spanish explorers and conquistadors. Read it and answer the following questions:
    (a) Give *two* reasons why the writer encouraged voyages of discovery by English sailors.
    (b) Mention *two* dangers sailors faced on voyages such as these.

(Junior Certificate Higher Level 2005)

DID YOU KNOW?

The Incas were far more advanced than the Europeans in some ways. They gave pensions to the old and disabled, some 350 years before most European countries did so!

SOURCE D

Richard Hakluyt, *The Principal Navigations, Voyages and Discoveries of the English Nation, 1589–1600.*

The kings of Spain and Portugal have enlarged their kingdoms, greatly enriched themselves and their subjects, and trebled the size of their navies. If we follow, there will be huge demand for English cloth, with great benefit for all those who work in the trade. A great number of men, but also children and women, who now have no work, will be found employment in making things which can be traded with those who live in new lands.

See what islands and ports you might find by sailing to the north-east, for it would be good that we should have the control over our own trade routes to India and China, and so bring ourselves great riches.

First and foremost…spread the happy news of Jesus to those who know nothing of him. Second…teach them about our knowledge of farming.

RESULTS OF THE DISCOVERIES

As the Spanish and Portuguese were later followed by the French, Dutch and British, huge changes occurred both in the lands they took over and in Europe itself.

Effects on the Colonies

Native civilisations were gradually destroyed by the Europeans. European rulers in the New World were there largely for the benefit of themselves and their home countries, so the natives lost out. Their lands were taken from them by European settlers who usually treated the natives badly.

While in theory, the Europeans looked after the well-being of the natives, in practice they often made **slaves** of them. As settlements in the New World grew and the demand for slave labour could not be met by the native population, millions of Africans were captured and brought to America. They worked as slaves on the coffee plantations of Brazil and the sugar plantations of the West Indies, in the silver mines of Bolivia and the cotton fields of Alabama. The first Africans to be taken directly across the Atlantic and sold into slavery were captured in 1532. From 1630 on, the demand for slaves increased. Historians believe that, over the next 200 years, 10 million Africans were sold into slavery, while 2 million died during transportation.

Natives died in their millions, either in battle, through slavery or from the many European diseases that the settlers brought with them; natives of America, Africa and the Indies had no immunity against

ailments such as influenza, measles and the common cold, let alone smallpox. In the Spanish lands alone – and the Spaniards were no worse than other colonisers – it is estimated that the number of natives dropped from 50 million in the late 15th century to little more than 4 million in the 17th century.

Europeans, especially from the Catholic countries of Spain and Portugal, brought **Christianity** with them and converted the natives. Sometimes this was done by persuasion, often by force. Missionaries from orders such as the Dominicans and Jesuits accompanied the explorers and armies, and so we find that today practically all of Central and South America is

Catholic. Many towns and cities in America have names of Christian origin, such as San Francisco, Sacramento, Sao Paulo, Santiago and hundreds more.

Native **languages** were replaced by European ones as the government, courts, schools and business dealings of the colonies were carried on in the languages of the European colonisers. Thus, Spanish and Portuguese are the languages of Central and South America, whereas English and, to a much lesser extent, French dominate in North America.

Effects on Europe

The discoveries and conquests brought about many important changes in Europe. By and large, the colonising countries achieved **great wealth**, with Spain becoming Europe's richest kingdom in the 16th century. The importance of Italy's great trading and seafaring cities began to decline at the same time. Spain itself came to be passed out in the 17th century by Britain. The British Empire became so large that it used to be said that the sun never set on it (in other words, the empire was spread all over the world, so it was always day somewhere in it).

As well as traditional products such as gold, gems, silks and spices, a huge **new array of goods** flooded into Europe. Tobacco, potatoes, pineapples and chocolate appeared there for the first time, along with drinks such as tea, coffee and rum. The English explorer and pirate Sir Walter Raleigh is credited with the introduction of tobacco into Europe and may very well have grown Europe's first potatoes on his estate near Youghal, Co. Cork, in the late 16th century.

As more European nations joined the hunt for riches and colonies, **wars** broke out between them. In the late 16th century, attacks by English ships on Spanish gold-carrying galleons were common and were one reason for Spain's disastrous attempt to invade England with the **Armada** (1588). War also broke out between the French and English in North America, and indeed rivalry over colonies and trade remained a constant source of bitterness between European nations until World War I (1914–18).

Finally, the new lands provided homes for millions of **European settlers**. South Africa, for example, became home to tens of thousands of Dutch settlers called **Boers**, who sought farmland that could not be found at home. Even people from non-conquering European lands were attracted by the opportunities that the newly discovered lands provided; it is said that there are five times as many people of Irish

> ## DID YOU KNOW?
> The world's second largest French-speaking city is Montreal (Canada), and the largest Spanish-speaking city is Mexico City (formerly Tenochtitlan). Today, there are ten times as many Portuguese speakers in Brazil as in Portugal.

> ## DID YOU KNOW?
> Despite the name, the first turkeys to appear in Europe were actually brought back from America.

descent in the United States as there are in Ireland itself, and many Irish first went to Australia as **prisoners** to penal colonies there.

SOURCE E

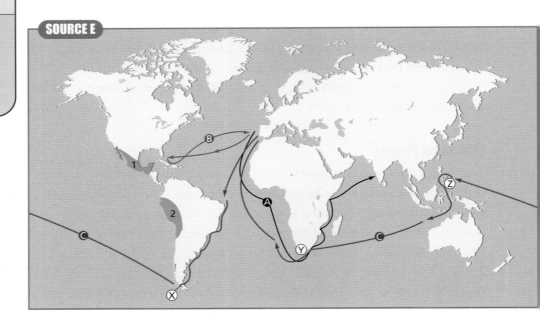

CAN YOU SAY?

15. For what products were (a) Brazil and (b) Bolivia famous?
16. Give *three* reasons why many natives died in European colonies.
17. Why are Spanish, Portuguese and English widely spoken in the Americas?
    (*Junior Certificate Higher Level 1992*)
18. What did Walter Raleigh grow at Youghal, Co. Cork?
19. Study the map in **Source E** above and answer the following questions:
    (a) Name the leader of each of the voyages of exploration marked **A**, **B**, and **C**.
    (b) Identify the straits marked **X**, the cape marked **Y** and the islands marked **Z**.
    (c) Name the civilisation in the area marked **1** that was conquered by Hernando Cortes in 1521.
    (d) Name the civilisation in the area marked **2** that was conquered by Francisco Pizarro in 1531.
    (e) Give *one* reason why the voyage of exploration marked **C** took place some years after the voyage of exploration marked **B**.
    (f) Name the rulers of Spain who sponsored the voyage of exploration marked **B**.
    (g) Select *one* of the voyages of exploration **A**, **B** or **C**, or any other exploration of your choice and discuss (i) why the exploration was undertaken, and (ii) the main consequences or results of the exploration.
    (*Junior Certificate Higher Level 1998*)

MINI-PROJECT

The following are five opinions on the voyages of discovery taken from *The Expansion of Europe, 1400–1600* (London: Longman, 1966) by Patrick Richardson. Read them carefully and then discuss *one* of these opinions:

1. They conquered, they traded and they settled.
2. Old civilisations were encountered and often destroyed.
3. The men and women of Africa and Europe, often unwillingly, moved from one continent to another.
4. Great religions came face to face and often into conflict.
5. The economy of Europe was revolutionised.

(Junior Certificate Higher Level 1994)

Or

Write an account of a native of a land discovered by Europeans during the Age of Exploration.

(Junior Certificate Higher Level 1998 and 2001)

Or

"Europe benefited, while the newly discovered lands and their peoples were exploited terribly." Do you agree? Write an account explaining your answer. Write six sentences or more.

(2003 Higher Level) (Similar question asked in Higher Level 2005.)

KEYNOTES

1. **Treaty of Tordesillas:** Spain • Portugal • Vespucci's evidence
2. **Conquistadores:** Hernando Cortes • Aztecs • Mexico • Tenochtitlan • Montezuma • Mexico City
3. **Francisco Pizarro:** Incas • Peru • Atahualpa • Cuzco • Manco Capac • Lima
4. **Results:** civilisations destroyed • slavery • native deaths • Christianity introduced • European languages • Europe affected • great wealth • new goods • rivalry and wars • settlers • prisoners

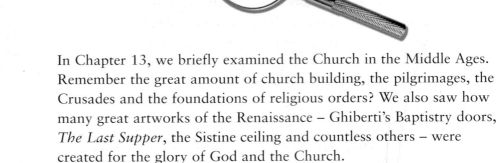

23 The Problems of the Church

In Chapter 13, we briefly examined the Church in the Middle Ages. Remember the great amount of church building, the pilgrimages, the Crusades and the foundations of religious orders? We also saw how many great artworks of the Renaissance – Ghiberti's Baptistry doors, *The Last Supper*, the Sistine ceiling and countless others – were created for the glory of God and the Church.

Yet, despite all these examples of the Church's popularity, there were many problems. We read about schisms, heresies and corruption. During the Renaissance, these problems got worse. Over the next four chapters, we will look at the problems and at the major changes that took place in the Christian world as a result. These events are called the **Reformation**.

ABUSES

We learnt earlier that a major reason for the foundation of the Cistercians and other strict monastic orders was the fear that many clergymen had become lazy and greedy. Although the new orders were successful in attracting devout, dedicated men and women to religious life, there always remained unsatisfactory clerics in the Church. A preacher in Strasbourg at the end of the 15th century claimed:

> **SOURCE A**
>
> *O Lord my God, how falsely now do even those live who seem most spiritual – parson and monks… Their study is not to do God's works but to conceal the Devil's works.*

Absenteeism

One result of the laziness of secular clergy, in particular, was **absenteeism**; in other words, clergy were absent from their duties. Given that travelling around in the 14th and 15th centuries was a slow process, it was common for the people in some parishes to go for weeks, or even months, without seeing a priest, hearing Mass or receiving the sacraments.

Pluralism

Sometimes, absenteeism was due to another abuse called **pluralism**. It has to be remembered that the Church had great wealth around Europe in the form of buildings, land, precious objects and the donations of churchgoers, kings and lords. So, the more parishes that a priest controlled, or the more dioceses a bishop held, the wealthier he could expect to be. It was not unheard of for one priest to have ten or more parishes; clearly, even if he wished to, he could hardly look after the spiritual needs of all the people of these parishes properly.

Pope Alexander V

Simony

Because the Church was so rich, another abuse called **simony** developed. This was the practice of buying Church appointments, especially positions in the upper levels of the Church, the **hierarchy**. Through payments of money, positions or land, people could bribe their way to become bishops, cardinals and, on at least one occasion, Pope. An account from 1492, the year of the election of Rodrigo Borgia as Pope Alexander VI, tells us:

> **SOURCE B**
>
> *Borgia openly corrupted many of the cardinals, some with money, others with promises of profitable places and benefices, of which he had many at that time in his power.*

> ### DID YOU KNOW?
>
> Cardinal Giuliano della Rovere (later Pope Julius II) was the abbot of several monasteries in the late 15th century, as well as being bishop of eight different dioceses in four different countries.

Nepotism

Once in positions of power, members of the hierarchy were sometimes guilty of **nepotism**. This term comes from the Latin for 'nephew' (*nepos*). It means giving important positions to relatives. Pope Sixtus IV (1471–84), for example, appointed six of his own nephews and cousins as cardinals – one of them was Giuliano della Rovere, whom we mentioned earlier. Pope Leo X (1513–21), whom we will read about in the next chapter, made cardinals of at least five of his cousins and nephews.

Indulgences

In the 14th and 15th centuries, it was commonly believed that when anyone except a saint died, the soul had to suffer in **Purgatory** for a time before being allowed into **Heaven**. **Indulgences** were reductions in the length of time to be spent in Purgatory. The Church granted these in return for special acts of devotion done by the person before death, such as going on a pilgrimage.

Erasmus.

In time, Christians could gain indulgences not just by going on a pilgrimage but by donating the cost of such a pilgrimage to the Church funds. From this grew the idea that the more money a Christian contributed to the Church in his or her lifetime, the shorter the soul's stay in Purgatory would be. Thus, indulgences, and hence entry into Heaven, were seen to depend on how much money you gave rather than on how good a Christian you were.

This practice of selling indulgences was one of the many abuses in the Church that Renaissance people began to question and criticise. Erasmus wrote in *In Praise of Folly* (1509):

Pope Leo X.

> **SOURCE C**
>
> *What shall I say of those who cry up and maintain the cheat of pardons and indulgences, who by these calculate the length of time each person should stay in Purgatory, and assign them a longer or a shorter sentence, according as they purchase more or fewer of these paltry pardons and saleable indulgences?*

CAN YOU SAY?

1. Identify and explain *three* abuses in the Church before the Reformation.
   (*Junior Certificate Higher Level 1993 and 2000, similar in 2002, 2003, 2004, 2005, 2009*)
2. What is the hierarchy?
3. What was Pope Alexander VI's real name?
4. Where does the word '**nepotism**' come from?
5. Name *one* Pope guilty of nepotism.
6. What was an indulgence supposed to achieve?
7. (a) In **Source A** above, what kind of people were being criticised?
   (b) In **Source B** above, how, according to the writer, did Borgia reach office?
   (c) In **Source C** above, what did Erasmus mean by 'saleable indulgences'?

OTHER FAULTS

Lifestyles

Other defects in the Church included the scandalous **private lives** of some Popes and members of the hierarchy. For example, Pope Innocent VIII (1484–92) had children, and his son married the daughter of none other than Lorenzo de Medici. As part of the marriage arrangement, Innocent VIII made Lorenzo's son, Giovanni, a cardinal at the age of 13; Giovanni later became Pope Leo X. Cesare Borgia, hero of Machiavelli's *The Prince*, was one of six children of Rodrigo Borgia, Pope Alexander VI.

Pope Innocent VIII.

Loyalty to Lords

The Church's problems were not found just in the hierarchy. In Chapter 13, we saw that many priests were appointed by the local lord of the manor, so they owed their loyalty to him rather than to the Church or the people.

Lack of Education

Lack of education was another problem; many secular clergy were unable to read the Latin Scriptures, and when explaining them to their people (congregation), they used a mixture of guesswork and superstition. The Church had no clearly defined **catechism** of ideas and beliefs, so it was common to find big differences in Catholic beliefs from country to country.

Corruption

Corruption and greed were also to be found among the ordinary clergy. Thomas More wrote in the early 16th century of how:

> **SOURCE D**
>
> *Some priest, to bring up a pilgrimage (and so money donations) in his parish, may devise some false fellow feigning himself to come seek a saint in his church, and there suddenly say that he hath gotten back his sight.*

Thomas More.

Politics and War

The Church's wealth also meant that it became heavily involved in international politics and so made further enemies. The Pope controlled large territories around Rome known as the Papal States (see map in Chapter 14) and on more than one occasion sent armies into battle against rival kingdoms. Giuliano della Rovere became Pope Julius II in 1503 and reigned until 1513; he was known as the 'Warrior Pope' because of his constant involvement in wars.

Although some people objected to Popes being involved in politics and wars on religious grounds alone, many European rulers also came to see the popes as political enemies. They also resented the fact that their subjects gave donations to the Church that might be used by a Pope in the future to wage wars against themselves.

CAN YOU SAY?

8. Explain briefly *one* of the problems or abuses in the Catholic Church about the year 1500 that led reformers to seek change.

   (Junior Certificate Ordinary and Higher Levels 1992)

9. Which pope was Lorenzo de Medici's son?

10. Explain in your own words what Thomas More describes in **Source D** above.

11. Which Pope was called the 'Warrior Pope'?

12. Why did some kings and princes dislike the Church's influence on their people?

In Florence, a Dominican friar named Savonarola suffered death in 1498 for attacking the Church's wealth and for encouraging people to lead lives of poverty and prayer.

Failure to Reform

It is very important to remember that, despite all the faults present in the Church, it still had millions of devoted followers and thousands of honest, God-fearing clergy. In the past, people who were called **reformers** criticised the abuses and faults that they found in the Church in an effort to improve matters. Men such as St Bernard and Ireland's St Malachy were great reformers of the early medieval Church and won a lot of support.

As the medieval Church became larger and more powerful, it was less anxious to listen to reformers. In 14th century England, **John Wycliffe** taught that Popes and bishops lost their right to be obeyed by people if they were evil themselves. **John Huss**, in 15th century Bohemia, attacked many Church teachings; consequently, he was convicted of heresy (see Chapter 13) and burned at the stake.

The medieval and early Renaissance Church refused to take notice of these obvious signs that not everyone was satisfied with it. In other words, the Church refused for so long to reform itself that eventually those who sought change simply broke away from it and founded new religions. We will meet these in later chapters.

THE INFLUENCE OF THE RENAISSANCE

Finally, if most of these problems had existed for centuries, why was it not until the 16th century that a major Reformation occurred? Some of the answer lies in the fact that the Church still had huge numbers of holy clergy who had the respect of the ordinary people, despite the corruption of some.

The Renaissance itself also contributed, being a time when people learnt to think and question for themselves. We have seen how old ideas in painting, medicine, astronomy and so on were often thrown out in favour of new ones. The new **Humanism** encouraged people to re-examine the relationship between humans and God. Humanist writers, such as Thomas More and especially Erasmus, pointed out faults in the Church and found an audience for their views when previously they might have been branded heretics. Petrarch once wrote in a letter to a friend:

> **SOURCE E**
>
> *Now I am living in France, in the Babylon of the West. Here reign the successors of the poor fishermen of Galilee; they have forgotten their origin. I am astounded, as I recall their predecessors, to see these men loaded with gold and clad in purple, boasting of the riches of princes and nations, to see luxurious palaces and heights crowned with fortifications... Instead of holy silence we find a criminal multitude... instead of soberness, drunken banquets, instead of pious pilgrimages, foul laziness; instead of the bare feet of the apostles, the war-horses of robbers fly past us, the horses decked in gold and fed on gold, soon to be shod with gold, if the lord does not check this slavish luxury.*

That great invention of the Renaissance, the **printing press**, brought education to growing numbers of people, allowing them for the first time to examine and discuss things for themselves. The result was that people began to doubt and disagree with Church practices that had been accepted without question for centuries before.

Remember the **great patronage** of the arts during the Renaissance by Popes and members of the hierarchy? Although this resulted in many great artistic treasures such as the *Pietà* and the Sistine ceiling, there was a negative result also. Some Christians realised that the money for these great Church artworks was coming essentially from the donations of often very poor people around Europe.

DID YOU KNOW?

Savonarola persuaded the people of Florence to stage a 'bonfire of the vanities' (1497), in which they threw perfumes, mirrors, musical instruments, carnival masks and even books by Petrarch into the flames to rid themselves of all ungodly pleasures.

Works, such as the great tomb that Julius II (above) commissioned Michelangelo to construct for him, made some Christians feel that this patronage was more for the glory of the churchmen themselves than for God or the Church in general.

In Chapter 15, we read of the efforts of artists such as Raphael and Michelangelo to rebuild **St Peter's Basilica** in the early 16th century. This was the most costly task the Church had ever undertaken. Once again, Christians around Europe were asked for help to meet the ever-rising costs of a project that was to take 109 years to complete. This proved to be 'the straw', as the saying goes, 'that broke the camel's back', and led to what became known as the Reformation.

CAN YOU SAY?

13. Give *two* reasons why many people thought that the Catholic Church was in need of reform in the early 16th century.
    (Junior Certificate Higher Level 2001 and 2004; Ordinary Level 2003)
14. From what countries were (a) Wycliffe and (b) Huss?
15. What did Savonarola mean by a 'bonfire of the vanities'?
16. Study **Source E** above, an extract from Petrarch criticising the lifestyles of the Popes of the 14th century.
    (a) Who are 'the successors of the poor fishermen of Galilee'?
    (b) Does the writer approve of what he saw? Mention *one* piece of evidence from the extract to support your answer.
    (Junior Certificate Higher Level 2002)
17. Mention *one* way in which the printing press helped the Reformation. *(Junior Certificate Ordinary Level 1995)*
18. Explain *one* other way in which the Renaissance influenced the Reformation.

NO MINI PROJECT BUT...

There is no mini-project with this chapter, but instead an important explanation. All the religions covered in the next few chapters are **Christian** because all believe in Christ as the son of God. Those Christian religions that opposed the Catholic Church were called **Protestant** because they protested against a decision to declare them illegal. In common usage, the word **Protestant** covers many different non-Catholic, but yet Christian religions. The next two chapters cover the origins of the three main Protestant religions in Europe – Lutheranism, Calvinism and Anglicanism.

KEYNOTES

1. **Abuses:** absenteeism • pluralism • simony • nepotism • indulgences
2. **Other problems: private lives:** loyalty to lords • lack of education • corruption • laziness • politics and war
   Hierarchy: Cardinal della Rovere (Julius II) • Alexander VI • Sixtus IV • Leo X • Innocent VIII
3. **Failure to reform:** Wycliffe • Huss • Savonarola
   Renaissance influence: Humanism • printing press • excessive Church patronage • rebuilding of St Peter's Basilica • Christian • Catholic • Protestant

Martin Luther and the German Reformation

24

SELLING INDULGENCES

The rebuilding of St Peter's Basilica was begun by Pope Julius II in 1506. His successor, **Leo X**, faced mounting costs as the work went on and, in 1517, he decided to raise funds from the faithful by offering a new indulgence. Anyone giving money to his collectors would gain a reduction in the Purgatory sentence for themselves or their relatives. In some areas, local members of the hierarchy were to be given a share of the money collected in order to win their help in persuading people to contribute.

In Germany, the young **Archbishop of Mainz** was deeply in debt as a result of simony – he had bought his way into several positions. He was delighted with the new indulgence idea and the 50 per cent 'cut' he was to get for encouraging contributions from his flock. With his support, indulgence 'sellers' travelled around Germany. One of them was a Dominican friar named **John Tetzel,** who promised that almost any sin could be forgiven in return for a donation to help rebuild St Peter's.

Educated, sincere Christians throughout Germany were horrified by Tetzel's actions. When Tetzel came to the area of Wittenberg in October 1517, one of them decided to speak out. His name was **Martin Luther**.

MARTIN LUTHER (1483–1546)

His Early Life

Martin Luther was born in 1483 near Eisleben in Saxony. His father was a fairly wealthy copper-miner and dealer who gave his son a good education at a number of different schools after the family moved to Mansfeld. At the age of 17, Luther entered the University of Erfurt, where his serious attitude to his studies earned him the nickname of 'the philosopher'.

Martin Luther.

Luther received a Bachelor of Arts degree the following year, 1502 – nowadays it takes at least three years to achieve this – and by 1505 he had obtained a Masters degree. His family hoped that he would become a lawyer, but Luther shocked them with the news that he was joining the order of Augustinian friars at Erfurt. Apparently, he took this decision as a result of a vow to St Anne. On his way to Erfurt in July 1505, he had been caught in a terrible thunderstorm; he prayed to St Anne for her protection and promised to become a monk in return. Luther later wrote:

> **SOURCE A**
>
> *Not freely or willingly did I become a monk, but walled around with the terror and agony of sudden death, I vowed a constrained and necessary vow.*

Nevertheless, Luther found himself well-suited to the strict life of a monk and was ordained a priest within two years of joining the order. Because of his previous university education, his superiors sent Luther to undertake advanced religious studies at the University of Wittenberg. Soon, Luther became a lecturer and then professor of **theology**, the study of a person's relationship with God.

'Justification by Faith Alone'

The more he studied theology, the more uncertain Luther became that he was on the right path to Heaven, or 'salvation' as he put it. He later wrote:

> **SOURCE B**
>
> *However righteously I lived as a friar, I felt myself in the presence of God to be a sinner with a troubled conscience, and I could not believe that my best efforts satisfied Him.*

Germany at the time of Martin Luther.

Luther struggled with his doubts for years. Finally, through studying St Paul's writings, he decided that the one essential thing for a Christian to have in order to be saved was **faith**. Rich or poor, powerful or weak would be saved, Luther concluded, not by money, pilgrimages or crusades, but by pure faith in God. He called this belief **Justification by Faith Alone.** For Luther, it did not matter if a poor man could not give as much to the Church, for example, as a rich man could – faith in God was what counted. This ran against the views of Pope Leo X and the preaching of John Tetzel.

In 1514, Luther began preaching in the local parish church at Wittenberg and, a year later, he was appointed to control the order's 11 monasteries in that part of Germany. He took part in many debates with other clergy, becoming more convinced all the time of 'Justification by Faith Alone'. So, when Luther heard of the arrival locally of John Tetzel, who was offering people salvation for money, he was outraged and decided to seek a debate with other churchmen and theologians about indulgences. He wrote down in Latin a list of 95 complaints for them to consider. This list was to become one of the most important documents in history.

CAN YOU SAY?

1. For what particular reason did Pope Leo X need money in 1517?
2. What deal was done between Leo X and the Archbishop of Mainz?
3. What did Luther's father want him to become?
4. (a) According to **Source A,** why did Luther became a monk?
   (b) In your own words, explain what troubled Luther according to **Source B.**
5. Who 'sold' indulgences in Wittenberg in 1517?
6. Why did Luther object to the sale of indulgences?

The Ninety-Five Theses

Because there were no newspapers, televisions or Internet in October 1517, the usual way to open the discussion of ideas was to display them in writing on a church door. Therefore, Luther nailed his **Ninety-Five Theses** to the door of the castle church in Wittenberg, attacking indulgences and other Church abuses. He then waited for other clergy to contribute their views. He also sent copies to the Archbishop of Mainz and to his own bishop.

Then something very important happened. Some individuals who agreed with Luther's theses had thousands of them **printed** and sent throughout Germany. This made a lot of people take notice and

Luther nails the Ninety-Five Theses to the church in Wittenberg.

caused great concern to the Church hierarchy. The **German Reformation** had begun. In the Ninety-Five Theses, Luther declared:

> **SOURCE C**
>
> *Indulgence improves no man, but only tolerates and allows his imperfection.*
>
> (Thesis No. 14)

Knowing that Pope Leo X supported these indulgences, Luther declared:

> **SOURCE D**
>
> *If the Pope knew of the actions of his corrupt preachers, he should prefer to see the Cathedral of St Peter's burnt to ashes than built on the skin, flesh and bone of his flock.*
>
> (Thesis No. 50)

Elsewhere, the theses even suggested that the Pope, as the richest man in Christendom, should build St Peter's himself.

CHURCH REACTION

Leo X's reaction was swift. In 1518, he sent a legate, Cardinal Cajetan, to try to get Luther to take back (**recant**) his theses. At a meeting, in October, Luther refused, as he did when debating with the theologian John Eck in 1519. Their arguments pushed Luther to become even more critical of the Pope and the hierarchy, declaring to Eck that 'a layman armed with Scripture is to be believed before a Pope or Church council without Scripture.'

Because indulgences, and other abuses such as simony and nepotism, were not mentioned in the Scriptures, Luther rapidly moved to the conclusion that Christians should rely on the Bible *alone*, not on the Pope. Eck reported to Leo X that a lot of people were agreeing with Luther:

> **SOURCE E**
>
> *All Germany is in revolution. Nine-tenths shout 'Luther' as their war cry and the other tenth cares nothing about Luther and cries 'Death to the Court of Rome'.*

Exsurge Domine

Having failed to make Luther recant, Leo X responded with a Papal Bull called *Exsurge Domine*. In it, he threatened to excommunicate Luther unless he recanted. On 10 December 1520, Luther and his students at Wittenberg publicly burned the Bull, along with works by Eck and other supporters of the Pope. Luther was then excommunicated.

At that time, Wittenberg lay within the borders of the Holy Roman Empire, ruled over by the same Spanish king who had financed Magellan, **Charles V**. He was persuaded by the Pope that Luther's heresy must be stopped; so, in 1521, Luther was summoned by Charles V to appear at the imperial conference known as the **Diet of Worms**. This strange-sounding name is explained by the fact that **Worms** is the name of the town in which the conference (called a **Diet**) was held.

> **DID YOU KNOW?**
>
> In 1520, 4,000 printed copies of a Martin Luther pamphlet sold out in just five days. Between 1517 and 1530, Luther was the world's best-selling writer with over 300,000 copies of his books and pamphlets printed, mostly in German.

The Diet of Worms

At Worms, Luther was called upon again to recant his criticisms of the Church. With his support growing all the time, particularly among local lords and princes, Luther replied:

> **SOURCE F**
>
> *Unless I am convicted of error by the testimony of Scriptures or by clear reasoning I cannot and will not recant anything... I put no trust in the unsupported authority of the Pope or of councils.*

Luther burns the Papal Bull at the East Gate of Wittenberg.

Emperor Charles V.

> **CAN YOU SAY?**
>
> 7. What did Luther want to achieve by nailing the Ninety-Five Theses to the church door?
> 8. Why did Luther's criticisms become widely known?
> 9. (a) Explain Luther's Thesis No. 14 in your own words, based on **Source C**.
>   (b) Name *one* 'corrupt preacher' attacked by Luther in **Source D**.
> 10. What was *Exsurge Domine* and what did Luther do with it?
> 11. (a) According to **Source E**, what were the *two* reasons why Germans were 'in revolution'?
>   (b) According to **Source F**, what would never convince Luther to change his mind?

LUTHER'S REFORMATION GAINS GROUND

Princes Support Luther

Luther giving Holy Communion to Frederick of Saxony. In what way does Luther look different from a Catholic priest?

Despite the fact that the Diet of Worms later passed the **Edict of Worms**, declaring Luther an outlaw, his support was so strong that not even the Emperor dared to act against him. Luther left Worms safely, but then, on his way back to Wittenberg, he suddenly disappeared. Many thought he had been murdered by agents of the Pope or the Emperor. Instead, he had been kidnapped by one of his own supporters – the local prince, **Frederick, Elector of Saxony**.

For Luther's own safety, Frederick sheltered him in his castle at Wartburg for almost a year, disguised as a nobleman called Junker Georg. Frederick and other German princes had long been angry that what little money many of their people possessed had been going in donations to Rome rather than to their own rulers.

Luther believed it was vital that people should take guidance from the Scriptures alone, so at Wartburg he began to translate the Bible into German with the aid of a young follower called **Philipp Melanchthon**.

Luther's Ideas Developed

By 1525, what began as an attempt to debate Church policies had turned into a full-scale split in the Catholic Church. All through, Luther stuck to his belief in (1) **Justification by Faith Alone**, and added that, because the Popes and Church councils had often been wrong, (2) **Christians should rely on the Bible alone for guidance**. These two ideas were the basis of what became a new religion, **Lutheranism**. As the row with the Catholic Church grew, Luther developed a systematic set of beliefs from these two ideas; these were known as Lutheran beliefs.

The Bible was now available in vernacular German. Because Luther believed that the study of the Bible was all that a Christian needed, he felt there was no need in his Church for priests or hierarchy. He simply relied on **ministers** to preach the scriptures. This was known as the **priesthood of all believers**. Also, because there was no mention in the Bible of ministers remaining unmarried, Luther believed **ministers could marry**. He himself married a former nun, Catherine von Bora, in 1525.

Catherine von Bora.

Having translated the Bible into German, Luther also composed prayers and services in the **vernacular language**, arguing that using Latin prevented many people from understanding the Bible or Mass. Also, because they were not mentioned in the Bible, **indulgences**, **praying to statues** and the wearing of special priest's clothing (**vestments**) were banned in Lutheranism.

Although the Catholic Church had, over the centuries, developed seven special sacraments, Luther found only two mentioned in the Bible – **Baptism** and **Holy Communion** – so these were the only **sacraments** in Lutheranism. A fairly complicated but important difference came in beliefs about the Eucharist. Catholics believe that, at the Consecration, bread and wine are transformed into the body and blood of Christ (**Transubstantiation**). Luther felt that the Bible's description of the Last Supper did not say this and decided on a belief called **Consubstantiation** – that bread and wine become the body and blood of Christ, while also *remaining* bread and wine.

CAN YOU SAY?

12. What was the main result of the Diet of Worms 1521?
    (Junior Certificate Higher Level 1998 and 2009)
13. Who protected Luther after the Diet of Worms?
14. What did many princes hope to gain by supporting Luther?
15. Who was Catherine von Bora?
16. Explain briefly *one* way in which Protestantism in the 16th century was different from the Catholic religion.
    (Junior Certificate Ordinary and Higher Levels 1992) [Can you explain *three*?]

LATER PROBLEMS

The Peasant Revolt

Inspired by Luther's teachings that all Christians were equal, a Peasant Revolt against local rulers broke out in Germany in 1524–25. Although Luther sympathised with some of the peasants' complaints against their lords and princes, he was horrified by the violence of peasant armies. He also had to consider that some of his strongest and most powerful supporters were the German lords, so he condemned the Peasant Revolt in a pamphlet entitled *Against the Murdering and Thieving Hordes of Peasants*. The revolt was eventually crushed by the nobles, leaving about 100,000 peasants dead.

SOURCE G

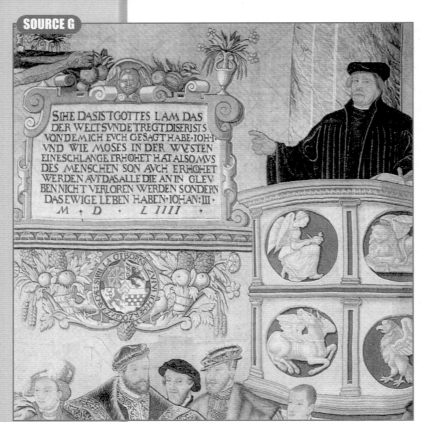

A 16th-century tapestry which shows Luther preaching a sermon.

The Diet of Augsburg

By 1530, German princes and the states they ruled were firmly divided into either Lutheran or Catholic camps. At a specially convened **Diet of Augsburg**, the Emperor Charles V tried to find common ground between the two sides but failed. Luther was still officially an outlaw, so the case for Lutheranism was made by Philipp Melanchthon, using a document written by Luther called the *Confession of Augsburg*.

All this time, Luther's support was growing. The ruling councils of more than half of Germany's cities adopted Lutheranism and by 1540 it had become the main religion of other countries such as Denmark and Sweden.

WARS OF RELIGION

After Luther died of a heart attack in 1546, Germany erupted into open religious warfare between Catholic and Lutheran states – the last thing Luther would have wished. Peace was finally restored in the **Peace of Augsburg** (1555). This allowed for both Catholics and Lutherans in the Holy Roman Empire and left it up to the rulers of each city or state to decide what their official religion would be.

DID YOU KNOW?

The Thirty Years War basically started after two Catholic governors of Bohemia were thrown out of a palace window in Prague (in what is now the Czech Republic) by Protestant opponents in 1618. Because *fenestra* is the Latin for a window, the event became known as the 'defenestration of Prague' (pictured right).

Although the Peace of Augsburg was an important step, it did not provide permanent peace. Between 1618 and 1648, northern Europe was engulfed in a series of wars between Protestant and Catholic states, known as the **Thirty Years War**. In the coming chapters, we will also see how the Reformation, which Luther began in 1517, spread throughout Europe.

CAN YOU SAY?

17. What precisely was Luther's attitude to the Peasant Revolt in Germany?
18. In the picture, **Source G**, above, are those listening to Luther wealthy people or peasants? Explain your answer by giving *one* detail from the picture and *one* fact not in the picture as proof.
19. Name *two* other countries where Lutheranism became popular.
20. What did the Peace of Augsburg decide?   (*Junior Certificate Higher Level 2009*)
21. When was the Thirty Years War fought?
22. In **Source H** below are extracts from the writings of Martin Luther. Read them carefully and answer the questions afterwards.

> **SOURCE H**
>
> *I was a good monk and...if ever a monk were able to reach heaven by monkish discipline I should have found my way there...if it had continued much longer I would, what with prayers, readings and other such works, have done myself to death.*
>
> *Since works justify no one and it is necessary to be just before he does a good deed, it is most clear that it is faith alone which by the pure mercy of God... justifies and saves the person...the Christian man needs no work and no law to be saved...by the grace of God and through his faith he has enough and is saved.*

(a) Why did Luther consider himself to be a good monk?
(b) Do you think Luther was happy as a monk? Support your answer by evidence from the passage.
(c) Why did Luther consider faith more important than good works?

(*Junior Certificate Higher Level 1996*)

KEYNOTES

1. **Sale of indulgences:** Leo X • rebuilding of St Peter's • Archbishop of Mainz • John Tetzel
   Martin Luther: Saxony • studied law • Augustinian friar • University of Wittenberg • 'Justification by Faith Alone'
2. **Luther's objections:** Ninety-Five Theses • printing
   Church reaction: John Eck • *Exsurge Domine* • Charles V • Diet of Worms • Edict of Worms
3. **The Reformation takes hold:** Frederick, Elector of Saxony • Wartburg Castle • German Bible • Philipp Melanchthon • **developing ideas** • authority of the Bible • 'priesthood of all believers' • married clergy • vernacular • two sacraments • no indulgences or statues • Lutheranism
4. **Consequences: support of princes** • Peasant Revolt • Diet of Augsburg • *Confession of Augsburg* • Peace of Augsburg • Defenestration of Prague • Thirty Years War

MINI-PROJECT

How many exact **reasons** can you find in this chapter for Luther's fight with the Catholic Church? Having done that, how many **results** can you find of his break with the Catholic Church? Again, rely on *only* this chapter.

Or

Write an account of a named religious reformer at the time of the Reformation.

Hints:

- name of the reformer
- important events in the reformer's life
- main beliefs
- results of the reformer's work

(*Junior Certificate 1998 and 2000 both levels, 2001 and 2006 Ordinary only, 2003 Higher and Ordinary – hints only given at Ordinary level*)

[*Note:* This question could be done on one of several reformers, most of whom you will come across in the next two chapters. However, see whether you can write 10 or 12 sentences just on Luther here, without the book.]

25

The drive for reform and for the setting up of new religions was felt in many countries during and after Luther's time. Historically, two of the most important reformations happened in Switzerland and England, though for very different reasons, as we will now see.

JEAN CALVIN (1509–64)

The Early Years

Although Martin Luther was the main personality of the early Reformation, the dominant one of the later Reformation was Jean Calvin. Born at Noyon in France, Calvin was the son of a church clerk and received a very good early education paid for by the Church. He later attended the University of Paris where he received a Master of Arts degree; he then went to the University of Orleans to study law.

Calvin converted to the Protestant faith in his early 20s. France was a strongly Catholic country and, in 1536, the King began to persecute French Lutherans. Calvin fled to Basel in Switzerland, where he studied theology.

In 1536, he published a book outlining his religious beliefs. Its title in English is *The Institutes of the Christian Religion* and it quickly established Calvin as one of the greatest Protestant thinkers in Switzerland. In the autumn of 1536, Calvin moved on to Geneva, south of Basel.

This city had just followed the lead of other Swiss cities such as Berne and Zurich – its council had broken with its Catholic bishop and declared Geneva a Protestant city. Calvin intended to pass through Geneva on his way elsewhere, but was persuaded by its Protestant preachers to help establish the faith there.

Calvinism

Like Luther, Calvin believed that the Bible, not the Pope or the hierarchy, was the only place where Christians should seek guidance.

DID YOU KNOW?

Before Calvin, another Reformer in Switzerland, named Zwingli, once showed his disagreement with the teachings of the Church by frying and eating sausages on Good Friday in Zurich. Catholic tradition has this as a day of fasting from meat, but the Bible says nothing against it.

The two also agreed on having vernacular services, that indulgences and the worship of statues and pictures were wrong and that clergy could marry – Calvin was married, though his wife died after only a few years.

However, Calvin's beliefs, as he explained them in *The Institutes*, differed from Luther's in significant ways. Whereas Luther believed in 'Justification by Faith Alone', Calvin thought that God decided, even before people were born, who would be saved and who would not. He called this **predestination**. In *The Institutes*, he explained it thus:

> **SOURCE A**
>
> *We assert by an eternal and unalterable decision God has once and for all decided both whom He would admit to salvation and whom He would condemn to destruction. We affirm that this decision, as it concerns the elect, is founded on His gracious mercy, totally regardless of human merit.*

Jean Calvin.

Those whom God had chosen for Heaven, Calvin called the **elect**; they were expected to show that they were God's chosen people by leading good, holy lives. So, whereas Luther believed that a person could be saved by faith in God during his or her lifetime, Calvin believed that God had already made that decision before the person was even born.

Calvin also differed with Luther over the sacraments. Whereas Luther agreed with two of the Catholic Church's seven sacraments, Calvin believed that only one was truly mentioned in the Bible – baptism. Instead of Luther's belief that bread and wine, as well as the body and blood of Jesus, were present in the Eucharist (Consubstantiation), Calvin felt the bread and wine were just symbols or reminders of Jesus, and nothing more.

However, Calvin agreed with Luther that there was no need for a Pope or a hierarchy. Calvin chose an ancient Greek name for his ministers. He called them **presbyters**, so the religion is often called **Presbyterianism**.

CAN YOU SAY?

1. Name (a) a religious reformer of the Protestant Reformation and (b) **one** major difference between his teaching and that of the Roman Catholic Church.
   (*Junior Certificate Ordinary Level 1993, both levels 1998 and 2000*)
2. What nationality was Jean Calvin?
3. Name Calvin's great book.
4. Why did Calvin settle in Geneva?
5. Explain **predestination** in your own words, having read **Source A**.
6. Explain any *two* other differences between Calvinism and Lutheranism, apart from predestination.
7. Why is Calvinism often called Presbyterianism?

Life in Calvin's Geneva

Calvin began preaching his beliefs in Geneva and organising the Reformation there between 1536 and 1538. However, his preference for using French ministers rather than Swiss ones led to him being forced out by the city council. Only when the council members changed in 1541 was he invited back and given almost total freedom to develop the Reformation there.

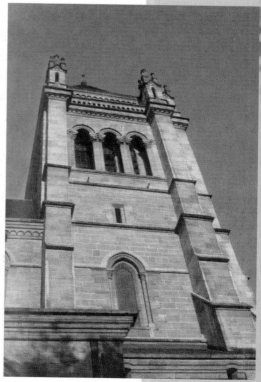

Calvinism in Geneva was based on a system devised by Calvin in a document entitled *Ordonnances Ecclésiastiques* (*Ecclesiastical Orders*) in 1541. There were four groups or 'orders' responsible for maintaining the Calvinist faith in what Calvin called the 'City of God'. (He saw Rome as the 'City of the Devil' – can you guess why?)

A meeting in a Calvinist church; there are no statues, holy pictures or crucifixes, and the pulpit is the most important feature.

Presbyters preached God's word to the people and administered baptism. **Doctors**, in fact, were teachers whom Calvin called the 'order of the schools'. **Elders** were chosen by the city council 'to have oversight of the life of everyone, to criticise in a friendly way those whom they see...to be living a disordered life.' Finally, **deacons** were appointed to look after the poor.

The main power in Calvin's 'City of God' lay with a **consistory** made up of presbyters and elders. As Calvinism grew in Geneva, the consistory ruled over its people in a very strict fashion. According to one writer:

> **SOURCE B**
>
> *All kinds of amusements, theatres, dances, cards etc. were banned as ungodly, as were also extravagance in dress and anything approaching silliness. Nobody was allowed to sell wine or beer, except a limited number of merchants licensed by the consistory.*

DID YOU KNOW?

Calvin attempted to set up taverns where people could drink moderately – *and* listen to Scripture-readings at the same time! But these drew very few customers and eventually the old taverns had to be reopened.

Sunday was a particularly special day, the **Sabbath**. No work or amusements were allowed on this day and taverns remained closed. People flocked to the cathedral on the hill, where it still stands overlooking Lake Geneva. There they were reminded of their duties as members of the 'elect'. While life in Geneva was undoubtedly very strict, most people seemed happy. John Ball, an Irish bishop visiting Geneva, wrote:

> **SOURCE C**
>
> *Geneva seems to me to be the wonderful miracle of the whole world. So many from all countries come here ... not to gather riches but to live in poverty ... Spaniards, Italians, Scots, Englishmen, Frenchmen, Germans, differing in customs, language and dress ... dwell together like a spiritual and Christian congregation.*

Foreign disciples of Calvin played a vital role in spreading Calvinism when they returned to their native countries after periods of instruction at his **seminary** (today the University of Geneva). Calvinism spread from Geneva across southern France in the 1550s and 1560s, as well as to the Netherlands, parts of Germany and to Scotland, where a follower of Calvin's named John Knox helped to make it a popular religion.

CAN YOU SAY?

8. What name did Calvin give to Geneva?

9. What work was done by (a) elders and (b) deacons in Geneva?

10. What was the *consistory*?

11. (a) Having read **Source B** above, list *two* ways in which Calvin's Geneva differed from a modern Irish city.

   (b) Name *three* nationalities mentioned in **Source C** and explain in your own words why they all went to Geneva.

12. Write an account of the following: Calvin's church in Geneva.
   (Junior Certificate Higher Level 2009)

13. Name *one* important religious reformer and *one* important teaching of that reformer.
   (Junior Certificate Ordinary Level 1996, and both levels 2001 and 2005)

14. Name a reformer and state *one* important effect he had on the country most associated with him.
   (Junior Certificate Ordinary Level 1997)

HENRY VIII

Between 1455 and 1485, England was gripped by a civil war between two families seeking the throne. It became known as the **Wars of the Roses** because each side had a rose as its emblem. The **House of York** was represented by a white rose, while the **House of Lancaster**, which eventually won the war, had a red rose. The leader of the victorious House of Lancaster was Henry Tudor; he became **King Henry VII** of England.

Henry VII reigned from 1485 to 1509; after 30 years of civil war, he worked hard to ensure peace in England and to leave his heirs in a strong position when he died. Thus, he arranged a marriage between his eldest son and heir, Arthur, and **Catherine of Aragon**, the daughter of Ferdinand and Isabella of Spain, one of Europe's most powerful kingdoms. Unfortunately, just a few months after the wedding in 1502, Arthur died, leaving Henry VII's second son, Henry, as heir to the throne.

Henry VII wanted to hold onto the marriage alliance with Spain, so he decided to have Catherine now marry his second son, Henry. Because the Old Testament forbade marriage to a brother's widow, special permission (**a dispensation**) was sought from the Pope – Julius II – and it was granted. Soon after succeeding his father to the throne (1509), Henry VIII married Catherine of Aragon. Their marriage was quite a happy one and, between 1509 and 1527, Catherine had several children. However, only one survived, a daughter called Mary.

DID YOU KNOW?

To this day, because Lancaster won the Wars of the Roses, the emblem of England is the red rose.

The rose is the emblem today of England's rugby team.

Modern British coin. Note the 'FD' after the queen's name.

Henry VIII.

DID YOU KNOW?

Henry VIII hated Martin Luther and was given the title **Fidei Defensor (Defender of the Faith)** by Pope Leo X in 1521 for writing a pamphlet attacking Luther. The kings and queens of England still use this title – that is what FD on the edge of a British coin represents.

Catherine of Aragon.

Like his father before him, Henry VIII wanted England to remain strong and united. For this, he was convinced he needed a son to succeed him as king. With Catherine in her 40s, it was unlikely that she would have any more children. Henry had also fallen in love with a young lady named **Anne Boleyn**. Thus, for his country's sake and his own, Henry decided to seek a divorce. His grounds were simple – the marriage to his dead brother's wife should not have been allowed in the first place and must be dissolved immediately.

Henry sent **Cardinal Thomas Wolsey**, his Lord Chancellor (roughly the same as a Prime Minister today), to seek permission from the Pope to divorce Catherine. Unfortunately for Henry, **Pope Clement VII** was then in dispute with the Holy Roman Emperor, Charles V. In fact, Charles's army had just invaded Rome and Clement was his prisoner. Charles V, as we saw in Chapter 24, was Spanish and was Catherine of Aragon's nephew. Clement was forced to refuse Henry VIII's request for a divorce.

Wolsey returned home empty-handed and Henry dismissed him as Lord Chancellor. He then decided on a solution to what had become known as 'the King's great matter'. He would make himself the head of the Church in England and so be able to grant his own divorce. This decision was the start of the **English Reformation**.

Pope Clement VII surrounded by Spanish soldiers.

CAN YOU SAY?

15. Henry VII became England's king after what wars?
16. Who was Henry VII's eldest son?
17. Why did Pope Leo X confer on King Henry VIII the title **Defender of the Faith**?

    (Junior Certificate Higher Level 1995)

18. Why did Henry VIII need a dispensation from the Pope to marry Catherine?
19. Why did Henry VIII, King of England, quarrel with the Pope?

    (Junior Certificate Ordinary Level 1993)

20. Who failed to get Henry his divorce?

The Reformation Parliament

In 1529, Henry set up what was called the Reformation Parliament. Although most of its members supported Henry's desire to break with Rome, one who did not was his new Lord Chancellor, **Thomas More**. In 1532, Henry dismissed More and then in 1535 had him beheaded for alleged treason, but really because More sided with the Pope on the issue of Henry's divorce.

Divorce

The Reformation Parliament was dominated by Henry's new Archbishop of Canterbury, **Thomas Cranmer**. In 1533, he granted Henry his divorce:

> **SOURCE D**
>
> *We, Thomas Archbishop, having first invoked the name of Christ and with God alone before our eyes, pronounce, decree and declare the nullity and invalidity of the said marriage and that the aforesaid most illustrious and most mighty prince Henry VIII, and the most high lady Catherine ought not to remain in the same pretended matrimony.*

Anne Boleyn on the way to her execution.

Head of the English Church

Along with Cranmer, Henry found another strong ally in **Thomas Cromwell,** who became his Lord Chancellor in 1532 and his closest adviser. The most important law put through the Parliament by Cranmer and Cromwell was the **Act of Supremacy** of 1534, breaking the control of the Pope over England's faith:

> **SOURCE E**
>
> *Be it enacted by authority of this present Parliament, that the King our Sovereign Lord, his heirs and successors … shall be taken, accepted and reputed the only Supreme Head on Earth of the Church of England.*

The Closure of the Monasteries

The English monasteries were loyal to the Pope and so a threat to Henry's new position. Cromwell felt that closing them and dispersing the monks and nuns would remove their opposition. It would also leave the lands owned by the monasteries in the possession of the head of the Church of England – Henry himself! Cromwell had promised to make Henry the 'richest sovereign that ever reigned in England'. So, using the claim that the monasteries were places of sin and corruption, they were shut in the **Act of Dissolution** (1536) and their lands sold to local lords, with a nice profit to the Crown.

Later Developments in Henry's Reign

Although marrying Anne Boleyn was one of Henry's main reasons for breaking with the Pope, he later had her beheaded on the grounds that she had been unfaithful to him. Anne had borne Henry one child, a daughter called **Elizabeth**, so Henry still did not have a male heir. His third wife was a Protestant called Jane Seymour and, in October 1537, she gave birth to a son, **Edward**; just 12 days later she died. However, at last, Henry had a male heir, and Edward later became King Edward VI.

Henry's break with Rome, sometimes called the **Henrican Reformation**, really only changed the leadership of the Church in England and dissolved the monasteries. He had always been a devout Catholic and still hated Luther, so until the day he died in 1547 he kept the Mass, the seven sacraments and most of the other Catholic practices. Although Henry VIII started the English Reformation, it would be incorrect to call his a Protestant Reformation. It was to be under the rule of his children that England really became a Protestant country.

CAN YOU SAY?

21. Why was Thomas More executed?
22. What was Thomas Cranmer's position during Henry VIII's reign?
23. In *one* sentence, what does **Source D** declare?
24. In your own words, what does **Source E** declare?
25. Who took charge of closing the monasteries?
26. Write an account of the following: Henry VIII and the Reformation in England.

(Junior Certificate Higher Level 2009)

27. This drawing attempts to illustrate Henry VIII's relations with the Church. Study it carefully and answer the questions below.

(a) Henry VIII has his two feet resting on P. Clemens. What is the evidence in the picture that P. Clemens is Pope Clement?

(b) What message is the artist attempting to convey to the people by having Henry VIII's feet resting on P. Clemens?

(c) What *two* other messages does the artist wish to give to the people by showing Henry VIII:
    (i) holding the sword in his right hand?
    (ii) giving the Bible to Cranmer, a Reformation bishop?

(d) Give *one* reason why the Catholic clergy on the right-hand side and in the forefront were right to be worried by the actions of Henry VIII.

(Junior Certificate Higher Level 1996)

MINI-PROJECT

Write an account of the following: *A follower of a particular reformer during the Reformation*. Name the reformer.

Hints:

- reformer's early life
- the teachings of that reformer
- why people followed that reformer
- how following that reformer affected the lives of his followers

Write at least 10 or 12 sentences, without looking at your book.

(Junior Certificate Higher Level 1994)

KEYNOTES

1. **Calvin:** Noyon ● University of Paris ● Basel ● *Institutes of the Christian Religion* ● Calvinism ● predestination ● the elect ● presbyters
2. **Geneva** ('City of God') ● *Ordonnances Ecclésiastiques* ● consistory ● elders ● deacons ● doctors ● Sabbath ● Strict lives ● University of Geneva
3. **Wars of the Roses** ● York ● Lancaster
   Henry VII: Arthur ● Catherine of Aragon ● dispensation
   Henry VIII: daughter Mary ● Defender of the Faith
4. **Henrican Reformation:** ● no male heir ● Anne Boleyn ● divorce rejected ● Pope Clement VII ● Wolsey
   Reformation Parliament: More ● Cranmer ● Cromwell ● Act of Supremacy ● Act of Dissolution

The Consequences of the Reformation

26

GENERAL CONSEQUENCES

New Christian Churches

The most obvious result so far of the Reformation was the setting up of new Christian religions around Europe. As well as the main Lutheran and Calvinist religions, there were several other smaller Protestant Churches. In Germany today, for example, there are over 20 different Protestant groups, all of which owe their beginnings to the Reformation.

In Scotland, Calvinism became the main religion thanks to the work of one of Calvin's students at Geneva, John Knox (c.1512–72). Knox was a former Catholic priest who came to think of Calvin's Geneva, during his six years there, as 'the most perfect school of Christ'. In Scotland, Calvinism came to be known as **Presbyterianism** or, sometimes, **Puritanism**.

The ships of the Spanish Armada.

In England, after the death of Henry VIII, the country went through a 50-year period of religious change. Under Henry's son, Edward VI, a Protestant state was set up between 1547 and 1553, thanks mainly to the influence of Thomas Cranmer. After Edward died, his Catholic sister Mary became queen. She had been reared a Catholic by her mother, Catherine of Aragon. Mary brought back the Catholic religion and had hundreds of Protestants, including Cranmer, executed. (Mary's persecution of Protestants earned her the nickname 'Bloody Mary'.) Following Mary's death in 1558, her sister Elizabeth turned back to a form of Protestantism again, with herself as head of what became known as the Anglican Church.

SOURCE A

A contemporary picture of the massacre of Protestants (Huguenots) in France on Saint Bartholemew's Day, 1572

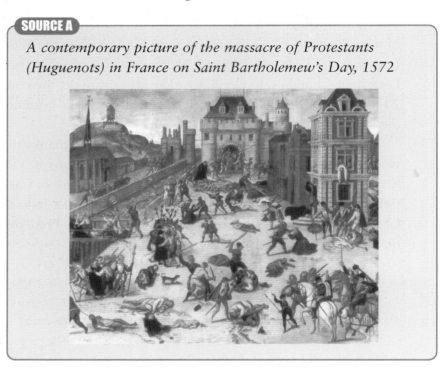

Conflict

Throughout Europe, disputes between Catholics and reformers became the long and bitter 'Wars of Religion'. In France, for example, an eight-year civil war took place. The worst incident in this war was the Massacre of St Bartholomew's Day; this was when over 20,000 French Calvinists (known as **Huguenots**) were massacred on the orders of the country's Catholic king on 24 August 1572. In many places, well after the Reformation ended, religious differences continued to cause violence between people and nations. The following is an extract from a letter from Catherine de Medici to her ambassador in Venice. She was the mother of the King of France at the time of the St Bartholomew's Day Massacre.

SOURCE B

The King is greatly troubled that in the heat of the moment certain Protestants were slain by the Catholics who remembered many evils, robberies and other wicked acts committed upon them... but now at last all is peaceful, so there is recognised only one king and one justice...because the King is determined, in view of the evils caused by differences of religion, to allow only his own religion.

DID YOU KNOW?

A later Pope actually ordered artists to paint loincloths over the original nudes of Michelangelo's Sistine paintings as part of the Catholic Church's efforts to 'improve' its image after the Reformation.

Increased Power of Rulers

The Reformation led to an obvious reduction in the power of the Pope, as more and more reformers rejected his authority. The new religions often relied on the monarchs of individual countries for protection or, as in the case of England, as Church leaders. Thus, the power of these kings and queens increased. Even Catholic monarchs became more important as the Pope and the Catholic Church relied increasingly upon them for support – Philip II of Spain is a very good case in point.

Art and Literature

Even in art and literature, the Reformation had an influence. The Reformation Churches gave an added push to **vernacular writing** because they used the native languages of their followers. As we saw earlier, Luther was Europe's best-selling writer in 1520. Books for and against the Catholic Church became an important feature of literature as a result of the Reformation. In the visual arts, too, artists such as Holbein, Cranach and Dürer devoted many of their paintings to **Protestant subjects**, while others, such as Michelangelo, remained devoutly Catholic.

Part of the end wall of the Sistine Chapel.

CAN YOU SAY?

1. Name *three* main Reformation religions.
2. Mention *two* effects of the Reformation in Europe during the period 1517 to 1648.
   (Junior Certificate Higher Level 2001 and 2005)
3. Who brought Calvinism to Scotland?
4. Name *one* English Protestant ruler and *one* Catholic one after Henry VIII.
5. From **Source A** above, identify *two* pieces of evidence to show that the soldiers were acting very cruelly. *(Junior Certificate Higher Level 2002)*
6. From **Source B** above, how does Catherine de Medici explain the killings? Use your own words. *(Junior Certificate Higher Level 2002)*
7. How did the Reformation make rulers more powerful?
8. How did the Reformation boost literature?

THE COUNTER-REFORMATION

The Reformation had a huge influence on the Catholic Church itself. As part of its efforts to prevent more people from leaving and to win back Protestants if possible, the church tried **punishment, improving** itself and **persuading** people about the Catholic religion. These three policies together came to be known as the **Counter-Reformation**.

Punishment

Long before the Reformation, the Catholic Church had set up a type of court that dealt with people who opposed its doctrines or who were accused of heresy. This was called the **Inquisition**. It had existed in some European countries during the Middle Ages. Now it became a powerful weapon in combating the Reformation. There were two main Courts of the Inquisition – the Roman Inquisition and the Spanish Inquisition.

The Roman Inquisition

The Roman Inquisition was founded by Pope Paul III in 1542. Run by six cardinals, it dealt with Protestants and any others whose views contradicted those of the Church – this was the court that tried Galileo (see Chapter 18). As the works of Luther and other Church critics became widely available in print, the Roman Inquisition also produced an *Index Librorum Prohibitorum* from 1559, listing all the books that good Catholics were forbidden to read.

The Spanish Inquisition

Spain had special courts for centuries, which dealt out harsh punishments to people not of the Catholic faith. Before the Reformation, these had been mostly Jews or Muslims (Moors). In the 16th century, the Spanish Inquisition turned its attention towards combating the new Protestant religions. It often arrested people who had no Protestant sympathies at all, but simply had said or done the wrong thing at the wrong time. King Philip II was very anti-Protestant. He declared in 1565:

> **SOURCE C**
>
> *Let all prisoners be put to death, and allow them no longer to escape through the neglect, weakness and bad faith of the judges. If any are too cowardly to carry out the sentences, I will replace them with men who have more courage and belief.*

Sentences

Although most victims of the Spanish inquisition were subjected to imprisonment or torture, some were executed. Execution was usually in the form of an *auto da fé* ('act of faith'). This generally occurred in a town square where the prisoner was tied to a wooden stake and surrounded by sticks and straw. These were then set alight, which ensured a slow and very painful death. If the victim recanted as the flames were being lit, he or she was quickly strangled – to ensure the soul would go to Heaven before another change of mind occurred!

Auto da fé.

Improving the Church – The Council of Trent

The Counter-Reformation sought to **improve** (reform) the teachings and conduct of the Church itself. To bring this about, Pope Paul III set up the **Council of Trent** in 1545. This was an assembly of the hierarchy, which met in three sessions over an 18-year period (1545–7, 1551–2 and 1562–3). The final decisions of the Council can be summed up in two main objectives.

Getting rid of abuses

Firstly, much was done to **abolish** the abuses and defects that we read about in Chapter 24. For example, (a) absenteeism, (b) pluralism, (c) simony and (d) nepotism were outlawed. Also, (e) indulgences could now only be earned by prayer and faith, not bought with money. Other defects would be dealt with by (f) setting up seminaries for training priests and (g) clearly explaining Church teachings in a new catechism.

Making Church doctrine clear

The Council of Trent also cleared up any doubts people might have had on Church **doctrine** (beliefs). It stated specifically that (a) Mass was a sacrifice, (b) it involved the complete change of bread and wine into Christ's body and blood

The Council of Trent.

(Transubstantiation) and (c) it should be said in Latin. Furthermore, (d) the Bible *and* the teachings of the Popes were accepted authorities on faith, so (e) the belief in seven sacraments was re-emphasised. Moreover, it stated that (f) faith in God *and* good works could ensure a person's path to salvation and (g) clergy should remain unmarried.

Overall, the Council of Trent did much to stamp out the worst of the Church's faults and strengthen its doctrine. Together with the Inquisition, it formed a vital part of the Counter-Reformation, which ensured the survival of the Catholic Church in Europe. Though smaller than before the Reformation, the Church was in some ways better after it.

CAN YOU SAY?

9. What was the Counter-Reformation?
(Junior Certificate Ordinary and Higher Levels 1995)
10. What famous scientist was tried before the Roman Inquisition?
11. What was the *Index Librorum Prohibitorum*?
12. What did the Spanish Inquisition do?
(Junior Certificate Higher Level 1993; similar in 2003)
13. In **Source C** above, who was Philip II criticising and why?
14. Describe *two* ways in which the Catholic Church responded to the Reformation.
(Junior Certificate Higher Level 1994)
15. State *two* reforms proposed by the Council of Trent.
(Junior Certificate Ordinary and Higher Levels 1994, 1998 and 2000)
16. How is it possible to suggest that the Catholic Church improved because of the Reformation?

Persuasion – New Religious Orders

The third approach of the Counter-Reformation involved **persuasion**. Several new Catholic **orders** were founded, who by preaching and leading good lives tried to win Protestants and non-Christians to the Catholic faith.

The **Capuchins** (1525) took on the strict way of the hermit's life as proposed by St Francis. Many devoted themselves to missionary and social work. They numbered 17,000 friars by 1571. Orders of nuns sprang up too, notably the **Ursulines** founded in Italy in 1535, and were devoted to charity and teaching work. The **Carmelites** had existed long before the Reformation, but they only became an enclosed order of nuns in 1562, with the very strict rule of St Teresa of Avila.

Ignatius Loyola and the Jesuits

Of all the new Catholic orders, none was more successful than the **Society of Jesus (Jesuits)** founded by the Spaniard **St Ignatius Loyola**. Born in northern Spain in 1491, Loyola followed the typical path of a nobleman's son by becoming a page, squire and finally a knight. There was nothing particularly religious about him. He described himself then as:

St Ignatius Loyola, the founder of the Jesuits.

> **SOURCE D**
>
> *A man given to the delights of the world, whose main delight consisted of fighting in wars, with a great and vain desire to win fame.*

At the age of 32, Loyola was very seriously wounded in both legs during the siege of Pamplona in 1521. While recovering, he read books about Christ and the saints. These books had a profound effect on him and he decided to devote his life to God. First, he lived the life of a hermit, praying up to seven hours a day in a cave at Manresa and then he went on a pilgrimage (on foot) to the Holy Land. While there, according to himself, he:

> **SOURCE E**
>
> *learned that it was God's will that he should not stay in Jerusalem, he wondered in his heart what he should do and finally decided to study for a time in order to be able to help souls.*

DID YOU KNOW?

Before going to Manresa, Ignatius Loyola spent three whole days confessing the sins of his life at the famous mountain top monastery of Montserrat, near Barcelona.

Loyola studied for the priesthood over the next 12 years. He had to learn Latin during this time and did so by joining a class of young boys. In addition, he began to write a book on his religious views called *The Spiritual Exercises*. Because of his extreme devotion and lack of concern for appearance, Ignatius Loyola was suspected of being a heretic for a time, with the result that he was imprisoned twice by the Spanish Inquisition, but released on both occasions.

Later, Loyola went to France. Finally, while studying in Paris, he and a group of followers formed themselves into the Society of Jesus (1534); they were recognised as a new religious order by Pope Paul III in 1540. The Jesuits

were committed to thorough training, poverty and loyalty to the Pope. Also, according to Loyola's *Constitutions*, they were:

> **SOURCE F**
>
> *ready to live in any part of the world where there was hope of God's greater glory and the good of souls.*

Organised as a sort of spiritual army, with Ignatius Loyola as the order's first **General**, the Jesuits became known as the **Soldiers of Christ**. Yet, their methods were those of teaching and example, not war. Loyola himself founded the Roman College and the Germanicum, a college that specialised in training German candidates for the priesthood.

In Europe, the order concentrated on areas where Protestantism was growing. Highly educated Jesuits left seminaries such as the Roman College and through their efforts succeeded in keeping the Catholic faith strong in Poland, Czechoslovakia and in southern Germany.

Loyola's Jesuits also had an influence on Church architecture. Determined to re-emphasise the Catholic Church's commitment to building magnificent churches with fine artwork, the Jesuits built many churches in the new Baroque style. The most famous of these was the Gesu in Rome.

Jesuits also went far beyond Europe to convert non-Christians to Catholicism in places such as Brazil, Ethiopia and India. The greatest Jesuit missionary was undoubtedly **St Francis Xavier** (1506–52),

St Francis Xavier preaching in India.

The Gesu church in Rome.

another Spaniard and co-founder of the order with Loyola. He spent 12 years in Asia, three of them in Malaysia. In India, he won thousands of converts and founded a seminary there to train priests. He had further success in Japan, but died of fever before entering China.

Ignatius Loyola himself died in 1556 and was declared a saint in 1622. His tomb lies in the Gesu, and the right arm of St Francis Xavier is kept there too in a special shrine.

CAN YOU SAY?

17. Where was Ignatius Loyola born?
18. Mention *one* contribution made by Ignatius Loyola to the Catholic Counter-Reformation. *(Junior Certificate Higher Level 1999)*
19. What is the full name of the Jesuits?
20. According to **Source D** above, what was Ignatius Loyola's main interest in life before 1521?
21. In **Source E** above, what decision did Loyola make?
22. Using **Source F** above, explain why the Jesuits travelled all over the world.
23. Who was the great Jesuit missionary of Asia?
24. Write an account of the Society of Jesus (the Jesuits).
(Junior Certificate Higher Level 2002; similar in 2009.
Aim to write at least six good sentences)

MINI-PROJECT

Return to the chapter on the problems of the Catholic Church (Chapter 24). Make a short list of these problems (headings will do) and write a sentence about each one, stating how it had or had not been changed by the Counter-Reformation.

KEYNOTES

1. **New religions:** Wars of Religion • Scotland's Presbyterianism • Anglicanism • St Bartholomew's Day Massacre • vernacular writing • powerful rulers
2. **Counter-Reformation:** Roman Inquisition • *Index Librorum Prohibitorum* • Spanish Inquisition • *auto da fé*
   Council of Trent: abolition of abuses • clarification of doctrine
   New orders: Capuchins • Ursulines • Carmelites
3. St Ignatius Loyola • Knight • Pamplona • Manresa • Paris
   Society of Jesus: Jesuits • *The Spiritual Exercises* • Soldiers of Christ • General • Baroque churches • St Francis Xavier • missionaries

27 Sixteenth-Century Ireland

After the Norman invasion, as we saw in Chapters 10–13, Ireland had its castles, manors, feudal system, towns, churches and monasteries like every other land in the Middle Ages. Yet, Ireland was unusual – though not exceptional – in a number of ways too, particularly in the fact that the island was controlled by different groups of people.

NORMANS AND IRISH

The descendants of the early Normans were, in many cases, still in Ireland. These families, such as the Fitzgeralds, Butlers and Burkes, still ruled over their lands and sometimes had local Irish 'kings' as their vassals. On the other hand, some parts of Ireland had never been fully captured by the Normans and some parts had even been won back by the Irish. Families such as the O'Neills, O'Donnells and McCarthys had their lands for centuries before the arrival of the Normans. In the Middle Ages, they still observed the same Brehon Laws and traditions, and spoke the same language as in Celtic times.

So, who really ruled medieval Ireland? Officially, the Kings of England did. Ever since 1172, when Henry II had been accepted by Normans and Irish alike as **Lord of Ireland**, each King of England had kept that title. Year after year, the Norman lords of Ireland, and several of the Irish ones too, paid their dues to the King of England in accordance with feudal tradition. In truth, however, as long as the English kings received a good income from their Irish subjects, they had little other interest in medieval Ireland.

Old English and Irish families in the 16th century.

The Normans 'Become' Irish

In the centuries after 1169, the Normans in Ireland slowly took on the language, pastimes, laws and dress of the Irish. Marriages between Norman and Irish families took place, and gradually the differences between the two groups disappeared. The Normans had, in many ways, become 'more Irish than the Irish themselves'. By 1400, the main difference between Normans and Irish was in name – the Normans being called **Old English** and the others **Irish**. The Irish comprised the overwhelming majority of the population.

> ### DID YOU KNOW?
> Gerald Fitzgerald, third Earl of Desmond, was praised in the Annals as 'a witty and ingenious composer of Irish poetry' in 1398. He was Ireland's most powerful Norman!

THE ENGLISH IN IRELAND

Officially, a 'chief governor', council of ministers and parliament (that first met in 1264) ran Ireland on behalf of the King of England. In practice, the Old English had only occasional dealings with this government, and the Irish had almost none at all.

The only parts of medieval Ireland that were truly 'English' and loyal to the Crown were big towns (such as Waterford, Kilkenny and Galway), and the area around Dublin, known as the **Pale**. It was extremely difficult for the English government to keep in contact with some towns because they were surrounded by wild countryside with hostile Irish inhabitants. Moreover, the towns depended on these Irish neighbours for their survival. A document from 1463 tells us:

> **SOURCE A**
>
> *The profit of every market, city and town in this land depends principally on the resort of Irish people bringing their merchandise to the said city and towns.*

The Pale.

It was also common for towns or settlements surrounded by Irish-ruled territory to be forced to pay **black rents** – in other words, ransoms paid to Irish chieftains to persuade them not to attack the town or settlement.

The Pale

Medieval Ireland's main city or 'capital' was Dublin. In the early 13th century, King John built three castles there to protect the royal taxes. As the centuries passed, Dublin and its surrounding countryside remained the stronghold of English power in Ireland. A report to the

The Dublin crest still shows the three castles.

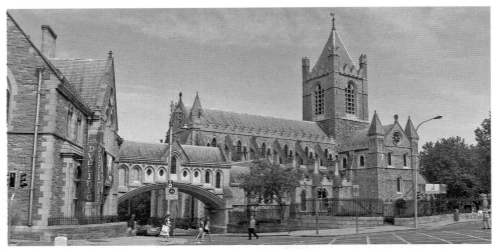

Christ Church, Dublin: A gothic cathedral that was begun in 1038.

SOURCE B

A Gaelic Irishman
A Woman from the Pale

English king in 1435 declared that it was only in the area around Dublin:

> *scarcely thirty miles in length and twenty miles in breadth, that a man might safely... go... to answer the King's writ and to do his commandments.*

This area was called the 'Pale' because around it there was a ditch and paling fence to stop attacks by the Irish or possibly even the Old English who lived beyond. English language, dress, customs and laws dominated in the Pale. English farming methods – based on **tillage** (crop-growing) – were widespread there, whereas the rest of Ireland still relied largely on cattle. Dublin merchants did most of their trade with England.

CAN YOU SAY?

1. Name *two* Norman families and *two* native Gaelic families in 16th century Ireland.
2. What title did English kings hold in Ireland?
3. What precisely did the terms **Old English** and **Irish** mean?
4. According to **Source A** above, why did towns depend on their Irish neighbours?
5. What parts of Ireland were truly loyal to the English Crown?
6. What were **black rents**?
7. Why did Dublin become Ireland's capital?
8. How did life in the Pale differ from life outside? Give *three* examples.

England Takes Control: The Fitzgeralds

With control only over a very small area of Ireland, some English kings in the 14th and 15th centuries had sent over special 'Lord Deputies' to govern Ireland for them. However, the Lord Deputy needed huge amounts of money to keep an English army in Ireland and to build castles beyond the Pale. Another idea was to find an Old English lord outside the Pale who was powerful enough to rule Ireland for the king. From 1468, the Fitzgeralds, Earls of Kildare, held the post of Lord Deputy.

The Fitzgeralds were the most powerful family in Ireland because of their rich Kildare lands, their strong castle at Maynooth, marriage alliances with the other powerful families and their closeness to the Pale. From Kildare, they could attack or protect the Pale as they wished. Even though the Fitzgeralds supported the House of York during and after the Wars of the Roses, both Henry VII and Henry VIII were happy to appoint the Earls of Kildare as Lord Deputies. That was the case, at least, until 1534.

Cannon being used for the first time in Ireland during the rebellion of Silken Thomas.

HENRY VIII AND IRELAND

By the 1530s, Henry VIII had a number of reasons for wanting to increase English control over Ireland. As we saw, the Fitzgeralds were Yorkist rather than Lancastrian supporters during the Wars of the Roses. The same was true of most Old English families, except for the Butlers. Therefore, Henry saw Ireland as a possible base of support for his enemies in England.

In addition, by 1534, Henry VIII had broken with the Pope and divorced Catherine of Aragon, making powerful enemies in Catholic Ireland outside the Pale. Henry was worried that Ireland would ally with Catholic rulers in Europe against him. He was also keen to set up a form of empire for England, as Spain was doing in America, and Ireland seemed an obvious place to start.

In 1534, Silken Thomas, son of the Lord Deputy Gearóid Óg Fitzgerald, rebelled against the Crown after hearing a false rumour that his father had been executed in London by Henry VIII. The rebellion was crushed and, in 1537, Silken Thomas and his five uncles were executed in London. Gearóid Óg died soon afterwards and the lands of Kildare were taken over by the Crown.

Maynooth Castle, the home of Silken Thomas.

Surrender and Regrant

Henry VIII was now determined to control Ireland by peaceful means. His idea for doing so was known as **Surrender and Regrant**. Both Old English and Irish rulers were to 'surrender' themselves and their lands to the king, and he 'granted' them their lands back, with an English title for good measure. 'The O'Neill', for instance, became the 'Earl of Tyrone'. Henry's scheme was accepted by 40 Irish and Old English lords, fearful that, if they refused the offer, they would suffer the same fate as the Fitzgeralds.

The scheme also had two important benefits for Irish rulers. Under Brehon Law, it was the family (or clan), and not the ruler, who owned the land. The new system made the ruler the owner of the land and so increased his wealth. Secondly, it guaranteed that the lord's eldest son would succeed to the title; Brehon Law did not. Indeed, according to Irish custom, the successor could be any member of the lord's family (derbhfine). Thus, many rulers gained security for their sons by accepting Surrender and Regrant.

SOURCE C

Irish chieftains submitting to the Lord Deputy.

Increasing English Control

The system made it easier for Henry to control Ireland. All who surrendered to him swore to accept him as their king – in 1541, he had himself declared **King of Ireland**. They also swore to accept English law and language. Part of the deal was that any lord who rebelled against the Crown would have his lands taken. This had far-reaching consequences, as we will see in the next chapters.

CAN YOU SAY?

9. Study **Source B**, illustrations by Lucas de Heere (c.1575) on page 252. From the picture, give *one* piece of evidence to suggest that the artist felt that the Gaelic Irish were uncivilised.
(*Junior Certificate Higher Level 2001*)
10. Why were the Kildare Fitzgeralds very powerful?
11. Give *three* reasons why Henry VIII wanted to control Ireland.
12. Explain **Surrender and Regrant**.
13. How did it (a) benefit Irish chieftains and (b) increase English control over Ireland?
14. Look at the picture, **Source C**, above.
    (a) Identify *one* difference in the clothing of the Irish (kneeling) and the English.
    (b) What is resting on the cushion beside the Lord Deputy?
    (c) What is this object meant to represent, in your opinion?

DID YOU KNOW?

As King of Ireland, Henry VIII introduced a new coinage to Ireland. At his suggestion, one side of the new coins bore a harp, an ancient musical instrument; it has become a symbol of Ireland and appears on Irish coins up to the present day.

THE IRISH REFORMATION

We saw how England and Scotland were both affected by the Reformation. From Henry VIII onwards, English kings and queens were heads of the English Church. As England tried to increase its control over Ireland, it was natural that its rulers would also try to get Irish people to accept their new religions and accept the monarchs of England as heads of the Church in Ireland. This would certainly make Ireland easier for England to control, if it could be achieved.

Just as in England, Henry VIII attempted to make the Irish Catholic Church accept him as its head, in place of the Pope. The Irish Parliament, dominated by loyal men of the Pale, passed an **Act of Supremacy** (1536), making Henry head of the Irish Church. As in England, the monasteries were closed and their lands were confiscated by the Crown and sold off.

During the reign of Edward VI (1547–53), Protestant laws were introduced in Ireland. Later, Queen Elizabeth I (1558–1603) introduced the **Elizabethan Church Settlement**, which made the Church of Ireland almost identical to the Church of England. Mass was outlawed and attending Church of Ireland services was compulsory. Elizabeth also set up Ireland's first university, **Trinity College** (1591), but no Catholics could attend.

One of the first English translations of the Bible, which was published in 1539.

Problems

However, these efforts to start an Irish Reformation met with little success. Henry VIII was supported by George Browne, Archbishop of Dublin, who was slow to bring in sweeping changes. Even the more dedicated Protestant Bishop John Bale had little effect.

The closure of monasteries never took place in areas ruled by the Gaelic Irish, where the government still had little influence. Furthermore, most of Ireland outside the Pale was Gaelic-speaking, yet the new English clergy spoke only English and the Protestant prayer books were written in English.

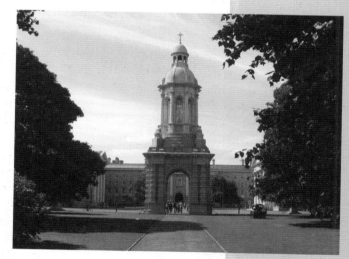

Trinity College, Dublin.

THE IRISH COUNTER-REFORMATION

Even when monasteries were closed, wandering friars kept Catholicism alive in Ireland through preaching, according to a report in 1539:

> **SOURCE D**
>
> *that every man ought, for the salvation of his soul, fight and make war against our sovereign lord the king's majesty.*

Finally, as the Counter-Reformation in Europe began to develop in the second half of the 16th century, Jesuits such as Fr David Wolfe came to Ireland and preached strongly against Protestantism. They set up Catholic schools and even helped young Irishmen to attend Catholic universities and seminaries in Europe. Later, these Irishmen returned to continue the struggle against the Reformation. A document from 1608 shows how little impact the Reformation had had:

> **SOURCE E**
>
> *Priests land here secretly in every port and creek... every town... is full of them... the people in many places resort to Mass in greater multitudes than for many years past.*

CAN YOU SAY?

15. State *one* way in which Ireland was affected by the Reformation.
   (*Junior Certificate, Higher Level, 1995 and 1997; two consequences asked for in 2006*)
16. Give *one* reason why Henry VIII closed the monasteries in Ireland.
   (*Junior Certificate Ordinary Level 1995*)
17. List *two* mistakes made by the English in trying to bring about an Irish Reformation.
18. Why did the friars, according to the 1539 report (**Source D**) above, urge war against 'the king's majesty'?
19. Who was the king at the time of that 1539 report?
20. How did the 1608 report (**Source E** above) explain the fact that people were going to Mass 'in greater multitudes' than before?

KEYNOTES

1. **Normans and Irish:** Henry II • 'Lord of Ireland' • Old English • Irish • the Pale • black rents • Dublin
2. **Growing English control:** Lord Deputies • Fitzgeralds of Kildare • Henry VIII • Gearóid Óg • Silken Thomas's rebellion • Surrender and Regrant • King of Ireland
3. **The Irish Reformation:** Act of Supremacy • Act of Uniformity • Elizabethan Church Settlement • Trinity College, Dublin • Archbishop George Browne • closure of monasteries • friars • Jesuits • Fr David Wolfe

The Munster Plantation

28

BACKGROUND TO PLANTATION IN IRELAND

In the last chapter, we saw how England had struggled to gain control over Ireland from the arrival of the Normans in 1169 until the middle of the 16th century. Over the coming two chapters, we shall see how all this changed in little over 100 years. By 1660, all of Ireland would be firmly under Crown control and most of the land would be owned by Protestant English and Scottish settlers. This chapter explains how this major change in Ireland began.

Henry VIII's scheme of Surrender and Regrant (see Chapter 27) stated that the lands of any lord who rebelled would be confiscated by the Crown. During the 1540s, the idea gained ground among English officials that when Irish lands were confiscated, they should be sold or rented to reliable settlers. This was called a **plantation**, with the new settlers being called **planters**. The idea was that it would make money for the Crown and prevent further rebellions.

LAOIS AND OFFALY

In the 16th century, the counties of Laois and Offaly were the bases of the O'Moore and O'Connor families respectively. Each family had a small army of highly armed soldiers called **kernes** (or **woodkernes**). During the 1540s, the kernes raided the lands of the Pale, stealing cattle and burning houses.

Rebellion Crushed

Several expeditions of English soldiers from the Pale drove the O'Moores and O'Connors back, but they escaped to the bogs and woods of the midlands and soon attacked the Pale again. The Lord Deputy, St Leger, tried to make peace with the two families. Other English officers wanted to crush them outright. English attacks provoked the O'Moores and O'Connors into rebellion, and, so, their lands were confiscated by the Crown in 1546.

DID YOU KNOW?

An account from 1533 tells us:

SOURCE A

All the butchers in Dublin hath not so much beef to sell as would make one mess of broth [a portion of soup]... and cause thereof is, they be nightly robbed; there hath been four or five raids... within this ten days, so that one butcher... hath lost 220 cows.

SOURCE B

An attack by woodkernes on English settlers.

Plantation

The confiscated land was divided into **estates** (large farms), some of over 1,000 acres (400 hectares). Loyal soldiers or people of the Pale could rent the estates in the better farming areas near the Pale very cheaply. Native Irish, but *only* those who could be trusted not to rebel, rented the poorest land, furthest from the Pale. Both counties were ruled by English **sheriffs**, based in new towns such as Maryborough (now Portlaoise). Every planter accepted English law, language and customs. All planters contributed to the defence and upkeep of roads, bridges and forts in the two counties.

A surviving plantation fort.

In the long term, this plantation was not very successful. The O'Moores and O'Connors continually attacked the planters who had taken their land. There were never enough English soldiers or forts to protect the planters properly. By 1600, the two counties were largely in the hands of the original families again. However, the plantation is important because it marked the beginning of a new policy. The English would use plantation again, having learnt from their mistakes here.

Trouble Elsewhere

In the early years of the reign of Queen Elizabeth I (1558–1603), another Irish rebellion was crushed. The rebel this time was Shane, leader of the O'Neill family of Ulster. After a long struggle, Shane was finally defeated and killed, but Elizabeth chose not to attempt an Ulster plantation because, by then (the 1560s), the Laois-Offaly Plantation was in difficulties. Instead, she placed what she thought were loyal members of the O'Neill family in control of their Ulster lands. You'll read about one of them, Hugh, in Chapter 29.

CAN YOU SAY?

1. In **Source A** above:
   (a) Why was Dublin so short of beef?
   (b) How many raids had there been in the previous ten days?
2. What was the Pale? *(Junior Certificate Higher Level 1995 and 2001)*
3. What was a plantation? *(Junior Certificate Higher Level 1995)*
4. In the picture above (**Source B**):
   (a) Where are the woodkernes coming from?
   (b) Why are they being led by a piper?
   (c) Describe the weapons carried by the woodkernes.
   (d) The two people marked 1 and 2 appear upset. What is upsetting them?
   (e) Describe what is happening in part **C** of the picture.
   (Junior Certificate Higher Level 1995)
5. Give *two* reasons why the Laois-Offaly Plantation was not really successful.
6. Who was Shane O'Neill?

PROBLEMS IN MUNSTER

The Fitzgeralds of Desmond had reasons to resent Queen Elizabeth I. They had remained strongly Catholic throughout the Reformation and feared that Elizabeth would try to force Protestantism on them. As part of her efforts to increase English control in Munster, Elizabeth encouraged Englishmen known as **adventurers**. These adventurers claimed to be descendants of the early Normans who had been granted lands in Munster by King Henry II. They now laid claim to these lands, which in reality belonged to the Fitzgeralds and other Old English families. Fearing for their future, the Fitzgeralds, and even native Irish families such as the MacCarthys, blamed the Crown for encouraging the adventurers.

Queen Elizabeth was the daughter of Anne Boleyn and so was closely related to the Butlers of

259

Ormond. Elizabeth was angered by clashes between the Butlers and their neighbours, the Fitzgeralds of Desmond, over territorial boundaries. Her response was to arrest both the Earl of Ormond and the Earl of Desmond and bring them to London in 1567. Ormond was quite well treated, but Desmond was held in the Tower of London, which was used as a type of prison. He was still there in 1569 and this provoked the Fitzgeralds into open rebellion.

The Desmond Rebellion

This First Desmond Rebellion was quickly crushed and its leader, the Earl's cousin, James Fitzmaurice Fitzgerald, fled the country. In 1573, the Earl of Desmond was released and his lands were given back to him. However, the rapid crushing of the rebellion had firmly established English power in Munster. Throughout the 1570s, Elizabeth's 'President of Munster', Sir John Perrot, built forts there and encouraged more adventurers to claim Irish and Old English lands. Elizabeth's Reformation policies were also forced on the people more strongly than ever before. Eventually, James Fitzmaurice Fitzgerald returned to Ireland and began the Second Desmond Rebellion in 1579.

A woodcut from the period done by the English artist John Derricke, which shows fighting during the Desmond Rebellion.

Although Fitzmaurice himself was killed, for a time the rebellion was very successful. The Earl of Desmond joined the rebels, as did some Leinster leaders. Fitzmaurice had tried to get help from Catholic rulers such as Pope Gregory XIII and Philip II of Spain. In 1580, 600 Italian and Spanish troops landed at Smerwick Harbour, Co. Kerry. However, success was to be short-lived.

An English army of 8,000 troops entered Munster. The Spaniards and Italians were surrounded and massacred at Dún an Óir, near Smerwick. The rebels elsewhere were beaten and the Earl of Desmond was killed by some Irish enemies in 1583. In crushing the rebellion, the English army also destroyed vast quantities of cattle and crops in rebel areas. Lord Justice Pelham explained:

SOURCE C

I give the rebels no breath to relieve themselves... they be continually hunted. I keep them from their harvest and have taken great preys of cattle from them.

Soon, there was widespread famine in Munster and an estimated 30,000 people died. Elizabeth's advisers urged her to ensure that Munster never troubled the Crown again by organising a plantation. The lands of the Earl of Desmond – almost 250,000 acres (more than 100,000 hectares) – and of his allies were confiscated by the Crown, and the **Plantation of Munster** began.

CAN YOU SAY?

7. Which families ruled (a) Desmond and (b) Ormond in the 16th century?
8. How was Queen Elizabeth related to Ormond?
9. Give *two* reasons why the Desmond Rebellions occurred.
10. Who was James Fitzmaurice Fitzgerald?
11. What happened at Dún an Óir in 1580?
12. (a) In Lord Justice Pelham's account above (**Source C**), how did he treat Munster's inhabitants?
    (b) Why do you think he did this?
13. State *two* results of the Desmond Rebellions.

THE PLANTATION OF MUNSTER

The 577,000 acres (230,000 hectares) to be planted were mapped out by a team of surveyors. In counties Kerry, Limerick, Cork and Waterford, estates were divided into lots of 4,000 acres (1,600 hectares), 6,000 acres (2,400 hectares), 8,000 acres (3,200 hectares) and 12,000 acres (4,800 hectares). Rents varied from one to three pence per acre, depending on the quality of the land, but very few estates cost more than £80 (€102) a year.

The size of the estates was much greater than those in the Laois-Offaly Plantation. That scheme had attracted only a few hundred planters, mostly from Ireland, but the aims of the Munster Plantation were much greater. A document from 1586 tells of how:

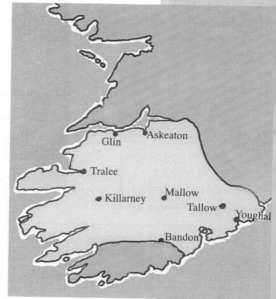

The Plantation of Munster.

SOURCE D

A number of gentlemen of Somerset, Devon, Dorset, Cheshire and Lancashire are making themselves ready to go to Munster, to plant two or three thousand English people there this year, and it is intended by them to plant above twenty thousand English people within a few years.

Undertakers

The new planters were expected to give certain guarantees or

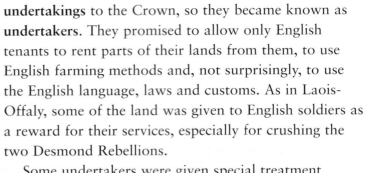

undertakings to the Crown, so they became known as **undertakers**. They promised to allow only English tenants to rent parts of their lands from them, to use English farming methods and, not surprisingly, to use the English language, laws and customs. As in Laois-Offaly, some of the land was given to English soldiers as a reward for their services, especially for crushing the two Desmond Rebellions.

Some undertakers were given special treatment because they had been loyal servants of the Queen. For example, Sir Walter Raleigh, who was a famous soldier and explorer, was given 42,000 acres (16,800 hectares) around Youghal for a rent of only £66 (€84) a year. He brought in English tenants and, as we saw in Chapter 22, planted the first ever potatoes in Ireland, having brought them back from his travels in America.

Walter Raleigh's house at Myrtle Grove, Youghal.

DID YOU KNOW?

Edmund Spenser was regarded as the greatest poet in 16th-century England. He received 3,000 acres (1,200 hectares) in north Cork and many of the descriptions in his famous poems, *The Faerie Queene* and *Epithalamion*, are based on the scenery of Cork.

Sir Walter Raleigh.

Edmund Spenser.

CAN YOU SAY?

14. Give *two* reasons why the English began a policy of plantation in Ireland.
(*Junior Certificate Higher Level 1999 and 2001*)
15. According to **Source D** above:
    (a) Where did the settlers come from?
    (b) How many English settlers were expected eventually?
16. What precisely were **undertakers**?
17. Where did (a) Raleigh and (b) Spenser settle?
18. Explain the term **plantation** as used in Irish history.
(*Junior Certificate Ordinary Level 1995*)

The Plantation in Action

The Munster planters felt safer living in groups because they feared attack by the natives, as had happened in Laois and Offaly. Thus, 'plantation towns' sprang up, such as Tallow (Co. Waterford), Mallow and Bandon (Co. Cork) and Tralee (Co. Kerry). Bandon was the most important plantation town, being described in 1622 as 'a large and beautiful town, consisting of about 250 houses, the inhabitants being all English'.

The new settlers introduced new farming methods and even set up small industries such as barrel-making and fisheries. Forests were cleared and the timber used to make charcoal, which was vital for the smelting of iron ore. Exports of timber, iron, fish and farm produce to England rose rapidly and the value of land in Munster had risen 500% by 1598. One settler described the advantages of living in Munster around 1590:

> **SOURCE E**
>
> *Their soil for the most part is very fertile, and apt [suitable] for wheat, rye, barley...and all other grains and fruits that England anywise doth yield. There is much good timber in many places... There is very rich and great plenty of iron stone [ore]...also there is great store of lead ore, and wood sufficient to maintain divers [several] iron and lead works for ever...A fresh salmon, worth 10 shillings in London (can be bought) for 6d [half a shilling]...You may keep a better house in Ireland for 50 pounds a year than in England for 200 pounds a year.*

For the native population, although many had died during the famines of the Desmond Rebellions, to some extent life went on as before. They paid rents now to 'New English' planters rather than 'Old English' lords. Some may even have found employment in industries set up by the planters, such as in the iron works owned by the Earl of Cork in west Waterford. However, there is no doubt also that many suffered from the strict enforcement of English law in Munster and many lost lands. If they did live in or near plantation towns, they were forced to live in poorer areas, often called 'Irishtowns'.

Problems

Despite all this, the plantation was not easy to maintain. Instead of the hoped-for 20,000 planters, little more than 4,000 English people settled in Munster. As a result, undertakers often had to take on Irish tenants (despite being forbidden to do so). In fact, most of the planted land was still being farmed and lived on by the native population. Many undertakers also had little interest in living in Ireland and were 'absentees'. Some, such as Raleigh, soon sold their interests. The main aim of the Munster Plantation was to make Munster English, but in reality that never happened.

DID YOU KNOW?

Tallow in Co. Waterford is known as 'Tulach an Iarainn' (the mound of iron) in Irish. The name comes from the huge iron works, set up there during the Munster Plantation by Richard Boyle. Boyle bought Walter Raleigh's estate in 1604 and his son, Robert Boyle, became one of the world's greatest scientists – read about Boyle's Law in an encyclopaedia.

Sir Christopher Hatton, a favourite dancing partner of Queen Elizabeth, had a fine house built on his estate in west Waterford, though he never even visited it in his lifetime.

The plantation agreement stated that settlers would be protected by the English army for seven years, but after that they would have to provide for their own defence. Few of them ever did this, so when their settlements were later attacked by the Irish, many planters were killed or fled back to England. Edmund Spenser's castle at Kilcolman, for example, was burnt down in 1598 and is still a ruin.

SOURCE F1

Youghal, Co. Cork, which was also a plantation town, developed near the estate of Sir Walter Raleigh.

SOURCE F2

The town walls of Youghal today.

CAN YOU SAY?

19. Having examined **Source E** above, name:
    (a) *Three* crops grown by the planters in Munster.
    (b) *Three* ways in which life was better than in England.
20. Look at both the drawing of Youghal (**Source F1**) and the modern photograph of its walls (**Source F2**) above.
    (a) From **F1**, give one piece of evidence to suggest that the town was well developed and wealthy. *(Junior Certificate Higher Level 2009)*
    (b) Identify *one* defensive feature of the walls that is still visible in **F2**.
    (c) Identify *one* feature of the walls shown in **Source F1**, but gone from the modern picture labelled **F2**. Can you give a reason for the change?
21. The document below, **Source G**, is an extract from an account of an attack by the native Irish against planters in Munster in 1598.
    (a) How did the undertakers react when the rebels attacked?
    (b) What was the author's attitude to the undertakers' reaction?
    (c) What did the Irish rebels find in the abandoned dwellings?
    (d) What happened to the 'faithful subjects' who were found by the rebels in the countryside?
    (e) Why does the author refer to the planters as 'faithful subjects'?
    (f) According to the document, the actions of the Irish rebels were unmerciful. Why do you think this was so?

(Junior Certificate Higher Level 1998)

SOURCE B

This document is an adapted extract of an account given by Fynes Moryson to the Duke of Ormond concerning an attack by the native Irish against the planters in Munster in 1598.

Neither did these gentle undertakers make any resistance to the rebels but left their dwellings, and fled to walled towns; yea, when there was such a danger in flight, as greater danger there could not have been in defending their own... I may not omit to acquaint your lordship that, at my coming into this province I found that the most part of the undertakers had most shamefully quitted and forsaken their castles and houses of strength before even the traitors came near them... whereby the rebels furnished themselves with arms and other munitions that before served against them. He that was abroad could not get home to save himself but was intercepted: he that was in a thatch house had no leisure to shift himself into a castle for defence but was slain by the way. He that was in the countrie had no respite (no time) to fly into the cittie: every base churle (Irish countryman) *laid hands on his next neighbour. Our selves, our goods were a prey onto them* (were attacked by them). *In 48 hours was all the mischief done all over the countrie. In the compass of 200 miles… were all your faithful subjects displaced, their goods surprised, themselves murdered… There should you have seen, some smothered out of houses, others hewn to pieces most unmercifully, others driven… into the waters where they were drowned; there should you have seen young infants scarce yet seasoned (3–4 years) lamentably brained, some dashed against the walls, others tumbled from high towers.*

Calendar of State Papers, Ireland, 1598–99, p. 291

KEYNOTES

1. **Plantation:** planters • Laois-Offaly • O'Moores and O'Connors • Pale • kernes • St Leger • Queen's County • King's County • sheriffs • estates
2. **Munster:** Fitzgeralds of Desmond • Elizabeth I • adventurers • Butlers of Ormond • James Fitzmaurice Fitzgerald • Sir John Perrot • Desmond Rebellions
3. **Plantation of Munster:** low rents • large estates • undertakers • soldiers • Raleigh • Spenser • Youghal • potatoes
4. **Progress of Plantation:** plantation towns • Bandon • Tallow • new farming methods • industries • exports • Richard Boyle • absentee owners • failure of plantation

MINI-PROJECT

Write an account of the following: *A settler in an Irish plantation of the 16th or 17th century.* Name the plantation.

You may use the following hints in your account.

Hints:

- settler's background
- why the settler came to Ireland
- conditions on which the land was granted
- results of the plantation

Write at least 12 sentences, without looking at your book.

(Junior Certificate, Higher Level, 1992, 1993, 1998, 2006; Ordinary Level, 1993, 1998, 2000: wording and hints vary, but essentially the same information was required).

The Plantation of Ulster and Beyond

29

BACKGROUND TO THE ULSTER PLANTATION

With much of Ireland relatively under control by 1590, Elizabeth's government in Dublin now turned its attention northwards towards Ulster. This province had never been brought under the control, in any meaningful way, of either the Normans or the English and was still very much a stronghold of the native Irish. It was densely wooded, with few roads, and was far from any English settlements.

Since the time of Shane O'Neill, Elizabeth's government had kept the peace in Ulster partly by blackmail; this included the kidnapping of **'Red' Hugh**, son of **The O'Donnell**, in order to force the important O'Donnell family to accept English officials. The O'Neills of Tyrone were the most powerful Ulster family and Elizabeth believed she had guaranteed their loyalty by appointing **Hugh O'Neill** as Earl of Tyrone. Hugh had been educated in England and even fought with the English forces in the Desmond Rebellion, so his loyalty seemed assured. She could not have been more mistaken.

Hugh O'Neill, Earl of Tyrone.

The new Lord Deputy **Fitzwilliam** encouraged adventurers to lay claim to lands controlled by Ulster families such as the Maguires of Fermanagh. All over Ulster, the presence of English sheriffs and officials caused great anger. Leaders such as 'Red' Hugh O'Donnell of Donegal and Hugh O'Neill felt under threat from these intruders. In addition, Ulster had remained strongly Catholic and efforts to impose the Anglican religion there met with opposition. By 1593, Hugh O'Donnell formed an alliance with the Pope to defend Ulster from Protestantism.

DID YOU KNOW?

Once, the 'loyal' Hugh O'Neill persuaded Queen Elizabeth to send him lead to fix his castle roof. Instead, he used it as ammunition against Elizabeth's own soldiers during the Nine Years War.

THE NINE YEARS WAR

In 1594, Maguire and O'Donnell defeated small groups of English in a series of battles; what we now call the **Nine Years War** had begun. Hugh O'Neill joined the rebels in 1595. He and O'Donnell wrote to **Philip II** of Spain:

Gallowglasses were generally more heavily armed than kernes.

The Ulster chiefs gathered large armies – O'Neill alone had 10,000 men, some of them hired soldiers from Scotland called **gall óglaigh** ('foreign soldiers'), or **gallowglasses** (as the Irish words were rendered in English).

Defeat

The most spectacular Irish victory in the Nine Years War was in 1598 at the **Yellow Ford,** north of Armagh. English losses were over 2,000 men, while the Irish lost 200. Success followed success and Irish chieftains outside Ulster joined the rebellion. Spanish soldiers came to help in October 1601, but landed at **Kinsale,** hundreds of miles from Ulster.

O'Neill and O'Donnell led their forces southwards to join them, but at the **Battle of Kinsale** on Christmas Eve, 1601, they were routed by a 20,000 strong English army, led by Lord Deputy **Mountjoy.** The 4,000 Spaniards surrendered, and within two years came the surrender of O'Neill and the other leaders at the **Treaty of Mellifont** (1603).

The Flight of the Earls

At Mellifont, the Ulster chieftains agreed to accept English rule in their lands – sheriffs and judges – and to abandon Irish traditions and any further thoughts of rebellion. Back at home, the defeated leaders met with anger from their people, as the Nine Years War had resulted in much famine and hardship, just as the Desmond Rebellion had done earlier in Munster.

With the decline in support from their people and increasing English control over Ulster, O'Neill and almost 100 leading members of Ulster's Irish families fled Ireland in an event known as the **Flight of the Earls** (1607). They sailed from Lough Swilly to Spain and Italy; O'Neill lived the rest of his life as an honoured guest of the Pope himself, dying in Rome in 1616.

Queen Elizabeth I died just before the Treaty of Mellifont in 1603. Being unmarried and childless, she was succeeded by her cousin, King

James VI of Scotland, who then became **King James I** of England. In Scotland, he had successfully introduced plantation schemes in areas where rebellious clans lived. Consequently, he was easily persuaded by England's officials in Ireland that the best guarantee of Ulster's future loyalty was through a plantation.

CAN YOU SAY?

1. (a) Explain how the English tried to make sure that the O'Neills and O'Donnells remained loyal.
    (b) Give *two* reasons why they did not remain loyal, and instead chose war.
2. When O'Neill and O'Donnell wrote to Philip II (**Source A**):
    (a) What did they want?
    (b) What did they promise in return?
3. What were gallowglasses? Explain *one* way in which they differed from kernes.
4. Where were the Irish defeated in 1601?
5. Give *two* reasons why the Flight of the Earls took place.
6. Who succeeded Elizabeth I as ruler of England in 1603?

THE PLANTATION OF ULSTER

In the early years of James I's reign, much of counties Antrim and Down was granted to two Scottish noblemen, Sir James Hamilton and Sir Hugh Montgomery. They brought over thousands of Scottish settlers as tenants to work the land and by 1609 these planters were well settled. However, it was really after the Flight of the Earls that the English officials decided on a much larger plantation, covering the lands of the defeated Irish lords over six other counties. In 1609, the **Plantation of Ulster** began in earnest.

DID YOU KNOW?

In 1605, a number of English Catholics tried unsuccessfully to blow up the Houses of Parliament with King James inside. This 'Gunpowder Plot' is commemorated with bonfires and fireworks each year in England on Guy Fawkes Night, 5 November. Fawkes was one of the plotters.

King James I of England.

The Gunpowder Plot of 1605 was foiled.

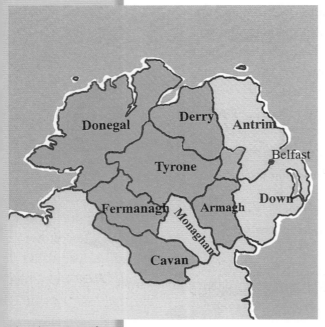

The Plantation of Ulster.

Organising the Plantation

The area to be planted covered six entire counties – Donegal, Derry (then called Coleraine), Tyrone, Armagh, Fermanagh and Cavan. In the Munster Plantation, less than 300,000 acres (121,000 hectares) had been successfully planted in the end. In Ulster, these six counties occupied four million acres (1.6 million hectares).

Lessons had been learnt from previous plantations – no-one was to be given more than 2,000 acres (900 hectares) of land, unlike the unmanageably large estates in Munster. In addition, conditions placed on the planters were much more strictly enforced than before, to prevent the later recovery of lands by the native Irish.

This description tells us of the work of the surveyors before the plantation:

> **SOURCE B**
>
> *About the end of July last they began their journey into Ulster where they lay in camp nine weeks, and during that time performed two principal things. They took inquisitions* [evidence], *the counties being divided into baronies, they made a description of every barony in a several* [separate] *map…The maps were finished, and herein as well the proportions for undertakers of all sorts as the Church lands already granted and signed* [assigned] *to forts, corporate towns, free schools, etc., are distinguished by sundry* [various] *marks and colours.*

Who Was Involved?

There were six distinct groups involved in the Ulster Plantation:

1. As in earlier plantations, land was rented to **undertakers**. Their estates were of either 1,000 acres (400 hectares), 1,500 acres (600 hectares) or 2,000 acres (800 hectares) and annual rents were very low, about £5.33 (€6.77) per thousand acres (400 hectares).

    The undertaker lands were located close to each other. For protection, undertakers promised to build a castle or stone house, depending on the size of their holdings, 'with a strong court or bawn about it'.

They **undertook** to have only English or Scottish tenants. Tenants' houses also had to be built in accordance with these conditions.

2. The largest group of planters were **servitors**, so-called because they had given service to the Crown as officials or soldiers in the Nine Years War. They were allowed to have some Irish tenants as long as they maintained strict control over them; consequently, servitors paid an annual rent of £8 (€10.16) per thousand acres (400 hectares). They were also to introduce English farming methods to their lands.

3. Earlier, smaller plantations had found it difficult to attract enough English or Scottish planters, and with a plantation of this size it would be impossible. Therefore, a third group of planters were the **native Irish** who, if they could prove they had remained loyal during the Nine Years War, could rent land at £10.66 (€13.54) per thousand acres (400 hectares). Their estates were always situated next to those of servitors, who were obliged to keep an eye on them.

4. Being particularly anxious to see the Ulster economy prosper, King James I reserved the entire county of Coleraine for **London craft guilds**. The county was renamed **Londonderry** soon afterwards. The guilds formed an 'Irish Society' and promised to build new houses in Derry and Coleraine as well as found new settlements. Again they were encouraged to use only English or Scottish tenants.

A view of the top of Derry's walls today. In the left of the picture is the Guildhall. This view shows the width of the wall to be that of a narrow street.

271

5. Some Ulster land was reserved for **special groups**. The lands of the Catholic Church were handed over to the Anglican Church of Ireland. Also, some land was set aside in each county to provide funding for a series of Royal Schools, which educated planters' sons. Trinity College, Dublin, Ireland's Protestant university, actually received 30,000 acres (12,100 hectares) of land in the Ulster Plantation to pay for its upkeep.

6. Finally, what of the Irish who lost their lands? Around 6,000 of the most troublesome, usually woodkernes who had fought in the Nine Years War, were transported to Sweden where they served as hired soldiers. Many of the rest endured harsh conditions trying to survive on the hills and bogs. Some became outlaws called **tories**, attacking the homes of planters or travellers in remote areas. The seeds of yet another rebellion were still there, as an observer warned in 1617:

> **SOURCE C**
>
> *It is dangerous to drive them from the homes of their ancestors, making the desperate seek revenge and even the more moderate think of taking to arms.*

CAN YOU SAY?

7. Which counties were involved in the Ulster Plantation?
8. List *two* ways in which this plantation differed from those which we studied in the last chapter.
9. In **Source B** above:
   (a) How long did the surveyors spend in Ulster?
   (b) Name *three* things that they marked on the maps they made.
10. List *three* conditions agreed to by undertakers.
11. What native Irish people received land?
12. Name *three* special groups who received free land.
13. What were *tories*?
14. Why did the observer of 1617 worry about the tories in **Source C** above?
15. **Source D** (next page) is a drawing of the vintners' settlement at Bellaghy.
    (a) Why did the settlers build a castle?
    (b) From the picture, give *one* piece of evidence to suggest that the native Irish lived in the houses marked Y. *(Junior Certificate Higher Level 2001)*

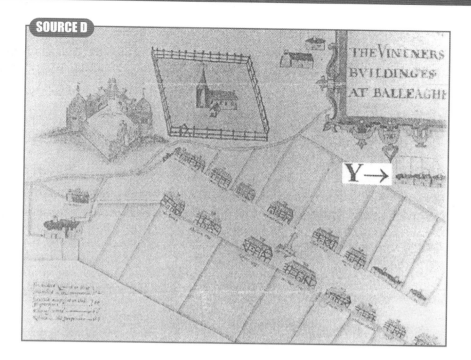

SOURCE D

THE VINTNERS BVILDINGES AT BALLEAGHE

Y→

Results of the Ulster Plantation

The most obvious result of the Plantation of Ulster was the large number of **English and Scottish people** now living in the province. By 1640, there were 40,000 Scots, with a slightly smaller number of English settlers. The new settlers formed the majority of the population in the planted counties, though Londonderry in particular remained mainly Irish as the guilds never brought over large enough numbers of tenants. To the native population, the city and county was still known simply as Derry.

The planters brought their **religions** with them. Whereas the English settlers were largely Anglican, the Scots introduced Presbyterianism (remember John Knox in Chapter 26). Catholic churches were sometimes taken over by the Protestant planters, but new Protestant churches were built too, notably the Gothic St Columb's Church of Ireland cathedral, which still stands in Derry.

There were some **religious tensions** among the settlers themselves. Members of the Anglican Church accepted the king as Head of the Church, but Presbyterians resented his plan to appoint bishops for them. However, the most important religious division was that between the Catholic native population and the Protestant settlers.

<blockquote>
DID YOU KNOW?

Protestants often referred to Catholics as 'Papists' because they were followers of the Pope, and *Papa* was the Latin term for 'Pope'.
</blockquote>

St Columb's Cathedral.

Religious division was to remain a source of near-continuous hatred, mistrust and even violence from 1609 onwards. Although earlier Irish plantations had too few Protestant planters to outnumber the native Catholic population, Ulster was different. The new settlers and their religions became firmly established there and helped to make Ulster the most loyal Irish province, where once it had been the most troublesome from Britain's point of view.

English planters brought **modern farming methods** with them and cleared much of Ulster's forests to make way for crop-growing, replacing the cattle-rearing preferred by the Irish. Many Scots were skilled in textiles (weaving cloth). The volcanic soil of north-east Ulster was ideal for the growing of **flax**, the raw material for the making of **linen**; over the next 300 years, Ulster became an important centre for linen making, while the rest of Ireland had very few industries. Farm produce and linen, sold in large quantities to Britain, made Ulster Ireland's richest province.

A drawing from 1622 of the villages of Magherafelt and Salterstown, built by the Salter's Company of London.

DID YOU KNOW?

English settlers began to colonise America at the same time as the Ulster Plantation. Many towns in Virginia, for instance, are similarly laid out to Ulster towns, though in 1650 no town in America was as large as Derry/Londonderry.

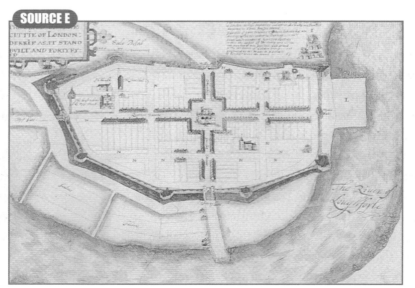

SOURCE E

Raven's sketch of Londonderry.

The planters also built **towns** in Ulster. The province had been almost untouched by the Vikings and Normans, and had few towns. 'Plantation towns' such as Belfast, Donegal, Enniskillen and Coleraine were now founded.

These towns had a central square (or 'diamond') where the main streets met and where the main buildings such as churches and guildhalls were situated. Leading out from the square lay carefully arranged streets and rows of houses, generally surrounded by a high wall. Thomas Raven's sketch of Londonderry on the previous page is typical of these plantation towns, which became centres of industry, trade and courts in the 17th century.

CAN YOU SAY?

16. From what countries did new planters come?
17. What were the *two* main forms of Protestant religion that they brought with them?
18. What changes in farming were introduced?
19. Give *two* reasons why linen production boomed after the Ulster Plantation.
20. Name *three* plantation towns in Ulster.
21. List *five* ways in which the plantation changed Ulster.
22. From **Source E**, identify *two* features which provide evidence that it was a plantation town. (*Junior Certificate Higher Level 2009*)
23. Why did the planners of plantations in Ireland not wish the English or Scottish planters to have Irish tenants? (*Junior Certificate Ordinary Level 1992*)

LONGER TERM EFFECTS OF PLANTATIONS

Cromwell's Plantation

After the Plantation of Ulster, roughly 40% of the land of Ireland was owned by Protestants. During the following 30 years, there were no major rebellions or wars in Ireland to trouble the Crown. King James I died in 1625 and was succeeded by his son, Charles I. It was during his reign that trouble flared again.

In the last chapter, we saw how native, or **Irish,** families who had lost their lands to settlers in the Ulster Plantation often attacked the planters. By 1641, Irish anger and the desire to recover lost lands led to a full-scale rebellion. Attacks on English and Scottish settlers took place and between 2,000 and 10,000 settlers were killed. Many more fled their homes in terror, for the safety of the Pale or of large towns.

While the rebellion was taking place in Ireland, England's King Charles I was overthrown by his own parliament. As a result, the

Oliver Cromwell

country came under the control of the leader of parliament, **Oliver Cromwell**. He held the title 'Lord Protector'. As soon as the king's forces had been defeated in England, Cromwell brought his army to Ireland to crush the rebellion here.

Cromwell's time in this country has gone down in Irish history as a time of terrible war and destruction. Most infamously, he was responsible for the massacres of many people in the towns of Drogheda and Wexford, and the forced deportation of thousands of Irish families once the rebellion had been crushed.

Cromwell also introduced a plantation that saw Catholic landowners (considered 'transplantable persons') driven from their land to the poorer land of Connacht. (This is where the phrase 'To hell or to Connacht' originates.) In their places, English soldiers and servitors were granted large farms and estates. The result was that by 1655, most of Ireland's land was owned by English or Scottish 'landlords', with the Catholic Irish who remained renting land as their tenants.

After Cromwell

Unlike the Ulster plantation, Cromwell's did not introduce tens of thousands of Protestant tenants into Ireland. It did, however, ensure that by 1700 around 90% of Irish land was owned by Protestants of English or Scottish origin. Only in Connacht did Catholics remain as the main landowners; elsewhere, they became tenants of the new Protestant **ascendancy** (wealthy land-owning class).

In Ulster, since the 1609 plantation, the majority of tenants as well as landowners had been Protestant settlers from England and Scotland, making Ulster even more loyal to the Crown. This also led, however, to centuries of bitterness between Catholics and Protestants in Ulster and elsewhere, nowadays called **sectarianism**.

The control exercised by English-speaking settlers in Ireland meant that the English language dominated in trade, business, landlord-tenant and official dealings. Gradually, the Irish language declined, remaining strongest in Connacht, where the dispossessed had been sent by Cromwell. The decline in the Irish language also meant that language-related **cultural activity** – songs, poetry, music, storytelling and so on – struggled to survive in many parts of the country.

Unlike with the Ulster Plantation, there was no real boom in town building after Cromwell. Outside of Ulster, Ireland remained a primarily **rural** country. Among the Irish living on the poorer land of the west, potato growing became popular after the 1650s. Their lands were often too poor to produce much else. This increasing reliance on potatoes over the next two centuries was to have terrible results, as we shall see in Chapter 40.

CAN YOU SAY?

24. Explain *two* challenges to the Catholic religion in Ireland after the plantations.
25. Name *one* plantation carried out in Ireland in the 16th or 17th century and the ruler who carried out that plantation.

(Junior Certificate Ordinary and Higher Levels 1996, and Ordinary Level 2001, two rulers asked in 2006 Higher Level)

26. Explain *one* of the following terms as used in British plantations in Ireland: undertaker, servitor, bawn, Irish papist, transplantable persons.

(Junior Certificate Ordinary and Higher Levels 1996)

27. Write about the consequences (results) of plantations in Ireland under each of *two* of the following headings:
    (a) Religion
    (b) Politics
    (c) Culture

(Note: Your answer may include both immediate and long-term results.)

(Junior Certificate Higher Level 1999, and – worded differently – 1997, 2001 and 2009)

KEYNOTES

1. **Rebellion in Ulster:** Hugh O'Neill • Hugh O'Donnell • Fitzwilliam • Nine Years War • Philip II • gallowglasses • Yellow Ford • Kinsale • Treaty of Mellifont • Flight of the Earls
2. **Plantation of Ulster:** King James I • undertakers • servitors • loyal Irish • London guilds • 'Irish Society' • tories
3. **Results: English and Scottish planters** • Protestant religions • tillage • flax • linen-manufacture • plantation towns
4. **Longer term effects:** rebellion • Cromwell's campaign • Cromwellian plantation • transplanting to Connacht • new landowners

MINI-PROJECT

Write an account of the following: *A native Irish landowner who lost land in a named plantation.*

Hints:
- name of plantation
- reasons for losing the land
- new conditions of life
- relations with the new planters

(Junior Certificate Ordinary Level 1994, 1999 and 2006; Higher Level, 1994 and 2000 – no hints given at Higher Level in 2000)

30 America moves towards revolution

Following Columbus' historic voyage in 1492, many Spanish and some Portuguese explorers claimed large areas in Central and South America. In the 16th century, other European explorers turned their attention northwards. As Spanish forces moved into North America, so too did explorers and soldiers from France, Britain, the Netherlands and even Russia, carving-up land between them. The French in particular took over an area almost as large as Europe itself, to the east, west and north of the great Mississippi River.

BRITAIN'S THIRTEEN COLONIES

Britain's lands in North America consisted of thirteen regions known as **colonies**, the first set up at **Virginia** in 1607. Over the next 150 years, many people from Britain settled these colonies, which were rich in land and raw materials. By 1750, the colonies had 1.7 million settlers (**colonists**).

As with other conquerors elsewhere, settling in these colonies meant driving out the native population, then known as **Indians** from Columbus' famous mistake in 1492 (see Chapter 22). Thus, to the west of the thirteen British colonies in 1750 lay not only the French territories but also tribes of angry natives whose lands had been taken from them.

By 1750, many settlers

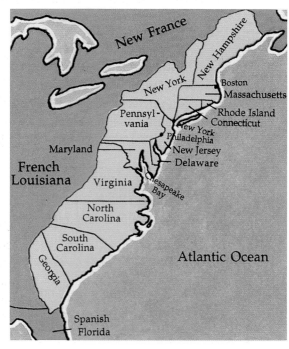

Britain's thirteen American colonies

in America had lost their links with their countries of origin. Most 'British' colonists in 1750 had never been to Britain and felt much more 'American' than 'British'. Yet, they were controlled by Britain. Laws in the American colonies were still made by the British Parliament, and their defence was in the hands of the British army, called **Redcoats** because of their uniforms.

The French and Indian War (1756–63)

From 1756 to 1763, the colonists and British Redcoats fought side by side, defending the colonies from a combined French and Indian attack. Victory allowed Britain to take over French lands, including Canada. Yet fighting in a seven-year war so far from home cost Britain £14·5 million per year. Despite the war, the American colonies were very prosperous and sold vast amounts of tobacco, grain, fish and raw cotton to Europe. Many in Britain, particularly the new king, George III, felt it only fair that the colonists should help to pay the costs of winning the French and Indian War (also called the **Seven Years War**). The way to do this was by imposing taxes on the wealth of the colonists.

The city of Boston in 1770

Britain had other reasons for wanting to control America. From the 1750s on, Britain had begun to build factories on a large scale. The American colonies were becoming more and more prosperous, and Britain needed a cheap supply of American raw materials to make goods such as cotton clothing. Also, America produced similar goods to Britain, such as iron, and Britain wanted to prevent America from competing with it for sales to the rest of the world.

Finally, Britain hoped to sell the products of Britain's factories to America. The result of all this was that Britain began to place taxes and trade restrictions on America, just as Americans were beginning to look for freedom from Britain. It was inevitable that serious conflict would arise.

CAN YOU SAY?

1. Name three European countries that gained land in North America in the 1600s.
2. What was Britain's first American colony?
3. How were the colonists in America similar to the Normans in Ireland?
4. List two results of the French and Indian War.
5. Who was the English king in the 1770s?
6. Give three reasons why Britain decided to impose taxes on America.

INCREASED TAXATION

For years, Britain's **Navigation Acts** forced the thirteen American colonies to sell some of their products, like rice and tobacco, to Britain alone. With no outside competition, Britain could buy the goods cheaply. America was also prevented from building up its iron industry as this might rival Britain's. Finally, America was to buy some goods, such as sugar, from other British colonies only, even though they could be bought more cheaply elsewhere. Most Americans put up with these restrictions in return for the protection of the Redcoats. However, now the British government tried to recover the cost of the French and Indian War by imposing even more taxes.

1. **The Stamp Act** (1765) placed taxes on a wide range of items such as legal documents, wills, newspapers, certificates – even playing cards and dice.
2. **The Quartering Act** (1765) made the colonies pay extra taxes to cover the cost of keeping (quartering) Redcoats in America.
3. **The Townshend Acts** (1767) imposed taxes on goods such as lead, glass, paper, paint and tea which America imported in large quantities. These taxes raised money for Britain but caused price rises in America.

Anger among Americans

American reaction to these new taxes was swift. Some colonists took to violence and attacked tax collectors. Some refused to buy British goods coming into America, while others adopted more political methods. Many felt that, as the colonies were not represented in the British Parliament, then the British Parliament had no right to make laws for and impose taxes on America. This was summed up in the cry, '**No taxation without representation**'.

British Reaction

The British response to the growing opposition in the colonies was confused. Parliament scrapped the Stamp Act but issued a **Declaratory Act** (1766) stating:

> **SOURCE A**
>
> *The British government has… full power and authority to make laws… to bind the colonies and people of America, subjects of the Crown of Great Britain, in all cases whatsoever.*

Force was also used and, in 1770, five American demonstrators against the Townshend Acts were shot dead by Redcoats. This incident became known as the **Boston Massacre**. Exaggerated accounts of it spread around the colonies, making Americans even more angry with Britain. Even when the Townshend Act was scrapped, Britain still insisted on keeping a tax on tea as, according to the British Prime Minister North:

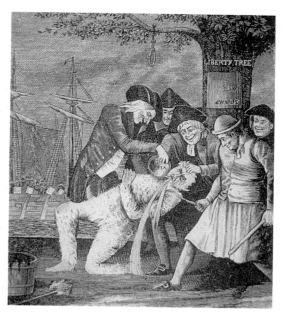

An American cartoon shows a tax collector being tarred and feathered.

SOURCE B

a mark of the supremacy of Parliament and... a declaration of their right to govern the colonies.

SOURCE C

The Boston Tea Party

Trouble arose again in 1773 when Britain introduced a **Tea Act**. This allowed the British East India Company (in which many British members of parliament owned shares) to sell its tea duty-free in the American colonies. The Americans saw this as a deliberate attempt to give the British company control of the American tea market. They felt that the Act was brought in to help Britain rather than America, and if they accepted it, others would follow.

Once again, Boston was the centre of opposition. On 16 December 1773 about 1,000 colonists, some dressed as Mohawk Indians, boarded three English tea ships in the city's harbour. They broke open the chests of tea and dumped all of them – 342 chests – into the sea. The **Boston Tea Party**, as the event became known, rallied all Americans to oppose British rule as never before. John Adams wrote at the time:

> **SOURCE D**
>
> *This destruction of the tea is so bold, so daring, so firm, intrepid and inflexible, and it must have so important consequences, and so lasting, that I... consider it an epoch in history.*

The Boston Tea Party.

The Intolerable Acts

The British response was severe. In 1774, a series of new laws was introduced – called the **Intolerable Acts** by the Americans. The most important of these was the closure of Boston Harbour. By now, hatred of the British and their taxes was so great that representatives from all thirteen colonies formed themselves into a sort of American parliament called the **First Continental Congress** (September 1774).

CAN YOU SAY?

7. Why did most Americans tolerate the Navigation Acts?
8. Which Acts taxed (a) playing cards and (b) paint?
9. List three different ways in which Americans showed their opposition to the Acts of 1765–67.
10. What exactly does 'No taxation without representation' mean?
11. In the picture of the Boston Massacre by Paul Revere (**Source C**), what details suggest that Revere hated the British?
12. (a) In **Source A**, what details might have angered Americans and why?
    (b) In **Source B**, why in your own words did Britain keep the tea tax?
    (c) Based on his comments on the Boston Tea Party (**Source D**), do you think John Adams was American or British? Why?

THE OUTBREAK OF WAR

The Congress

The Congress which met at Philadelphia declared its opposition to the British. One delegate, Patrick Henry from the colony of Virginia, spoke in favour of all-out rebellion:

> **SOURCE E**
>
> *Is life so dear, or peace so sweet, as to be purchased at the price of chains and slavery? Forbid it, Almighty God! I know not what course others may take, but as for me, give me liberty or give me death.*

Throughout the thirteen colonies, secret groups prepared to resist the British by force. Weapons began to be stockpiled in hiding-places. The Continental Congress encouraged the part-time civilian armies (**militias**) in each colony to prepare for war. Meanwhile, the British General Gage was made Governor of Massachusetts, the colony in which Boston was situated. He decided to seize hidden American weapons before these could be used.

The First Shots

On 18 April 1775, word reached the Boston home of a man named **Paul Revere** that Gage and some eight hundred Redcoats were going to seize the weapons' of the Massachusetts militia at the town of Concord, near Boston. Revere rode through the night to Lexington and raised the alarm so that the militia could recover their guns before the British arrived.

At **Lexington** a force of just seventy-seven Americans fought a brief battle with the British. Later, when the British troops arrived at Concord, they were routed by a force of several hundred American militiamen. The first shots in the **American War of Independence** had been fired.

After the Battles of Lexington and Concord, a **Second Continental Congress** met in May 1775 and appointed an experienced soldier from Virginia to take charge of a new **American Continental Army**. His name was **George Washington**. Days later, the Americans were defeated by the British in the **Battle of Bunker Hill**, but not before 1,000 British soldiers had died – three times as many as the number of American deaths.

The Battle of Bunker Hill.

*Paul Revere's ride,
18 April 1775*

Independence Declared

There was now no turning back. The American Continental Congress decided that the goal must no longer be just to end taxes or the sale of British tea – it must go beyond that. On 4 July 1776, the Congress issued one of the most famous documents in history, the **Declaration of Independence**. Largely the work of **Thomas Jefferson**, the declaration outlined twenty-six different complaints against the British and included some startling new ideas:

> ### SOURCE F
>
> *We hold these truths to be self-evident, that all men are created equal, that they are endowed by their Creator with certain unalienable Rights, that among these are Life, Liberty and the pursuit of Happiness. That to secure these rights, governments are instituted among Men, deriving their just powers from the consent of the governed. That whenever any Form of Government becomes destructive of these ends, it is the Right of the People to alter or to abolish it, and to institute new Government...*
>
> *The History of the present King of Great Britain is a history of repeated injuries and usurpations, all having in direct object the establishment of an absolute tyranny over these states. We, therefore, the Representatives of the United States of America... do solemnly publish and declare, that these United Colonies are, and of Right ought to be, Free and Independent States; that they are Absolved from all Allegiance to the British Crown...*

CAN YOU SAY?

13. In **Source E** above, what evidence is there that Henry hated British rule?
14. Who was the British Governor of Massachusetts?
15. What were the first two battles of the war?
16. Who was chosen to lead the American forces?
17. Who chiefly wrote the *Declaration of Independence*?
18. Study the extract above from the American *Declaration of Independence* (**Source F**), 4 July 1776 and answer the following questions:
    (a) State the 'unalienable Rights' each man has as mentioned in the source.
    (b) From whom do governments get their 'just powers'?
    (c) Why did the representatives of the United States of America absolve themselves 'from all Allegiance to the British Crown'?

(Junior Certificate Higher Level 1992)

KEYNOTES

Background: thirteen British colonies • 'Americans' • Indians (Native Americans) • Redcoats • French and Indian War • George III • taxation

Taxation and Reaction: Navigation Acts • Stamp Act • Quartering Act • Townshend Acts • Declaratory Act. • No taxation without representation • Boston Massacre • Tea Act • Boston Tea Party • Intolerable Acts.

Outbreak of War: First Continental Congress • Philadelphia • militias • Paul Revere • Lexington • Concord Second Continental Congress • Continental Army • George Washington • Bunker Hill • Thomas Jefferson • Declaration of Independence

George Washington

GEORGE WASHINGTON (1732–99)

George Washington, at the age of twenty, inherited his family's 8,000 acre (3,200 hectare) estate at Mount Vernon, Virginia. There, he introduced many modern farming methods and enjoyed farming; in his own words:

> **SOURCE A**
>
> *It is honourable, it is amusing and, with superior judgement, it is profitable.*

Washington also had an interest in politics and became a member of Virginia's own assembly in 1755. Standing 6 feet 2 inches tall (roughly 1 metre 90 centimetres), he proved himself a fine athlete and, in the French and Indian War, he also distinguished himself as a soldier. He once wrote to his brother:

> **SOURCE B**
>
> *I have heard the bullets whistle, and believe me, there is something charming in the sound.*

When Washington retired from the army, he married a widow named Martha Dandridge. She already had two children and owned some 15,000 acres (6,000 hectares) of fine Virginia land. Washington was now one of the wealthiest landowners in the colony. He was angered by Britain's efforts to tax America and he vowed in May 1774:

> **SOURCE C**
>
> *I will raise 1,000 men, subsist them at my own expense, and march myself at their head for the relief of Boston.*

At first, Washington was not convinced that America should seek full independence from Britain, but his views gradually changed. He was chosen as one of Virginia's seven delegates to the First Continental Congress in 1774 and to the Second Congress in 1775. After Lexington and Concord, Congress chose Washington as commander-in-chief of its army.

Mixed Fortunes at War

Upon taking charge of the American forces in 1775, Washington turned them into an impressive fighting force of 20,000 men.

In March 1776, the Americans under Washington won a great victory and drove the British, led by General **Howe**, out of **Boston**. The Americans captured 200 cannon and hundreds of rifles, supplies badly needed against the better-equipped Redcoats.

Unfortunately, success at Boston was short-lived. When Washington tried to hold the city of **New York** against General Howe's army, he failed. The city was very spread out and included a number of islands. Howe's force of some 25,000 men and thirty warships was too strong for the Americans. When Washington made the mistake of allowing the British to occupy the high ground at **White Plains** just outside New York, his men were bombarded by British cannon and forced to retreat.

Washington won some minor victories at **Princeton** and **Trenton**, where a Co. Wexford-born sailor named John Barry (1745–1803) served with distinction. However, in 1777 things got worse for the Americans. Howe's army of 18,000 men, reinforced by some German troops called **Hessians**, attacked **Philadelphia**. Not only was Philadelphia the largest city in America, but it was also the home of the Continental Congress. With a much smaller army and desperately short of equipment, Washington was defeated. The Congress had to flee from Philadelphia, and Generals Howe and Cornwallis occupied the city for the British on 26 September 1777.

American disappointment at the loss of Philadelphia was made up for at the **Battle of Saratoga** the following month. There, the American army led by General Horatio **Gates** defeated and captured an English force of 8,000 men. The victory was seen by many as a turning-point for the

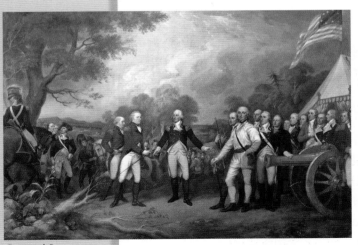

General Burgoyne surrenders to General Gates at Saratoga, 17 October 1777.

Americans and, for a time, some members of the Continental Congress even thought of appointing General Gates as commander-in-chief in place of Washington.

CAN YOU SAY?

1. Based on **Sources A**, **B** and **C**, what kind of personality did George Washington have? Write three points.
2. Which city did the Americans capture in March 1776?
3. Give two reasons why Washington was defeated at White Plains.
4. On the British side, what were Hessians?
5. Which British generals occupied Philadelphia?
6. Name two of the original thirteen colonies that broke away from England in the late 18th century. (*Junior Certificate Higher Level 1998*)

FROM DEFEAT TO VICTORY

Washington at Valley Forge

Having been defeated at both White Plains and Philadelphia, Washington needed to regroup his forces during the winter of 1777–78. They camped at a desolate spot north of Philadelphia called **Valley Forge**. There, with the Congress beginning to lose its faith in Washington, and in freezing conditions, the men endured great hardship. Many died from hunger.

> **SOURCE D**
>
> *Christmas dinner, little more than flour and scraps of beef, is over. The men lie on the damp ground in the open air or in makeshift tents and huts, too weak from cold and hunger to know the difference between waking and sleeping.*

On 23 February 1778, Washington reported that no one had had meat in two weeks. On that same day Washington's weakened and demoralised army received a welcome boost with the arrival of a German baron, called **Frederick von Steuben**. A former captain in the great Prussian army, he reorganised the Americans into a disciplined, fully-organised army along European lines. He gave the Americans fresh spirit and confidence.

French Help

The Americans received another great boost in February 1778. Britain's traditional enemy, France, joined the war on America's side. Since 1776, France had given muskets, gunpowder and other supplies to the Americans. Individual Frenchmen too, like the **Marquis de Lafayette** (1757–1834), had helped the Americans.

Now, Lafayette and the American representative in Paris, **Benjamin Franklin**, persuaded **King Louis XVI** to send a 6,000 strong army and a fleet of ships to assist the Americans against his great enemy, Britain.

The arrival of the French was decisive. Up to then, the powerful British navy had controlled the seas off the east coast of America. The small American navy had been no match for the powerful British warships. With the French taking part, the British no longer had complete control.

Yorktown

On land, French forces combined with Washington's men and over the next two years the Americans gained the upper hand in the war. Then, in mid-1781, 7,000 British troops under **General Cornwallis** were surrounded at **Yorktown**. Washington had some 9,000 American troops, assisted by 5,000 Frenchmen, while a French fleet anchored in Chesapeake Bay to prevent a British escape by sea. The British resistance began to crumble. Finally, in October, a section of the army led by the Marquis de Lafayette himself tore through the remaining British defences and General Cornwallis surrendered.

The Americans storm the British defences at Yorktown, 14 October 1781.

Victory at Last

Victory at Yorktown decided the outcome of the war. The will of King George and the British government to continue fighting faded away. The Redcoats began to return home in January 1782 and the following month the British Parliament voted to abandon the war effort. Peace negotiations began in Paris between British representatives and a team of Americans comprising Benjamin Franklin, John Jay and John Adams. In the **Treaty of Versailles**,

September 1783, Britain recognised the independence of the thirteen American colonies and withdrew all troops from American soil.

Washington resigned from his position once the war was over and returned to his farm. He also received a grant of land from the Congress as a token of its gratitude, along with £24,700 (€31,363) in expenses. Yet his 'retirement' was not to be permanent; his country would call upon him one more time a few years later.

CAN YOU SAY?

7. Where did Washington's army spend the winter of 1777–78?
8. According to **Source D**, (a) what did the soldiers eat and (b) where did they sleep at Valley Forge?
9. Who was Frederick von Steuben?
10. What help did France give America before 1778?
11. How many men had Washington at Yorktown?
12. What were the effects of French involvement in the American Revolution? (*Junior Certificate Higher Level 1994*)
13. What treaty ended the war in 1783?

Results of the war

Americans celebrate 4 July as the date of the founding of their nation because on that date in 1776 the *Declaration of Independence* was published. Certainly, it is possible to say that America was an independent nation from that day. It elected its own Congress, ran its own army and on 14 June 1777 even adopted its own flag. This became known as the **Stars and Stripes**, with a red or white stripe representing each of the thirteen colonies that had fought the British. The number of stars was to increase to fifty over the years, representing the fifty states which make up the USA today. *The Star Spangled Banner*, written in 1814, later became the US national anthem.

Democracy established

The changes brought about by American independence involved much more than just a new flag or an anthem. In many respects, simply by overthrowing its foreign rulers, America set a pattern for many other nations to follow. In 1787, a special convention was called which established the new United States of America as a democracy. While democracy itself was an ancient Greek idea, it had died out thousands of years before. The democratic system is based on 'the

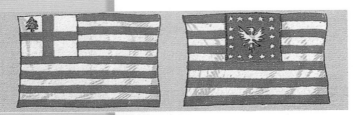

The Stars and Stripes today with (above) two early flags of the American War of Independence.

wishes of the people' (Greek **demos** – 'people' and **kratos** – 'rule').

America chose a parliament called the **United States Congress** to make its laws. This was based in the new capital city which was named after **George Washington**. It had two sections or houses, the **Senate** and the **House of Representatives**. Each state appointed two senators to the Senate, while the members of the House of Representatives were elected by the male citizens, one for every 30,000 voters. The Congress met on **Capitol Hill**.

The day-to-day running of the country was placed in the hands of a president. This was another major change brought about as a result of the War of Independence. Up to then, every independent nation had been ruled by a monarch who succeeded to his/her position by right of birth. The American president was elected democratically for a term of four years. George Washington was chosen as the country's first president in 1789 and, ever since, presidents have lived at the **White House**, Washington.

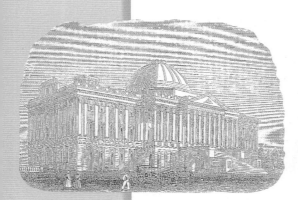

The Capitol Building in 1848; begun in 1793 it was still unfinished.

Mount Rushmore in South Dakota, a giant sculpture which features the heads of four American Presidents: George Washington, Thomas Jefferson, Theodore Roosevelt and Abraham Lincoln. Work on the eighteen-metre high sculpture was begun in 1927 and completed in 1941.

AMERICA'S IMPACT ON IRELAND

The success of the Americans in gaining independence had a very big impact in countries around the world, including Ireland.

We saw in the last chapter that a lot of America's anger towards Britain developed from the controls that Britain held over the American economy. This was similar in Ireland where a group who had even promised to support Britain against Americans, known as the Irish Volunteers, quickly came to realise that Ireland was suffering because of **economic controls** as America was.

Many Irishmen used the fact that Britain was weakened by its war with America to gain more control over their own affairs. In the Irish parliament, a **Patriot Party**, led by **Henry Grattan**, tried to demand free trade and more say for Irish Parliament members in how Ireland was run. Eventually, Britain agreed to **legislative independence**, giving the Irish parliament the right to make laws (legislate) for Ireland with or without Britain's approval.

Henry Grattan.

After 1776, Ireland and other countries now saw how it was indeed possible to win **freedom through war**. Time and again, Irish rebels had tried to gain freedom from English control through war but always failed. The Americans' success encouraged some Irishmen in the late 18th century to try again, led by a man called Theobald Wolfe Tone. We will read about their efforts in Chapters 37 and 38.

Another important link between American revolution and Ireland was the fact that a number of soldiers in the American forces were of **Irish descent**. Even in the 1700s, many Irish had emigrated to America and their success in helping the colonies gain independence undoubtedly inspired those at home seeking freedom from Britain.

The Americans taught Ireland another important lesson in the manner in which they were able to call on **foreign aid**, particularly in combating the might of the British navy. Just as the Americans did in the 1770s, Irishmen seeking freedom after that would realise that help from Britain's great enemy, France, was vital to any prospects of a successful Irish revolution.

An Irish stamp featuring John Barry.

Many writers in the 18th century period known as **the Enlightenment** had pushed the idea that all men were equal and should have an equal say in the government of their country. This was the core idea in the American Declaration of Independence. As a document written in English, the Declaration was immediately inspiring to Irishmen of different religions and backgrounds to unite in search of independence. It was no accident that they would choose the name 'United Irishmen' for their movement.

Ireland took a final very important lesson from the American Revolution. The Americans had defeated the British and established an independent country. It was also a country in which people were able to elect their own government (a **democracy**). In Ireland, and across Europe in particular, democracy would become the goal of many peoples in the following decades.

CAN YOU SAY?

14. Name (a) the American flag and (b) its national anthem.
15. What does the word democracy mean?
16. Name the two sections of America's parliament.
17. How long is a US president's term of office?
18. Explain four ways in which events in America inspired some people in Ireland to plan a revolution. [Two effects of the American War of Independence on Ireland were asked for on the Junior Certificate Higher Level paper, 2002]
19. Explain the influence of the American Revolution on events in France during the late eighteenth century. (*Junior Certificate Higher Level 2003, 2004*)

MINI-PROJECT

Write an account of the role of George Washington in the American Revolution.
[Without looking at your book, try to make at least ten points on his role in the revolution.]
(*Junior Certificate Higher Level 1994*)
or
Write an account of a person living in America during the period of unrest and revolution in the late eighteenth century.
(*Junior Certificate Higher Level 1999 – No hints given*)
or
A supporter of a named revolutionary leader during the period,1770–1803.
(*Junior Certificate Higher Level 2006 – No hints given*)

KEYNOTES

George Washington: Mount Vernon • Virginia • commander-in-chief.
Course of the war: General Howe • Boston capture • White Plains • Princeton
• Trenton • John Barry of Wexford • loss of Philadelphia • Hessians
• victory at Saratoga • General Gates.
From defeat to victory: Valley Forge • Frederick von Steuben
• Marquis de Lafayette • King Louis XVI • French join in • victory at Yorktown
• Cornwallis surrenders • Treaty of Versailles.
United States established: Stars and Stripes • Star Spangled Banner • democracy
• Washington • US Congress • Senate • House of Representatives • Capitol Hill
• President • White House • Inspiration to Irish revolutionaries • Wolfe Tone
• John Barry • Value of foreign aid • Democracy

32 France: Background to Revolution

THE ANCIEN RÉGIME

The second great revolution of the 18th century took place in France from 1789 onwards. The background causes of the **French Revolution** were more varied and complicated than those of the American War of Independence, and go back to the Middle Ages. France, like the rest of Europe, had a **feudal** system of government. Absolute power was held by a monarch (king or queen) and nobles. In 1789, the King of France was **Louis XVI** and the political system which he led was known as the **Ancien Régime** ('old system').

The Nobles of France

The nobles of the Ancien Régime were divided into two groups. One was the **hierarchy** (higher levels) of the Catholic Church, known as the **First Estate**. Ever since the Reformation, the Catholic Church had remained very strong in France. It owned large estates of land and several churchmen had risen to positions of great power, even prime ministers.

The other branch of the French nobles was made up of great landowners such as dukes, counts, barons and marquises. These were often called the **aristocracy** or **Second Estate**. They too were wealthy and held most of the main positions in the French government, army and courts.

Louis XVI, King of France.

Marie-Antoinette, Queen of France

Taxes

Apart from land and power, the First and Second Estates enjoyed one other privilege under the Ancien Régime. They paid very little tax. As in other feudal systems, most of the taxes were paid by poor peasants in the countryside and workers in the cities. Peasants paid a crippling land tax (*taille*) to the state; both workers and peasants paid a tax to the Church called a *tithe*. Also, people had to pay high prices for food and other goods because of duties placed on these by the state. Among these were the *gabelle* (a salt tax). In addition to all these taxes, peasants had to pay rent to their noble landlords, buy goods from them and even had to carry out free repair work (*corvée*) on their local roads.

The Third Estate

During the 18th century, industries developed and France's cities grew in size. An important result of this was the rise of a new group of people known as the **Third Estate**. This 'middle class' included factory owners, businessmen, lawyers, doctors and other professionals. They were well educated and often very wealthy through their businesses or professions. Yet, the Third Estate had few of the privileges of the nobles. It paid high taxes and very few of its members ever rose to power in the government, army or courts.

SOURCE A

A FAUT ESPERER Q'EU JEU LA FINIRA BEN TOT

Dissatisfaction

We have seen that many French people were deeply unhappy under the Ancien Régime. Peasants and workers resented the taxes and laws which kept them poor. The middle class (or '**bourgeoisie**'), which made up the Third Estate was angry because of the taxes too but also because despite their wealth and education they were denied power. These groups greatly outnumbered the King, nobles and churchmen, but until the reign of Louis XVI, they had been kept down by strict laws and by force. Prisons like the **Bastille** in Paris were constantly full with people who criticised the government or who had failed to pay their taxes.

The result of all of the dissatisfaction we have seen was that many French people were desperate for change. In 1789, events unfolded which were to turn this anger into revolution.

CAN YOU SAY?

1. What was the feudal system called in France?
2. What people belonged to the (a) First, (b) Second and (c) Third Estates?
3. Name three taxes paid by French peasants and explain what each one was for.
4. Study **Source A** above showing a poor French peasant from about 1789 carrying a nobleman and a clergyman on his back, and answer the following:
   (a) Who, according to the cartoonist, were the dominant classes in France?
   (b) Do you think this source is biased or not? Give one reason.
   (c) What does the cartoon try to tell about the treatment of the peasants by the clergy and nobility? (*Junior Certificate Higher Level 1992*)

 THE DEMAND FOR CHANGE

The Ideas of the Enlightenment

A great movement called the **Enlightenment** swept France in the eighteenth century. It was made up of a group of French writers and philosophers ('lovers of wisdom') who sought to bring about change. Instead of accepting the Ancien Régime, men like **Montesquieu** (1689- 1775), **Voltaire** (1694-1778) and **Rousseau** (1712-78) attacked it in their writings.

Jean-Jacques Rousseau

Voltaire was particularly opposed to the privileged position of the Church in France, arguing for freedom of religion. Rousseau once wrote:

SOURCE B

The primary source of evil is inequality; inequality has made possible the accumulation of wealth. The words 'rich' and 'poor' are only relative terms; wherever men are equal, there will be neither rich nor poor. Wealth leads to luxury and idleness.

Ideas of equality inspired the French middle class in particular to seek an end to the privileges enjoyed by the nobles. In short, a growing desire for change emerged during the Enlightenment, change that would bring down the Ancien Régime.

The Royal Family

Louis XVI's palace at **Versailles**, 22 kilometres south-west of Paris, was a colossal building with hundreds of rooms and servants. Here the royal family and some nobles lived lives of feasting, hunting and gambling. Without doubt, the ordinary people resented their wealth, especially when they themselves were poor and hungry. Louis XVI's wife, **Marie-Antoinette**, had a reputation for spending huge sums of money on expensive food, clothing and jewellery. She was also hated because she came from Austria, a traditional enemy.

Palace of Versailles

Public Anger

Envy of the royal family's wealth grew among the peasants in 1787–89 in particular, when bad harvests left many of them on the verge of starvation. The price of wheat doubled in the space of two years. Food prices rose, bringing hardship to workers in the towns and cities. In addition, unemployment was rising as French factories struggled against powerful competition from fast-growing British industries.

France 'Broke'

Despite everything, Louis XVI was not entirely a despot. He allegedly felt for the suffering people in his kingdom. He had shown some willingness to improve France; prisons like the Bastille were being shut down, and torture was being used less and less. Louis could have helped his people by reducing their heavy taxes, but he did not. There was one major problem – France was bankrupt! During the previous fifty years, France had been involved in four major wars at an estimated cost in today's currency of €254 million. Rather than cut taxes, Louis was faced with having to find extra money simply to keep the country going.

The Estates General Called

Things were so bad with France's finances that even the range of taxes that the government had was not enough to raise the money needed. Louis decided that a complete change in the entire tax system was needed and he called a meeting of the **Estates General** to do this. The Estates General was a sort of parliament made up of representatives of the First, Second and Third Estates, but it had not actually met in 175 years!

While the First and Second Estates hoped to use the Estates General to defend their privileges, the Third Estate was inspired by the writings of the Enlightenment and the example of the Americans in 1776. They were determined to seek greater political power and to force the Church and nobles to pay more taxes. Many ordinary peasants and workers pinned their hopes on the Estates General also, believing that if the Church and nobles were forced to pay more taxes, then everyone else would have to pay less. The opening of the Estates General was set for Versailles on 5 May 1789.

The opening of the Estates General, 5 May 1789.

CAN YOU SAY?

5. What, in your own words, was the Enlightenment?
6. According to Rousseau what was 'the primary source of evil' (**Source B**)?
7. What did Rousseau believe wealth led to?
8. Name (a) Louis XVI's main palace and (b) his queen.
9. Why did the peasants grow more angry from 1787 on?
10. What had caused France to run up huge debts by 1789?
11. What exactly was the Estates General?
12. What did the Third Estate expect the Estates General to do?

FROM ESTATES GENERAL TO REVOLUTION

The Voting Issue

Throughout France, the Third Estate outnumbered the First and Second Estates, so it had 610 representatives out of a total of 1,201 voting delegates in the Estates General. This meant that it could outvote the combined numbers of the Church (300) and the nobles (291). Of course, the First and Second Estates realised that this could be damaging for them. Thus, they proposed a *vote par ordre* (**voting by Estate**). This meant that when decisions were being made, the First Estate would agree on its view and then cast a single vote. The Second would do the same and the Third Estate likewise.

If this was agreed upon, it would almost certainly mean that the First and Second Estates would join forces and defeat the Third Estate 2:1 every time. Thus, the Third Estate would be left with even less power than it already had and probably a lot more taxes.

From the start, the Third Estate deputies refused to *vote par ordre*. On the other hand, the First and Second Estates refused to attend a joint meeting with the Third Estate, where they would be outvoted. Several members of the Church and some nobles, including the **Marquis de Lafayette** (hero of the American Revolution), supported the demands of the Third Estate for a new, fairer system. Finally, on 17 June the Third Estate voted to form itself into a **National Assembly** regardless of whether the other Estates joined it or not.

The Tennis Court Oath

SOURCE C

The determination of the Third Estate to achieve their aims grew when they were locked out of their meeting place at Versailles on the morning of 20 June. This was as a result of an error, but the Third Estate deputies believed that it had been done on purpose. The Assembly members moved instead to the nearby royal tennis court and took the **Tennis Court Oath**, swearing:

> **SOURCE D**
>
> *Never to break up and to meet wherever the circumstances dictate until the constitution of the kingdom is set up and laid on firm foundations.*

King Louis XVI was uncertain what to do next. He partly accepted the need for change, but he was a weak man, and was being pressurised by Marie-Antoinette and the nobles who wanted the Assembly broken up. Reluctantly, Louis sent a messenger to the Assembly, calling on its members to disperse, return to the Estates General and *vote par ordre*. One deputy, **Mirabeau**, replied to the king's messenger:

> **SOURCE E**
>
> *Sir, you are a stranger in this assembly, you have not the right to speak here... Return to those who have sent you and tell them that we shall not stir from our places except at bayonet point.*

Growing Support

With 830 members of the original Estates General now in the National Assembly, news reached Louis that a mob of 30,000 citizens of Paris was ready to attack Versailles in support of the Assembly. To the ordinary people of France, the National Assembly was their best chance yet for a new France in which there would be greater justice and equality. Louis finally gave in and ordered the remaining members of the First and Second Estates to join the National Assembly.

It seemed that a great victory had been won by the Third Estate and those who wanted to end the Ancien Régime. However, under further pressure from advisers, Louis sacked his prime minister, **Jacques Necker**, who was believed to support the calls for reform. Worse still, Louis was found to have stationed seventeen army regiments around Versailles and Paris. The Assembly leaders and their supporters in Paris feared that the troops were to be used to break up the new Assembly. People from some of the poorer parts of Paris demonstrated in support of the Assembly, urged on by a lawyer named **Camille Desmoulins**.

The attack on the Bastille

In Paris, there was a huge fortress and prison called the **Bastille** where people were locked up for years without any form of trial. To the people of Paris it was a symbol of the hated Ancien Regime. It also contained a large supply of gunpowder, and fearing an attack from the army, the people needed arms. On 14 July 1789, a mob of workers, craftspeople and small business owners attacked the Bastille. These people were known as *Sans Culottes* ('without breeches'), because they were poor and wore trousers instead of the expensive breeches then in fashion. After a confused attack in which almost 100 *Sans-Culottes* were killed, negotiations with the Bastille defenders took place. Meanwhile, two men forced down the drawbridge by breaking its chains and this allowed the mob to enter the prison. Only seven prisoners were being held in the Bastille at the time and these were set free. The commander of the defenders, the Comte de Launay, was beheaded.

The fall of the Bastille had a huge impact. Most of Paris now rose in rebellion against the king. Bailly, the leader of the National Assembly, was elected Mayor of Paris, and a **National Guard** under Lafayette was formed to protect the Assembly. Louis and his ministers were devastated. Those ministers who had opposed the Assembly

resigned, Necker was given his job back and the troops were withdrawn from around Paris. Clearly, Louis had lost control.

On 17 July, he was forced to come to Paris and put on the type of hat worn by those who had stormed the Bastille; on the hat there was a rosette or **cockade** of red, white and blue ribbons. The Assembly had won a great victory. But the French Revolution was not over – it had, in fact, only begun.

The storming of the Bastille.

CAN YOU SAY?

13. What did *vote par ordre* mean exactly?
14. Why did the Third Estate oppose *vote par ordre*?
15. In the painting, **Source C**, what suggests that the artist was a supporter of the Tennis Court Oath?
16. In your own words, what did the Tennis Court Oath (**Source D**) mean?
17. What do you think Mirabeau meant about only moving from the Assembly 'at bayonet point' (**Source E**)?
18. Give two reasons why the *Sans Culottes* stormed the Bastille.
19. Give three immediate changes which came about after the fall of the Bastille.
20. Mention two causes of the French Revolution.
    (*Junior Certificate Higher Level 1999 – worded differently in 1993*)

MINI-PROJECT

You are a *Sans Culotte* in France in 1789. Write an account of the events in your life up to July of that year.

Hints:

- Taxes.
- Hopes for the National Assembly.
- Attitude to the monarchy.
- Role during the attack on the Bastille.

[Write about ten or twelve sentences, without looking at your book.]

KEYNOTES

Ancien Régime: Mount Vernon • Louis XVI • First Estate • Church • Second Estate
- lay nobles • taxes • *tailles* • *tithes* • *gabelle* • *corvée* • Third Estate
- middle class (bourgeoisie)

Demand for change: Enlightenment • Voltaire • Rousseau • Versailles
- Marie-Antoinette • bad harvests • rising unemployment • France bankrupt
- summoning of the Estates General.

From Estates General to revolution: *vote par ordre* • Lafayette • National Assembly
- Tennis Court Oath • Mirabeau • Necker • Desmoulins • Bastille • *Sans Culottes*
- the National Guard • cockade • 14 July 1789.

The Revolution completed

DESTRUCTION OF THE ANCIEN RÉGIME

After the triumph of 14 July 1789 (**Bastille Day**) the National Assembly began demolishing the Ancien Régime. Noble titles were abolished – everyone was now known as a **citizen** or **citizeness**. Control of the courts, which was in the hands of the nobility, was given now to elected judges. All the feudal dues owed by peasants to their noble landlords were abolished. Church lands were confiscated by the state and in 1790, the **Civil Constitution of the Clergy** was introduced. Under this, religious orders were banned, bishops and parish priests were in future to be elected like any other officials, and the pope's rulings were to be virtually ignored in France.

While some nobles tried to resist the Revolution, most chose to flee from France, hoping to return with help to crush it. The Church was equally angry at the changes, and only seven bishops and half the nation's priests accepted the Civil Constitution. Clearly, the Revolution still had a long way to go.

The Rights of Man

Perhaps the most important reform passed by the National Assembly was the *Declaration of the Rights of Man and the Citizen* on 26 August 1789. Like the American Declaration of Independence before it, this set out new ideals of freedom and equality, firmly based on the Enlightenment. It stated:

> **SOURCE A**
>
> *"Therefore the National Assembly recognises and proclaims the following rights of man and of the citizen: Men are born free and equal in rights. The purpose of all political associations is the preservation of the natural rights of man. These rights are: liberty, property, security and resistance to oppression. Liberty consists in being able to do whatever does not harm others. No man ought to be uneasy about his opinions, even his*

> *religious beliefs, provided that this actions do not interfere with the public order established by law. The free communication of thought and opinion is one of the most precious rights of man: every citizen can therefore talk, write and publish freely."*

The aims of the Revolution were later summed up in the famous slogan **Liberty**, **Equality**, **Fraternity**, meaning that all Frenchmen were free, equal and brothers.

The Reaction of Louis XVI

The **tricolour** flag of the Revolution that Louis had been forced to accept after Bastille Day had the royal colour of white hemmed in by red and blue, the traditional colours of Paris. This symbolised that the king was now under the control of the people of Paris. In addition, Louis had to accept the *Declaration of the Rights of Man.*

In October 1789, a Paris mob marched to Versailles and forced the royal family to move to the Tuileries Palace in Paris. Louis had now lost most of his power and feared for his life. He and Marie-Antoinette decided that they had to escape in order to get help abroad. Marie-Antoinette's brother was Emperor Leopold of Austria. On 20 June 1791, dressed as servants, the king and queen escaped with their children from the Tuileries. Their coach headed for the eastern border, there to meet up with supporters who would bring them to safety. Unfortunately, Louis was recognised twice along the way and the coach was stopped in the town of Varennes. Its inhabitants had been warned in advance and blocked the road. The royal family was brought back to Paris. The Revolution now entered a new and more bloody phase.

A revolutionary poster declaring Liberty, Equality, Fraternity or Death

DID YOU KNOW?

The so-called Flight to Varennes might have worked but for the fact that Marie-Antoinette had insisted on bringing servants with them. Thus, the coach was overloaded and could only travel at the rate of 11 kilometres per hour.

The women of Paris bring Marie-Antoinette and her children back to the city from Versailles, October 1789.

CAN YOU SAY?

1. List two ways **each** in which (a) the lay nobles and (b) the clergy lost their privileges after Bastille Day.
2. What was the slogan of the French Revolution?
3. In your own words give the views of the *Declaration of the Rights of Man* (**Source A**), on (a) power, (b) the law and (c) taxes.
4. Explain the meaning of the colours on the tricolour.
5. What was the slogan of the French Revolution? Explain its meaning.
6. Give two reasons why Louis wanted to escape.

THE END OF THE MONARCHY

The Changes Continue

In October 1789, the Assembly moved from Versailles to the **Palais Bourbon** in Paris. Members who wanted to make gradual changes sat on the right wing of the building, while those who wanted sweeping changes sat on the left wing. The modern political terms **left wing** and **right wing** originate from this. The Flight to Varennes had shown Louis to be an enemy of the Revolution. A new constitution was agreed upon in September 1791 which removed all his remaining powers and prevented him from making any laws in the future. Laws were now to be passed by a new parliament, the **Legislative Assembly;** France was now a **constitutional monarchy.**

War

Most kings and princes in Europe were alarmed by the Revolution. Many were family relations of Louis or Marie-Antoinette. Also, they feared that if the Revolution wasn't crushed, its ideas would spread to their countries and threaten them. On 20 April 1792, war between France and Austria began.

DID YOU KNOW?

Just four days after the outbreak of war, an army engineer named Rouget de Lisle composed a marching song to rally the French troops. It became a favourite of units from Marseilles and was called *La Marseillaise*; it has been the French national anthem since 1795.

The Palais Bourbon in Paris, as it is today.

The Second Revolution

Most French army officers were nobles and, since 1789, many had fled abroad. Thus, the army was very short of leadership. Austria, meanwhile, had received help from bands of French *emigrés* (nobles who had fled from France) and from the King of Prussia, determined to restore Louis XVI to full power in France. Throughout 1792, the French army struggled badly in the war, so hatred of the royal family grew. It was also widely believed that Marie-Antoinette was a spy for Austria.

The attack on the Tuileries, 10 August 1792.

With foreign soldiers already moving into France, the Sans Culottes of Paris invaded the Assembly on 10 August 1792, demanding the right to vote and to carry arms. They also attacked the Tuileries, where the royal family was living, and killed many of the guards. The mob demanded that Louis be dethroned and France made a **republic**. All of the mob's demands were agreed to; a newly elected parliament called the **National Convention** would bring them into law. This so-called **Second Revolution** took place in September 1792 and saw many nobles and churchmen killed.

The Death of Louis XVI

In December 1792, the most extreme step possible was taken. The Convention put Louis on trial as an enemy of the Revolution. Louis was found guilty on 14 January 1793, and the Convention voted by 387 to 334 that he should be executed.

Since April 1792, the execution of criminals and enemies of the Revolution had been carried out by **guillotine**. It had been introduced to France by Dr Guillotin, a member of the first National Assembly, as a more effective and painless method of execution than hanging. It killed the victim swiftly by cutting his/her head off (**decapitation**). On 31 January 1793, Louis was brought to a square in the centre of Paris. One eye-witness wrote:

SOURCE B

Paris, 23 January 1793, Wednesday morning. My dearest Mother, I commend to you the spirit of the late lamented Louis XVI. He lost his life on Monday at half past ten in the morning, and to the very last he maintained the greatest possible courage.

He wished to speak to the people from the scaffold, but was interrupted by a drum-roll and was seized by the executioners, who were following their orders, and who pushed him straight under the fatal blade. He was able to speak only these words, in a very strong voice: "I forgive my enemies; I trust that my death will be for the happiness of my people, but I grieve for France and I fear that she may suffer the anger of the Lord."

The King took off his coat himself at the foot of the scaffold, and when someone sought to help him he said cheerfully: "I do not need any help." He also refused help to climb onto the scaffold and went up with a firm brisk step. The executioner wanted to cut his hair; he refused saying that it was not necessary. But on the scaffold the executioner tied his hands behind his back (this was when the king spoke to the people), and then cut his hair.

After his death his body and head were immediately taken to the parish cemetry and thrown into a pit fifteen feet deep, where they were consumed by quicklime. And so there remains nothing of this unhappy prince except the memory of his virtues and of his misfortunes.

The execution of King Louis XVI.

CAN YOU SAY?

7. What does the term **constitutional monarchy** mean?
8. Give two reasons why the Revolution worried kings and other rulers in Europe.
9. What was *La Marseillaise*?
10. List three changes brought about in the 'Second Revolution' of August – September 1792.
11. Give one reason why Louis XVI of France was executed in January 1793. (*Junior Certificate 1996*)
12. Based on the account in **Source B** above:
    (a) Mention one thing that happened when Louis tried to speak.
    (b) Why did Louis 'grieve for France'?
    (c) Do you think that Louis met his death bravely? Give two reasons for your view.
    (d) What was the attitude of the author to the execution of the king? Write down one example of evidence from the text that supports your answer.
    (e) Explain, briefly, why Louis was executed. (*Junior Certificate Higher Level 2000*)

Robespierre and the Jacobins

The execution of Louis XVI occurred as a new group of politicians began to dominate the National Convention. These were known as the **Jacobins** and were strongly supported by the workers and the *Sans Culottes* of Paris. The Jacobins – called after the old monastery in which they first met – were a form of political party whose aim was the complete destruction of all enemies of the Revolution.

The most famous Jacobin leader was a young lawyer from Arras named **Maximilien Robespierre (1758–94)**. In 1789, he was elected as a Third Estate delegate to the Estates General. He immediately showed himself to be a very active politician, speaking over 500 times in the National Assembly. Robespierre was also very strict in his manners, dress and behaviour, earning himself the nickname the 'Incorruptible' because of his honesty.

The Reign of Terror

When the Jacobins came to control the Convention, a special group of twelve men was appointed to run the country and to weed out the counter-revolutionaries. This was called the **Committee of Public Safety** and from July 1793 Robespierre became its most important member, declaring:

> **SOURCE C**
>
> *It is our leniency towards traitors that is ruining us... what we need is swift, hard and inflexible justice.*

DID YOU KNOW?

Every day a group of Parisian women gathered around the guillotine to watch the executions. They generally did their knitting as they watched, and were called *Les Tricoteuses* (**tricoter** is French for 'to knit').

Under Robespierre, the work of the Committee of Public Safety came to be known as the **Reign of Terror**. To please their *Sans Culottes* supporters, strict price controls were enforced on bread and other goods. Anyone overcharging was liable to be guillotined.

In September 1793, the Committee passed a **Law of Suspects** that gave it great powers to arrest and punish enemies of the Revolution, often on flimsy evidence. The number of prisoners trebled in three months. The guillotine was widely used too – twenty-two Girondins, leading opponents of the Jacobins, were executed in October. Marie-Antoinette suffered the same fate on 16 October, charged with plotting with Austria against France.

In the Vendée region of western France, a peasant revolt erupted against Robespierre's harsh treatment of the clergy. It was crushed and thousands of people were killed. By June 1794, the number of executions by guillotine alone had reached almost two hundred a week. Even former heroes of the Revolution such as Bailly, Desmoulins and Georges Danton were guillotined for opposing the Reign of Terror.

The End of Robespierre

Eventually, Robespierre went too far. In July 1794, he tried to have deputies who disagreed with his religious views arrested. A number of them rallied support in the Convention and succeeded in getting an order for his arrest. By then, even the *Sans Culottes* had had enough. Robespierre and his supporters were arrested at the town hall (Hotel de Ville) in Paris. During his arrest Robespierre was badly wounded in the face; it is unclear whether or not this was as a result of attempted suicide. On 28 July 1794, Robespierre was guillotined, along with 108 of his supporters. The Reign of Terror was over.

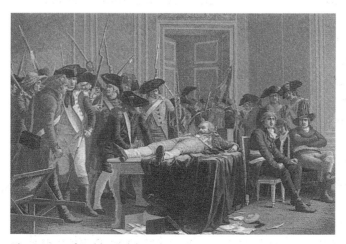

The arrest of Robespierre.

CAN YOU SAY?

13. What group of politicians became popular after the execution of Louis XVI?
14. Name Robespierre's (a) profession and (b) his home town.
15. How many men sat on the Committee of Public Safety?
16. What do you think Robespierre meant by 'swift, hard and inflexible justice' in **Source C**?
17. What did the Law of Suspects involve?
18. How did Jean-Paul Marat die?
19. Why did Robespierre lose support in the end?
20. Where was he captured and when was he executed?

Beyond the Revolution

The death of Robespierre saw the Revolution in France begin to settle down. A new five-member committee ruled France from 1795 onwards. They were known as the **Directory**. It maintained order in France and there was no return to the harsh régime of Robespierre and the cruelty of the Terror. There were other changes of government after this, and even returns to monarchs for a time in the 19th century. However, most of the core ideas of the Revolution survived, despite the efforts of those inside France and outside it to wipe them out.

Since April 1792, France was at war with Austria, Prussia and the emigré nobles who wanted to restore the monarchy. At first, the war went against France. Then, under Robespierre, **conscription** was introduced, forcing all able-bodied men to serve in the army. This improved matters a great deal and France began to defeat its enemies. By 1795, however, more countries were at war with France and by 1799 the list of France's enemies included Austria, Britain, Russia, Turkey, Naples and Portugal. Despite the changes in France brought about by the Revolution, if its forces were defeated in this war, everything could be destroyed. Therefore, the French people and government came to rely more and more on their army generals to protect the Revolution. Eventually, one general named Napoleon Bonaparte became not only head of the army but of the country as well.

The French Revolution, like the American before it, had a great impact on other countries, including Ireland. It again proved that force could be successful in overthrowing a country's rulers, and the *Declaration of the Rights of Man* also reinforced the idea that countries should be run as democracies. The belief in revolution and

democracy were at the core of the ideas that emerged in late 18th century Ireland, which we will see in the next chapter.

France spent many years after 1789 fighting wars against its enemies. Its most troublesome enemy was probably Britain because the British navy was the best in the world and made it impossible for France to invade Britain, an island. When a group of revolutionaries was founded in Ireland during the 1790s, the French saw a chance to get at Britain another way, by helping the Irish revolutionaries against the British and perhaps use Ireland as a route for invading Britain. We will see the results of this in the next chapter.

CAN YOU SAY?

21. What was the Directory?
22. Why did some countries go to war with France in the 1790s?
23. Name five countries which were at war with France in 1799.
24. List three changes brought about by the French Revolution.
25. Explain three ways in which the French Revolution influenced Ireland.
26. Write an account of the following: *The "Reign of Terror" during the French Revolution* and *The consequences of the French Revolution*.
    (*Junior Certificate Higher Level, 2004 and 2008*)

MINI-PROJECT

Write an account of the following:
A named revolutionary leader in America or France in the late 18th century or early 19th century.

Hints:
- Early life.
- Revolutionary activities.
- Reasons for becoming a revolutionary.
- Success or failure.

(*Junior Certificate Ordinary Level 1992, 1994 and 1998; Higher 1997, 2005 – hints vary*)
or
Write an account of the following:
A supporter of the government describes how revolution broke out in America or France or Ireland during the period,1770–1815. (*Junior Certificate Higher Level, 2001*)

KEYNOTES

Destruction of the power of nobles and clergy: Civil Constitution
  • *Declaration of the Rights of Man and the Citizen* • Liberty, Equality, Fraternity
  • tricolour • Flight to Varennes

End of the monarchy: constitutional monarchy • outbreak of war • *La Marseillaise*
  • Second Revolution • republic • Convention • guillotine • execution of Louis XVI
  • Jacobins

Robespierre: Committee of Public Safety • Reign of Terror • Law of Suspects
  • executions of Girondins • execution of Marie-Antoinette • Danton
  • death of Robespierre

Beyond the Revolution: Directory • war and conscription • Napoleon
  • survival of revolutionary ideals • influence on Ireland

34 Background to Irish Rebellion in 1798

● EIGHTEENTH-CENTURY IRELAND

We saw in Chapters 28 and 29 how plantations greatly affected Irish history. After 1691, even more Catholic landowners lost their property. Irish Catholics supported the Catholic King James II in his war for the English throne (1688–91) against the Protestant King William of Orange. When William's forces claimed victory in 1691, Protestantism was in full control in Ireland.

William of Orange.

William of Orange.

During the 1700s, the position of Irish Catholics worsened, as a series of **Penal Laws** was introduced. These forbade Catholics from owning valuable property, receiving an education or attending Mass. Catholics could not become teachers, doctors, lawyers or officers in the army or navy.

Restrictions on Catholics owning land were important. No Catholic could buy land from a Protestant; if a Catholic landowner's son became a Protestant, he would inherit everything in law when his father died, leaving his still-Catholic brothers with nothing. Thus, while 14% of land was Catholic-owned in 1700, by 1778 that was down to just 5%.

Poverty on the Land

Whether the landowners were Catholics or Protestants, the tenants who tried to survive on their small rented farms had a constant struggle. While methods of farming in Britain had improved greatly, Irish farmers were either too suspicious or too poor to have any interest in new methods of agriculture and scraped out an existence on potatoes and a few animals and chickens.

A peasant cottage in the west of Ireland during the 1780s; most Irish people lived in conditions such as these.

Other Angry Catholics

While the vast majority of Irish Catholics in the 18th century were tenant farmers, in towns and cities, especially Dublin, there was a growing Catholic 'middle class' of shopkeepers, doctors and businesspeople. Though richer than Catholics living in the countryside, they too had grievances.

All Catholics working agricultural land had to pay 10% of the value of their produce in **tithes** to support their local Church of Ireland. Many of the Catholic middle class had to send their sons abroad to be educated because of the ban on Catholic schools or universities. Most of all, the Irish Catholic middle class was angry because it had no political power. No Catholic could hold office in the British army, the courts or government. Throughout the 18th century, an Irish parliament co-operated with Britain in the government of Ireland, but again no Catholics could be elected to it. Thus, Catholics really had no say in the running of their country, though they made up three-quarters of the population.

By the 1790s, the Penal Laws had mostly been abolished – Catholics could vote (if wealthy enough), become barristers and buy land. The government even allowed a training college for priests (a seminary) to be set up at Maynooth – 100 years earlier priests had been considered criminals.

Yet, for the Catholic tenants, there remained their poverty, the tithes and the hated landlord system. For richer Catholics, there was still no political power and no chance of being admitted to parliament. For some of these Catholics, the only solution seemed to be to seek an end to British control over Ireland. In other words, some thought of rebellion.

The Irish Parliament building at College Green in Dublin.

MORE DISSATISFACTION

Angry Presbyterians

The notion of unhappy Catholics planning to oppose British rule in Ireland was not a new one. What was unusual in the 18th century was that many Irish Protestants, too, felt dissatisfied with British rule. These people were members of Protestant Churches other than the Church of Ireland. They known as **Non-Conformists** or **Dissenter**s. ('Dissenting' and 'not conforming' both basically mean having different opinions from most others, in this case on matters of religion) Like Catholics, Non-Conformists such as **Presbyterians** were forced to pay tithes to support the Church of Ireland, and were barred from parliament and high office.

British Control over Ireland's Trade

Non-Conformists and members of the Church of Ireland were generally the wealthiest people in Ireland. They were the main landowners and also owned the few large industries located in the country. The huge linen industry in Ulster was controlled by Presbyterians of Scottish and French origin.

With Britain's industries growing rapidly (as we will see in Chapter 36 and later), its government feared competition from Irish products. Thus, Britain began to control Ireland's trade strictly. As early as 1699, Ireland was forbidden to sell woollen textiles to Britain. A later restriction was placed on linen and other Irish goods when these threatened British producers' markets.

Despite all this, most Irish Protestant businesspeople and landowners remained loyal to Britain. The 15,000-strong British army in Ireland was, after all, protecting them from possible attack by Catholics.

Calls for Political Reform

The final reason for Protestant anger with Britain concerned the system of government itself. Ireland had its own parliament but the power of this parliament was very restricted. The most powerful man in Ireland's government was the **Viceroy** (also called the **Lord Lieutenant**), who was appointed by Britain. Also, the British parliament could make laws for Ireland, but any laws which the Irish parliament wanted to pass had to be approved by Britain first. Quite simply, Ireland's Protestant parliament could do little governing without Britain's permission.

> ### DID YOU KNOW?
>
> British control over Ireland's affairs was such that Ireland even had to pay pensions to people on Britain's behalf. An ambassador from Sardinia received £1,000 (€1,270) annually from Irish taxes, while a deposed Queen of Denmark got £3,000 (€3,809), which was an enormous amount of money at the time.

CAN YOU SAY?

1. What group of people did the Penal Laws affect?
2. What percentage of Irish land was owned by Catholics in (a) 1700 and (b) 1778?
3. Why did Irish agriculture remain fairly backward in the eighteenth century?
4. List two reasons why the Irish Catholic middle class in the 1780s was unhappy.
5. List two reasons why Irish Dissenters (Non-Conformists) were unhappy in the eighteenth century.
6. In 1699, what product was Ireland forbidden to sell to Britain? Why was this done?
7. Why did Protestant businesspeople put up with British restrictions over their exports?

Wolfe Tone (1763–98)

Theobald Wolfe Tone was the son of a Protestant Dublin carriage-maker. He studied law at Trinity College and qualified as a barrister at the age of 26. Yet he was much more interested in politics than in law.

Tone was angry that the Irish parliament admitted only Protestants. Though a Protestant himself, he felt religion should not divide Irishmen. In fact, in 1791 he first made his mark on politics with a short pamphlet called *An Argument on Behalf of the Catholics of Ireland*. In it, Tone called for Catholics to be admitted to parliament, after centuries of 'absolute slavery': *If ... long suffering be preparation, there are no men under Heaven better prepared than the Catholics of Ireland.*

Theobald Wolfe Tone

A **Catholic Committee**, set up to fight for representation in parliament (**Catholic Emancipation**), was so impressed by Tone's views that its leader, **John Keogh**, hired Tone as the committee's secretary at £200 (€254) a year.

The United Irishmen

Tone's views on equal rights for all religions were also popular among Presbyterians. He visited Belfast in 1791 and met with **Samuel Neilson, Henry Joy McCracken** and an old friend from Cork named **Thomas Russell**. In October 1791, these men became the founders, with Tone, of the **Society of United Irishmen;** the following month a branch was organised in Dublin by the Protestant politician, **James Napper Tandy**.

The United Irishmen. From left to right they are: Samuel Neilson, Michael Dwyer, John Sheares, William Corbett, Arthur O'Connor, A.H. Rowan, William Jackson, W.J. MacNevin, Matthew Teeling, Robert Emmet, Henry Sheares, Wolfe Tone, J. Napper Tandy, T.A. Emmet, James Hope, Thomas Russell, Henry Joy MacCracken, Lord Edward Fitzgerald.

The society's aims were to bring about equal rights for all religions in an Ireland free of British control. Each member took an oath, promising:

> **SOURCE A**
>
> *that I will use all my abilities and influence in the attainment of an impartial and adequate representation of the Irish people in parliament... to forward a brotherhood of affection, an identity of interests, a communion of rights, and a union of power among Irishmen of all religious persuasions.*

Developing the French Connection

In Chapter 30, we read how governments around Europe feared the spread of the ideals of the French Revolution. Calls for 'representation of the Irish people' and a 'brotherhood' among all Irishmen clearly show the influence of the French Revolution on the United Irishmen. In fact, Tone's first meeting in July 1791 with his Ulster co-founders took place during celebrations of the second anniversary of Bastille Day, the day on 14 July 1789 that the French Revolution had begun.

In 1793, Irish Catholics were given the vote but still could not enter parliament. Disappointed Catholics now began to join the United Irishmen, believing that stronger action was needed to achieve reforms and end British control over Ireland. The authorities became suspicious of the United Irishmen. Their support for revolutionary France was well-known and the suspicion deepened when in February 1793 Britain and France went to war.

Government spies kept a very close eye on the activities of Tone and the United Irishmen. France might very well support them in the hope of using Ireland as a base from which to attack Britain. By now, Tone believed that only an armed revolution would achieve his aims. He wrote to the French in 1794 that:

> **SOURCE B**
>
> *The great bulk of the people would probably throw off the yoke if they saw any force in the country sufficiently strong to resort to for defence.*

A parade in Belfast on 14 July 1792, which was held to celebrate the third anniversary of Bastille Day.

CAN YOU SAY?

8. What was Wolfe Tone's religion?
9. In what way did Tone impress the Catholic Committee in 1791?
10. What does the term Catholic Emancipation mean?
11. Where and when was the Society of United Irishmen founded?
12. In your own words, what, according to the oath taken by members of the United Irishmen, were the society's aims (**Source A**)?
13. In your own words, what did Tone's letter to the French (1794) want them to do (**Source B**)?
14. Explain why the United Irishmen celebrated Bastille Day.

MOVING TOWARDS REBELLION

Government Measures

The failure of Tone's early efforts to get French help for a rebellion led to Tone himself fleeing to America in June 1795. In February 1796, he went from there to France to seek help in person. Meanwhile, the government decided to stamp out any threat of rebellion by a combination of force and laws.

Two types of local force were set up, comprising Irishmen loyal to the Crown, aimed at weeding out likely rebels. Firstly, **militias** of Catholic tenants loyal to the government and under the command of Protestant officers, were formed throughout Ireland. Then, in 1796, regiments of **yeomen** were also set up, comprised of 30,000 Protestant tenants.

A recently erected monument in memory of the United Irishmen in County Wexford.

New legal measures were introduced too. The United Irishmen were declared illegal. An Arms Act made it illegal to import guns. The Insurrection Act of February 1796 made administering a secret oath punishable by death. This Act also gave the authorities the right to search homes for arms without a warrant and to arrest suspected rebels without charging them.

The Activities of the United Irishmen

The government's use of these harsh tactics convinced the United Irishmen that no more reforms would be introduced. Most of them were by now determined to make Ireland a republic, completely independent of Britain, electing its own government. Their numbers increased as they were joined by new recruits from illegal Catholic tenant groups such as the **Defenders**. This was a secret society dedicated to attacking landlords who mistreated their Catholic tenants or charged very high rents.

Tone and others had tried to get Protestant tenants to join the United Irishmen also but with little success. The religious bitterness between groups like the Defenders and the Protestant **Peep o' Day Boys** was just too great for Tone to overcome. On one occasion in 1795, a full-scale battle (the **Battle of the Diamond**, near Armagh) took place between these two groups, and over twenty people were killed.

Captain Swayne of the North Cork Militia torturing a victim in Prosperous, Co. Kildare.

DID YOU KNOW?

Lord Edward Fitzgerald had been sacked by the British army for attending a banquet in honour of the French Revolution.

Under the government measures, some leaders of the United Irishmen were arrested, including Samuel Neilson and Thomas Russell. However, others took their place, notably a young member of the Irish parliament called **Lord Edward Fitzgerald** (1763–98). As an ex-army officer, Fitzgerald was chosen in 1797 to organise the military preparations for a rebellion.

SOURCE C

The French attempt to land at Bantry Bay, December 1796.

SOURCE D

Extract from a speech by Wolfe Tone, 1798
From my earliest youth, I have regarded the connection between Ireland and Great Britain, as the curse of the Irish nation; felt convinced that, whilst it lasted, this country could never be free or happy. I determined to apply all the powers, which my individual efforts could move, in order to separate the two countries. That Ireland was not able, of herself, to throw off the yoke, I knew. I therefore sought for aid, wherever it was to be found. Under the flag of the French Republic, I sought to save and liberate my own country.

CAN YOU SAY?

15. Where did Wolfe Tone go in February 1796 and why?
16. Why did the government set up militias?
17. Explain one feature of the Insurrection Act.
18. Explain why an event like the Battle of the Diamond was so disappointing to a man such as Wolfe Tone.
19. Who was Lord Edward Fitzgerald?
20. **Source C** and **Source D**
    (i) Why did the fleet sent by the French in 1796, shown in **Source C**, fail to land?
    (ii) In **Source D**, what does Wolfe Tone consider to be the 'curse of the Irish Nation'?
    (iii) Give two reasons why Wolfe Tone sought military help from the French.
    (Junior Certificate Higher Level 2008)

Tone and the French

Throughout 1796, Wolfe Tone worked in France persuading the government there to provide help for an Irish rebellion. With France at war with Britain, capturing Ireland might give the French army an ideal base from which to invade Britain. After months of effort, Tone finally succeeded, promising the French:

> ### SOURCE E
> *I will stake my head there are 500,000 men who would fly to the standard (flag) of the Republic (France) if they saw it once displayed in the cause of liberty and their country.*

France supplied 13,975 men, forty-three ships and its greatest general, **Lazare Hoche.** The invasion fleet sailed from Brest on 16 December 1796, with Tone on board. Within a day, problems began when fog and bad weather separated the ships. Contact was lost with more than half the fleet, including Hoche's own ship, the *Fraternité*. The remaining ships continued to Bantry Bay, Co. Cork, under the second-in-command, General Grouchy.

Arriving on 22 December, the fleet had only fourteen ships and 6,000 soldiers left. Grouchy waited for two days for Hoche to arrive. Then, when it had been decided to land without him, the weather worsened again. Though the fleet remained at anchor in the bay from 24 December to 29 December, it was impossible to land the troops. The chances of surprising the British had been ruined. Tone wrote in his diary:

> ### SOURCE F
> *Dec. 29: At four this morning, the commodore made the signal to steer for France; so there is an end of our expedition for the present, perhaps forever.*

A French frigate, La Surveillante, which sank off Whiddy Island in Bantry Bay on 1 January 1797. The wreck is now being investigated by underwater archaeology.

More Government Measures

Following their narrow escape from a French invasion, the authorities stepped up their efforts against the United Irishmen. The *Northern Star*, the United Irishmen's Belfast newspaper, was closed down. Government spies joined the United Irishmen to inform on their leaders.

Ulster was where the United Irishmen had been formed, so early in 1797 the British army, led by General Lake, entered the province.

Assisted by militias and yeomen, it captured over 6,000 weapons. Homes were ransacked, and people tortured and killed in an effort to root out rebels.

Through spies and informers, the government obtained information on most of the leading United Irishmen and, in March 1798, many of them were arrested. In May, Lord Edward Fitzgerald was captured. With Tone back in France, it seemed the rebellion was over before it had started.

During the struggle to arrest him, Lord Edward (in white shirt) was seriously wounded and he died later from his wounds.

After Ulster, Lake's forces moved into Leinster. Their methods of torture included the half-hanging of victims until they gave information on the whereabouts of rebels and weapons. Others were pitch-capped, having lighted tar poured over their heads, or were flogged on wooden triangles. While arms and rebels were captured, the actions of the soldiers, militias and yeomen angered some people so much that they became rebels. Throughout Leinster, small uprisings of tenants occurred – most rebels were armed with nothing more than pikes. These long wooden shafts with metal spikes on them were no match for the enemy's guns and cannons. Rebels were quickly defeated in areas of south Leinster such as Carlow and Wicklow, but it was quite a different story in Co. Wexford. Even though Wolfe Tone, the man who had done most to encourage rebellion, was back in France, and United Irishmen were thin on the ground in the county, it was to be in Wexford that the 1798 rebellion really began.

CAN YOU SAY?

21. List three things done by the government before 1797 to prevent rebellion.
22. Who were the Defenders?
23. What position was Lord Edward Fitzgerald given in the United Irishmen?
24. Why did France agree to give help to an Irish rebellion?
25. (a) How, according to **Source E**, did Tone claim the French would be greeted in Ireland?
    (b) What were Tone's emotions on 29 December, 1796, according to his diary (**Source F**)? Use your own words.
26. Give two reasons why the French expedition of 1796 failed.
27. List three things done by the government in 1797–98 to prevent a rebellion.
28. Write on: The main events during the 1798 Rebellion.
    (*Junior Certificate Higher Level, 2004*)

MINI-PROJECT

Write on: *A supporter of the government describes how revolution broke out in Ireland during the period 1770-1815.* (Junior Certificate Higher Level, 2001 – no hints given) *[Just deal here with how the 1798 rebellion broke out, as you haven't seen what happened after that year yet.]*
or
Write on: *Reasons for the failure of the 1798 Rebellion in Ireland.*
(Junior Certificate Higher Level, 2008)
or
The results of the 1798 Rebellion in Ireland. (Junior Certificate Higher Level 2003, 2004)

KEYNOTES

1. **18th-century Ireland:** Penal Laws
    Poverty of tenants: rents • backwardness • tithes
    Catholic middle class: no vote • no seats in parliament • no schools/universities
    Presbyterians: no seats in parliament • Dissenters/Non-Conformists
    • trade restrictions over Ireland • Irish parliament restricted
2. **Theobald Wolfe Tone:** *Argument on Behalf of the Catholics of Ireland*
    • Catholic Committee secretary • Society of United Irishmen • demand for reform
    • demand for revolution • failure of Tone's first plans • suicide of Jackson
3. **Activity from 1796 to 1798:** Government measures • militias • yeomen • laws.
    • Tone and France • Hoche • Bantry expedition • weather
4. **Background to rebellion:** further government measures • closure of *Northern Star*
    • spies • arrests of United Irishmen leaders • death of Fitzgerald
    • Lake's forces enter Leinster • Carlow and Wicklow • Wexford

35 1798 Rebellion and Its Aftermath

REBELLION IN WEXFORD

In March 1798, regiments of soldiers, yeomen and the North Cork Militia entered Co. Wexford, searching for arms and rebels. They embarked on a campaign of great brutality. Although there were very few members of the United Irishmen in Wexford, stories of torture and murder made the Wexford people determined to resist the invaders.

At **Boolavogue**, the local Catholic curate raised a makeshift army of peasants, mostly armed with pikes. The priest's name was **Fr John Murphy**. When they were confronted by a force of 110 members of the North Cork Militia at **Oulart Hill**, the peasants won a complete victory; only two officers and three privates in the militia escaped with their lives. With growing confidence and with weapons captured at Oulart Hill, Fr Murphy's 'army' of rebels occupied Camolin and Ferns. **Enniscorthy** then fell to them and a camp of supposedly 6,000 rebels was established at **Vinegar Hill**, looking down on Enniscorthy.

Soldiers and local Protestants had taken refuge in the towns of Wexford and New Ross. However, when the rebels attacked **Wexford**, the garrison fled and the town fell to the United Irishmen. When prisoners were freed from the town jail, one of them turned out to be a prominent United Irishman named **Bagenal Harvey**. He was made leader of the rebellion and Co. Wexford was declared a republic.

Despite the rebels' heroism against much better armed opponents, and their dreams of freedom, their indiscipline sometimes turned into deeds that were completely against the beliefs of the United Irishmen. Though Bagenal Harvey was a Protestant, over 200 Protestant civilians were massacred in June 1798 in a barn at **Scullabogue** and on **Wexford Bridge**.

SOURCE A

Defeat

By 5 June, **New Ross** was the only major town in Co. Wexford not in rebel hands. It was an important port and crossing point on the River Barrow, and was defended by some 1,200 men under General Johnson. After fierce fighting, the part of the town on the Wexford side of the river was taken by Harvey's men. However, the British regrouped on the other side of the river, counter-attacked and drove the rebels out of the town. This is known as the **Battle of New Ross**.

The Battle of New Ross.

The rebels never fully recovered from the New Ross defeat. An army under General Lake crossed the New Ross bridge and finally cornered over 15,000 rebels at their **Vinegar Hill** camp on 21 June. Although the rebels outnumbered the enemy, their pikes and a few muskets could not withstand the cannons and cavalry charges of General Lake's men. The result was a crushing defeat – the rebels were routed, and their leaders were arrested and executed. Bagenal Harvey was hanged on Wexford Bridge and Fr Murphy was killed a few days later in Co. Kilkenny.

The Ulster Rebellion

Before 1797, Ulster had been the main stronghold of the United Irishmen. The campaign of terror by the yeomen and the militia, however, had succeeded in capturing many guns and intimidating the population. Thus, the rising in Ulster was much smaller than the one in Wexford. Also, unlike Wexford, where the rebels were mainly Catholic, the rebels in Ulster were mostly Presbyterians.

In Co. Antrim, **Henry Joy McCracken** raised an army which in June 1798 took over the towns of Larne, Randalstown and Ballymena. However, after a fierce battle for **Antrim** town, the rebels were defeated. Soon afterwards, McCracken was captured and hanged in Belfast. Antrim's example spread to Co. Down where **Henry Munro** raised a 7,000-strong rebel force, over twice as large as McCracken's had been. After an initial victory at Saintfield, Munro's forces were routed by the cannon fire of the militia and army at **Ballynahinch**. Munro was later betrayed by an informer and was hanged outside his own front door at Lisburn.

SOURCE B

General Lake's forces attack the rebel camp on Vinegar Hill.

CAN YOU SAY?

1. Write down two reasons why there was a rebellion in Ireland in 1798.
   (*Junior Certificate Ordinary Level 1997, Higher Level 2000*)
2. Who led the first rising in Co. Wexford?
3. Where was the main Wexford rebel camp established?
4. Who was Bagenal Harvey?
5. Examine the picture, **Source A** on page 329, and explain how the massacre of Scullabogue was carried out.
6. List three differences between the British forces shown in **Source B** and the Irish shown in the picture of the Battle of New Ross.
7. Who led the rebellions in (a) Antrim and (b) Down?
8. Who became the Lord Lieutenant of Ireland in 1798?

The Year of the French

While all these events were taking place in Ireland, Tone was in Paris, desperately trying to get French help. He deeply regretted not being in Ireland with the rebels:

> **SOURCE C**
>
> *I cannot express the rage I feel at my own helplessness at this moment; but what I can do? ... From the blood of every one of the martyrs for the liberty of Ireland will spring, I hope, thousands to revenge their fall.*

Humbert

Unfortunately for Tone, his friend, General Hoche, had died of pneumonia in 1797 at the age of 29. However, the French eventually agreed to help and in August 1798, with the rebellion almost over in Ireland, General Humbert sailed for **Killala,** Co. Mayo, with three ships and 1,000 men. They landed there on 24 August and the local Protestant bishop's residence became the French headquarters.

The surrender of General Humbert.

Several thousand Mayo men joined Humbert's force, though most were unarmed. Once again, the British commander sent to crush the uprising was General Lake. Facing well-equipped and superbly organised troops for the first time in Ireland, Lake's men were routed in an encounter nicknamed the **Races of Castlebar** because of the speed with which the British fled.

Humbert's mission, however, was too little and too late to rally Ireland again to full rebellion – that had ended two months before. Furthermore, expected reinforcements of 9,000 men failed to arrive from France. Thus, though Humbert crossed the Shannon into Co. Longford, his mission was doomed. Most of his Irish followers were dispersed by the British at **Granard** and then his remaining 850 men were cornered at **Ballinamuck**. On 8 September, following a 30 minute engagement with Cornwallis' newly arrived army of 5,000, Humbert surrendered.

Bompard

Meanwhile, a second French fleet commanded by Admiral **Bompard** had left Brest. It consisted of nine ships, carrying 3,000 troops. Tone was on board one of the ships, the *Hoche*. In October 1798, as the French sailed into Lough Swilly, Co. Donegal, they were intercepted by British warships. Only three of the French ships escaped.

The *Hoche* was one of the ships that was captured. Tone was soon recognised and taken to Dublin to face trial.

The Death of Wolfe Tone

At his trial, Tone was convicted of treason and sentenced to be hanged. However, he requested that, as an officer in the French army, he should be executed by firing squad. When his request was denied, Tone cut his own throat with the penknife he had been given for sharpening writing quills. Unfortunately, he failed to cut the carotid artery and for a week he lingered on in great pain before dying on 19 November 1798.

So ended the 1798 Rebellion and the **Year of the French.** The loss of life involved was estimated at between 25,000 and 40,000, including many innocent civilians on both sides. The scale of the rebellion is further demonstrated by the fact that some 70,000 pikes alone had been captured by the authorities by August, even before the arrival of the French.

Lack of organisation and weapons, especially cannon, along with insufficient French help and plain bad luck had all combined to defeat the rebels. The British forces had been severely tested during the rebellion and once it was crushed, the British government decided that it needed to keep firmer control over Ireland. We will see how it proposed to do this in the following pages.

The 1798 Rebellion

Theobald Wolfe Tone described the objectives of the rebellion in the following terms:

> **SOURCE D**
>
> *To subvert the tyranny of our execrable government, to break the connection with England, the never failing source of all our political evils, and to assert the independence of my country, these were my objects. To unite the whole people of Ireland, to abolish the memory of past dissensions, and to substitute the common name of Irishman, in place of the denominations of Protestant* (Anglican), *Catholic and Dissenter* (Presbyterian), *these were my means.*

CAN YOU SAY?

16. Using Tone's own comments (**Source C**), how do you think he felt when in France he heard of the Irish rebellion?
17. Who led the French forces at Killala?
18. What were the **Races of Castlebar**?
19. Give two reasons why Humbert eventually failed.
20. Who commanded the French fleet that sailed to Lough Swilly?
21. On which ship was Tone captured?
22. Explain one way in which Ireland was affected by the French Revolution. (*Junior Certificate 1996 and Higher Level 1998*)
23. Study the extract (**Source D**) from the writings of Theobald Wolfe Tone on page 332 and answer the questions.
    (a) Why did Tone want 'to break the connection with England'?
    (b) What do you think was Tone's attitude to differences in religion?
    (c) Is this a reliable source for information on the attitudes of most Irishmen to religious differences?
        (Give **one** reason to support your answer.) (*Junior Certificate Higher Level 1992*)

1798 – THE POLITICAL AFTERMATH

The Act of Union

The 1798 rebellion was a major shock for the Protestant Irish ascendancy and for Britain. The British prime minister, **William Pitt,** decided that Ireland should be made part of Britain to keep it under control and lessen the risk of another French invasion. Thus, in 1799, he proposed an **Act of Union**. This would abolish the Irish parliament; Irish MPs would represent their people at the British parliament in Westminster instead. The new state would be called the **United Kingdom of Great Britain and Ireland.** Pitt hoped to convince Irish Catholics to accept this by promising them representation in the Westminster parliament, in other words **Catholic Emancipation.**

At first, Grattan and the Irish parliament refused to accept the Union. In 1800, however, through a mixture of persuasion, coercion and bribery with money and positions, Pitt got the Irish MPs to pass the Act of Union. It became law on 1 January 1801. For the next 120 years, this Union with Britain and the desire of many to end it would dominate Irish politics.

Robert Emmet's Rebellion

In the first half of the 19th century, some Irish opponents of the Union with Britain tried to break it by force. One of these was **Robert**

Emmet, the younger brother of a leading United Irishman (Thomas Addis Emmet). In 1803, Robert Emmet used £3,000 left to him in his father's will to plan a rebellion. He bought weapons and ammunition, and stored them in two houses in Dublin. Unfortunately before plans were complete, an explosion in one of the stores put the government on alert. Fearing arrest, Emmet quickly staged an immediate rising for 23 July 1803. However, it turned out to be little more than a riot. Only about 100 men turned up and some of these were drunk. On the way to attack Dublin Castle, headquarters of the British

Monument to Robert Emmet located on Massachussets Avenue, Washington DC, in the US.

authorities in Ireland, what was in effect a mob attacked and killed the Chief Justice, Lord Kilwarden. Some minor scuffles between the mob and the military then took place, but by late evening it was all over. Hardly a shot had been fired. Emmet escaped, but he was captured a month later while visiting his fiancée, Sarah Curran. He was convicted of treason, hanged and then beheaded at Dublin's Thomas Street on 20 September 1803. It would be forty-five years before another rebellion against British rule in Ireland took place.

The execution of Robert Emmet in front of St Catherine's Church in Thomas St., Dublin.

Daniel O'Connell (1775–1847)

After the Act of Union in 1801, King George III blocked plans to introduce Catholic Emancipation. William Pitt resigned as prime minister in protest at this. In 1823, Daniel O'Connell from Co. Kerry founded the **Catholic Association** to campaign for Catholic Emancipation. About 400,000 Catholics joined the Catholic Association.

O'Connell succeeded in getting four Protestant supporters of Emancipation elected to Westminster in 1826. Then, in 1828 O'Connell himself won a seat in the Clare by-election, even though the law said that he could not take the seat because he was a Catholic. Though O'Connell was very much a constitutional rather than a physical force nationalist, the British government feared an Irish rebellion if as a Catholic he was prevented from taking his seat. As a result, Catholic Emancipation was made law in 1829 and for the first time, Catholics sat in Westminster.

Daniel O'Connell.

Next, O'Connell began a campaign for **Repeal of the Union**; he wanted the Union between Britain and Ireland abolished and an Irish parliament established in Dublin again. Therefore, he founded the **Repeal Association**. All around Ireland, he held what were called **monster meetings** which were attended by thousands of people. When in 1843 the British authorities banned O'Connell's monster meeting at Clontarf, many followers wanted him to lead a rebellion. However, O'Connell had attended school in France where he had witnessed some of the bloody events of the French Revolution and he was totally opposed to violence. He declared:

> **SOURCE E**
>
> *"The freedom of my country is not worth the shedding of a single drop of Irish blood."* — Daniel O'Connell

With his reluctance to use violence, support for O'Connell faded and by the time he died in 1847, Repeal was almost a lost cause.

DID YOU KNOW?

Daniel O'Connell actually died in Genoa, Italy, on his way to Rome to seek help from the Pope. O'Connell's heart was removed after he died and sent to Rome, and his body now rests under a 50-metre high round tower in Glasnevin Cemetery, Dublin.

A monster meeting at Clifden, in 1843. It was said of O'Connell: 'You could hear his voice a mile off, as if it were coming through honey.'

CAN YOU SAY?

17. Why did William Pitt propose the Act of Union?
18. What did the Act of Union mean for Ireland?
19. Who staged a rebellion in Dublin in 1803?
20. Why did that rebellion fail?
21. Explain in your own words what being an Irish **nationalist** meant in the 19th century.
22. Again, in your own words, what was the difference between a physical force nationalist and a constitutional nationalist?
23. What did Daniel O'Connell's campaigns for (a) Catholic Emancipation and (b) Repeal mean?

MINI-PROJECT

Write an account of the following:
A named revolutionary leader in Ireland in the late 18th or early 19th century.
Hints:
- early life
- revolutionary activities
- reasons for becoming a revolutionary
- success or failure

(Junior Certificate 1995, Ordinary Level 2000, 2001, 2003 and 2006 – hints vary. Higher Level 2006 with no hints.)

Or

Write an account [seven or eight points at least] on either *The influence of the French Revolution on Ireland* or *The consequences of the unsuccessful rebellion of 1798 in Ireland.* *(Junior Certificate Higher Level 2003)*

KEYNOTES

1. **Wexford:** Fr John Murphy • Boolavogue • North Cork Militia • rebel victories at Oulart Hill and Enniscorthy • camp at Vinegar Hill • capture of Wexford • Bagenal Harvey • massacres at Scullabogue and Wexford Bridge • failure at New Ross • final defeat at Vinegar Hill.
    Ulster: Henry Joy McCracken (Co. Antrim) • Henry Munro (Co. Down) • Ballynahinch • new Lord Lieutenant Cornwallis.

2. **The Year of the French:** Humbert at Killala • Races of Castlebar • defeat at Granard and Ballinamuck • Bompard at Lough Swilly • ships captured • Tone arrested • convicted of treason • suicide.

3. **Aftermath:** Act of Union (1800) • William Pitt • Ireland loses its parliament • part of the United Kingdom • Robert Emmet • 1803 Rebellion • physical force nationalist • Daniel O'Connell • constitutional nationalist • Catholic Emancipation • repeal.

36

Background to the Industrial Revolution

● A DIFFERENT TYPE OF REVOLUTION

Whereas both the American and French Revolutions, referred to briefly back in Chapter 30, involved violence and the overthrow of old rulers and régimes, this is not true of all 'revolutions'. The word itself simply means a complete turnaround, as in the 'revolution' of a bicycle wheel. In history, the word is used to indicate a complete change in things. North America and France both had political revolutions, hugely changing the way in which these countries were governed.

Britain in the 18th and 19th centuries also went through a revolution, but this was not to do with politics. Britain's **social revolution** concerned the way in which people worked and lived.

Since ancient times, goods were made by hand by craftspeople in small workshops or in their own homes. This was known as a **domestic system** (or **cottage industry**). Yet, in the second half of the 18th century, huge changes occurred which saw the building of machines and factories on a massive scale, and the production of more goods than ever before. These changes were so great and rapid that they earned the name **the Industrial Revolution** and Britain itself became known as the **Workshop of the World**.

Why It Happened

By the late 18th century, Britain's sailors and soldiers had explored and conquered a huge area of the world. From the colonies of its **empire**, Britain was able to obtain cheap raw materials for its industries, for example cotton, metal and rubber. The goods that Britain made from these raw materials could also be sold back to the colonies, using the world's largest fleet of trading ships.

Britain produced great inventors. The most important invention was probably the **steam engine** of **James Watt** (1736–1819). Though not the first ever steam engine, Watt's machine inspired hundreds of other inventions used in manufacturing, transport and other areas.

The steam engine relied on water heated in a boiler by a coal fire.

DID YOU KNOW?

Though James Watt invented the steam engine, his name is most commonly used today in describing the strength of electric light bulbs.

Steam from the water rose through a pipe into a cylinder where it pushed a metal block, called a piston, upwards. When the piston reached a certain level, the steam escaped through an opening (valve) and the piston fell down, only to be pushed up again straight away as more steam entered the cylinder from the boiler. This happened continuously and the power from this engine could be used to operate pumps, drive machinery or turn wheels.

Steam engines were made from **iron** and their boilers were heated by **coal**. Britain was lucky in that all over the island large amounts of iron ore and coal lay under the ground. The mining of these became a huge industry and provided the raw materials for many other industries.

James Watt.

Britain's **population** grew quickly in the 18th and 19th centuries. Important changes in agriculture had made more food available and better medical knowledge also helped people to live longer. With more people, goods were in greater demand – clothing, knives, forks and so on. Businesspeople bought machines, built factories and hired more and more workers to produce these goods.

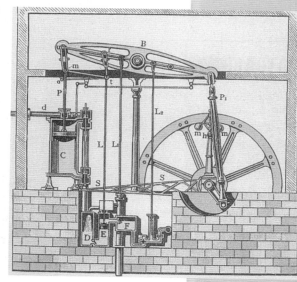

Watt's steam engine.

CAN YOU SAY?

1. What does a **social revolution** mean?
2. What does the term **cottage industry** mean?
3. What nickname did Britain earn during the Industrial Revolution?
4. Mention *one* way in which the Industrial Revolution helped Britain's overseas trade.   (*Junior Certificate Higher Level 1995*)
5. Give *two* reasons why the Industrial Revolution began in Great Britain.

(*Junior Certificate 1994, 1998 [Higher], 2000, 2002 and 2008 [Higher]*)

339

THE TRANSPORT FACTOR

Britain's Industrial Revolution depended a lot on improvements in transport. To produce and transport lots of goods, wider and firmer **roads** were needed. Some of the best of these, as well as the bridges and tunnels the roads needed in places, were designed by the engineers Thomas Telford and John Macadam. These were built by gangs of workers known as **navvies** (short for **navigators**). Canals were also built, providing a cheap means of transporting goods on flat-bottomed boats called barges. Of all these transport improvements, the economist Adam Smith (1723–90) wrote:

> **SOURCE A**
>
> *Good roads, canals and navigable rivers, by diminishing the expense of carriage* (transport costs) *put the remote parts of the country more nearly upon a level with those in the neighbourhood of a town. They are, upon that account, the greatest of all improvements.*

Thomas Telford designed the great Menai Suspension Bridge in Wales as part of the route from London to Holyhead, the main port linking Britain and Ireland.

Little did Adam Smith realise that even greater improvements were to come in this transport 'revolution'. Once again, James Watt's steam engine, capable of turning a wheel, was to have a huge impact. **Richard Trevithick** (1771–1833) altered Watt's engine to make it capable of moving a wheeled carriage along an iron track. In doing so, he invented the **steam locomotive**.

Building on Trevithick's idea, **George Stephenson** (1781–1848) built a locomotive called the *Rocket*, which was able to travel at almost 50 kilometres an hour – Trevithick's *Catch-Me-Who-Can* had done only 16 kilometres an hour in 1808. Soon, the steam locomotive became the quickest and cheapest method of transport in Britain. Over the next 30 years, 12,800 kilometres of railway track were laid, boosting industry, trade and tourism.

SOURCE B

Stephenson's Rocket.

Steam power was also used in **steamships**. In 1838, the *Sirius* became the first steam-powered ship to cross the Atlantic. The great railway engineer Isambard Kingdom Brunel improved matters by using steam-powered propellers, as well as paddle wheels, to build large ships solidly of iron.

Brunel's greatest ship was the *Great Eastern*, launched in 1858. It weighed 27,000 tonnes and could carry 4,400 people. Steamships gradually replaced sailing ships; being larger and capable of travelling against the wind with little difficulty, they could cross the Atlantic in half the time it took sailing ships.

CAN YOU SAY?

6. According to Adam Smith (**Source A**), what did transport improvements result in? Use your own words.
7. What was George Stephenson's locomotive called and what was its top speed?
8. Using the picture of the *Rocket* (**Source B**), explain *two* ways in which it differed from a modern train engine.
9. Write about the following: Improvements in transport during the Industrial Revolution.
   (Junior Certificate Higher Level 2008)
10. Looking at the *Great Eastern* below (**Source C**), explain *two* ways *each* in which it differed from (a) the ships of Columbus and (b) modern ships.

SOURCE C

The Great Eastern, *launched in 1858, was the largest ship in the world at that time.*

A REVOLUTION IN AGRICULTURE

From 1200 to 1700, little changed on the land. The lords of the manor were still there, though they were now called squires or landlords. Their land was still rented and farmed by peasants, though the treatment of the peasants was usually better than that of the medieval serfs.

Although very little had altered in farming from what we saw in medieval times, a number of discoveries and inventions changed it greatly at this time, in what is called an **Agricultural Revolution**. These changes made it possible for the Industrial Revolution to happen when it did.

It is also very important to realise that all of these changes took place in Britain but very few of them affected Ireland. We will see the results of this in Chapters 36 and 37.

SOURCE D1

Strip-farming and the open-field system.

One of the main drawbacks in agriculture was crop rotation. Farmers did not have fertilisers, so they had to leave one field in three empty (**fallow**) every year to allow it to regain soil nutrients. Consequently, one-third of the land produced no food in any given year. A progressive agricultural reformist, **Charles Townshend**, found that instead of leaving fields fallow, turnips, clover or grass could be grown which would put back vital chemicals such as nitrogen, into the soil. This four-crop rotation was known as the **Norfolk system**.

On each large field, a cycle of (a) wheat, (b) turnips, (c) oats or barley and (d) clover or grass was used over a four-year period. The

Norfolk system also boosted cattle-rearing. Up to the 1730s, most cattle had to be slaughtered in winter time because of lack of food (**fodder**). Now, stored turnips and hay made from dried grass fed them in the winter. With more fodder available, the numbers of farm animals in Britain shot upwards and people were better fed.

The Norfolk system.

Landlords made their tenants accept an idea called **enclosure**. Instead of strips scattered throughout the estate, a tenant was given his land all together in one small farm. Now there was no longer any need to spend time travelling from one strip to another. The fields of these farms would be **enclosed** with fences, ending the old open-field system. With more crops and animals to sell, landlords could now make more money and, if their tenants made more money too, they could be asked for higher rents.

Common land, where everyone's cattle once grazed, was enclosed and this prevented the spread of disease among animals. This in turn helped cattle numbers to grow. Whereas landlords and large farmers benefited, small farmers were often unable to meet the higher rents demanded for their land. Many moved to the towns or cities in search of work in the new industries.

Greater numbers of cattle and sheep were now grazing on fields of clover and grass, and their 'droppings' fertilised the soil. Thus, when under the Norfolk system, wheat and other crops were sown in these fields the following year, the crop-yield increased.

Several individuals contributed greatly to the Agricultural Revolution. Jethro Tull invented a **seed drill**, pulled by a horse or ox.

SOURCE D2

How the village and district pictured above would have looked after enclosure.

This machine sowed seeds neatly in straight rows with no waste. The old broadcast method, where seeds were scattered by hand, had meant that many seeds were destroyed by the weather or eaten by birds.

In 1834, an American named Cyrus McCormick invented a **mechanical reaper**. This was a simple horse-drawn cart with a vibrating cutting blade. It was pulled along the straight rows of cereals which had been sown by seed drills and as it went it cut the crop neatly. This all meant that crop-harvesting was now done more quickly than before and was also much cheaper as far fewer labourers were needed.

Robert Bakewell developed **selective breeding**. He took the largest male and female animals on his farm, and instead of killing them for meat, he allowed them to breed on a sort of stud farm. Their offspring, inheriting their parents' qualities, were also generally large. Bakewell repeated this process year by year and gradually the average size of his cattle and sheep increased. Bakewell set a trend which other farmers began to follow. In this way, farmers increased the size of their animals and so meat became more plentiful in Britain.

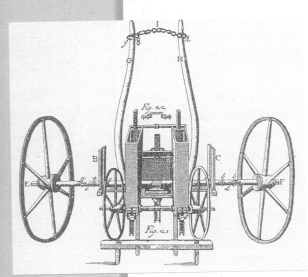

The seed drill invented by Jethro Tull.

The Impact of All This

The Agricultural Revolution helped the growth of industry in Britain. The larger quantities of fresh food available led to an increase in population. This in turn supplied the workers for the factories of the Industrial Revolution and the people to purchase those factories' products. Changes, such as enclosure, and inventions, such as the seed drill and the mechanical reaper, meant that fewer workers were needed in agriculture. This again boosted the Industrial Revolution because, whether they liked it or not, thousands of cottiers, labourers and small farmers poured into the industrial towns and cities looking for work.

All the improvements in agriculture meant that less people could now produce more food. Thus, Britain was well able to cope with the dramatic population shift that saw more than half of its people living in towns and cities by 1850. A hundred years earlier, four in every five people lived on the land.

Harvesting corn by hand.

CAN YOU SAY?

11. Examine both **Source D1** and **D2** above. Using what you see in the drawings, identify *three* changes that occurred in the countryside as a result of the changes in agriculture.

12. How did the Norfolk system encourage farmers to enclose their land?

13. State *one* advantage of the enclosure movement in England in the late 18th century.
   (Junior Certificate Higher Level 1995, similar in 2003 and 2008)

14. Why was Tull's method of seed sowing better than the old broadcast method?

15. Complete this sentence: Robert B_____ was a successful animal breeder.
   (Junior Certificate Higher Level 1993)

16. Mention *two* effects of the Agricultural Revolution on Britain.
   (Junior Certificate Higher Level 2004)

17. Mention *one* factor that made possible the Agricultural Revolution in England.
   (Junior Certificate Higher Level 1999)

KEYNOTES

1. **Industrial Revolution:** domestic system/cottage industry • Britain – the Workshop of the World • British Empire • inventors • Watt's steam engine • coal and iron • population growth • banking • political stability

2. **Transport:** Telford • Macadam • navvies • bridges • tunnels • canals • barges • steam power • Stephenson • the *Rocket* • steamships • I K Brunel

3. **Farming: crop rotation:** Charles Townshend • Norfolk (four-crop) system **Enclosures:** end of strip-farming and commons • more food produced • seed drill • mechanical reaper • selective breeding • agriculture boosts industry • more food • population boom • migration to towns

Working in the Industrial Revolution

37

We have seen how important both transport and agricultural developments were in helping Britain's Industrial Revolution to happen. Naturally, there were thousands of industries involved in this eventually. However, as we turn to examine the sort of work, and working conditions, facing the people who lived in Britain between 1800 and 1850, we will focus on the main industries of the time: textile manufacture, mining and steel production. They will give us a very good picture of what work was like.

Cottage industry – the woman standing is spinning the yarn while the woman seated is winding it onto a spindle.

TEXTILE WORK

Before the Industrial Revolution, textiles or cloth were nearly always handmade. The raw materials varied from sheep's wool to fluffy fibres from plants such as flax (from which linen was made). Turning these into cloth involved several stages, but two were particularly important. **Spinning** involved stretching out the fibres into long strands and winding these together into a continuous spool of thread (**yarn**) with the aid of a **spinning-wheel**. The yarn was then made into cloth by a process called **weaving**, in which overlapping threads were slowly woven together on a device called a **loom**. Although cleaning, dyeing and other processes were also necessary, spinning and weaving were the vital stages in cloth making.

Before the mid 18th century, practically every cottage in the countryside had a spinning wheel for turning the home-produced wool or flax into thread or yarn. Every district too usually had its local part-time weaver who wove the yarn into cloth for his customers on his handloom. All this **cottage industry** was slow and it did not involve massive machinery, quantities of goods or large factories. A number of important inventions changed all that, so that, by 1800, cottage industry had been generally replaced by **factories**.

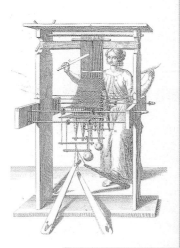

A medieval handloom.

The Growth of a Textile Industry

We need not concern ourselves much with inventors here. It is enough for us to know that inventions such as John Kay's **flying shuttle** and James Hargreaves's **spinning jenny** set in motion the change from cottage industry to mass production in the 18th century.

Spinning Jenny

Although Kay's invention made weaving twice as quick as before, Hargreaves's enabled one spinner to make eight times more yarn. **Sir Richard Arkwright** then developed a water-powered spinning machine called a **water-frame**, which produced stronger thread than the spinning jenny. Eventually, Samuel Compton combined both Hargreaves's and Arkwright's inventions into what he called a **mule**, with one operator able to make 48 spools of thread at one time. Edmund Cartwright brought steam power to weaving using a **power loom**, allowing a handful of machine workers to manufacture cloth at a pace that 100 weavers could only dream of before.

From our point of view, one thing matters in all of this. Machines such as water frames, mules and power looms needed huge buildings

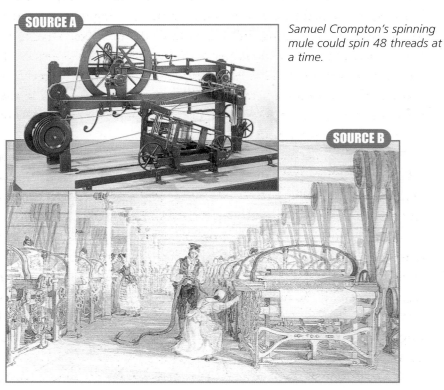

SOURCE A

SOURCE B

Samuel Crompton's spinning mule could spin 48 threads at a time.

Cartwright's steam-powered loom in use in a cotton-mill near Preston in 1834.

to house them. By 1800, huge 'factories' (often called **mills**) were to be found all over Britain. These employed thousands of workers, with the cotton mills of Lancashire and woollen mills of Yorkshire in particular turning out hundreds of times more cloth than ever before. The revolution in cotton production, for instance, saw the imports of raw cotton from Britain's colonies grow from 2.3 million kilogrammes in weight (1771) to 240 million kilogrammes by 1841.

CAN YOU SAY?

1. Name the *two* main processes in textile production.
2. Explain what is meant by **cottage industry**.
3. Explain the term **mass production**.
4. Name *two* pieces of equipment used in textile production before the Industrial Revolution.
5. Looking at **Sources A** and **B** above, explain *one* way in which working at *each* of these machines differed from working with those used before the Industrial Revolution.

COAL AND IRON

Changes often lead on to other changes. For example, improvements in transport helped textile production, both in bringing raw materials to the mills and in getting finished cloth to the markets. Thanks to agricultural improvements, larger and more plentiful supplies of sheep meant more wool for the mills of Yorkshire, for example, to turn into textiles. The invention of steam power and the rapid growth in the textiles industry were very important too in giving a push to the rest of the Industrial Revolution.

Steam power needed a fuel supply to heat its boilers, namely coal. Likewise, iron was needed to build steam engines and textile-making machinery. The **mining** of coal and iron ore became major industries, and factories then also sprang up near supplies of these materials.

Whether mining for coal or iron ore, passageways had to be cut underground to reach the **seams** where the coal or the ore lay. Sometimes these passageways sloped gently from the surface to the seam below, and the miners could walk into the passageway to work. The coal or the ore was carried out in baskets, or, later on, pulled in wagons or carts along small railway lines by people called **hurriers** or by animals such as dogs or 'pit ponies'.

Where the **coal** or the **ore** lay deep underground, a tunnel (**shaft**) was dug straight down. Tunnels led from the shaft to where the coal or iron ore lay. Here the miners worked, making more tunnels as they went. Tools were simple – pickaxes and shovels, as well as carpentry equipment for erecting wooden props to prevent tunnels from caving in.

New inventions also helped the development of mining. Steam engines were used to keep deep mines from flooding, by pumping the water out. Later, steam engines were used to bring miners and the coal or the ore to the surface in lifts, to power cutting machines and ventilation systems.

Mining became a major part of the Industrial Revolution. For example, by 1844 the Northumberland and Durham Coalfield alone produced 5 million tonnes of coal a year and employed 50,000 people. The table below shows how much mining expanded there, which was typical of mines all over Britain.

SOURCE C

Date	1753	1800	1836	1843
No. of mines	14	40	76	130

Iron ore and coal were the essential raw materials for iron and steel manufacture. When coal was heated in an airtight chamber, it became **coke**, a substance that was found to be useful in heating and smelting iron ore more cheaply than ever before.

The quality of iron was also improved on, by a process known as puddling and rolling. In basic iron, known as **pig iron**, unwanted particles of carbon and other substances (**impurities**) often remained after smelting, weakening the metal. In a process called puddling, molten (melted) pig iron was stirred around in order to bring impurities to the surface, where hot air burned them away. The iron was passed through giant rollers before it cooled and hardened. The resulting **wrought iron** was used for a wide variety of products such as shovels and plough blades.

Soon after 1850, another major improvement in iron production came when Henry Bessemer invented a cheap means of making something even harder than wrought iron – **steel**. The great centre of steel-making in Britain was Sheffield, where Bessemer himself had a foundry. To this day, knives, forks, scissors and blades of all sorts from Sheffield are sold around the world.

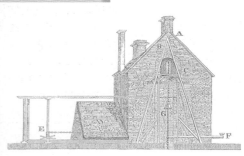

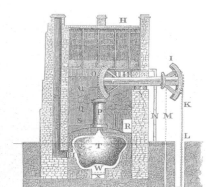

Newcomen's engine being used in a mine in Cornwall.

CAN YOU SAY?

6. Textile production gave a boost to what other industries? Explain why.
7. Explain why steam power was useful in the mining industry.
8. Using the table (**Source C**) of the growth of the Northumberland and Durham mining industry above, say (a) how many mines were opened between 1753 and 1836 and (b) between 1836 and 1843. Explain why this was so, based on what you have read.
9. What was coke and what was it used for during the Industrial Revolution?
10. Describe briefly one major improvement in iron production that took place during the Industrial Revolution. (*Junior Certificate Ordinary and Higher Levels 1994*)

THE SCRAMBLE FOR WORK

For a lot of the people who left rural Britain to work in industries, the attraction of a regular job with steady wages was far greater than that of the lives they left behind as peasants, where a bad harvest or animal disease could have caused them serious hardship. However, particularly as the Industrial Revolution expanded rapidly in the first half of the 19th century, working conditions for these people also had many serious drawbacks.

It is fair to say that in 1800 the ordinary factory worker or miner spent more **time at work** than away from it. Work usually began at 5.30am and the shift lasted between 12 and 16 hours. This routine went on six days a week, with Sunday being the only day off. Holidays did not exist and anyone missing from work lost their wages and often the job too.

As the Industrial Revolution went on, more and more people moved to the cities in search of work. This made it easy for employers to find replacements for any workers they sacked. Also, because of **competition for jobs**, people were prepared to work for lower and **lower wages** rather than be unemployed. Those without work could face starvation, as there was no unemployment payment, sick pay, pensions or social welfare at the time of the Industrial Revolution.

Wages became so low that often all the members of a family – men, **women** and children – had to work to make ends meet. Amazingly, employers were obliged to pay women only half as much as men. In the textile industry particularly, women outnumbered men, as this table from 1839 shows.

DID YOU KNOW?

A weaver at the Brocklehurst silk factory earned 16½ shillings (€1.05) a week in 1821, yet in 1831 the same weaver's pay was down to 6 shillings – 38 cent a week!

Women at work in a Lancashire cotton-mill in 1851.

SOURCE D

Industry	Women working %	Men working %
Cotton	56.5	43.5
Wool	69.5	30.5
Silk	70.5	29.5
Linen	70.5	29.5

Female labour was also widely used in mining; here, women hauled or pushed cartloads of coal and ore weighing more than they did themselves, through tunnels to the mine shaft. The tunnels were low and narrow, so that they could not stand upright and often had to crawl.

Children at work in a Lancashire coalmine. While the hurrier *on the left pushes the cart, the child on the right (the* trapper) *is responsible for opening and closing the doors to prevent the build-up of poisonous gases.*

Child labour was an awful feature of the Industrial Revolution – because wages were so low, children had to work to help support their families. Another survey from 1839 tells us that out of 420,000 factory workers, 193,000 of them were under 18 years of age. In textile factories, children were used for getting into awkward places between and under machines to fix broken threads that adults could not reach. In mines too, children pulled heavy carts along tiny tunnels through which adults could not pass. In the mines of Cornwall, where 19,000 men worked, a further 11,000 jobs were filled by women and children.

As jobs became available in Britain, tens of thousands of **immigrants** arrived there, seeking work in factories, mines or as 'navvies' building roads, bridges and railways. Many of these were Irish.

> **SOURCE E**
>
> *These Irishmen... insinuate themselves[1] everywhere. The worst dwellings are good enough for them; their clothing causes them little trouble, so long as it holds together by a single thread; shoes they know not; their food consists of potatoes and potatoes only; whatever they earn beyond these needs they spend upon drink. What does such a race want with high wages? The worst quarters of all the large towns are inhabited by Irishmen.*

[1] *'insinuate themselves'* = find their way in

CAN YOU SAY?

11. How long was the average worker's day in 1800?
12. What happened if you missed a day's work?
13. What caused wages to fall as the Industrial Revolution progressed?
14. According to the table above (**Source D**), which branches of the textile industry employed (a) most men and (b) most women?
15. According to **Source E** above:
    (a) In what kind of dwellings did the Irish live?
    (b) Why does Engels believe that the Irish do not require high wages?
    (c) According to Engels, what is the only food of Irish workers?
    (d) Do you find any evidence of bias in this passage? Briefly explain your answer.

(Junior Certificate Ordinary Level 1998)

WORKING AND SURVIVING

Not only were the hours long and the work hard, **factory discipline** was very harsh. Remember that a day's wages might be no more than one shilling – 12 old pennies or about 6.3 cent. Yet, for being just a few minutes late, a worker could be fined three pennies. Similar fines were imposed for using bad language, for smoking, breaking pieces of equipment, singing or whistling. In 1844, James Leech, a workers' leader, complained of one factory where over £35 (€44) a week was taken in fines, and of a supervisor who was sacked because he collected only £30 (€38) in one particular week.

DID YOU KNOW?

Methane has no smell, so miners brought caged canaries down with them. If there was a leak of gas, it would kill the bird quickly and this warned the miners to get out before an explosion occurred. This is where the phrase 'a canary in the coal mine' originated.

Accidents at work were extremely common. In the mines, many died in gas explosions, flooding or cave-ins. Most British iron ore and all its coal contained a chemical called **carbon**. Unfortunately, carbon gases such as **methane** often built up in mines; these would explode if they came into contact with a naked flame. Miners had to use flaming torches and candles to see what they were doing underground, as no electric light existed before 1850. Even after **Sir Humphrey Davy** invented what was called the **Miner's Safety Lamp**, explosions were common dangers.

SOURCE F

This is an extract from the *Memoirs* of Joseph Robert Clynes, the son of an Irish immigrant in Britain.

" In 1851, when he was a quiet farm worker in Ireland, a Parliamentary Act which he did not understand was passed and Patrick Clynes, with hundreds of others suffered the cruelties of eviction, and was left to find a new way of living. He could not find it in Ireland: but the cotton boom in Lancashire was attracting thousands of machine-minders, and he went to Oldham, where he worked in a mill.

My father, from his twenty-four shillings, paid a penny or two a week each for myself and my brother and five sisters, so that we should receive an education he had missed. When I had achieved the manly age of ten I obtained half-time employment at Dowry Mill as a "little piecer". My hours were from six in the morning each day to noon; then on to school for the afternoons.

The noise was what impressed me most. Clatter, rattle, bang, the swish of thrusting levers and the crowding of hundreds of men, women and children at their work. I remember no golden summers, no triumphs at games and sports, no walks through dark woods or over hills. Only meals at which there never seemed to be enough food, dreary journeys through smoke-fouled streets, in mornings with tiredness and in evenings when my legs trembled under me from exhaustion."

- Shilling = old coin worth roughly 6 cent.

Factory workers operated huge machinery with very few safety precautions. In one seven-week period in 1843, the *Manchester Guardian* newspaper reported six deaths in local industrial accidents, four of the victims being children. Also, thousands of workers lost fingers, hands or other limbs from being caught by rotating belts in steam-powered machinery. The future leader of the Irish Land League, Michael Davitt, lost his entire right arm in a Lancashire cotton-mill accident in 1857, when he was just 11 years old.

For most workers, the **damage to health** was more gradual. A report from a Factory Inquiry Commission in 1836 blamed:

SOURCE G

The inevitable necessity of forcing their mental and bodily effort to keep pace with a machine … Continuance in an upright position during unnaturally long and quickly recurring periods … Loss of sleep in consequence of too long working hours … Low, crowded, dusty or damp workrooms, impure air, a high temperature and constant perspiration.

Miners commonly developed severe lung complaints – the average lifespan of a north of England miner in 1840 was just 47½ years. Those working in the textile mills were exposed to chemicals in the bleaching and dyeing processes. Conditions in the textile mills were warm and damp, and the windows were kept closed. This was to prevent the threads drying out and breaking. Workers breathed in air full of dust and fibre particles, making lung diseases such as tuberculosis widespread. In the steel industry, one Sheffield doctor found that fork grinders, who inhaled tiny metal particles at their work, died on average between the ages of 28 and 32.

In the next chapter, we will see how some improvements, but by no means huge ones, were brought about in the working and living conditions of British workers by the mid 19th century.

DID YOU KNOW?

Up to 1840, because of their size, children as young as five or six were employed to climb inside chimneys and clean them. Many inhaled so much that they died of lung complaints before ever becoming adults. Those who survived were in such poor health that they could never work again.

CAN YOU SAY?

16. List *three* things for which a worker could be fined.
17. Why did miners bring canaries down with them?
18. **Source F** above is from the memoirs of Joseph Robert Clynes, son of an Irish immigrant in Britain. Read it and answer the following questions:
    (a) Why did his father suffer the 'cruelties of eviction'?
    (b) Explain why his father chose to go to Oldham.
    (c) Why did his father pay 'a penny or two a week each for myself and my brothers and five sisters'?
    (d) At what age did Joseph start work? What was his job?
    (e) Briefly describe the conditions in the factory.
    (f) Do you think Joseph had happy memories of his childhood? Give *two* pieces of evidence from the extract to support your answer.

    (Junior Certificate Ordinary Level 2002)

19. Using **Source G** above, identify in your own words *three* reasons given for the poor health of workers.
20. Why were Sheffield fork grinders so unhealthy?

KEYNOTES

1. **Textiles:** spinning and weaving • flying shuttle • spinning jenny • water-frame • mass production • factories • mule • power loom • Yorkshire wool • Lancashire cotton
2. **Mining:** seams • mines • shafts • hurriers • coal • coke • pig iron • wrought iron • puddling and rolling • Bessemer • cheap steel • Sheffield
3. **Fighting for work:** hours of work • competition for jobs • lower wages • women working • child labour
4. **Working and surviving:** gas explosions • Miner's Safety Lamp • canaries • flooding • cave-ins • machinery accidents • damage to health

MINI-PROJECT

Write an account of:
A factory or mine owner during the Industrial Revolution in Britain, c.1850.

(Junior Certificate Higher Level 2005)

Or

A worker in a coal mine *or* a textile factory during the Industrial Revolution.

(Junior Certificate Higher Level 2003)

(You will find some more information that might be useful about the owners in the next chapter but challenge yourself here to see whether you can find enough material from only Chapters 33 and 34 to write 10 or 12 good points.)

Living in Industrial Britain

38

THE CLASS SYSTEM

The revolutions in agriculture and industry made many people very rich. In the countryside, many of the wealthy landowners, known as the **aristocracy** (or **upper class**), benefited from the enclosure of land and became richer.

In the towns and cities, another class of wealthy people was created by the Industrial Revolution. This was the **bourgeoisie (middle class)**, which consisted of the factory-owners and those people whose services were increasingly in demand, such as doctors, lawyers and shopkeepers. These people made their money through their inventiveness and effort, whereas the wealth of the aristocracy came from land that was passed on from generation to generation.

Belgrave Square in London in 1860.

Some members of the middle class, in fact, became much wealthier than many in the landowning upper class. Many of the beautiful Georgian and Victorian buildings in cities such as London, Glasgow and Manchester were originally the homes of the Industrial Revolution's rich middle class. Such people hired servants, cooks and butlers to look after them.

However, by far the largest number of people affected by the great changes that these revolutions brought about were the ordinary people. The changes in farming and the possibilities of employment in the factories led thousands to leave the British countryside and move to the towns and cities. The story of this **working-class** population (sometimes called the **proletariat**) is very different from that of the middle and upper classes.

THE GROWTH OF TOWNS

For reasons we have seen earlier, Britain had a rapidly **increasing population** in the 19th century. Between 1801 and 1851 alone, the population more than doubled, going from 9 million to 22 million. The growth was most obvious in the towns and cities, as increasing numbers arrived from the countryside. The following population table for Yorkshire woollen towns gives an idea of the remarkable changes that occurred.

Town	Population 1801	Population 1831
Bradford	29,000	77,000
Halifax	63,000	110,000
Huddersfield	15,000	34,000
Leeds	53,000	123,000

SOURCE A1

Sheffield in 1800.

SOURCE A2

Sheffield in 1874.

The rapid growth of towns and cities resulted in severe **overcrowding**. The new inhabitants either packed into the existing buildings with one or sometimes two families to a room, or into tightly crammed houses built near the factories by employers. (Such awful districts are known as **slums**.) Edwin Chadwick wrote in 1842 of one such slum:

SOURCE B

Shepherds Buildings consists of two rows of houses with a street seven yards wide between them; each row consists of what are called 'back and front' houses, that is two houses placed back to back. There are no backyards; the privies [toilets] are in the centre of each row, about a yard wide... each house containing two rooms... In one of these houses there are nine persons belonging to one family... There are 44 houses and 22 cellars and all cellars are the same size. The cellars are let out [rented out] as separate dwellings; these are dark, damp and very low, not more than six feet between the ceiling and the floor. The street between the two rows is seven yards wide, in the centre of which is a common gutter... into which all sorts of refuse [rubbish] is thrown; it is a foot in depth. There is always a quantity of putrefying [rotting] matter contaminating [fouling] the air. At the end of the rows is a pool of water... and a few yards further on, a part of the town's gasworks.

Pollution and Disease

Few British towns or cities had water or sewerage systems that could cope with the huge population increase. As in the Middle Ages, it was still common for waste to be simply dumped near people's homes. Even when towns had sewers, the waste went from the sewers directly into nearby rivers from which the town got its drinking water.

Air pollution was also common in industrial centres. Smoke from factory furnaces and from coal fires in people's homes combined to make a deadly mixture of **smog**, which frequently covered 19th-century London and other cities. Naturally, these various forms of pollution meant that disease was very common. As we saw, many workers suffered from lung diseases caused by their working conditions. Many people living in towns and cities also suffered from these diseases, caused by air pollution.

A London slum in the middle of the 19th century.

Perhaps the greatest killer disease was **typhoid**, caused by dirt and the lack of fresh drinking water. Epidemics were common and most large towns built special fever hospitals to cater for sufferers from typhoid and other killer diseases such as cholera, smallpox, scarlet fever and consumption (tuberculosis). In 1843, over 10,000 people died of typhoid in Glasgow alone. Death rates among new-born babies were particularly high. The following table shows the contrast between death rates in the cities and the countryside:

SOURCE C

Out of 10,000 deaths	
In Rutland (a healthy agricultural district) 2,864 died under five	115 lived to over 90
In Preston (a cotton-manufacturing town) 4,947 died under five	41 lived to over 90
In Leeds (a wool-manufacturing town) 5,286 died under five	31 lived to over 90

CAN YOU SAY?

1. List *three* reasons for population growth in industrial towns.
2. Looking at **Sources A1** and **A2** above, identify *two* changes that occurred in the appearance of towns because of the Industrial Revolution.
3. Having read **Source B** above:
   (a) Give *two* points of evidence to show that there was overcrowding in Shepherds Buildings.
   (b) Why was the air foul-smelling there?
   (c) From the evidence in the extract, what type of work do you think some of the people had? Give a reason for your answer.

   (Junior Certificate Higher Level 1999)
4. Name *three* common diseases in industrial towns.
5. In the table of death rates above (**Source C**), which place had (a) the highest number of child deaths and (b) the greatest number of people living beyond 90? Offer *three* suggestions why this was so.
6. Mention *one* fact about housing conditions for the workers in towns during the Industrial Revolution.

   (Junior Certificate Higher Level 2001)

LIFE OUTSIDE OF WORK

For the adults who lived and worked in such appalling slum conditions, many took to **heavy drinking**. Manchester had over 1,000 licensed public houses in the 1840s, as well as hundreds of illegal ones (**hush shops**). One official in Glasgow estimated that 30,000 workmen got drunk every Saturday night. Considering that many of these were badly paid to begin with, drinking led to increased **poverty**, with many families selling their few possessions to local pawnshops for extra money.

For the rich, the wealth that the Industrial Revolution brought meant that their **diets** were very good. Meat was available in larger quantities than ever before, as well as imported goods such as wine, tea, coffee and even chocolate and sugar from the colonies. The poor, however, rarely had meat and relied for food mainly on grain products, such as porridge (gruel) and bread, and most drank ale. Even for them, however, the Agricultural Revolution had made sure that those on the land produced enough food to ensure that starvation or famine were things of the past.

Poverty, dreadful living and working conditions, alcoholic drink and the lack of an organised police force in many areas resulted in higher levels of **crime**, mainly robberies and violent attacks. Look at the following table of arrests for criminal offences in Britain:

1805 –	4,605 arrests
1815 –	7,898 arrests
1825 –	14,437 arrests
1835 –	20,731 arrests

Because child labour was so widespread, little or no **education** was provided for working-class children. There was no state-run school system until well into the mid 19th century, and what few 'ragged schools' existed were run by charities or religious groups such as Quakers and Methodists. A survey in the 1830s revealed that in cities such as Liverpool, Leeds and Newcastle, less than half the children under 15 went to any school. Those who did attend studied reading, writing and arithmetic. Yet, because children were often ill, or working, or unable to pay the small fee required, many of them learnt little.

For the children of the wealthy, Britain had some of the most famous private schools (strangely enough called 'public' schools) in the world, including Eton, Harrow and Rugby, as well as world-famous universities such as Oxford and Cambridge.

DID YOU KNOW?

When a boy at Rugby school picked up the football during a game and ran off with it, the game now known as rugby was born. The boy's name was William Webb Ellis and the World Rugby Cup today is named after him.

With little **leisure time** and few recreational facilities (other than pubs), industrial workers had few pastimes. Sports that involved gambling, such as bare-knuckle boxing, cock and dog fighting and badger-baiting, were all popular. Most of these dated back to medieval times.

Yet, several modern sports, such as cricket, rugby and soccer, also developed during the mid 19th century. Of these, soccer was most associated with the industrial towns. It originated years before in street 'kickabouts' with few rules, but by the 1870s proper rules and organisations such as the Football Association and Football League had been established. Many of today's English Premier League teams began as factory teams in the second half of the 19th century.

Bearing in mind what we have just read about sports and pastimes, we should never forget that the basic working conditions endured by most people, especially young people, remained very hard for over a century. Before we move on to look at efforts to improve the conditions of workers, it is worthwhile reminding ourselves of these often grim conditions:

DID YOU KNOW?

Manchester United FC was founded by workers of the Lancashire and Yorkshire Railway Company based at Newton Heath. Several early Nottingham Forest players worked at the city's great Raleigh Bicycle Company. Why do you think Sheffield United are nicknamed the 'Blades' and Stoke City are the 'Potters'?

SOURCE D

From an interview with Sarah Carpenter and James Patterson, factory workers, in *The Ashton Chronicle*, 23rd June 1849.

Sarah:
"They took me into the counting house and showed me a piece of paper with a red sealed horse on which they told me touch, and then to make a cross, which I did. This meant I had to stay at Cressbrook Mill till I was twenty-one.

Our common food was oatcake. It was thick and coarse. This oatcake was put into cans. Boiled milk and water was poured into it. This was our breakfast and supper. Our dinner was potato pie with boiled bacon in it, a bit here and a bit there, so thick with fat we could scarce eat it, though we were hungry enough to eat anything. Tea we never saw, nor butter. We had cheese and brown bread once a year. We were only allowed three meals a day, though we got up at five in the morning and worked till nine at night.

We had eightpence a year given to us to spend: fourpence at the fair, and fourpence at the wakes. We had three miles to go to spend it. Very proud we were of it, for it seemed such a sight of money, we did not know how to spend it."

James:
"I worked at Mr Braid's Mill at Duntruin. We worked as long as we could see. I could not say at what hour we stopped. There was no clock in the mill. There was nobody but the master and the master's son had a watch and so we did not know the time. The operatives were not permitted to have a watch. There was one man who had a watch but it was taken from him because he told the men the time."

Source: Spartacus.co.uk

Playing football in a London street.

CAN YOU SAY?

7. State *one* serious problem (apart from overcrowding) faced by those living in industrial towns in England in the early 19th century.

(Junior Certificate Higher Level 1995)

8. Mention *one* fact about diet or health among workers in towns in Britain during the Industrial Revolution.

(Junior Certificate Ordinary Level 2004)

9. Give *three* reasons why working-class children often did poorly at school.

10. List *three* gambling-based sports popular during the 19th century.

11. Mention *two* effects of the Industrial Revolution on the lives of ordinary people.

(Junior Certificate Ordinary Level 1998)

12. Read **Source D** above, taken from an interview with Sarah Carpenter and James Patterson, factory workers, and published in the *Ashton Chronicle*, 23 June 1849.

   (a) Why did they make Sarah touch the red sealed horse and make a cross?

   (b) What food were they given in the mill once a year?

   (c) How much did she get to spend per year?

   (d) Why do you think the master did not want workers to know the time?

   (e) From your study of this time, name *two* other problems that factory workers faced.

(Junior Certificate Higher Level 2006)

The Earl of Shaftesbury.

IMPROVING CONDITIONS

Conditions remained very difficult for the average workers up to the middle of the 19th century and well beyond it. However, some employers and politicians realised that things were much worse than they should be and tried to bring about improvements. **Robert Owen** was probably the most famous of the 'benevolent' employers.

The **Earl of Shaftesbury (1801–85)** also did much to improve working conditions. He persuaded parliament to pass an important **Factory Act** in 1833, which made it illegal to force children aged 9 to 13 to work more than 54 hours a week (roughly twice the time you spend at school now!). No one under 9 could be employed in a factory, and those between 14 and 18 could work 'only' 68 hours a week.

The use of children to clean chimneys was banned (1840), and by 1842 it was forbidden to employ women – or children under 13 – in mines. Shaftesbury had found boys as young as four or five working in some coalmines. The **1844 Factory Act** reduced working hours to 12 per day for women and 6 and a half for children up to the age of 13. Finally, in 1847, came the **Ten Hours Act**. This limited women, and children under the age of 18, to just ten hours working a day.

SOURCE E

Maddened men, armed with sword and firebrand, . . . rushed forth on errands of terror and destruction.

A cartoon which shows a group of angry Luddites about to smash machinery.

In terms of improving living conditions, **Edwin Chadwick (1800–90)** produced a very important *Report…on the Sanitary Conditions of the Labouring Population* (1842). This laid the basis for a wave of improvements in public health care – the appointment of local health officers in every district, pollution and disease control, providing clean running water and so on. Without doubt, such measures did much to slowly improve the living conditions of Britain's workers and their families.

It would be wrong to think that everything was hugely better for workers by 1850 than it had been in 1800. However, the work of people such as Owen, Chadwick and Shaftesbury did bring about the slow improvement of workers' conditions. Not all factory and mine owners accepted these demands for change. For example, a lot of employers simply cut wages when they were unable to get people to work for the same long hours as before.

Sometimes, workers involved themselves in protests against their employers. **Luddites**, for example, were workers' groups who broke into factories and smashed machinery because, after 1800 in particular, workers were losing their jobs as more and more machines were developed to do the work instead. Several Luddites were hanged for their actions.

In the late 18th century, groups of workers began to form **trade unions** to seek better wages and conditions from their employers. These early trade unions faced great obstacles and repression under the **Combination Acts** until 1824. It was not until the second half of the 19th century that unions became fully legal. They were granted the right to go on strike only in the 1870s.

Other workers formed a movement called the **Chartists**, demanding more of a say in the running of the country (i.e. politics) for the working class. During the 1830s in particular, Chartists' demands for the right to vote for all adult males, more workers in parliament and other reforms were very loud indeed. Very few of these demands were achieved at that time but slowly, those who ruled Britain began to move in the direction of real **political reforms**.

A **Reform Act** in 1832 gave more seats in parliament to the industrial cities of northern England than they had had before, taking them from rural areas that had few people in them. However, it would be nearer the end of the 19th century before most British working men could vote, and it would be 1918 before any women could.

In many European countries that experienced industrial growth after Britain, poor living and working conditions inspired workers to join revolutionary movements, to assassinate politicians or kings, and even to stage revolutions. Britain's moves to reform before such events came about helped it to remain at relative peace as the Workshop of the World until the end of the 19th century.

DID YOU KNOW?

Six English farm labourers tried to form a trade union in Tolpuddle (Dorset) in 1834. They were each sentenced to seven years penal servitude in Australia. However, this harsh sentence caused such anger that they were released after two years. They became known as the **Tolpuddle Martyrs**.

SOURCE F

CAUTION.

WHEREAS it has been represented to us from several quarters, that mischievous and designing Persons have been for some time past, endeavouring to induce, and have induced, many Labourers in various Parishes in this County, to attend Meetings, and to enter into Illegal Societies or Unions, to which they bind themselves by unlawful oaths, administered secretly by Persons concealed, who artfully deceive the ignorant and unwary,—WE, the undersigned Justices think it our duty to give this PUBLIC NOTICE and CAUTION, that all Persons may know the danger they incur by entering into such Societies.

ANY PERSON who shall become a Member of such a Society, or take any Oath, or assent to any Test or Declaration not authorized by Law—

Any Person who shall administer, or be present at, or consenting to the administering or taking any Unlawful Oath, or who shall cause such Oath to be administered, although not actually present at the time—

Any Person who shall not reveal or discover any Illegal Oath which may have been administered, or any Illegal Act done or to be done—

Any Person who shall induce, or endeavour to persuade any other Person to become a Member of such Societies,

WILL BECOME

Guilty of Felony,

AND BE LIABLE TO BE

Transported for Seven Years.

ANY PERSON who shall be compelled to take such an Oath, unless he shall declare the same within four days, together with the whole of what he shall know touching the same, will be liable to the same Penalty.

Any Person who shall directly or indirectly maintain correspondence or intercourse with such Society, will be deemed Guilty of an Unlawful Combination and Confederacy, and on Conviction before one Justice, on the Oath of one Witness, be liable to a Penalty of TWENTY POUNDS; or to be committed to the Common Gaol or House of Correction, for THREE CALENDAR MONTHS; or if proceeded against by Indictment, may be CONVICTED OF FELONY, and be TRANSPORTED FOR SEVEN YEARS.

Any Person who shall knowingly permit any Meeting of any such Society to be held in any House, Building, or other Place, shall for the first offence be liable to the Penalty of FIVE POUNDS; and for every other offence committed after Conviction, be deemed Guilty of such Unlawful Combination and Confederacy, and on Conviction before one Justice, on the Oath of one Witness, be liable to a Penalty of TWENTY POUNDS, or to Commitment to the Common Gaol or House of Correction, FOR THREE CALENDAR MONTHS; or if proceeded against by Indictment may be

CONVICTED OF FELONY,

And Transported for SEVEN YEARS.

COUNTY OF DORSET, Dorchester Division.	C. B. WOLLASTON, JAMES FRAMPTON, WILLIAM ENGLAND, THOS. DADE, JNO. MORTON COLSON.	HENRY FRAMPTON, RICHD. TUCKER STEWARD, WILLIAM R. CHURCHILL, AUGUSTUS FOSTER.
February 22d, 1834.		

G. CLARK, PRINTER, CORNHILL, DORCHESTER.

This notice was printed and circulated in Dorset just one week before the Tolpuddle Martyrs were arrested.

CAN YOU SAY?

13. In *one* sentence, why was the Earl of Shaftesbury important for workers of the Industrial Revolution?
14. List *three* improvements to health care that came about through the work of Edwin Chadwick.
15. In **Source E** above, is the cartoonist a supporter of the Luddites or not, in your opinion? Give *one* reason for your view.
16. Look at **Source F** above and explain *two* reasons in your own words why these men were wanted by the law.
17. What were Chartists looking for?
18. What change did the 1832 Reform Act make in British politics?
19. Explain in your own words why Britain never had a revolution in the 19th century.

KEYNOTES

1. **Class system:** aristocracy • bourgeoisie (middle class) • proletariat (working class) • contrasting living conditions • population growth in towns • overcrowding • slums • pollution • diseases
2. **Lifestyle:** drinking • poverty • pawnshops • rising crime • gambling • education • reading • writing • arithmetic • boxing • cock and dog fighting • badger-baiting • soccer • Football Association
3. **Improving conditions:** Robert Owen • Lord Shaftesbury • Factory Acts • Ten Hours Act • Edwin Chadwick • Luddites • Chartists • trade unions • illegal • Tolpuddle Martyrs • Political reform • Great Reform Act

MINI-PROJECT

Write an account of the following: *A factory worker or mine worker in England c.1850.*
Hints:
- working conditions
- living conditions
- health and diet
- pastimes and entertainment

[Write about 10 or 12 sentences, without looking at your book.]

(Junior Certificate Ordinary Level 2005 and 2008, similar in 1996 and 2003, with slightly different hints given)

Or

The Industrial Revolution in Britain had a major impact on people's lives. In the light of the above statement, write an account of the effects of the Industrial Revolution on *one* of the following aspects of everyday life in Britain:
- housing and diet
- health and leisure activities
- education

Try to write at least *six* good points on whichever one of these you choose.

(Junior Certificate Higher Level 2004)

366

Irish Society in the Early 19th Century

39

○ **COMPARING IRELAND AND BRITAIN**

Cities and Industries

We saw in Chapters 33–35 how in the early 19th century, Britain was the Workshop of the World. The Act of Union of 1801 joined Britain and Ireland together in the United Kingdom. But did Ireland have a revolution in industry and agriculture like its neighbour?

There is no doubt that some parts of the country were as industrialised as most of Britain. Ulster, in particular, had huge textile industries. The linen industry had grown rapidly there since the 17th century. By 1811, 50,000 people worked in the textile industry centred around Belfast. Shipbuilding was once a small industry in Belfast, but during the first half of the 19th century, the company of Harland and Wolff became the largest shipbuilder in the world.

Dublin, Ireland's capital city, had a population of 250,000 in 1850. Though it had large industries such as woollen manufacture and Guinness's brewery, its prosperity mostly depended on the fact that it

How many changes can you see between the scene from 1850 and today's view?

O'Connell Street in Dublin (then called Sackville Street) in about 1850. Nelson's Pillar is in the background.

367

was the chief trading port with Britain. In 1835, Henry Inglis, a Scottish visitor, wrote of:

> **SOURCE A**
>
> *the numerous private vehicles that fill the streets... the magnificent shops for the sale of articles of luxury and taste, at the doors of which, in Grafton Street, I have counted upwards of twenty handsome equipages [teams of horses]... the number of splendid houses, and legion of liveried [uniformed] servants.*

Problems

Ireland's cities had similar problems to Britain's. In 1844, Friedrich Engels wrote:

> **SOURCE B**
>
> *The poorer districts of Dublin are among the most hideous and repulsive to be seen in the world ... [they] are extremely extensive, and the filth, the uninhabitableness of the houses and the neglect of the streets surpass all description.*

The Father Mathew statue in Patrick St., Cork.

Other Irish cities had the same problems – overcrowding, dirt and, of course, sickness. In an 1817–18 **typhus** epidemic (caused by infected food and water), 25% of the population of Limerick and 95% of people in the slum areas of Waterford caught the disease. As in Britain, **crime** was also a serious problem in Ireland's cities. So too was **alcohol**, despite the efforts of people such as Cork's **Fr Theobald Mathew** to encourage **temperance** (avoiding alcohol).

Transport

Signs of an Irish transport revolution dotted the countryside. An efficient coach-travel system was set up in Clonmel by the Italian **Charles Bianconi** in 1815 – by 1845, his coaches travelled 5,600 kilometres a day around Ireland. Ireland also had two large canals, the **Royal** and the **Grand**, which made it possible to travel from Dublin to Limerick or Waterford by water.

In 1834, **William Dargan** built Ireland's first railway line from Dublin to Kingstown (now Dún Laoghaire), and by the

Charles Bianconi, 1786–1875

1850s, all the main cities were linked by rail. The railways boosted trade and were especially important in helping farmers to transport livestock and other produce to city markets or to ports for shipment to Britain. Passenger transport also grew rapidly, boosting tourism at seaside resorts and making it easier for people to travel to cities or to ferry ports in search of work.

Yet, No Industrial Revolution

So we see that in several ways, Ireland's cities resembled those of Britain during the early 19th century. To say that we had an Industrial Revolution, however, would be incorrect. Apart from the northeast and a handful of cities, Ireland had few factories or large industries. This was partly because we had little or no coal or iron, and we were very slow to adapt to the use of steam power. Ireland didn't have any colonies to supply it with raw materials; indeed, Ireland was itself part of the British Empire.

Although officially part of the United Kingdom from 1801, goods produced in Ireland did not have the same chances of being sold in Britain because of a system of tariffs and extra transport costs. With the union of Ireland and Britain, mass-produced goods from British factories were sold here without customs duties and were often cheaper than home-produced goods. As the 19th century progressed, Ireland lost industries rather than gained them because of British competition. Bandon, for example, had 2,000 handloom weavers in 1825, but only 100 by 1837.

CAN YOU SAY?

1. Which was Ireland's most industrialised province in the early 19th century?
2. (a) According to Henry Inglis (**Source A**), what was Grafton Street in Dublin famous for?
   (b) What evidence does Inglis give that Dublin was a city of great wealth (**Source A**)?
3. According to Friedrich Engels (**Source B**), why were the poorer districts of Dublin 'hideous and repulsive'?
4. State *two* ways in which the coming of the railways affected life in Ireland around the middle of the 19th century. *(Junior Certificate Higher Level 1993)*
5. List *three* transport improvements in 19th century Ireland.
6. Give *three* reasons why Ireland had no Industrial Revolution.

CHANGE IN RURAL IRELAND

Population Growth

Just like Britain, Ireland had a massive growth in population in the early 19th century. Between 1781 and 1841, Ireland's population more than doubled from 4 million to 8.1 million. Britain's more than doubled also, from 8.5 million (1781) to 18.5 million (1841). A more plentiful food supply, improvements in farming methods and health care, and cleaner cotton clothing again all played a part. In Ireland, there was also a tradition of marrying young and this was another reason for the growth, with most people having large families.

There was one important difference between the two countries. By 1841, most of Britain's population lived in cities and earned its living from industry or trade. Ireland, however, still had over 70% of its population living in the countryside and depending on farming for survival.

ID YOU KNOW?

n official survey from 838 claimed that there vere 32 million acres 13 million hectares) of and being farmed in ritain and 14 million cres (6 million hectares) n Ireland. Yet, Ireland ad 75,000 more farm abourers than Britain!

SOURCE C

Castletown House in Celbridge, Co. Kildare is a good example of the kind of luxury that the really wealthy landlords lived in.

Prosperous Farmers

Most landowners in 19th-century Ireland were the descendants of settlers from the earlier plantations. Some of these **landlords** had estates of 40,000 acres (16,000 hectares) or more, and most lived comfortably in large mansions filled with servants, fine furniture and works of art. If a landlord preferred to live in Britain (in other words, he was an *absentee landlord*), then he generally hired a **land-agent** to run his estate for him.

Most of the land on an estate was rented out to Irish tenants. The size of farm occupied by each tenant varied, as the following table shows (1845):

SOURCE D

	No. in 000s	Average farm size
Wealthy farmers	50	80 acres (32 hectares)
Strong farmers	100	50 acres (20 hectares)
Family farmers	200	20 acres (8 hectares)
Poor farmers	250	5 acres (2 hectares)
Cottiers/Labourers	1,000	1 acre (0.4 hectare)

The wealthy or strong farmers did well. The enclosure of land and the introduction of machinery helped them to produce more food than ever before. Many farmers, particularly in the eastern half of the country, exported produce to Britain and made handsome profits. By 1846, almost one million head of livestock were being exported each year, along with millions of tonnes of grain.

Other Issues

Catholic Emancipation (see Chapter 32) gave the more wealthy farmers in Ireland some **voice in politics**, with nearly 40 Catholic MPs getting into Westminster in the years after 1829. Unfortunately, they were still greatly outnumbered by British-based MPs. It was also true that when Catholic Emancipation came in, another law was introduced which took the right to vote away from many of the people who had supported O'Connell in the first place.

Irish farmers, both rich and poor, had to pay **tithes** to support the upkeep of their local Protestant Church, even if the farmers were Catholics. This tithe was basically a tax of 10% of the farmer's income and it dated back to medieval times. It resulted in quite a deal of violence in Ireland in the 1830s, often called the **Tithe War**, until tithes were more or less abolished.

A very important development in rural Ireland was the setting up of free **primary** (or **national**) **schools** in 1831. These schools sprang up all over Ireland, funded by the government and local parish. They gave good, basic education to Irish children, at a time when many of similar ages in Britain were working in factories and mines. Everything was taught through English so that, even with the great benefit of education for children, these schools are also believed to have lessened the amount of Irish that was spoken in rural Ireland.

How many differences can you spot between this scene and what you might find in a modern school?

Entertainment

Hurling matches were played between entire parishes with few rules and many injuries. Sometimes, rival groups (**factions**) fought running battles with each other (**faction fights**). These most commonly occurred at big fairs such as those at Donnybrook near Dublin or the Old Lamas Fair in Antrim:

> **SOURCE E**
>
> *The most numerous class of cases at most assizes [court sessions] is ... 'fair' murders; that is, homicides committed at fairs ... The factions have chiefs, who possess authority. Regular agreements are made to have a battle; the time agreed on is generally when a fair takes place.*
>
> (Henry Inglis, 1835)

SOURCE F

A donnybrook is a term used to describe a serious brawl or fight; it has its origins in the notorious fairs that were held at Donnybrook in Dublin, where RTE has its headquarters today.

CAN YOU SAY?

7. What was the main difference between the growing Irish and British populations in the 19th century?
8. In the table above (**Source D**), how many Irish farmers had (a) 5 acres or less and (b) 50 acres or more?
9. Explain *one* good and *one* bad result of Catholic Emancipation for Irish farmers.
10. Why was there a Tithe War in Ireland during the 1830s?
11. How did national schools damage the Irish language from 1831 onwards?
12. (a) According to Henry Inglis (**Source E**), what was the most common type of case heard in Irish courts?
    (b) What evidence does Inglis (**Source E**) give that these faction fights were highly organised affairs?
13. List *five* activities that you can see in the picture of the fair. (**Source F**).

DISASTER LOOMING FOR THE POOR

The boom in Irish agriculture, particularly for wealthy farmers, led to an increase in demand for farm labourers. After 1800, it became common for these labourers to receive part of their wages in the form of tiny plots of land rather than in cash. They often had less than an acre (0.4 hectare) on which to support their families and were forced to move to Britain for part of the year in search of work. (Moving away temporarily like that is called **migration**, whereas moving away permanently is called **emigration**.) There they would labour in British factories or work as navvies building railways and canals.

Irish farm labourers leave for England to work on the harvest.

Even with small plots of land and migration, some poor families had to seek food and shelter in local **workhouses** for several months every year. Set up in 1838, these institutions were run by **Boards of Guardians** made up of landlords, strong farmers and businesspeople in every district. The families of many cottiers and labourers, as well as the poor of the cities, used to enter the workhouses when food was scarce in the period leading up to the potato harvest.

Inside the women's section of a workhouse.

Those who remained on the land had to find some means of survival. Often, if a farmer had several sons, the solution lay in **subdivision**. This meant dividing up the land among all the sons when the farmer died. For example, if a farmer with 5 acres (2 hectares) had five sons, then each would receive a 1 acre (0.4 hectare) plot when he died.

A farmer who lived on such a tiny plot of land was generally called a **cottier**. By 1845, there were about one million cottiers and labourers in Ireland. When one includes their families, we find that a staggering 4.7 million, well over half the country's people, lived on farms of an acre (0.4 hectare) or less. This was *the* great difference between Irish and British conditions.

SOURCE G

Depending on the Potato

Ireland's huge population of cottiers and labourers lived in extreme poverty most of the time. Their farms were too small to make cattle-rearing possible. In general, the further west these cottiers and labourers lived, the worse their land, so it was unsuitable for growing wheat or other grain crops that were cultivated in Britain. By 1800, the staple food of these people was the **potato**.

Potatoes are a nourishing food and packed with vitamins. Ever since Sir Walter Raleigh had introduced them to Munster (c.1590), they had become increasingly popular among Ireland's poor. Potatoes were more suited to Ireland's marshy soil and damp climate than other crops. Their 'yield' was high. That means that even an acre (0.4 hectare) of land could produce enough potatoes to feed a family of six for at least six months. Some families were even able to rear hens or a pig or two, using potato skins to feed them. Put simply, the potato was the difference between life and death for many.

Read the two accounts from the 1840s that follow:

SOURCE H1

Account 1
"There are no means of finding out exactly the number of persons who were dependent on potatoes for their support, but it must have formed a large portion of the population of all the western counties, and was not inconsiderable even in the eastern counties of Leinster and Ulster. Perhaps it may be estimated at 2,000,000."

SOURCE H2

Account 2
"The hovels which the poor people were building as I passed, solely by their own efforts, were of the most miserable desxcription; their walls were formed, in several instances, by the backs of fences; the floor sunk in ditches; the height scarcely enough for a man to stand upright; a few pieces of grass sods the only covering; and these extending only partially ofer the thing called a roof; the elderly people miserably clothed; the children all but naked."

In such conditions of poverty, people generally grew a potato type called a 'lumper'. This was less tasty than other varieties but gave a very high yield and never suffered from rot as was the case with other types.

In bad years, life for those at the poorest end of Irish farming meant only one thing – a struggle to survive. In many years in the 18th and early 19th centuries, survival was extremely difficult. In 1845–48, for many, it was to become impossible.

CAN YOU SAY?

14. In the pictures of a landlord's home (**Source C**) and a poor farmer's home (**Source G**, above), can you identify *four* differences between the two?
15. Give *two* ways in which life in a workhouse was unpleasant.
16. What was a cottier in 19th-century rural Ireland?
17. Explain why the numbers of (a) *labourers* and (b) *cottiers* rose in the early 19th century.
18. Give *three* reasons why many poorer Irish farmers depended on potatoes in the 19th century.
19. (a) From **Source H1** above, how many people does the author believe were dependent on the potato arout 1840?
    (b) Do you think the author of **Source H2** above is shocked by what he has seen? Give *one* piece of evidence from the account to support your answer.

(Junior Certificate Higher Level 2004)

KEYNOTES

1. **Irish industries and cities:** Ulster • Belfast • textiles • Dublin • rich and poor • crime • drink • disease • Bianconi's coaches • Royal and Grand Canals • William Dargan • railways
2. **Rural Ireland:** population growth • landlords • land-agents • prosperity for some • voice in politics • tithes • national schools • hurling • faction fights • fairs
3. **Disaster looming for the poor:** labourers and cottiers • migration • workhouses • subdivision • dependence on potato • lumpers • danger of disease and starvation

MINI-PROJECT

Keeping in mind what we learnt earlier about Britain's Industrial Revolution, list at least *six* ways in which life in industrial England differed from that in rural Ireland around the mid-19th century. Consider things such as population, employment, housing, entertainment and so on.

In the previous chapter, we saw that Ireland's poor lived mainly in rural areas and, in many cases, depended hugely on the growing of potatoes for their survival. One commentator wrote in 1844:

> **SOURCE A**
>
> *These people live in the most wretched clay huts, scarcely good enough for cattle pens, have scant food all winter long or… they have potatoes, half enough thirty weeks of the year, and the rest of the year nothing.* [When supplies run out in the spring] *wife and children go forth to beg and tramp the country with their kettle in their hands. Meanwhile, the husband, after planting potatoes for the next year, goes in search of work either in Ireland or England and returns at the potato harvest to his family.*

This type of poverty and dependence on the potato was to result, in 1845, in one of the greatest human disasters the island has ever known.

THE POTATO BLIGHT

On 20 August 1845, Dr David Moore at Dublin's Botanical Gardens was the first to notice that a new potato disease had come to Ireland. This was *phytophthora infestans*, more simply known as **potato blight**. It was a kind of fungus that spread in warm, moist conditions and attacked first the stalks above ground, and then the potatoes below. Sometimes the potatoes seemed healthy when first dug, but later turned into a sticky mess when pressed. The crop was totally unfit to eat.

This potato blight first appeared in America in 1843. It was spotted in Belgium and Britain early in 1845. However, these regions produced a variety of other crops, so that few people depended on the potato alone. Ireland, on the other hand, was on the brink of disaster.

DID YOU KNOW?

Strangely enough, potato blight came to Ireland because of improved farming methods. A new type of fertiliser called **guano** (made from dried bird-droppings) was imported to Europe from South America. It is believed to have contained the blight particles (**spores**).

377

SOURCE B

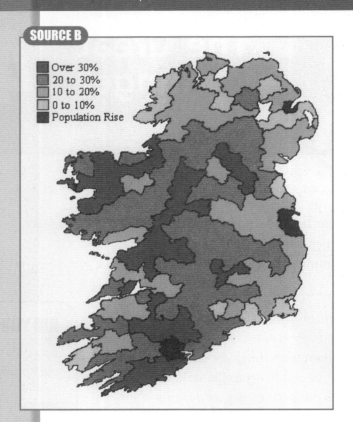

- Over 30%
- 20 to 30%
- 10 to 20%
- 0 to 10%
- Population Rise

Foretaste of Disaster

In 1845, blight affected only about one third of Irish potatoes. It had been a good year for growth and by August much of the crop had already been harvested and stored away. The loss of one-third of the crop was not a new occurrence. Bad weather had damaged crops before; thousands had died from starvation in 1741, 1816 and other years.

Many people believed that the blight was just a one-year problem. However, in 1846 at least two-thirds of potatoes were unfit to eat. Now the prospect of real starvation faced the hundreds of thousands of cottiers and labourers, mostly in the western half of the country, who depended almost entirely on the potato.

CAN YOU SAY?

1. Give *three* reasons why many Irish farmers depended heavily on potatoes.
2. According to the writer of **Source A**:
   (a) When did potato supplies usually run out?
   (b) Normally, how long did the potato crop last?
   (c) When supplies ran out, what did husbands do?
3. What was the blight during the 1840s in Ireland?

   (*Junior Certificate Ordinary Level 2001*)
4. Explain why there was no widespread panic when the blight struck in 1845.
5. **Source B** is a map showing the population decline in Ireland between 1841 and 1851. Name *one* part of the country that experienced:
   (a) a rise in population during this period.
   (b) a fall in population greater than 30% during this period.

   (*Junior Certificate Higher Level 2004*)

THE FAMINE

Slow Government Reaction

When the Famine first struck, the government in Britain took little notice of the situation. This was partly because it expected the blight to be gone by 1846 and also because it didn't fully realise the total dependence of the Irish peasants on the potato. In Britain, blight also destroyed potato crops, but farmers there almost always had other crops to fall back on. The British government believed in a policy of non-interference, known as *laissez-faire*. It did not see it as a government's duty to get involved in the daily lives of the people, and so unemployment benefit and health insurance were not provided. Much of the effort to help the starving in Ireland had to come from voluntary and charity groups.

Workhouses

From 1845 onwards, tens of thousands headed for the **workhouses**; at this time there were 123 workhouses countrywide. Families were split up in the workhouse – men were held in one section and boys in another, and there were separate sections for women and young children, and girls.

Conditions were deliberately bad – no entertainment, few comforts and just enough food for survival – to discourage even more people from trying to get in. Yet, by early 1847, Ireland's workhouses were filled to overflowing with 116,000 people.

The workhouse at Clifden in Galway, January 1850.

As people began to starve, their bodies weakened and so they were more likely to catch infections and die from them. In workhouses especially, diseases spread rapidly among the closely packed inmates, so that many who entered the workhouses to save themselves never came out alive. As the Famine progressed, many people who were dying went to the workhouses, just hoping for a proper burial.

> **SOURCE C**
>
> *The father and the mother were enquiring ... about Síle and Diarmaidín. Both children were not long dead when the parents became aware of it. All these poor people could speak Irish. The authorities were unable to speak the language or*

could only speak it badly. The poor people could learn of each other's welfare unknown to the authorities. As soon as the father and the mother heard of their children's deaths they were so stricken with grief and loneliness that they were unable to remain in the place. Both had been separated but they were able to contact each other. They decided to escape.

The wife's name was Cáit. Pádraig escaped from the workhouse first. He stopped at the top of Bóthar na Sop to wait for Cáit. After some time he saw her coming but she was walking very slowly. She had fever. They continued up towards Carraig an Staighre and arrived at the place where the mass grave was. They knew that the two children were buried in that grave with hundreds of other bodies. They stood by the graveside and cried bitterly ... they left the graveside and headed northwest towards Doire Liath where their cabin was ... they felt the pangs of hunger and Cáit was sick with fever so they had to walk slowly ... they met neighbours.

They were given something to drink and a little food but because they had come directly from the workhouse, and because the woman had the dreaded fever, people were afraid to invite them into their houses. Pádraig simply lifted his wife on his back and headed northwest towards the cabin ... he reached the cabin which was cold and empty without fire or heat.

On the following day, a certain neighbour came to the cabin and went in. He saw the two inside, dead and the woman's two feet were resting on Pádraig's chest as if he was trying to warm them. It seems that he realised because of the coldness of her feet that Cáit was about to die so he rested her feet on his chest to warm them.

Charities

As news of the Famine spread, many charities came to the aid of the people. The **Society of Friends** (Quakers) set up **soup kitchens** around the country and fed thousands of people on rice that they got from fellow Quakers in America. In all, groups from at least 19 different countries sent aid to Ireland, including £470,000 from a British association and £2,000 from Jamaica.

CAN YOU SAY?

6. Explain what the term *laissez-faire* government meant.
7. **Source C**, taken from *Mo Scéal Féin* by an tAthair Peadar Ó Laoghaire, describes the plight of a poor family in Macroom Workhouse, Co. Cork, during the Famine. Peadar Ó Laoghaire was about eight years of age at that time.
   (a) What did Pádraig and Cáit (parents of Síle and Diarmaidín) do when they heard that their children had died?
   (b) It seems that the members of the family were separated from each other. Mention *two* points of evidence from the passage to support this opinion.
   (c) What advantage was a knowledge of Irish to the poor people in the workhouse?
   (d) 'People were afraid to invite them into their houses.' According to the author, why was this so?
   (e) What did Pádraig do when he realised that Cáit was about to die?

   (Junior Certificate Ordinary and Higher Levels 1996)

   (f) What was a workhouse? Why did people like Pádraig and Cáit go to workhouses during the Famine?

   (Junior Certificate Ordinary Level 1996)

8. How did the Society of Friends help Famine victims?

Sir Robert Peel

What the British government did for Irish famine victims was largely because of the efforts of the Conservative Party leader, **Sir Robert Peel**, who disliked the *laissez-faire* attitude of many British politicians. As starvation became widespread, Peel read reports of thousands dying of hunger-related diseases such as the 'bloody flux'. This is where the victims coughed up their own blood before dying of hunger and exhaustion. He began sending shipments of **maize (Indian corn)** to Ireland. This had to be soaked in water to make it soft enough to eat and people who were used to potatoes found it difficult to digest. Because of its yellow (sulphur) colour and its hardness, it got the nickname **'Peel's brimstone'**. However, there is little doubt that the Indian corn saved lives and its arrival marked the end of *laissez-faire* government.

In November 1845, Peel set up a **Relief Commission** to distribute grain to food depots around the country and to sell it at cost price to **local relief committees**. Their job was to raise money locally to buy food and to sell it to the poor in any area where the local workhouse was already full. However, those who most needed food had no money and no way of earning it. **Public works schemes** were put in place to provide employment for these people. By 1846, almost

Sir Robert Peel.

Memorial to the Great Famine in Dublin

400,000 people were involved in building roads, walls, bridges and sometimes quite useless constructions called 'follies', simply to provide them with employment. It was harsh, physical, outdoor work and people who were weak from hunger were often unable to do it. Those who were strong enough to work received roughly one shilling (5 cent) a day, but food shortages had forced up prices, so most still found it impossible to feed their families properly.

Despite the availability of some employment and income, many were left to survive, if they could, by poaching fish and wildlife on landlords' estates, or by trying to steal potatoes. They risked severe punishment if caught. The register from Kilmainham Gaol (Jail), lists people jailed during the Famine in 1847 and many were imprisoned for stealing small amounts of food (see page 12).

Black '47

1847 proved to be the worst year of the Famine. There was virtually no blight that year, but because almost no seed potatoes had been kept since 1846, the potato crop was very small. To make matters worse, typhus epidemics were spreading like wildfire among the already weakened people. Many people moved into the towns and cities seeking work and shelter, and brought the disease with them. Thus, it spread even more rapidly. One Cork doctor wrote:

> **SOURCE D**
>
> *During the first six months of that dark period, one-third of the daily population of our streets consisted of shadows and spectres* [ghosts], *the impersonations of disease and famine, crowding in from the rural districts, and stalking along to the general doom – the grave – which appeared to await them at the distance of a few stops or a few short hours.*

Despite all the efforts of charities, government and officials such as Poor Law Guardians, almost a quarter of a million people died in Ireland in the year known as **Black '47**.

The End of the Famine

There is no precise date for the end of the Great Famine. While many consider 1845 to 1848 to be the key years, the starvation lasted much longer than that. Over 40,000 more people died in 1850, for instance, than in 1846, one of the 'official' Famine years.

A combination of relief efforts, improved weather which restricted the blight and the development of a spray to prevent blight all helped eventually. The spray was basically a mixture of copper sulphate (bluestone) and washing soda, and versions of it are still used by potato growers today.

CAN YOU SAY?

9. Which British politician was mostly responsible for ending the *laissez-faire* policy towards Ireland?
10. What were (a) 'Peel's brimstone' (*2005 Higher Level*) and (b) follies?
11. In what ways did public works schemes cause problems?
12. Why was 1847 known as Black '47?
13. In the Cork doctor's account (**Source D**):
    (a) What caused the streets to be full of 'shadows and spectres'?
    (b) Where did these people come from?
    (c) What, in his opinion, was going to happen to them all?

THE RESULTS OF THE FAMINE

Whereas the 1841 census had recorded a population of 8,175,000, the 1851 census showed it to be 6,552,000, a drop of 1,623,000. The true decrease was probably more like **2 million**, as the population in 1851 should have been over 8,500,000 according to the previous rising trends. At least one million people died of starvation or disease. The cottiers and many of the farm labourers simply disappeared. After the Famine, the population continued to fall – the first census since 1841 that recorded a population increase in Ireland was not until 1966!

The Famine put an end to the subdivision of land that had made farms so small in the first place. Now, the **eldest son** inherited all his father's land. Younger sons were forced either to move to the cities for work (migrate) or to emigrate from the country for good. After the Famine, younger sons had no prospects of inheriting land, so they tended not to risk getting married as early as before. **Later marriages** generally resulted in fewer children being born, again causing a drop in population.

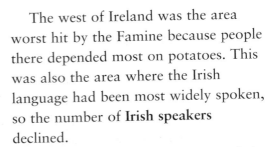

...migrants on the ...uayside in Cork, ...ay 1851.

The west of Ireland was the area worst hit by the Famine because people there depended most on potatoes. This was also the area where the Irish language had been most widely spoken, so the number of **Irish speakers** declined.

Many landlords who had struggled to get starving tenants to pay rent during the Famine **evicted** them afterwards and turned their lands over to cattle farming. There thus began a change from being largely a crop-growing (**tillage**) island to a cattle-rearing (**pasture**) one.

The most lasting result of the Famine was **emigration**. Although it had been common before – particularly to industrial Britain – during the Famine its importance increased greatly as thousands attempted to flee the country to escape disease and starvation. Afterwards, the end of subdivision, the high rate of evictions and the lack of industrial employment in Ireland made emigration a virtual necessity for many. The main destinations of Irish emigrants were Britain, USA, Canada and Australia.

During the Famine, emigration reached 200,000 a year. The ships were often small and unseaworthy, and because many of their tightly packed passengers died of hunger and disease on board, they were called **coffin ships**. The worst voyages were the transatlantic ones to Canada and the USA.

James Brendan Connolly, 1896 Olympic triple jump champion.

DID YOU KNOW?

The first winner of a title in the inaugural modern Olympic Games of 1896 was James Brendan Connolly of the USA. He was the son of Irish emigrants from the Aran Islands who had settled in Boston.

On board a coffin ship.

SOURCE E

Tuesday, 6 July
Two men (brothers) died of dysentery and I was awakened by the noise made by the mate, who was searching for an old sail to cover the remains with. In about an hour after, they were consigned to the deep, a remaining brother being the solitary mourner. He continued long to gaze upon the ocean, while a tear that dropped from his moistened eye told the grief he did not otherwise express. I learned in the afternoon that he was suffering from the same complaint that carried off his brothers.

Thursday, 8 July
The captain had a great dread of the coast of Newfoundland which, being broken into deep bays divided from each other by rocky capes, is rendered exceedingly perilous [dangerous], more especially, as the powerful currents set [run] towards this inhospitable shore. We kept a lookout for some vessel coming from the gulf, in order to learn the bearings [direction] of land but did not perceive one during the day.

Friday, 9 July
A few convalescents appeared upon deck. The appearance of the poor creatures was miserable in the extreme. We now had 50 sick, being nearly one half the whole number of passengers. Some entire families, being prostrated [unable to stand], were dependent on the charity of their neighbours, many of whom were very kind ... The brother of the two men who died on the sixth instant followed them today. ... The old sails being all used up, his remains were placed in two meal-sacks and a weight being fastened at foot, the body ... fell into the deep and was no more seen. He left two little orphans, one of whom – a boy, seven years of age – I noticed in the evening, wearing his deceased father's coat. ... The remainder of the man's clothes were sold by auction ... and the 'Cant', as they called it, occasioned jibing and jesting, which it was painful to listen to, surrounded as were the actors by famine, pestilence and death.

Thousands of passengers died on board or soon after arrival. For those who survived, a whole new life awaited. In cities such as Boston and New York, the Irish tended to live in the poorest areas and work in the lowest paid jobs. Areas such as the Bronx in New York virtually became 'little Irelands' in their own ways. In time, certain jobs became dominated by the Irish, the police forces in Boston and New York being good examples. Many earned enough money to be able to send the fare home for other members of the family to join them. Thus, the **emigration drain** of the young Irish population continued.

The immigrants brought with them a deep hatred of landlords and of Britain. Many blamed Britain for the Famine; they maintained that there had been sufficient food in Ireland to keep the people alive but that it had been exported by greedy, cruel landlords. This hatred and bitterness would eventually result in Irish-Americans being the main financial backers of later **revolutionary groups** in Ireland, including those that took part in the 1916 Rising.

SOURCE F

As a result of the Famine many families were broken up. This was in a good way due to the tempting offers to emigrate. This was what was called 'Free Emigration'. Everyone who left paid a pound and the English government paid the rest. This was freely accepted for years after the Famine with the result that it was always the young members of the family that left. When they became well off they persuaded the parents to go. It was usually to America or Australia they emigrated. It often happened in the poor mountainous districts of West Cork that only the aged parents were left to keep the little homestead. They were often unable to pay the rent except they got help from across [the Atlantic] and the result was that evictions were numerous. The most [majority] of the landlords were of no help to the suffering people. They oftentimes took from them the solitary cow or goat which was their sole support. If a family was suspected of receiving money from America the rent was sure to be raised, so the poor people got no choice anyway.

CAN YOU SAY?

14. During the Famine how many people (a) died and (b) emigrated?
15. Why did the practice of subdividing holdings decline after the Famine?

(Junior Certificate Ordinary and Higher 1994)

16. Why did the Irish population continue to fall after the Famine? Give *three* reasons.
17. Give *two* consequences for Ireland of the Great Famine of the 1840s.

(Junior Certificate Higher Level 2003)

18. **Source E**, taken from Robert Whyte's *1847 Famine Ship Diary – The Journey of an Irish Coffin Ship*, describes the voyage of the *Ajax*, which sailed from Dublin on 30 May, 1847, for Grosse Île, Canada.

   (a) Describe how they buried the two brothers who died of dysentery.
   (b) 'The Captain had a great dread of the coast of Newfoundland.' Give *two* reasons for his fear.
   (c) Why did Robert Whyte consider it painful to listen to the 'jibing and jesting' during the auction of the dead man's clothes?
   (d) What was the attitude of the author towards the emigrants? Support your answer by evidence from the passage.
   (e) What evidence is there in the passage to support the author calling the ships 'coffin ships'?
   (f) How many days did it take the *Ajax* to sail from Dublin to Newfoundland?

(Junior Certificate Ordinary and Higher 1996)

   (g) How many Famine emigrants were aboard the *Ajax*?

(Junior Certificate Ordinary Level 1996)

19. Write an account on the contrasting lifestyles in rural Ireland and industrial England around 1850.

(Junior Certificate Higher Level 2006) [Aim for around *six* good sentences]

20. **Source F** above is an account by Maighread Ní Dhonnabhain of Drimoleague, Co. Cork, describing what she knew of life around Drimoleague, Co. Cork after the Famine. Read it and answer the following questions:

   (a) Mention *two* effects of emigration on the people of west Cork.
   (b) 'The most of the landlords were of no help to the suffering people.'
   Give *two* pieces of evidence to support that view.

MINI-PROJECT

Write an account of the following: *A person who emigrated from Ireland about 1850.*
Hints:
- reasons for emigrating
- conditions in the country to which the person emigrated
- difficulties settling into the new country
- the emigrant's attitude to Ireland

[Write at least 12 sentences, without looking at your book.]

(Junior Certificate Higher Level 1993, 1998; Ordinary 1998, 1999 – hints vary)

Or

A tenant farmer in Ireland c.1850.
Hints:
- home and family
- relations with the landlord
- crops and livestock
- fairs and markets

[Write at least 12 sentences, without looking at your book.]

(Junior Certificate Higher Level 1995)

KEYNOTES

1. **The Famine strikes:** 1845 • blight • one-third crop destroyed • worse in 1846
   • little help • government's *laissez-faire* policies • workhouses • charities (Quakers)
   • soup kitchens • donations from abroad • government action • Sir Robert Peel
   • 'Peel's brimstone' • Relief Commission • local relief committees
   • public works schemes • follies • Black '47
   Results: deaths and emigration • end of subdivision • later marriages
   • continued fall in population • west of Ireland worst hit
   • decline of the Irish language • change from tillage to pasture
   Emigration: coffin ships • to Britain, USA, Canada, Australia • Irish communities in these countries • retained love of Ireland • deep hatred of Britain

Notes

Notes

Notes

Notes

Notes

Notes